AMERICAN EVANGELICALS

Bloomsbury Advances in Religious Studies

Series Editors: Bettina E. Schmidt, Steven Sutcliffe, and Will Sweetman

Founding Editors: James Cox and Peggy Morgan

Bloomsbury Advances in Religious Studies publishes cutting-edge research in the Study of Religion/s. The series draws on anthropological, ethnographical, historical, sociological and textual methods amongst others. Topics are diverse, but each publication integrates theoretical analysis with empirical data. The series aims to refresh the interdisciplinary agenda in new evidence-based studies of "religion."

Appropriation of Native American Spirituality, Suzanne Owen
Becoming Buddhist, Glenys Eddy
Community and Worldview among Paraiyars of South India, Anderson H. M. Jeremiah
Conceptions of the Afterlife in Early Civilizations, Gregory Shushan
Contemporary Western Ethnography and the Definition of Religion, Martin D. Stringer
Cultural Blending in Korean Death Rites, Chang-Won Park
Free Zone Scientology, Aled Thomas
Globalization of Hesychasm and the Jesus Prayer, Christopher D. L. Johnson
Individualized Religion, Claire Wanless
Innateness of Myth, Ritske Rensma
Levinas, Messianism and Parody, Terence Holden
New Paradigm of Spirituality and Religion, Mary Catherine Burgess
Orthodox Christianity, New Age Spirituality and Vernacular Religion, Eugenia Roussou
Post-Materialist Religion, Mika T. Lassander
Redefining Shamanisms, David Gordon Wilson
Reform, Identity and Narratives of Belonging, Arkotong Longkumer
Religion and the Discourse on Modernity, Paul-François Tremlett
Religion as a Conversation Starter, Ina Merdjanova and Patrice Brodeur
Religion, Material Culture and Archaeology, Julian Droogan
Secular Assemblages, Marek Sullivan
Spirits and Trance in Brazil, Bettina E. Schmidt
Spirit Possession and Trance, edited by Bettina E. Schmidt and Lucy Huskinson
Spiritual Tourism, Alex Norman
Theology and Religious Studies in Higher Education, edited by D. L. Bird and Simon G. Smith
The Critical Study of Non-Religion, Christopher R. Cotter
The Problem with Interreligious Dialogue, Muthuraj Swamy
Religion and the Inculturation of Human Rights in Ghana, Abamfo Ofori Atiemo
UFOs, Conspiracy Theories and the New Age, David G. Robertson

AMERICAN EVANGELICALS

Conflicted on Islam

Ashlee Quosigk

BLOOMSBURY ACADEMIC
LONDON • NEW YORK • OXFORD • NEW DELHI • SYDNEY

BLOOMSBURY ACADEMIC
Bloomsbury Publishing Plc
50 Bedford Square, London, WC1B 3DP, UK
1385 Broadway, New York, NY 10018, USA
29 Earlsfort Terrace, Dublin 2, Ireland

BLOOMSBURY, BLOOMSBURY ACADEMIC and the Diana logo are trademarks of
Bloomsbury Publishing Plc

First published in Great Britain 2021
This paperback edition published 2023

Copyright © Ashlee Quosigk, 2021

Ashlee Quosigk has asserted her right under the Copyright, Designs and Patents Act, 1988,
to be identified as Author of this work.

For legal purposes the Acknowledgments on p. xiv constitute an extension
of this copyright page.

All rights reserved. No part of this publication may be reproduced or transmitted in any
form or by any means, electronic or mechanical, including photocopying, recording, or any
information storage or retrieval system, without prior permission in writing
from the publishers.

Bloomsbury Publishing Plc does not have any control over, or responsibility for,
any third-party websites referred to or in this book. All internet addresses given in
this book were correct at the time of going to press. The author and publisher regret
any inconvenience caused if addresses have changed or sites have ceased to exist,
but can accept no responsibility for any such changes.

A catalogue record for this book is available from the British Library.

A catalog record for this book is available from the Library of Congress.

ISBN: HB: 978-1-3501-7558-7
PB: 978-1-3502-4323-1
ePDF: 978-1-3501-7561-7
eBook: 978-1-3501-7560-0

Series: Bloomsbury Advances in Religious Studies

Typeset by Deanta Global Publishing Service, Chennai, India

To find out more about our authors and books visit www.bloomsbury.com and sign up
for our newsletters

Dedicated to my parents, Mabel Baldes and John Baldes, to whom I will always be grateful. Your wisdom is truly a garland to grace my head and a chain to adorn my neck (Proverbs 1).

Do not judge by appearances, but judge with right judgment.

—John 7:24

CONTENTS

List of Illustrations	viii
Preface	ix
Foreword	xi
Acknowledgments	xiv
Abbreviations	xvii

Chapter 1
PREPARING FOR BATTLE: AN INTRODUCTION TO THE STUDY ... 1

Chapter 2
EXTERNAL ENEMIES AND INTERNAL STRIFE: A HISTORICAL REVIEW OF EVANGELICALISM AND ITS CONFLICTS ... 15

Chapter 3
THE GREAT DIVIDE: EVANGELICAL IDENTITY AND CONFLICTING MORAL AUTHORITIES ... 45

Chapter 4
EVANGELICAL LEADERS: CONFLICT AND DIVERSITY IN PLACES OF POWER ... 79

Chapter 5
EVANGELICAL CONGREGANTS: STRIFE, VARIETY, AND MODERATION ... 107

Chapter 6
COMPLEXITIES OF EVANGELICAL VIEWS ON ISLAM: COMPARATIVE PERSPECTIVES OF LEADERS AND CONGREGANTS ... 141

Chapter 7
MAKING SENSE OF THE CONFLICT: WHERE DO WE GO FROM HERE? ... 155

Appendix 1: Qualitative Approaches: Justification of Methods and Data Analysis ... 179
Appendix 2: Biographical Reflexivity, Researcher Identity, and Ethical Considerations ... 185
Appendix 3: Additional Demographics and Level of Engagement with Muslims ... 192

References ... 199
Index ... 217

ILLUSTRATIONS

Figure

3.1 Progressive-Traditional Spectrum with Categories — 72

Tables

4.1 Leadership: Stated Moral Authority and Evidential Moral Authority with Demographics — 85
5.1 Mercy and Adams River Congregants: Stated Moral Authority and Evidential Moral Authority with Demographics — 120
A.1 Leadership and Mercy and Adams River Congregants: Gender Ratio — 193
A.2 Leadership: Demographics — 194
A.3 Mercy and Adams River Congregants: Demographics — 195

PREFACE

Personally, the intersection between Muslims and Christians has always held interest for me due to the influence of my Pakistani mother, of Indian heritage, who grew up in the Pakistani city of Karachi. Although Karachi is a bustling Muslim-majority city, my mother was a Christian and lived at the Seventh-Day Adventist Lodge in Karachi and she attended a private Catholic school. At school, she formed friendships with Muslim classmates. As she grew older, persecution of Christians increased in Pakistan, prompting my grandparents to emigrate to the United States with my mother in 1975, when she was eighteen. Growing up, I was fascinated yet conflicted by stories of my mother's Muslim friends in Pakistan. Clearly, she valued these friendships and cared about these Muslim friends, but I wondered how she maintained those friendships even as she knew about the subtle persecution of her family members by Muslims.

After 9/11, my interest in interactions between Christians and Muslims only increased. The topic of Islam became a frequent discussion point, both in the general media and in Evangelical circles. I questioned what a Christian response to Islam and Muslims should look like, and these questions, among other factors, led my husband and me to attend an Evangelical conference on Islam in 2012.

In one of the talks I met another attendee, an older Pakistani man, and we began to chat. I found out, to my amazement, that he knew my grandparents and had lived in Karachi as well, not far from them. He told me things in Pakistan had taken a sharp turn for the worse for Christians in the decades after my family emigrated to America. He said he leads underground Bible studies in Pakistan, where any man who converts faces the possibility of a death sentence. The danger is so great that he counsels the new convert to immediately flee the country. He told me he personally knew of new converts who had been murdered due to the strict Islamic teaching that apostasy (conversion from Islam to another religion) and blasphemy (derogatory remarks against Muhammad or the Qur'an) can be punishable by death. His account resonated with me as I understood more clearly the dangers my family escaped from by coming to the United States and the dangers other Pakistani Christians now faced.

At the same conference, however, I also heard some of the most positive and accepting perspectives on Islam that I had ever heard. Both at the conference and in subsequent conversations with Evangelicals I knew, I was confused by the variety of messages I received from Evangelicals regarding Islam. It seemed many Evangelicals I heard speak or that I asked about Islam told me something different, often in conflict with what others had said. For example, some Evangelicals felt the Qur'an had truth in it, whereas others believed it to be evil and full of lies. In addition, some felt Muslims and Christians worship the same God, while others rejected this view due to their belief in the nature of God being triune. These are not small issues. This lived experience of Evangelicals disagreeing with one another on Islam did not match up with stereotypical perception that all Evangelicals saw Islam as the enemy, and I wanted to know more.

This book began during that time of questioning in 2012. It is undeniable that research feels more meaningful when it is personal. I have heard it said that research is really me-search. In many ways this book is no different. I dove into the questions, read, listened, laughed, analyzed, cried, achieved answers, and developed theoretical and methodological advances to the study of religion along the way. Due to the quite individual nature of some of the questions themselves, specifically questions about where we derive our sense of right and wrong, I hope you find this research to be, at the very least in that way, me-search as well.

FOREWORD

I was honored to be asked to write the foreword of Ashlee Quosigk's book *American Evangelicals*. This book is important on several fronts. It is my hope that the issues she brings out will inform our debate about Evangelical Christianity, religious tolerance, and religious identity. This book touches on all three topics and encourages us to think more deeply about them. I will look at those topics in that order.

This book is a clear reminder that Christians are not a monolithic group. Many individuals realize that not all Christians fit into a right-wing conservative Christian stereotype, but there is still a tendency among the media, scholars, and others to lump Evangelicals together as a single group. While the Evangelical label provides some predictive value in identifying the particular subgroup of Christianity that a person self-identifies with, the common label may make it too easy to paint all members of that group with the same brush. Quosigk prompts us to question what we think we know about Evangelicals, illustrating that this group is far more nuanced than our most basic stereotypes about them. Contrary to common belief, not all Evangelicals are attempting to proselytize non-Christians, and many of them see members of non-Christian religions as fellow brothers and sisters. Even if it is true that they, as a group, are more particularistic than other Christians, we need to be careful about automatically applying this image, or any other, to all Evangelicals.

This example leads me to think about other master stereotypes that are often attached to Evangelicals. For example, there has been recent talk about Evangelical activism on behalf of President Donald Trump (Fea 2018, Scala 2020). This focus suggests that Evangelicals and other conservative Christians focus more on political accomplishments than those of other religious identities do. Yet recent research indicates that it is atheists who are per capita more engaged in politics, with white Evangelicals lagging behind most other groups (Burge 2020). This study disproves the stereotype of Evangelicals as uniquely engaged and aggressive political activists. Given the underrepresentation of conservative Christians in academia (Ecklund, Park, and Veliz 2008), it is not surprising that careful analysis of this group is often replaced by ungenerous stereotypes. We need works like this one to help us move beyond those stereotypes and gain a more complete understanding of this religious group.

In addition to offering a greater understanding of Christian Evangelicals, this text also touches on the topic of religious tolerance. Clearly there are varying levels of religious tolerance among Evangelicals. In this they are not different from other religious groups, as we should expect variation of tolerance among members of any given group. In Quosigk's work, this tolerance—or rather intolerance—is seen in the desire of some Christians to convert Muslims. In contrast, other Christians, who envision Muslims as fellow believers who need not conform to Christian faith, can be seen as tolerant. While Evangelicals may be more likely to engage in conversion than not, the impulse to convert will vary.

But we now gain a chance to move deeper into thinking about what is occurring in this particular situation. Should we define tolerance as a lack of desire to convert others to our beliefs and causes? If this definition holds true for the Evangelical, then it is easy to see how it is also true for the Muslim. But is it also true for those with political agendas? Is it intolerant to attempt to convince the conservative Evangelical to accept same-sex marriage? If we saw a MAGA hat on his or her head, was it intolerant to try to convince that person to vote for Biden? In other words, are attempts at conversion only intolerant in the religious world or is it true whenever we attempt to push a doctrine onto those who do not already believe in it?

Of course, the pushback to the argument of political proselytization is that politics deals with issues of this world while religion focuses on the next world, which none of us can see. However, is it fair to acknowledge the assumptions of priority and reality connected to such an assertion. Many religious individuals perceive their beliefs to have very real effects in this world. And can we not argue that religious belief can and does change individuals in ways that can be profound and beneficial? To take only a single dimension as an example, there is plenty of work indicating the benefits of religiosity to health (Lawler-Row 2010, Levin, Chatters, and Taylor 1995, Aukst-Margetić and Margetić 2005). We can argue with those who promote religious conversion about whether the specific conversion outcome they are seeking is a desirable one. But the impulse to convert transcends conservative religionists, and perhaps we would do well to think about this desire in other spheres of life. If doing so alters our definition of tolerance, then such a process can lead to a better definition of that concept.

Finally, I do not want to ignore what Quosigk is doing with her observations of religious identity. Her discussion of stated and evidential moral authority touches on a subject that gets too little attention among scholars of religion. It is tempting to merely accept a self-identification as the end of our assessment of religious identity. But it is vital to go one step further and ask whether that religious identity has saliency in an individual's personal philosophy of life. As indicated by Smith and Denton (2009), many young Christians identify as Christian, yet their philosophy about their religion does not match up with an orthodox understanding of that faith.

When I teach sociology of religion, I point out to my students that we are all searching for meaning and purpose. Many turn to a traditional religion to find those qualities while others may rely on secular ideologies (e.g., feminism, environmentalism, humanism). But what often happens is that individuals who are members in a religious denomination or church still rely upon a secular ideology to deal with questions of meaning, purpose, and identity. I think of such individuals when I consider the Evangelicals in Quosigk's sample who have a mismatch of stated and evidential moral authority. I suspect that there are many more such individuals than we realize. Quosigk's approach provides a means of identifying and studying such situations.

Quosigk is an exceptionally talented young scholar. She is tremendously thorough in her analysis which she supports with a multitude of quotes from her interviewees. This process allows her interviewees to speak for themselves and refrains from overinterpretation which makes her work stand out in rigor and credibility. Her innovative methods help guard against problems often associated with researcher bias.

Her work has tremendous implications for the understanding of religious intragroup conflict spanning from the macrolevel (e.g., government and church policy) to microlevel (e.g., individual interactions). I am delighted to support her work. Her findings encourage us to go beneath the surface and rethink some of our assumptions about conservative Christians, tolerance, and religious identity.

George Yancey
Professor at Institute for Studies of Religion and Sociology at Baylor University

ACKNOWLEDGMENTS

I would like to thank several individuals who helped make this book become a reality. A number of professors that I encountered during my years at university stand out as I consider how this book came to fruition. I am humbled and appreciative for them and the contributions they provided during my journey to publication. This book began as a doctoral dissertation at Trinity College Dublin, then moved to Queen's University Belfast (QUB). At both schools, I benefited from the support and critique of Gladys Ganiel, who read numerous drafts and spent countless hours offering feedback. Gladys was incredibly hospitable, and I'm honored to call her a friend. John Brewer of QUB took the project under his wing and offered valuable insight regarding my data. Gladys and John are both academic mentors to me and greatly benefited the book.

At the University of Texas San Antonio (UTSA), Kolleen Guy guided me in my new role as an Honors history instructor and propelled me into doctoral studies. Bruce Daniels assisted me during my time at UTSA and beyond and aided the improvement of my writing, and Ann Eisenberg welcomed me into the Honors College faculty at UTSA.

My thanks also to the following professors: at the University of Georgia (UGA), Sandy Martin for his encouragement of my research, the extension of it, and his warm welcome to me as Visiting Scholar at UGA's Department of Religion; at Kennesaw State, my former history professor Gerrit Voogt—by enduring his fascinating classes, I learned what it meant to study history well; at Baylor University, I thank Thomas Kidd for his important historical work on Evangelicalism and Islam; at Georgia Highlands College, I thank Leslie Johnson for sharpening my public speaking skills during a memorable communication class and at the University of Virginia, I thank James Hunter, the creator of the moral authority argument, for his continued scholarship contributing to the study of truth and his kind words regarding my research. I am also grateful to the library staff of four distinguished universities: Trinity College Dublin, Queen's University Belfast, University of Texas at San Antonio, and Kennesaw State University.

Much appreciation goes to a number of scholars who offered helpful comments and suggestions: Peter Riddell, Mathew Guest, David Livingstone, Sean Oliver-Dee, George Yancey, Richard McCallum, Veronique Altglas, Richard Zetter, Warren Larson, Abby Day, Dan Brubaker, Cheryl Lawther, Jeff Killbride, Thomas Messick, Robert Miller, Richard Shumack, David Tombs, Daniel Janosik, William McMillan, Mark Durie, and the late Peter Berger, Keith Small, and Nabeel Qureshi. Their support reminds me of the ancient proverb: "As iron sharpens iron, so a friend sharpens a friend" (Proverbs 27:17).

I am grateful to a number of individuals from Bloomsbury Academic, including my gracious publisher, Lalle Pursglove, for her shepherding this book through to publication; Lily McMahon, for her guidance with preparing the manuscript; and Camilla Erskine and James Cox, for believing in the project.

The book has been through multiple drafts over the years. I am especially grateful to my dear friend Jamie Santa Cruz, as her encouragement of this project was instrumental and her editing improved the work. By careful proofreading, Rose Focht also benefited the work. Many thanks to Emily Woodhull for her help on the manuscript, particularly with style and accessibility.

My deepest gratitude goes to the people who opened themselves up and spoke with me about their thoughts on a variety of sensitive topics. I name no names to protect your privacy and safety. I am forever grateful.

Sweet friendships have refreshed my soul as I scribbled away on this book (Proverbs 27:9). Special thanks to Laura Penn, Amrin Wesley, Carrie Clowers, Leah Evans, Bridget Cochran, Kristy Rostad, Erica Thomas, Amy Flack, Wendy Diego, Sheeja Santhosh Abraham, Ruth Malhotra, Jennifer Cheek, Emily Jones, Naddia Strickland, Aimee Pitzo, Tayla Lowe, Megan Edwards, Brent Hartnett, James Roe, Alex Hernandez, Seth Dixon, and Johnathan Thompson.

My special thanks goes to a number of families: the Bazs, the Baldeses, the Quosigks, the Eakins, the Binghams, the Quisenberrys, the McKissicks, the Martins, the Clowers, the Kumars, the Bigners, the Cosbys, the Pinsons, the Maloneys, the Greens, the Tibbetts, the Marshalls, and the Blacks. To all my extended family, near and far, thank you for blessing my life.

I also greatly appreciate the support from New Covenant Church, First Asian Indian Baptist Church, Raccoon Creek Baptist Church, Crosspoint City Church, Cartersville First Baptist Church, Bethel Worship Center, Creekside Fellowship Church, Woodstock First Baptist Church, Crescent Church, Belfast Church of Christ especially James Black, Younis Farhat, Jeremy Morton, Mulligan Price, Scott Johnson, Michael Abernathy, Patrick Miller, and James Griffin.

A number of family members have shown me love throughout this process. The person who has had the strongest influence on the project is my beloved husband of fourteen years, Benedikt Quosigk—a brilliant scholar—who has spent countless hours working alongside me, discussing nearly every detail. Beyond his intellectual contributions, he has been my rock, strong and faithful, and the hands-on sacrificial father to our children. I respect and admire you, my love. Thank you for your words of affirmation and acts of service. Life with you is half as hard, and twice as good (Mark 10:8).

On my home front, the children are all young, with one yet to make his or her arrival as of this writing. These four precious children have been a significant part of this project, as all but one has arrived since its inception. I treasure you beyond words. Mothering you has shown me what it means to lay down my life for someone else (Proverbs 22:6). Your playfulness, desirousness, and pure joy have meant not one dull lonely moment during this project. The love each of you gives Mama is indescribably satisfying (Psalms 127:3-5).

In many ways my parents are responsible for anything about this book that is down to earth, clear, and makes good sense. I appreciate that you raised me as the last person anyone ever thought would be an academic, including myself. You've been my biggest critics while simultaneously my greatest encouragers.

Thanks to my mother, Mabel Baldes, who has been a steady presence of support. Her daily hands-on help and solid advice have been a comfort. She offers treasures of wisdom, perseveres under difficulty with an unshakable joy, and her sacrificial love and care are beautiful examples for me to admire. Many women do noble things, but you surpass them all (Proverbs 31:29-31).

To my father, John Baldes, I am grateful for the long conversations about everything during my childhood years and into the present. Now that I am a mother, looking back, I am aware it was sacrificial of him to ask me questions and get me talking about right and wrong. While I do believe he was genuinely curious about what his little girl thought about this and that world issue, patiently he also wanted to let me practice the art of thinking and communicating. Your wisdom and voice of reason have been a rich resource for me (Proverbs 20:7). I'm blessed to be your daughter.

Thanks to my first friend, my brother John Baldes. Together we enjoyed too many church services to count, basketball, raising puppies, joy, pain, and all that growing side-by-side entails (John 1:41). I continue to look up to you. You enrich my life with your unique insight, laughter, and tangible help in times of difficulty. Thanks also to my caring sister-in-law Marianne Baldes and dearly loved nephews, John Dylan Baldes and Hayden Mitchell; John Dylan may be happier than anyone to hold "Auntie's" book in his hands.

It's clear to me that life is short. Every breath truly is a miracle. My most exuberant thanks are to God, the maker of heaven and earth, and the giver of life, hope, and salvation, who has opened every door to allow me the opportunity to write this book (Colossians 1:16). I praise the Father, praise the Son, and praise the Spirit, Three in One (2 Corinthians 13:14).

ABBREVIATIONS

A Common Word (ACW)
American Board of Commissioners for Foreign Missions (ABCFM)
English Standard Version (ESV)
Insider Movements (IMs)
Islamic State of Iraq and al-Sham (ISIS)
National Association of Evangelicals (NAE)
New Evangelical Partnership for the Common Good (NEP)
Qur'an and Christ conference (QAC)
Southern Baptist Convention (SBC)

Chapter 1

PREPARING FOR BATTLE

AN INTRODUCTION TO THE STUDY

Religion is behind the violence and jihad we're seeing in Europe, the Middle East, Asia, and here in this country. It's a religion that calls for the extermination of "infidels" outside their faith, specifically Jews and Christians. It's a religion that calls on its soldiers to shout "Allahu Akbar" ("God is Great" in Arabic) as they behead, rape, and murder in the name of Islam. Radical Islamists are following the teachings of the Quran. We should call it what it is.

—Franklin Graham

I was raised as an evangelical Christian in America . . .
Islamophobic evangelical Christians . . . must choose. Will they press on in their current path, letting Islamophobia spread even further amongst them? Or will they stop, rethink and seek a more charitable approach to our Muslim neighbors?

—Brian McLaren

Introduction

At the height of the Covid-19 pandemic, the *New York Times* published an article titled "The Road to Coronavirus Hell Was Paved by Evangelicals" (Ernst, 2020; Stewart, 2020). The article, written by popular journalist Katherine Stewart, argues that Evangelicals are to blame for America's "incompetent response" to the virus. Stewart depicts Evangelicals as dangerous religious nationalists who deny science and willfully ignore facts. Evangelical Christians (a particular subset within Christianity), who make up the largest religious group in America, have often been the scapegoat for societal problems, and most are aware of the disdain toward them from many outsiders (Brown, 2020; McMillan, 2013; Lindsay, 2007).

The late sociologist of religion Peter Berger argued that the "American intelligentsia" has looked down on and stereotyped the nation's Evangelical population, which he regarded as the most dynamic element of the religious landscape in the United States (2010, 2008, 2006, 2002, 1999).[1] This stereotyping of Evangelicalism has been acknowledged by numerous other scholars of religion as well, including many specializing in Evangelicalism (Shields and Dunn, 2016; Yancey, Reimer, and O'Connell, 2015; Bean, 2014; Guest et al., 2013; Hutchinson and Wolffe, 2012; Needham-Penrose and Friedman, 2012; Elisha, 2011; Mitchell and Ganiel, 2011; Yancey, 2011; Hankins, 2009; Tobin and Weinberg, 2007; Lindsay, 2007; Marsden, 2006; Reimer, 2003; Smith, 1998; Noll, 1994). For example, Yancey (2011) found that between 40 and 50 percent of professors would be less likely to hire a prospective employee for their department if that candidate were either an Evangelical Christian or Fundamentalist Christian, and Tobin and Weinberg (2007) found that 53 percent of college professors surveyed admitted to having negative feelings about Evangelicals. Yancey, Reimer, and O'Connell (2015) argue that these types of negative opinions about Evangelicals are a result of the perception of Evangelicals as intolerant, politically/religiously conservative, antiscience, as well as less educated and low status (which serves as a boundary marker for the educational elite). They also found that academics studied were not only less likely to personally identify as a conservative Protestant but also likely to have less contact with them. According to Yancey, Reimer, and O'Connell, this lack of contact "may lead to an ignorance of conservative Protestants that feeds into negative stereotypes toward them" (2015: 331).

Dominant Western stereotyping of Evangelicalism tends to present all Evangelicals as one and the same: they are often typecast as backward, uneducated conservatives living in the Bible Belt of the southern United States, where they consume Fox News, pack a gun, idolize Donald Trump, use hate speech when discussing Islam, and protest abortion even while supporting the death penalty. Southern Evangelicals in particular have been depicted condescendingly as rural and anti-intellectual by much of the national media. These negative perceptions and stereotypes have not gone unnoticed by Evangelicals themselves. Many know that they are considered simpletons and/or extremists by outsiders, and Evangelicals often contrast their own views and actions against the stereotypes about Evangelicals (McMillan, 2013; Lindsay, 2007).

This book challenges these stereotypes. Although I do not deny that some Evangelicals fit well within the clichéd framework described earlier, my study seeks to shed light on the diversity and complexity of thought that exists within Evangelicalism. Beyond arguing about whether these specific stereotypes are accurate, I question to what extent any stereotype or description can accurately apply to Evangelicals as a whole.

The possibilities for analysis of Evangelical thought seem infinite. Thus, I have necessarily been selective in topics to examine. The findings presented in

---

1. I have capitalized "Evangelical," as Richard McCallum set this important precedent in his study of Evangelicals and Muslims in the UK context (2011). This was chosen in order to balance the capitalization of the word "Muslim," since both are used to refer primarily to a person as a member of a faith community (McCallum, 2011).

this book illustrate Evangelical diversity on a single topic, rather than providing a comprehensive picture of all possible diversity within this religious group. Specifically, I focus on illustrating the variety of attitudes held by various Evangelicals regarding Islam and Muslims. Drawing on my research and interviews with Evangelical leaders and congregants, this book details the—perhaps surprisingly— diverse views Evangelicals hold on Muhammad, the Qur'an, politics, and the relationship between Christianity and Islam. I demonstrate that Evangelicals are a varied group, that their thinking is often more complex than outsiders allow, and that stereotypes are often inadequate to capture who Evangelicals are and what they believe. In fact, Evangelical views diverge dramatically enough to have caused serious internal conflicts within this group. While many both inside and outside of Evangelicalism are well aware of the battles between Evangelicals and their larger culture, and between Evangelicals and Muslims, there is less awareness of the internal battles raging among Evangelicals. Disagreement among Evangelicals regarding how to understand and interact with Muslims is an example of one such battle.

Why Study Evangelical Attitudes toward Muslims?

Tension between Evangelicals and Muslims is not new: the two religions are founded on opposing exclusive truth claims that have long put the two religions at odds with each other. Islam, like Evangelicalism, is a monotheistic religion, usually believed to be based on revelations to the Prophet Muhammad in the seventh century after Christ. The two religions recognize many of the same prophets, and both hold Jesus in high esteem. But the religions also diverge significantly in a number of areas, perhaps most significantly on the question of who Jesus was (Muslims reject the Evangelical claim that Jesus is God) and how to best live a life pleasing to God.

While conflict between the two religions has existed for centuries, the United States is currently seeing escalating tensions between Evangelicals and Muslims. In the post-9/11 era many Evangelicals support the so-called war on terror, and that war has in turn worsened the relationship between Evangelicals and Muslims (Pew, 2019, 2017b). In addition, many are concerned about the influx of money to American universities from Saudi Arabia (some estimate Saudi gifts to be over $1 billion a year to US universities), and how the perceived repercussions that come with that money may alter the way Islam is portrayed in US institutions of learning (Sokolove, 2019). Adding to the tension between the two religious groups is the fact that Islam is attracting an increasing number of American converts, and sometimes these converts come directly from Christian circles. Like Evangelicalism, Islam is an evangelistic religion, meaning the religion encourages the faithful in its ranks to actively seek converts. While it is difficult to estimate how many people convert to Islam in the United States each year, the appeal of Islam is evident. A 2007 Pew report found that two-thirds of all converts to Islam in the United States come from Protestant churches (Pew, 2007). One US counterterrorism expert testified that 80 percent of prisoners who convert while in prison convert to Islam, and some studies estimate that between 30,000 and 40,000 American prisoners are converting to Islam each year in correctional institutions alone (Hirsi Ali, 2015; Waller, 2003; Dix-Richardson, 2002).

Not only are tensions between Evangelicals and Muslims already high, but there is also reason to think that the tensions are likely to continue. Christianity and Islam are already the world's two most dominant monotheistic religious groups, and both are continuing to grow steadily. Peter Berger noted there to be two "particularly powerful religious explosions—resurgent Islam and dynamic evangelical Protestantism"—and he believed the growth of these two groups to have great global significance (Quosigk, 2016; Berger, 2008).[2] According to Pew population projections, Christians and Muslims are on track to make up an even greater majority share of the world's population by 2060 than they do now (Pew, 2017c). Thus, whatever problems exist between these two opposing faiths are set to endure. Not only will the two groups be interacting more often and in more places, but their interaction will increasingly affect other religious groups, including the religiously unaffiliated (those who identify as atheist, agnostic, or have no particular religion), who "are projected to decline as a share of the world's population" due to low birth rates (Pew, 2017c).

One of the ways Evangelical attitudes toward Muslims might impact others is at the polls. As one of the single largest religious groups in the United States, Evangelicals are a significant voting bloc and political force. Their thoughts about Islam can have significant social and political consequences, influencing US foreign affairs and immigration policy. For example, Evangelical support may have significantly influenced the restrictive travel policies proposed by Donald Trump in January 2017 at the start of his presidency—policies that were widely viewed as attempting to restrict Muslim travel in the United States. Pew found white Evangelicals to be more approving of these policies than other groups, and the push for restrictive policies toward certain Muslim-majority countries has encouraged sociologists to continue their exploration of the role of race in the 2016 election of Donald Trump. For example, sociologist Gerardo Marti argues that the "ban on Muslim refugees from entering the United States was a reflection of the racial bias" held by the Trump administration and that Trump's views on terrorism and immigration can "certainly be tied to a Christian nationalist sentiment" (2020: 13, 241). Whitehead and Perry also noted the importance of Christian nationalism (a "cultural framework" that ties religious identity with race, nativity, citizenship, and political ideology), arguing that it was an important predictor of whether or not an Evangelical voted for Donald Trump in 2016 (2020: x).

---

2. Berger argued that the "rise in evangelical Protestantism has been less noticed by intellectuals, the media, and the general public in Western countries, partly because it more directly challenges the assumptions of established elite opinion" (Quosigk, 2016; Berger, 2008).

The sheer size and influence of Evangelicalism make it imperative to have a clear understanding of who Evangelicals are and what they believe on nearly every topic, including Islam. Yet despite the importance of an accurate understanding of Evangelicalism's relationship to Islam, there is a limited body of work on Evangelical Christianity and Islam in the United States. Few studies have examined American Evangelical attitudes toward Islam and even fewer use qualitative methods. Most studies use quantitative data, such as surveys, that is limited to rigidly definable variables, rather than more in-depth, less structured qualitative approach that examines thought patterns, reasoning, and motivations. Most of these studies simply encourage the typecast of Evangelicals as monolithically hostile toward Muslims.[3] The internal variation and discussion among Evangelicals on topics related to Islam and about the way that contemporary Evangelicals should relate to Muslims is a story that is rarely, if ever, being told.

To address that lack, this book provides an in-depth exploration of how Evangelicals relate to Muslims and how Evangelicals view topics such as Muhammad, the Qur'an, interfaith dialogue, politics, and syncretism (the attempted blending of opposing religions) between Christianity and Islam.[4] In particular, my work focuses on Evangelicals in the southern United States, the group of Evangelicals most strongly stereotyped as uneducated extremists. Through a rich assortment of stories and quotations, this study offers new insights into how Evangelicals think about Islam and how their views impact their politics and their social relationships. It demonstrates that Evangelicals are actually complex in their theological, moral, and political attitudes about Islam. In addition, it demonstrates that not all Evangelicals are resolutely opposed to Islam, as might be assumed based on dominant stereotypes; rather, Evangelicals advocate varying stances toward Islam. At one end of the spectrum are those who believe the Islamic religion to be inspired by the devil and who seek to convert Muslims, but on the other end are those who greatly admire Islam and even deem some aspects of Islam superior to Christianity. Many Evangelicals fall somewhere between these two extremes.

Furthermore, this book offers insight into *why* Evangelicals differ among themselves. Specifically, it explores the assumptions that guide individuals' perceptions of the world, which are known as a person's moral authority (e.g., orthodox authority such as the Bible or progressivist authority such as subjective intuition). It demonstrates how moral authority varies among Evangelicals and

---

3. There has been some recent theological and political work focused on exploring Evangelical views of Islam and/or Muslims in the United States (e.g., Bhatia, 2016, 2015; Hoover, 2004), and this work has come some way in exposing diversity. However, studies in the field of sociology are surprisingly lacking. Cimino (2005) and Bok (2014) offer helpful articles that explore US-based Evangelical literature on Islam. But these articles do not examine the views of everyday rank-and-file Evangelicals. Furthermore, there is minimal attention given to the diversity found within their content analysis data.

4. While exploration of Muslim views of Evangelicals would also be a topic worthy of research, it is beyond the scope of this book.

explains how Evangelicals' moral authority influences their views on Islam. Correlating individuals' opinions to their moral authority makes the findings applicable to Christian-Muslim relations worldwide as everyone appeals to moral authority, irrespective of their geographic location. My hope is that recognition of the differences in Evangelical thinking will enable a more sophisticated cultural conversation about Evangelicals and their relationship to Muslims, which can in turn lead to more accurate understandings and better conflict management.

The Theory behind This Book: Christian Smith's Ingroup/Outgroup Hypothesis and James Hunter's Moral Authority Argument

My research and analysis draw on established theories set forth by sociologists of religion. Theories are statements about how and why certain perceived facts about the world, particularly the social world, are connected. They are valuable because they help make sense of how and why certain phenomena are happening around us. Studies can be designed to test whether relevant theories apply to a given situation, and researchers can analyze the extent to which a theory may explain their research results.

In addressing the question of unity (or disunity) among Evangelical thought on Islam, I draw on the work of Christian Smith. In his work on subcultural identity theory, Smith laid out his "ingroup/outgroup hypothesis." This theory holds that "intergroup conflict in a pluralistic context typically strengthens in-group identity" (1998: 113). In other words, if a group experiences a threat from or conflict with a source outside their group, their group will become more strongly unified. Applied to Evangelicalism and Islam, Smith's theory suggests that the existence of conflict between Evangelicals and Islam should strengthen Evangelical identity and promote uniformity in Evangelical views of Islam. My work explores both the merits and limitations of Smith's hypothesis as they apply to intra-Evangelical conflicts on Islam.

Anticipating that Evangelicals do not hold unified views on Islam, as Smith's theory suggests they should, I employ a second theorist's work to explore the reasons for such disagreement. James Hunter is best known for his popular culture wars thesis, which analyzed the emerging cultural polarization in the United States in the early 1990. Hunter's thesis was further articulated and refined in later work exploring how the culture war has played out in the various eras, including in the present exploration of the relationship between science and morality (Hunter and Nedelisky, 2020; Hunter, 2019; Hunter and Nedelisky, 2018; Hunter and Fiorina, 2007; Hunter and Wolfe, 2006b). Hunter perceived hot-button cultural topics such as homosexuality and abortion to have two definable polar opposite positions and thus sought to understand from where these extreme impulses derive. He then created the culture wars thesis, arguing that moral authority was at the root of the divide. This moral authority argument is what I apply in this book. Hunter argues that all people are drawn toward one of two polarizing impulses, namely an "orthodox" impulse, which reasons based on divine authority and revelation, or a "progressive" impulse, which reasons based on personal experience and subjective intuition. These impulses reflect fundamentally different moral authorities, or moral "assumptions," that guide individuals' "perceptions of the world" (1991: 119).

According to this theory, if someone is drawn to a progressive impulse on one topic, this may indicate that they appeal to a progressive source of moral authority to guide their lives. In other words, people are drawn to one of these extremes because, consciously or not, they have aligned their lives according to one of two very different moral authorities. With respect to Evangelicals in particular, some Evangelicals may gravitate toward an orthodox (i.e., traditional) view of moral authority, while others gravitate toward a progressive view. These differing conceptions of moral authority may then translate to contrasting views on a variety of other issues, such as social and political matters. I use Hunter's moral authority argument as a theoretical model to explore why some Evangelicals seem to be dividing on the topic of Islam rather than uniting together. Smith's and Hunter's theories help shape the study's main objectives and provide a framework for exploring if and why Evangelicals differ in their viewpoints. Using these theories as a starting point, my study seeks to gain insight into the level of cohesiveness within Evangelicalism on the topic of Islam and Muslims; it also seeks to understand how differing moral authorities may be catalyzing internal conflicts within Evangelicalism on the topic of Islam.

One advantage of using the moral authority argument to explore Evangelical views of Islam and Muslims is that it transcends politics. There is a common tendency to attribute viewpoints to an individual's political convictions, but this approach does not consider the deeper motivations for adhering to a particular philosophy. Studying moral authority helped me explore and analyze the root cause of differences between people and the differences in the fundamental assumptions that guide our perceptions of the world. An individual's moral authority matters and motivates, and that spills over into how one views Islam, Muslims, interfaith dialogue, and politics, rather than the other way around. The conclusions within this book will hold even under different political circumstances.

Not only are the theoretical models I chose the most relevant for my project, but they are also accessible, and they make good sense to people beyond academia. This is particularly true of Hunter's culture wars theory (which is the theory I explore the most). This accessibility was important for me when I was planning how best to examine Evangelicalism: I wanted to incorporate theories that were tangible, relatable, and that I could talk with family and friends about. The goal was accomplished.

Objectives of This Study

The overarching aim of my research has been to discover how American Evangelicals view Islam and approach Muslims. Specifically, this book has three distinct objectives: (1) to elucidate Evangelical attitudes on the topic of Islam and show how Evangelicals are engaging in dialogue about Islam; (2) to illustrate the extent to which Evangelicals are (or are not) reacting to Islam with increased internal cohesion, as Smith's theory suggests they should; and (3) to show the extent to which interviewees' highest moral authorities explain divergent Evangelical attitudes on topics such as interfaith dialogue with Muslims, Muhammad, the Qur'an, engagement with Muslims, and missiology (e.g., how Evangelicals should interact with and minister to Muslims).

I fulfilled my research objectives by employing qualitative methods, with the main approach being open-ended interviews (discussed further in Appendix 1). To uncover Evangelical attitudes on Islam, it was important to ask Evangelicals questions and get them talking, rather than merely relying on quantitative survey data that can often leave many questions unanswered. Thus, I conducted lengthy interviews with a range of Evangelical leaders who have prominent voices on Islam, such as mega-church pastors, renowned Christian apologists, and Evangelical professors and best-selling authors. I also conducted similarly extensive interviews with Evangelical congregants from two different congregations that are actively engaged with the Muslim community, for a total of seventy-two interviews. At the time of the interview, most of my seventy-two interviewees were living in the "Bible Belt" of the United States—a region in the southern part of the country characterized by a large population of "born again" Evangelical Christians. Most interviewees were living in urban or suburban areas within the Bible Belt (the urban/rural divide is addressed in Chapter 4). These interviews offered me the data I needed to gain a detailed understanding of my interviewees' moral authorities and to conduct an in-depth analysis of intra-Evangelical conflict on Islam.

In the process of fulfilling my research objectives, I found that while Hunter's theory went great distance in explaining the reasons for divergent viewpoints, it did not fully account for some of the nuance reflected in my results. As a sociologist, another objective of any study where theory is employed is to evaluate the theory itself. When a theory does not perfectly fit, the immediate conclusion should not be to dismiss the theory altogether. In some cases, there is opportunity to refine or advance the theory. These advancements can be useful not only for the study at hand but also for future researchers. In the case of Hunter's moral authority theory, there are two specific areas in which his theory can be advanced, and presenting those two advancements is another of the book's objectives.

First, whereas Hunter highlighted two ideal type categories of moral authority (the orthodox/traditional and the progressive), and whereas culture wars literature after Hunter has generally retained this binary conceptualization, I argue that it is helpful to think in terms of a *spectrum* of views regarding moral authority. This spectrum ranges from the progressive on one end to the traditional on the other, but it includes hybrid views in between. Specifically, I added two new hybrid categories—Progressive-Traditional and Traditional-Progressive—to provide four different categories rather than the traditional two.

Second, I draw an important distinction between an individual's *stated* moral authority (the authority an individual claims to have when asked about it directly) versus an individual's *evidential* moral authority (the authority an individual demonstrates indirectly via how he or she actually appeals to moral authority when reasoning about various topics). In other words, the moral reasoning that individuals apply when they are explaining their viewpoints may not necessarily reflect the authority they say, and may even believe, they follow.

My introduction of the concept of evidential moral authority has value in two senses. First, distinguishing between the two types of moral authority provides a more nuanced indication of an individual's true moral authority. Although my interviewees generally stated that they follow similar moral authorities, my evidential analysis suggests that interviewees' moral authorities actually varied considerably in practice. I argue that because evidential moral authority reflects how an individual actually reasons (and not just how they claim to reason), analysis of evidential moral authority is the better indicator of an individual's *true* moral authority. Second, this advancement allows for a bridge between quantitative and qualitative study. While evidential moral authority can certainly be illustrated qualitatively in the content of a respondent's answers, it also lends itself to being measured quantitatively, in a way that can produce numerical data. In the case of my study, although it is primarily qualitative in nature, I was also able to introduce a qualitative measure: I established an individual's evidential moral authority by counting the instances of interviewees' usage of traditional moral authority terminology in their responses to questions regarding Islam and politics. The concept of evidential authority allows researchers to compliment qualitative data with a quantitative component.

A Few Definitions

Although the term "Evangelical" is likely familiar, it is important to discuss the use of the term in this book. When referring to Evangelicalism historically, this book follows the work of many other scholars of Evangelicalism in appreciating the definition of Evangelicalism proposed by historian David Bebbington (e.g., Ganiel, 2008; Guest, 2007; Reimar, 2003; Noll, 1994). Bebbington (1989) identified four qualities that capture the essence of Evangelicalism and that have together come to be known as the "Bebbington quadrilateral." The four qualities are conversionism (one must be converted or "born again" or have experienced the "new birth"), activism (Christians cooperate in the mission of God through evangelism and charitable works), biblicism (the Bible is the inspired word of God), and crucicentrism (stress on the atoning sacrifice of Christ on the cross as a historical event necessary for salvation). Bebbington's quadrilateral is flexible enough to allow for changes over time (e.g., his definition can accommodate early American Evangelicalism's unique emphasis on the Holy Spirit and revival) while still providing enough characteristics to distinguish Evangelicalism from other types of Christianity. Still, as Noll points out, Bebbington's fourfold list of Evangelical distinctives "have never by themselves yielded cohesive, institutionally compact, easily definable, well-coordinated, or clearly demarcated groups of Christians" (Noll, 1994: 8). Thus, these characteristics are broad enough that they can include a variety of conservative Protestantisms in the Evangelical fold, including Fundamentalists, Pentecostals, and Charismatics, even though some members of these various Protestant groups prefer to stress their differences from other Evangelicals rather than celebrating their common Evangelical emphases.

This description provides a general historical definition of the term "Evangelical" and may be helpful in distinguishing Evangelicals from other Christian groups. However, my use of the term in this book also practically includes anyone who self-identifies as an Evangelical. Most Evangelicals in the general population may not articulate their affiliation in terms of the Bebbington quadrilateral, but if they are representing themselves as Evangelicals, they are also included in my use of the term. The individuals I interviewed were given the opportunity to self-identify as Evangelicals, and I did not attempt to evaluate whether they met the criteria described earlier. (Chapters 4 and 5 offer further discussion of this self-identification, as well as rationale for the inclusion of some individuals who declined to self-identify as Evangelicals.) Those who call themselves Evangelicals, speak as Evangelicals, partake in Evangelical activities, and cite Evangelicalism as an influence on their lives are the people who contribute to the perceptions of Evangelicalism in the United States, whether or not they fall strictly within the historical definition. For that reason, I accept self-identification alone as grounds for inclusion in my study and for being labeled as an Evangelical.

Another consideration regarding the use of the term "Evangelical" is the limitation of any generalities that can be made regarding the group as a whole. One limitation of my study is that I am not able to determine how much of the diversity I have found might be reflected in US Evangelicals as a whole. This is due to the fact that my sample of seventy-two interviewees (comprising both congregants and leaders) was small and mostly included Evangelicals who are engaged with Islam and/or Muslims. Therefore, the findings I present are specific to the Evangelicals interviewed for my study. When I generalize my findings, I am generalizing about how my findings apply to the entirety of my *sample* of Evangelicals, not how they apply to the entirety of *all* Evangelicals.

Another key term that occurs repeatedly throughout the book and requires definition is the "dominant historical Evangelical perspective" on Islam. In Chapter 2, I present a precise articulation of the historic, traditional Evangelical view of Muslims—that is, the view of Muslims that predominated among Evangelicals in Evangelicalism's earliest years. Then, throughout the rest of the book, I compare current Evangelicals' views on Islam with that traditional set of Evangelical beliefs on Islam. To characterize how my interviewees' views relate to the dominant historical perspective, I describe their views as either "aligned with the dominant historical Evangelical perspective" or "out of step with the dominant historical Evangelical perspective." In this way, the book is able to compare and contrast the views of various Evangelicals with an objective point of reference.

The term "conflict" is included in the subtitle of my book, and the same term appears frequently in my presentation of Evangelical history (Chapter 2), as well as throughout the rest of the book. In this context, "conflict" generally refers to a struggle of ideas and to a battle over the definition of reality. In the case of this book, the battle is specifically over the definition of what Islam is and how one should engage with Muslims. The term "conflict" is warranted because it accurately captures the state of disharmony in which Evangelicalism now finds itself regarding how to answer the questions of exactly what Islam is and how best to approach Muslims. There are clear and oppositional positions that battle against the other, and which often appear to those most fervent within the battle as irreconcilable, which leads to various degrees of division (Yancey and Quosigk, 2021). To a lesser extent, other conflicts are also introduced, including conflict between Evangelicals and the larger culture, and conflict between Evangelicals and Muslims. These conflicts are very real, and they are also well established and documented. The conflicts within Evangelicalism, however, are much less apparent, and it is these conflicts that the book strives to bring to light.

What to Expect: An Overview of the Chapters

Chapter 2, "External Enemies and Internal Strife: A Historical Review of Evangelicalism and Its Conflicts," provides a timeline of the major eras of Evangelical history in America, giving specific attention to two major themes—the "enmities" Evangelicals experienced with outgroups during each era, as well as the internal division that they experienced among themselves during these same periods. It demonstrates that Evangelicals have always held diverse perspectives on important issues in their societies and that they are far from a monolithic group of Christian believers. The chapter devotes particular attention to tracking the relations between Evangelicals and Muslims, looking at the enmity expressed between the two groups throughout their history and the division among Evangelicals over how to respond to Islam. It also details the contemporary intra-Evangelical conflict over how much Evangelicals can and should borrow from Islam in their missiological activities as some seek to win Muslims to Christianity. This chapter also details the dominant view of Muslims that American Evangelicals had in Evangelicalism's earliest years. This discussion of the dominant historical Evangelical view of Islam is an important background for Chapters 4, 5, 6, and 7, where I will discuss how interviewees' views on Islam either aligned with or diverged from this dominant historical perspective.

Chapter 3, "The Great Divide: Evangelical Identity and Conflicting Moral Authorities," grounds my study in research surrounding identity studies in the sociology of religion, and it also outlines the theoretical and empirical themes that have guided my research. It explains the ingroup/outgroup hypothesis and the merits and limitations of the hypothesis in regard to Evangelical views of Islam. In addition, it articulates how Hunter's moral authority argument sheds light on why there is intra-Evangelical conflict on Islam. Finally, the chapter ends with articulating my refinements to Hunter's theory. It explains my development of four moral authority categories and the Progressive-Traditional spectrum rather than the traditional binary model—one of my key conceptual contributions. This chapter also articulates my distinction between stated moral authority and evidential moral authority. These conceptual developments arose directly from my analysis of the empirical data.

Chapters 4, "Evangelical Leaders: Conflict and Diversity in Places of Power," and 5, "Evangelical Congregants: Strife, Variety, and Moderation," delve into the data. Chapter 4 draws from my qualitative study of Evangelical leaders—leaders who are actively engaged with Islam in one form or another and who have had to decide among a wide variety of approaches regarding both how to think about Islam and how to interact with Muslims. Chapter 5, by contrast, draws from my interviews with congregants from two Evangelical churches in the urban southern United States. These are churches that have dedicated significant time and energy to learning about Islam, conducting missionary trips to areas with significant Muslim populations, and serving Muslims locally and abroad. One congregation is Southern Baptist and the other, while technically nondenominational, also leans Baptist in orientation (Southern Baptist congregations make up the largest Protestant denomination in the United States).

Both of these chapters empirically address two key questions: (1) To what extent are Evangelicals reacting to Islam with increased internal cohesion? (2) How might the moral authority of interviewees elucidate Evangelical attitudes on topics relating to Islam, Muhammad, the Qur'an, interfaith dialogue, missiological strategies for winning over Muslims to Christianity, and initiatives aimed at bridging divides between the two groups? While there are unique arguments within each chapter, most of my significant arguments are similar in both Chapters 4 and 5. In both of these chapters I argue that there is considerable diversity and conflict within Evangelicalism on Islam that appears to challenge Smith's version of the ingroup/outgroup hypothesis. I also articulate how my data point to an affirmation of Hunter's moral authority argument. Simultaneously, both chapters also give attention to ways in which my data refine Hunter's thesis: namely, that most Evangelical leaders in my sample did not congregate on the extreme Evangelical right or the extreme Evangelical left, but rather have moderate hybrid identities when categorized by their evidential moral authority. Most interviewees with traditional evidential moral authorities held positions on Islam consistent with the dominant historical Evangelical perspective, and most interviewees with progressive evidential moral authorities held stances out of step with historical Evangelical thinking on Islam. However, I also give considerable space to detailing the outliers who deviated from this pattern. Ultimately, I suggest that Hunter's moral authority argument is legitimate and illuminative, but that categories of moral authority are more fluid than might be imagined.

Chapter 6, "Complexities of Evangelical Views on Islam: Comparative Perspectives of Leaders and Congregants," the third and final analysis chapter, takes a comparative approach. Much of the literature that has built up around Hunter's culture wars thesis is concerned with determining the extent to which perspectives of leaders are similar to the perspectives of everyday people in the pews. Thus, following the examination of leaders and congregants separately, I then compare them to each other with the goal of providing an overall sense of how leaders and congregants are different and how they are similar. It also compares the four different categories on the Progressive-Traditional spectrum, pointing out the unique characteristics (demographically and otherwise) of the interviewees in each category. In large measure, this analysis shows that leaders and congregants generally exist in the same moral universe, in that most appeal to both progressive and traditional sources of moral authority when talking about Islam, Muslims, and related issues. However, my findings confirm Hunter is correct that leaders are still leading the culture war and are more polarized. The comparison between leaders and congregants and the comparison of individuals in each of the four categories of moral authority illustrate the complexities of Evangelicalism and the variety of ways Evangelicals make use of moral authority and discuss Islam.

Chapter 7, "Making Sense of the Conflict: Where Do We Go from Here?" concludes the book by discussing why this research is important and explaining my conceptual and empirical contributions to understanding Evangelicalism in the United States. Regarding my conceptual advancements, I articulate the usefulness of my creation of the Progressive-Traditional spectrum and of my distinction between stated moral authority and evidential moral authority. Regarding my empirical contributions, I discuss the richness and diversity I was able to uncover and explain how these empirical findings fill a void in the existing literature. This chapter articulates five key findings and explains how these key findings support or challenge the theories of Smith and Hunter, as described in Chapter 3. It also explores how my findings compare to recent arguments in the study of Evangelicalism, considers the limitations of my study, and discusses areas ripe for future research. Lastly, this chapter explains the usefulness of this work for a variety of groups, including sociologists, policymakers, interfaith practitioners, Muslims and Evangelicals, and others interested in the evolving religious scene in America, where the Muslim population is anticipated to increase.

The book contains appendices that present a justification of the research design and provide necessary technical information about my study. The appendices also include biographical reflexivity as to how my identity impacted the data collection and additional information regarding demographics of my study and engagement levels with Muslims.

Conclusion

Examining how Evangelicals' moral authority orientations shape their attitudes toward Muslims, Islam, and each other is useful not only for improving our understanding of domestic issues; it can also improve our understanding of *global* dynamics. As previously noted, Christianity and Islam are currently the world's largest religions and are projected to continue increasing their respective shares of the world's population relative to other religions. Thus, the specific focus of this portion of my research—the question of how US Evangelicals view Islam—is important on a global scale. More generally, this research also illuminates the vast range of beliefs that coexist under the umbrella of Evangelicalism. If Evangelicals appeal to differing moral authorities on this one topic, they presumably do so on others as well. These findings suggest that US Evangelicalism is far from the unified, monolithic group it is so often portrayed to be. Instead, it is not only diverse but overflowing with internal conflict. Such conflict is not a recent development in Evangelicalism, and we begin with a historical review of both the internal and external conflicts that have characterized Evangelicalism in past centuries.

Chapter 2

EXTERNAL ENEMIES AND INTERNAL STRIFE

A HISTORICAL REVIEW OF EVANGELICALISM AND ITS CONFLICTS

Both read the same Bible and pray to the same God, and each invokes His aid against the other.
—Abraham Lincoln on American Christians in the North and the South, Second Inaugural Address, March 4, 1865

Evangelicalism and Its Conflicts throughout History

Before delving into the diversity of views that exists among Evangelicals with respect to Islam in the present, it will be useful to briefly survey the origins and history of the Evangelical movement. Historically, traditional Evangelical Christians have held an exclusivist faith, believing that there is only one way to obtain salvation from God: through Jesus Christ, with an acceptance of his death and resurrection on the cross (Kidd, 2009). Thus, any creed, belief, religion, or culture that does not affirm this to be true, according to traditional Evangelicalism, is considered false, and religious groups that hold "errant" views are usually considered outgroups. Historically, traditional Evangelical Christians have also been missional, believing it to be their duty to fulfill the Great Commission found in the Gospel of Mark (16:15) to "Go into all the world and proclaim the gospel to the whole creation" (The Bible ESV, 2007). From this perspective, outgroups should be offered Christianity, and Evangelicals hope for their conversion. But Evangelicals' belief in exclusive truth has also led to conflict with outgroups. Outgroup ideologies (i.e., ideologies that do not conform to Evangelical truths derived from the Bible) are viewed as being opposed to truth and are considered evil. For Evangelicals, Islam poses a unique threat as a rival evangelistic monotheistic faith that disputes the divinity, death, and resurrection of Jesus (Kidd, 2009).

Evangelistic exclusivism leads directly to the first abiding theme of Evangelical history explored in this chapter, namely, the continuity of conflict and division between Evangelicals and outgroups. It can be argued that Evangelicalism thrived partially by constructing Evangelical identity in opposition to various outgroups. Over the course of time, Evangelicals perceived themselves as having an "enemy" or "enemies" who have posed some sort of threat and against whom they must struggle. The specific "enemies" have varied depending on the era, but they have included Catholicism, communism, and Islam, among others (Kidd, 2009; Noll, 1994).[1] One perceived adversary, Islam, has remained an enemy throughout the centuries (albeit to varying degrees during different periods). In other cases, those who were considered enemies at one time are no longer viewed so suspiciously, as is the case with Catholics (many Evangelical leaders, although they typically hold serious theological reservations about Catholicism, do not refer to the Pope as the antichrist, as was once commonplace). Regardless, as they have wrestled with these opponents, Evangelicals have sometimes resorted to violence (Lincoln, Gates, and Yacovone, 2009; Noll, 2006). In this chapter I will survey some popular enemies of Evangelicalism and examine the ways these enmities have played out with special attention to Islam.

The second abiding theme explored in this chapter relates to the diversity within Evangelicalism throughout its history. As argued in Chapter 1, dominant Western stereotyping tends to present Evangelicalism as monolithic. Statistics from polls, a certain degree of syncretism between Evangelical culture and nationalism, and inflexible stances regarding sexuality and other religions given as public remarks by Evangelicals have led many academics to lump Evangelicals into the category of "intolerant."

I do not deny that some Evangelicals fit well within these stereotypes. However, for better or worse, there is certainly more diversity within Evangelicalism than is commonly understood. Thus, the second theme explored in this chapter is the perpetual variation within Evangelicalism throughout the movement's history. Though often perceived and presented by outsiders as unified and monolithic, Evangelicalism is actually diverse and constantly in flux, changing "over time in response to the changing assumptions of Western civilization" (Bebbington, 1989: 19). The diversity, which has largely been attributed to a lack of controlling authority to adjudicate the meaning of Scripture and to an abiding individualism, has led at times to intense internal conflict between various Evangelical factions, sometimes testing the cohesiveness of the movement itself.

In this chapter, I will proceed first with a discussion of the origins of Evangelicalism, exploring how people came to identify as Evangelicals. I will then identify and describe major eras of Evangelical history in America, giving specific attention to the two major themes outlined earlier—the "enmities" Evangelicals experienced with outgroups during each era and the internal division that they experienced among themselves during these same periods. Through this discussion, it will become clear that Evangelicals have a long history of not only constructing their identity in opposition to others but also identifying the internal conflict about who the "enemy" is and how that enemy should be treated. My purpose is not to provide an exhaustive historical account. Rather, I identify historical patterns in

1. My list of Evangelical enemies is far from exhaustive; others have included Judaism, Deism, and Hedonism.

order to illuminate how the current diversity in Evangelical perspectives on Islam is in continuity with wider historical, religious, and sociological trends.

Disagreement over Date of Evangelical Emergence

The origins of Evangelicalism are much debated both by lay Evangelicals and by scholars of Evangelicalism.[2] David Bebbington, author of the popular and controversial *Evangelicalism in Modern Britain*, argues that eighteenth-century Evangelicalism has close ties with the Enlightenment and that the Enlightenment should be considered the origin of the movement (1989: 74, 36). Other notable scholars of Evangelicalism have also noted the fusion of Enlightenment ideas and the American Evangelical heritage (Marsden, 2006; Noll, 2002; Hatch, 1989). However, the argument that the rationalist spirit of the Enlightenment strongly influenced Evangelical leaders is a bold assertion, as earlier scholars often "thought of Evangelicalism as its [the Enlightenment's] antithesis" (Urdank, 1991: 241). In contrast to these assertions, lay Evangelicals typically trace their beliefs directly to Jesus and the early church apostles. Many Evangelicals consider their beliefs "as handed down doctrines unaltered from generation to generation" and "would find these claims regarding change over time due to wider cultural forces unsettling" (Haykin and Stewart, 2008: 30). In their view, the true gospel of the Christian Church was concealed and proscribed by the abuses of the Catholic Church during medieval Catholicism, but the true Evangelical gospel was still proclaimed even during this period by a handful of brave believers such as Augustine, Jan Huss, Thomas à Kempis, and John Wycliffe (Kidd, 2007).

This chapter takes a middle view: "Evangelicalism" as understood today had its origins in the early sixteenth-century Protestant Reformation and was "formed in the transatlantic context of the two centuries after the Reformation," not fully

---

2. Bebbington (1989) feels that Evangelicalism in its modern form emerged in the 1730s. This is when activism was really expanded from how Reformers and Puritans had previously understood it. The emotional confidence experienced by the Awakening Reformers (like the Wesley's) led them to engage in passionate witnessing and good works. It was not until the eighteenth century that the modern Protestant missionary movement was developed, which Bebbington perceives as a clear outworking of Evangelical activism. Bebbington sees Wesley as being influenced by John Locke and Enlightenment ideas, which emphasized trusting one's senses. He even goes so far as to say "the evangelical version of Protestantism was created by the Enlightenment" (Bebbington, 1989: 4). This close connection between the Enlightenment and the "emergence of Evangelicalism," however, has been challenged. *The Emergence of Evangelicalism: Exploring Historical Continuities* is full of eighteen scholarly critiques of the "emergence from Enlightenment" and expresses an opinion that there is more continuity between Evangelicals and preceding awakenings of Christianity (Haykin and Stewart, 2008). Bebbington himself has modified his original dating of Evangelicalism; he wrote in 2008 that "the chronology of the early stages of Evangelicalism needs to be extended in both directions" (Haykin and Stewart, 2008:428).

coming into its own until the First Great Awakening (1740s–1780s) that took place in colonial America (Hutchinson and Wolffe, 2012: 211).

The Reformation

Evangelicalism, as usually understood today, was not a recognizable movement at the time of the Protestant Reformation. But given that Evangelicalism is a form of Protestant Christianity, which proliferated during a sixteenth-century protest against Catholicism, its first external "enemy" was the Roman Catholic Church. Those who were united in protest against the Roman Catholic Church during the Protestant Reformation experienced considerable internal conflict as they struggled to determine which precise doctrines would define Protestantism. These early Protestants' opposition to Catholicism and their internal conflicts foreshadow the kind of processes and debates that would become characteristic of Evangelicalism.

The Protestant Reformation was initiated by Martin Luther, who in 1517 penned his *95 Theses* (Baylor, 2012). In the theses, he critiqued the Catholic Church's selling of indulgences and sharply criticized the church's extra-biblical theological doctrines (Bainton, 1950). Luther saw himself as calling the Catholic Church back to New Testament Scripture and back to Christ and the humble life to which Christ called his followers. His consequential work *The Freedom of a Christian*, published in 1520, expanded his criticisms (Oberman, 1989). Luther asserted that freedom is godly and that Christian liberty trumps extra-biblical Catholic law. Against Catholic doctrine, he further argued that good works were not tallied up and weighed by God on judgment day; rather, they were inevitable fruits of true faith (MacCulloch, 2003). Luther hoped to reform the Catholic Church, not break away; but when the Catholic Church rejected his critique and called instead for his excommunication, a new Protestant identity formed, and the powerful Catholic institution became Protestantism's first enemy (Baylor, 2012; Oberman, 1989; Bainton, 1950).

Though Protestants, the forerunners of Evangelicals, viewed the Catholic Church as a common enemy, this common enemy was not enough to keep their movement united. Most all Protestants agreed on the Lordship of Christ and abided by the rudiments of Luther's theology, but various Protestant leaders such as John Calvin and Ulrich Zwingli each emphasized differing aspects of their Protestant faith (Jensen, 1981). Among their many points of disagreement were doctrinal issues like predestination and behavioral issues such as when to support a war—disagreements that continue among their followers to this day. The early tendency toward diversity was only encouraged by Luther's translation of the Bible into the vernacular, which brought the Bible to the common people (MacCulloch, 2003; Bainton, 1950). Their new access to Scripture allowed individual believers to develop a scriptural understanding apart from ecclesiastical institutions, fostering a culture of individualism and freedom of interpretation, which in turn led to schism (Quosigk, 2017; Scribner and Benecke, 1979). Violence and warfare erupted across Europe in the wake of the Reformation as some factions of Christians—Protestants and Catholics included—inspired by both religious and sociopolitical motivations, sought to solve their disagreements at the point of the sword (Quosigk, 2017; Scribner and Benecke, 1979). Though some of the violence occurred between Catholics and Protestants, much of it occurred *within* Protestantism, as dominant Protestant groups sought to suppress minority dissenting groups, including Puritans, Mennonites, Anabaptists, and Quakers, among others (Kidd, 2007; Watt, 2006; Jensen, 1981). As a result of the ongoing warfare, "Christendom" was broken up into single political states of differing religious professions (Quosigk, 2017; MacCulloch, 2003).

The New World

The radical changes the European Reformation set into motion spread well beyond the Alps, extending over the Atlantic to the European colonies in North America (Bainton, 1950). Although some European immigrants to colonial America came for wealth, a considerable number came to escape religious persecution. Thus, alongside the dominant Protestant groups that settled in the New World, there were a variety of dissenting Protestants, persecuted by Catholics and Protestants alike, who streamed across the ocean in the sixteenth and seventeenth centuries to achieve a higher level of religious freedom (Noll, 2002). These included French Huguenots, German Pietists, Dutch Lutherans, and English Puritans, among others (Noll, 2002; Jensen, 1981).

As Protestants poured across the Atlantic to colonial America in search of religious freedom, many of them retained a sense of being in conflict with outsider faiths. Judaism, Hedonism, and (in the seventeenth and eighteenth centuries) Deism were all viewed as theological threats, but two particularly threatening enemies in this period were Catholicism and Islam (Kidd, 2009).

Historically Traditional Views on Islam from Okeley, Williams, and Edwards: Catholicism and Islam as Enemies of Colonial Protestantism

It is understandable that anti-Catholicism would be a common denominator for colonial Protestants, since the settlers had a strong connection to the Reformation movement (the English established Jamestown, located in present-day Virginia, a mere sixty-one years after Luther's death). Multitudes of colonial Protestants saw themselves as true heirs of the Reformation and aspired to ignite a similar reformation in the colonies, continuing in the heritage of Luther, Calvin, and other Reformation leaders as they established communities in the New World. Settlers brought with them a courageous sense of divine purpose: they believed they were a part of establishing a biblical "city on a hill" (Noll, 2002). The hope for a colonial reformation contained an inevitable need to vanquish anything seemingly Catholic or popish, leading to a shared sense among Evangelical-leaning Protestants of being "embattled" against Catholicism (Kidd, 2009).

Islam, too, was viewed as a significant theological enemy. Protestant Christians in America derived their impressions of Islam by reading captivity narratives, through which they learned of the enslavement of North Americans by Muslims in Africa, and by reading pamphlets, printed treatises, or sermons about Islam (Kidd, 2009: 2). Although they had little direct exposure to Islam, early Americans "certainly conversed about Islam regularly" and not in a positive light (Kidd, 2009: 4). Accounts of Muslim leaders being "sexual predators" were routine, and Muhammad was said to have gained "a number to be his followers" by promising "a sensual paradise" that they would enter through martyrdom in jihad (Edwards et al., 1793: 436–39, 50–5). They argued that the successes Muslims enjoyed in making converts were mostly attributed to the sword and threats of violence. In seventeenth- and eighteenth-century America, it was not abnormal to consider Islam a religion of the devil (Kidd, 2009).

These two enemies, Islam and Catholicism, were often linked together in early America, especially in the eschatological and narrative writings of the early English Protestants. Both religions were thought by colonial Protestants to be systems characterized by "irrationality and superstition," and in Protestant eschatological works in early America, the leaders of Catholicism and Islam were often associated with the antichrist—Muhammed being the antichrist of the East and the Pope the antichrist of the West (Kidd, 2009: 9). Rhode Island Baptist leader Roger Williams, for example, hoped that New England would "flourish when the Pope and Mahomet, Rome and Constantinople are in their ashes" and that Protestants might witness "the Pope and Mahomet flung into the Lake that burns with Fire and Brimstone" (Williams, 1676: A3–6). Williams also expressed the belief, widely shared at the time, that the destruction of Islam (simultaneous with the destruction of Popery) would be followed by the conversion of many Jews. Jonathan Edwards, a Puritan preacher perhaps most famous for his "Sinners in the Hands of an Angry God" sermon, similarly connected Islam and Roman Catholicism as the two powerful kingdoms that the devil raised up to combat the kingdom of Christ (McDermott, 2000). Edwards proclaimed that the "Mahometan kingdom" is like the Roman Church "of mighty power and vast extant" and set up by the devil as the antichrist of the East. "Mahomet" (Muhammad), who "was to be considered as the head next under God, published 'his Koran' which he pretended to have received from the angel Gabriel." Muhammad was also deemed by Edwards as "being a crafty man" who took advantage of his ignorant followers who were already "greatly divided in their opinions of religious matters" (Edwards, 1793: 436–9, 504–5). Edwards argued that "Islam represented intellectual regression" and "the suppression of free thought," that it won followers due to "sexual rewards," and that it lacked miracles that others could attest to (McDermott, 2000: 167–75).

In early American narrative literature, demonstrating the connection between Catholicism and Islam became a rhetorical tool to attempt to discredit both belief systems and show the superiority of Protestant Christianity. This is exemplified in the stories of escaped or redeemed captives of "Barbary" pirates who wrote captivity narratives describing their experience as a captive in an Islamic culture. They shared their stories about being Christian slaves to Muslims. For instance, the 1675 narrative of William Okeley, an English captive, compared practices of Islam with practices of Catholicism. Okeley told of the "notorious" hypocrisy of Algerian

Muslims who celebrated "Ramedan, which is their Lent" by fasting during the day but then gluttonously partook in feasts and sex by night which would "neither spare man in their rage, nor woman in their lust." Okeley felt the hypocrisy so extreme that it might only be compared with perhaps "the Popish Carnevals" of Catholicism (1676: 13–27). Narratives such as Okeley's became so popular that some poor alms-seekers in colonial America sought the favor of passersby by claiming to have obtained injuries by the Turks, which left bodily damage so great that it inhibited their ability to work (Kidd, 2009: 3). Although the Barbary pirates became less active in the mid-eighteenth century, the captives' narratives lived on in the colonial imagination, stirring fear, anger, and disapproval regarding Islam within the Protestant community.

The Great Awakening

Although the Evangelical movement had its roots in the Protestant Reformation and the earlier Christian Church, the movement began to come into its own as a recognizable movement distinct from other forms of Protestantism in the eighteenth century. As the movement became increasingly well defined, Evangelicals continued to experience conflict both with outsiders and among themselves. During this period, the primary outside "enemy" of Evangelicalism was the system of religious establishment in the colonies; internal conflict, meanwhile, centered on theological questions about a number of things—for example, how the Holy Spirit manifested itself, how to determine when a believer had experienced true conversion, and how to find the proper place of Islam in eschatology.

Following the European model, most of the colonies at the beginning of the eighteenth century had an official state church supported through taxation. In the New England colonies, the state church was primarily the Congregational Church; in the southern colonies, the established church was primarily the Church of England, though its strength was not much felt outside of the cities and towns. However, by the middle of the century, colonial dissenters were beginning to grow critical of these establishments, and the state-sponsored churches of the day became the new Evangelical "enemy."

This disenchantment with established religion occurred largely as a result of the revival movement known as the First Great Awakening, which swept the colonies beginning in the 1730s and ending in the 1780s at the closure of the American Revolution (Kidd, 2007). During the decades of the Awakening, traveling preachers such as George Whitefield, John Wesley, and Samuel Morris crisscrossed the colonies, breaking with the tradition of preaching in church buildings and instead making use of fields and parks for open-air preaching. These revivals were so quantitatively and qualitatively powerful that some historians have considered them to be the beginning of Evangelicalism itself. Indeed, their lively messages promoted what are recognized today as one of the defining elements of Evangelicalism: a deeply emotional religious experience, which they taught was legitimate and even essential to genuine faith. Though similar to English Evangelicalism, Evangelicalism in America was distinct in the sense that it was more enthusiastic and carried less decorum and less respect for tradition. Thomas Kidd points out that early American Evangelicalism gave special attention to the person of the Holy Spirit. Kidd writes, "Early American Evangelicalism was distinguished from earlier forms of Protestantism by dramatically increased emphasis on *seasons of revival,* or *out pouring of the Holy Spirit,* and on *converted sinners experiencing God's love personally*" (2007: xiv).

By the 1760s Evangelical preachers from the North, many being Presbyterian or Baptist, had begun to minister in the "southern backcountry," among the "isolated and scattered white settlers," which began the continual growth of Evangelical churches in the southern regions (Kidd, 2008: 17–18). At the time of the American Revolution, Evangelicals were still outnumbered in the South, but the seeds were planted for what would soon become America's "Bible Belt."

Colonists, caught up in the Evangelical revival fervor, became increasingly disenchanted with the state-sponsored religious establishment. Although the established churches were Protestant, and although some members of these established churches were themselves Evangelicals, most Evangelicals found them to be too similar to Catholicism. The dissenters typically shared a fondness for a demonstration of personal faith more intense than was generally found in the formal printed prayers of Anglicanism, and the desire for a more fervent church and a more graceful God led many to pursue alternatives to the usual high church services. As the First Great Awakening swept the colonies and the Evangelical movement grew, Evangelical dissenters (Puritans, Quakers, Presbyterians, "Zinzendorf-ers," Baptists, and Methodists, among others) began to push for the "disestablishment" of religion. Baptists pleaded with Virginia's government to remove "every species of religious as well as civil bondage" (Petition of Hanover Presbytery 1776, as cited in James, 1971: 71–2). They again used examples from within Catholicism and Islam to show the error of state establishments of religion. Establishment, they said, "was used to cruelly establish Islam in Muslim lands, and Catholicism in catholic lands—did Protestant Virginia want to follow the example of Muslims and Catholics?" (Kidd, 2010: 182). Evangelical Baptist ministers such as Isaac Backus and John Leland led a push for religious freedom and protection of rights of religious minorities; they were intimately acquainted with religious persecution, as the establishment in Virginia persecuted many Baptists. But though the early American Evangelicals pressed for religious liberty and separation of church and state, they were not seeking the sort of modern, quiet, private, apolitical faith or secular republic that has more recently been encouraged in the United States; rather, they sought a "combination of public religion and religious freedom" (Kidd, 2010: 40, 243; see also Pew, 2017e). They hoped that all men could "speak freely without fear" and "worship according to his own faith, either one God, three Gods, no God, or twenty Gods; and let government protect him in doing so" (Leland, 1791, as cited in Kidd, 2008: 140).

But while the Evangelical dissenters united against formal institutionalized religion and agreed on the importance of a personal faith, they certainly did not agree among themselves on everything. One major point of disagreement among Evangelicals was the question of who was really converted. The revivals challenged traditional leadership criteria and aided the leveling of societal distinctions as credentials like education became less important than whether or not individuals had the Holy Spirit dwelling within them. As traditional distinctions faded in importance, the churches went through a rapid period of change. Prior to this period, only white educated males filled church leadership roles. During the revival era, however, people like Samson Occom, a Mohegan Indian, and John Marrant, an African American, were received as Evangelical preachers. Lay, uneducated people began experiencing dreams, visions, healings, revelations, bursts of uncontrollable laughter, and trances; they attributed these outworkings to the Holy Spirit. Sometimes the minister would not experience the same type of manifestations that their congregants were experiencing, and some congregations began to question whether their pastor was really converted. All ministers were challenged to prove their devotion. In this counter-institutional process, some ministers failed and were dismissed.

In addition to arguing over who was truly converted and who was not, Evangelicals also argued among themselves over how far the bodily manifestations of the Holy Spirit could go. While some claimed the Holy Spirit came upon them and worked supernaturally inside of them (e.g., through a healing or a vision), others claimed these individuals were delirious. These arguments were sometimes very passionate and dramatic. One example of this passion is James Davenport. Davenport, a leading radical itinerant of the Great Awakening who attracted many followers, critiqued some fellow Evangelical ministers who were only moderately or cautiously supportive of the revivals. Davenport felt the theological teaching of some of these ministers was too influenced by the views of Reformation-era theologian Jacob Arminius, and he considered them to be not fully converted. He and his followers held book burnings in which they burned books authored by some very popular and enthusiastic colonial ministers, including Increase Mather, Benjamin Coleman, and Charles Chauncey. Claiming to be under the influence of the Holy Spirit, Davenport then challenged his followers to burn their fancy clothing as well, on the grounds that fine clothing was a worldly barrier between people and God. But when Davenport stripped off his own "plush breeches" (pants) and threw them into the fire, his act sparked criticism. Davenport later changed his mind about being under the influence of the Holy Spirit in calling for clothes burning and claimed an ailment in his leg had made him delirious (Smith, 2012: 144).

A third point of disagreement, perhaps less urgent than the previous two conflicts but still significant, concerned the place of Islam in the end times. As in seventeenth-century Protestant literature, Islam was often discussed jointly with Catholicism in Evangelical eschatological writings, and anti-Islamic and anti-Catholic thought were both prevalent. However, as Evangelicals read prophetic Scriptures and sought to interpret them, various authors came to somewhat different conclusions about the role of Islam in biblical prophecies about the end times. Some interpreted the prophecies with a heavy emphasis on the role of Islam in end times, while others downplayed Islam and perceived scriptural prophetic references to be pointing instead to Catholicism, rather than Islam. One example of these differing views is the way Evangelicals interpreted the sixth vial—the drying up of the Euphrates—found in Revelation 16:12. Some eighteenth- and nineteenth-century writers connected the Euphrates with Islam, suggesting that the ruin implied in this verse referred to the ruin of the Turkish Empire, which was ruled by Muslims. In 1762, for example, a Connecticut pastor wrote that he saw the sixth vial as representing the Turks and "as soon as their 2 stumbling Blocks viz. popery & Turkish Power are removed that will come in suddenly"— meaning that once the Turkish Empire and the Catholic Church were gone, the stage would be set for the mass conversion of the Jews (Allen, 1762, as cited in Kidd, 2009: 29). Thomas Wells Bray believed Revelation 16 predicted the Turkish downfall, but he felt more broadly that the downfall would extend to all forms of ecclesiastical or civil tyranny (Bray, 1780: viii–59). Others, however, disagreed with this interpretation and did not see reference to either the Turks or Islam in the sixth vial. Timothy Dwight, for example, believed the Euphrates symbolized Roman spiritual strength, thus connecting the Euphrates with Catholicism (1812: 11), while others such as David Austin, agreeing with Jonathan Edwards, felt the drying of the Euphrates symbolized the drying up of the wealth and means of antichristian churches and territories in general (Austin, 1794: 272, 297).[3]

The Revolutionary War

During the Revolutionary era, beginning around 1765, portions of the American population began to rebel against Britain. There were a variety of political and economic reasons for the animosity between the colonists and the British crown, but there was also a religious dimension to the hostility: many colonial Protestants, including Evangelicals, increasingly began to associate the British monarchy with the Catholic Church. Not all Evangelicals viewed the British crown as a pseudo-Catholic threat, however, and some maintained loyalty to the crown. As a result, the revolutionary period saw Evangelicals not just at odds intellectually but physically at war with one another.

The Church of England, Britain's established church, was technically Protestant, but it was the Protestant denomination most similar to Catholicism in doctrine and worship style. Accordingly, many of the colonists became increasingly suspicious that there was cooperation between Rome and London. As the revolutionary crisis developed, colonists began to perceive that the political actions of the British were

---

3. From the Revolution to the mid-nineteenth century an unprecedented amount of prophetic writings occupied American presses. Eschatological speculation became more widely acceptable than ever before in American society. Often the eschatological predictions asserted that both the Islamic kingdom and the Catholic kingdom would eventually be defeated. Islam became a popular player in the end-time predictions of many Evangelicals by the 1840s. Evangelicals continued to place Islam in their eschatological scenarios but they did not agree on specific prophetic scriptural references.

driven by Catholicism and that the colonists' religious freedom was under threat. Increased taxes, for example, appeared to Evangelicals as a "secular version of the threats they faced against their right to worship God as their Bibles instructed them to do" (Kidd, 2010: 63). The civil and ecclesiastical oppression from the British crown was seen as Popery. Israel Holly, a patriot Evangelical clergyman, believed the British crown was secretly backed by Catholic power. Holly felt that if Britain continued to impose itself on the colonists then "away must go our Bibles" and then we will be made to "pray to the Virgin Mary, worship images, [and] believe the doctrine of Purgatory, and the Pope's infallibility" (1774: 19, 21–2). For many Evangelicals, supporting the British crown was tantamount to supporting Catholicism. The spiritual and civil spheres were conflated, and revolutionary conflict was clothed in religious terms, as some Evangelical ministers publicly claimed that God was on the side of the patriots.

Even those Protestants who were not opposed to establishment in principle were wary of the Anglican establishment in particular. For example, Congregationalists in New England (some of whom were Evangelicals and some of whom were not) were supportive of the concept of state-supported religious establishments, and they believed that rulers deserved obedience unless they promoted immorality or tyranny. However, they held memory of times in English history (1640s and 1680s) when they had been oppressed by what they believed to be ungodly British kings and thus they feared the growth of the Church of England. Congregationalist Evangelicals used past examples of ungodly British tyranny to protest against British power in the colonies. During the revolutionary period, a variety of distinct Evangelical groups (including Baptists, Presbyterians, Methodists, Congregationalists, and others) banded together in the battle against the enemy of British tyranny.

Although the majority of Evangelicals viewed the British monarchy and the Anglican establishment as a threat, they were by no means in full agreement among themselves on the role of the government in religious affairs. As seen previously, Evangelicals tended to oppose state-sponsored religious establishments. In their view, the combination of civil and religious authority was a scheme of the devil, since it made politicians, rather than Christ, head (Rich, 1775: 11). Their hope was that, as church-state establishments were eradicated, "Americans might set the stage for the downfall of the Antichrist, the coming of the millennial kingdom, and the return of Christ" (Kidd, 2010: 168). However, some Evangelicals, especially those aligned with the Anglican and Congregationalist churches, did not share this view. These latter Evangelicals supported a strong relationship between church and state on the grounds that the government needed a Christian establishment to maintain communal morality. Some of these Evangelicals "had no intention of subverting the established order, for they themselves were supported by it" (Kidd, 2010: 45).

Largely because of their disagreement about the proper relationship between church and state, Evangelicals were also divided on which side to support in the war—or whether to engage in war at all. Isaac Backus, an Evangelical minister in colonial America, in describing the revolutionary period, wrote, "True religion is directly opposite to wars" (1871: 264). Following Backus's rationale, some Evangelicals refused to fight at all. In some ways, however, the pacifist position was a difficult one for Evangelicals to take, given that several of the formative *documents* of Protestantism, including the *Augsburg Confession,* the *Helvic Confessions, The Scots' Confession,* and the *Westminster Confession,* had all sprung from armed and doctrinal controversy (Noll, 2006: 15). Accordingly, most Evangelicals were willing to take up arms and generally they aligned with the cause of the patriots. A minority, however, were loyalists. Single congregations were sometimes split, as was the case with one Baptist congregation in Cambridge, New York, whose members "but a few days before had set together at the table of the Lord," yet all too soon were "arranged in direful hostility against one another, amidst the clangor of arms and the rage of battle. Brother fighting against brother!" (Benedict, 1813: 551). Loyalists were subject to harassment by patriots, and this sometimes meant Evangelicals supporting violence against one another. Such was the case with hostility displayed toward Methodists during the war. John Wesley, one of the leaders of Methodism, spoke out against the revolutionaries in England. His loyalty to the British crown caused Methodist ministers in revolutionary America to face persecution, including by fellow Evangelicals, as many were suspicious of the ministers' allegiance. Francis Asbury, a popular Methodist minister, went into hiding and some preachers were put in jail for alleged loyalist tendencies.

The Nineteenth Century, Slavery, and the Civil War

The enemy of religious establishments became less of a threat to Evangelicalism upon the conclusion of the War of Independence against Britain. In the aftermath of the Revolution, Evangelicals shared many common beliefs. For example, they felt that Christianity was superior to other faiths, that a culture of egalitarianism was best, and that the Islamic world needed to be proselytized. They typically had little respect for high church formalism and class distinctions. However, in the nineteenth century, the Civil War again revealed rifts among American Evangelicals. Slavery in particular was extremely divisive for Evangelicals, but other issues divided them as well, including the role of Islam in Bible prophecy and questions about how best to share their Christian faith with Muslims.

In the nineteenth century, much of the Western world was undergoing a process of secularization, but the United States experienced less secularization and less hostility to Christianity than did European countries. Indeed, after the Revolutionary era, the nineteenth century saw the rapid expansion of Evangelicalism. The Second Great Awakening, which swept through the new nation beginning in the late eighteenth century, encouraged the growth of the Baptists and Methodists, whose denominations tended to be heavily Evangelical in orientation. New Evangelical sects also emerged, while high churches continued to lose power. Women, African Americans, and uneducated men became more influential as they were offered power and some leadership positions within the Evangelical movement (Kidd, 2007). More Evangelicals began to believe in "free will," the notion that God gave people the liberty to choose to be saved, rejecting Calvin's doctrine of predestination. On a visit to the United States in 1848, Reverend James Dixon, an English Methodist minister, noticed the American confidence in self-determination, observing that Americans "are all life, elasticity, buoyancy, activity . . . men moving as if they had had the idea that their calling was to act, to choose, to govern—at any rate to govern themselves" (1849: 122).

At the start of the American Civil War, Protestantism dominated the United States. Most regions of the country were overwhelmingly Protestant, and this Protestantism was typically "of a readily identifiable evangelical type" (Noll, 2006: 14). The census of 1860 reported that Protestant institutions made up 95 percent of the churches in the United States, with the main Evangelical denominational families (Baptists, Congregationalists, Methodists, and Presbyterians) accounting for almost 75 percent of all churches (Noll, 2006: 14–15).

By the nineteenth century, an increasing number of Americans were growing distraught by the presence of slavery on American soil. The equality of all human beings by virtue of their creation by God had been the battle cry for the revolutionaries and was solidified in the Declaration of Independence, and this belief in equality was now thrusting many Americans into "a state of profound moral doubt" over slavery (Kidd, 2010: 252). This angst soon spawned a robust antislavery movement, and Evangelicals were at the forefront of it. Indeed, Northern Evangelicals, both black and white, made up the bulk of its ranks.

Although the abolitionist movement provoked incredible religious energy among Evangelicals in the North, it created great tension with many Evangelicals in the South, who were unwilling to entertain abolition. Southern Evangelicalism in this period was becoming increasingly conservative and separatist; there was "a trend toward schism in the southern country, contrasted with ecumenical tendencies in the North" (Reimer, 2003: 26). Accordingly, one denomination after another split in two over the issue of slavery: Presbyterians in 1837, Methodists in 1844, and Baptists in 1845 (Reimer, 2003: 26).

During the Civil War, Americans on both sides of the Mason-Dixon line believed that God was on their side. Evangelical ministers in both the North and the South used the Bible to defend their respective positions on slavery, and pulpits in Confederate and Union territory alike were turned into "instruments of political theology" (Noll, 2006: 1). In his 1865 Second Inaugural Address, Abraham Lincoln acknowledged the religious conviction behind both sides, observing, "Both read the same Bible and pray to the same God, and each invokes His aid against the other." Christians were fighting Christians. He accepted that God could not answer the prayers of victory from both sides and even suggested the terrible consequences of the ongoing war are "the judgments of the Lord and are true and righteous altogether" (Lincoln, 1865, as cited in Gates, 2009: xlviii–xlvix).

Topics unrelated to slavery also occupied the minds of Evangelicals in antebellum America. One of these was the conversion of the Islamic world. Due to divergent interpretations of biblical prophecies, there was disagreement among Evangelicals as to what would happen with respect to Islam prior to the establishment of the kingdom of God. Some held that Muslims would be destroyed, but many believed that Muslims would be won over via conversion. This latter view, in combination with the spiritual incitement of the Second Awakening, prompted an interest among Evangelicals in missions to Muslims. The creation of the American Board of Commissioners for Foreign Missions (ABCFM) in 1810 was representative of this new missionary impulse, and travel and missionary literature in this period also point to the importance American Christians put on their commission to the Muslim world. The missionary literature in this period popularized the view of Islam as being difficult to proselytize and stressed that Western Christians would need to exert a lot of effort in evangelizing Muslims (Heyrman, 2015; Kidd, 2009). The literature also promoted Christian exclusivism and superiority, and held that Islamic culture was a degraded culture in need of the hope that only the Christian gospel could give.

While there was general agreement about the need to proselytize Muslims, there were no clear-cut answers about how to accomplish this. One issue was that many missionaries were working in regions where proselytizing Muslims was illegal, such as in the Middle East. Therefore, missionaries in these areas often began to aid and missionize distant forms of Christianity, like Orthodox Christians or Christian Armenians living in Muslim lands, as this *was* legal. Missionaries hoped that the Muslim majorities in these countries would come to Jesus once they saw their Christian neighbors being awakened to the power of the gospel. While this method did create stronger ties between American Christians and Christians in the Muslim world, it also meant that Protestant missionaries rarely talked to actual Muslims. The few successful conversion stories were widely circulated, but direct Muslim evangelization was rare (Heyrman, 2015). Some Christians wondered why Western Christians continued to neglect Muslims and frowned upon the strategy of working with the indigenous Christian groups, rather than with Muslims themselves. These thinkers pointed out that some sects of Islam (such as the Shi'is of Persia) were open to hearing the gospel, and they held that Western Christians should take the gospel directly to Muslims (Kidd, 2009).

The Early Twentieth Century and the Rise of Modernism

At the dawn of the twentieth century, Evangelicals had to grapple with an increasingly pluralistic, modern world. Many Evangelicals felt oppressed by the worldview of moderns, and they increasingly perceived modernism as a threat. At the same time, however, the question of how much to embrace modernism also divided Evangelicals among themselves, eventually resulting in a bitter fundamentalist-modernist split.

By the 1920s, American Evangelicals believed they were living in a country that was turning away from Christ. A number of shifts in the culture of early twentieth-century America seemed to indicate that the United States was no longer a country rooted in the Bible. Some public schools, for example, began to adopt curricula that embraced religious pluralism (rather than teaching Christian distinctiveness); they also promoted Darwinian evolution over the biblical creation account. According to Marsden, these changes were all key components of the philosophical movement known as "modernism" (2006). A parallel shift was taking place in higher education as American universities, most of which had been founded as explicitly Christian institutions, "became more secularist in attitude and orientation" (Jacobsen and Jacobsen, 2008: 9). Other changes, including the growth of cities, the continued expansion of industries, and all that went along with having participated in the First World War, contributed to a more doubtful worldview that morality was not black and white, and left the nation with questions about the credibility and relevance of traditional forms of Christianity. In this cultural climate, some Americans responded with a rejection of certainty of belief and a rejection of Christianity, which they assumed would fade away with the expansion of the modern state. They saw belief in the Bible as the authoritative Word of God as "a manifestation of cultural lag that time and education eventually would eliminate" (Marsden, 2006: 4).

During this period, the shifts caused by modernism prompted many Evangelicals to fight back in an attempt to rescue schools, churches, and the culture in general from the onslaught of modernism. Many Evangelicals saw themselves in a spiritual battle, and they set out to "purge the churches of modernism and the schools of Darwinism" (Marsden, 2006: 5). To many Evangelicals, modernist developments were signs of biblical prophecy being fulfilled. Evangelical ministers, Bible institutes, conferences, radio personalities, publishers, and evangelists all attempted in earnest to reassert the authority of the Bible and the doctrine of salvation through Christ alone.

Much of the modernist challenge came from outside Evangelical ranks, and in that sense it was an external threat. However, it also produced internal conflict, stemming from variation in the degree to which Evangelicals felt connected to modern ideals. Some theologians, while still maintaining many acknowledged Christian beliefs, felt comfortable embracing modernism. They began to question the authority of the Bible, leading to the Bible being studied with more critical methods and with a more leftist theology. Instead of emphasizing the message of eternal salvation through trust in Christ's atoning work, they tended to emphasize a social gospel that concentrated on political action, which sought to realize the kingdom of God on earth by aiding the progress of civilization (Marsden, 2006: 120). Their liberal theologies continued to gain influence in higher education institutions before the First World War. On the other hand, those who maintained a more conservative view of the Bible became known as fundamentalists, a term derived from a widely distributed series of booklets *The Fundamentals*, published between 1910 and 1915. The booklets focused on a broad defense of the Christian faith and of saving souls, which some Evangelicals felt was desperately needed to combat modernism. The various volumes in *The Fundamentals* included contrasting perspectives on Darwin's theory of evolution (Livingstone, 1984; see also Livingstone et al., 1999). Some Evangelical contributors defended Darwin's original ideas from what they perceived as the unwarrantable godless "doctrine of evolution" that sprang up in the aftermath of Darwin's scientific contributions; they accepted the essentials of Darwinism on the assumption that God was a part of the creative process (Wright, as cited in Livingstone, 1984: 148). However, other contributors included creationist Evangelicals such as George McCready Price, Harry Rimmer, and William Jennings Bryan, whose views eventually won out and succeeded in leading much of the Evangelical flock to adopt a more literalistic approach to the Bible (Livingstone, 1984: 157–68).

The most spectacular demonstration of the fundamentalist-modernist controversy occurred in 1925 during the highly publicized Scopes Trial, which concerned a ban on the teaching of evolution in public schools. Held in the small southern town of Dayton, Tennessee, the trial was named after the defendant John Scopes, a young biology teacher. Scopes willingly violated Tennessee's Butler Act, which prohibited the teaching of the theory of evolution in public school (Hutchinson and Wolffe, 2012). The trial prompted heated debates about the place of the Bible in education and the accuracy of the biblical account of human origins. Although conservatives who opposed evolution won the case and the teaching of evolution in public schools was banned for a time in Tennessee, fundamentalists solidified their anti-intellectual reputation with the non-Christian elite and more progressive-leaning Christians. The dividing walls between the modernists and the Biblicist Christians grew higher. Because of their perceived backwardness, fundamentalist Evangelicals lost much of their credibility and influence in American society. Fundamentalists largely retreated out of the public eye during the next couple of decades (Wilkinson, 2012). Meanwhile, the more liberal theologies overtook much of the mainstream denominations and prominent theological schools and seminaries, with their cultural influence peaking in the 1930s (Sutton, 2013: 6).

The impact of the modernist-fundamentalist divide was broad, and one of its far-reaching effects was on the issue of missions, specifically missions to Muslims. Some Christians were swayed toward a modernist style that embraced a social gospel approach and focused on service and education in Muslim territories. Meanwhile, fundamentalists tended toward direct proselytization, prioritizing evangelism and conversion more so than their services to the community.

A good illustration of the latter approach is a missionary conference that took place in Cairo, Egypt, in 1906. Egypt had a long history of colonization by various groups, including Ptolemaic, Roman, and Arab groups, and was considered to be under British rule at the time of the 1906 missionary conference (Hopewood, 2020; Mark, 2009). Delegates from almost thirty missionary agencies attended the conference, the purpose of which was to develop a plan for directly ministering to Muslims. Some organizers of the Cairo conference had a negative view of Islam and feared that there could be a resurgence of Islamic colonization in Christian lands if missionaries did not take the commission to go into the entire world seriously, so they hoped to energize the missionaries to evangelize Muslims. Organizers were also were concerned that polytheists and animists, particularly in Africa, would turn to Islam if they did not hear the gospel. One of the delegates whose views were particularly influential in shaping American perceptions of Islam was Samuel Zwemer, an Evangelical missionary within the "Reformed Church in America" denomination. Zwemer, consistent with traditional Evangelical beliefs, held that Islam could not save its adherents; in his view, the "supreme need of the Moslem world is Jesus Christ" (Zwemer, 1911, as cited in Vander Werff, 1977: 231). He supported direct evangelization of Muslims, although he favored blending this approach with a modernist social gospel approach. Zwemer hoped to achieve a mission strategy that combined "philanthropy, education, and direct evangelistic appeals" (Kidd, 2009: 62). Regarding West Africa (where, he said, "it is Islam or Christ!"), Zwemer called for a Holy War waged with peaceful Christian weapons like "the Sword of the Spirit, which is the Word of God" (Zwemer, 1907: 233-4, 256).

In contrast to the approach of direct proselytization championed by Zwemer and others at the Cairo conference, the modernist approach to missions is reflected in the views of Cyrus Hamlin. Hamlin received his religious education in the congregational tradition of the United Church of Christ. He can be assumed to have considered himself at least moderately Evangelical early in his missionary career, in the sense that he was a Christian missionary purposefully venturing to Muslim lands. However, at the end of the nineteenth century, Hamlin, then head of the ABCFM school and seminary in Turkey, cut ties with ABCFM "over the primacy of education over direct evangelism" (Kidd, 2009: 54). Hamlin came to believe that Muslims would progress when they were civilized by good education and by technologies, like the steamboat and telegraph. More exposure to modern Western culture would help to "soften the prejudices of the Muslim mind" (Hamlin, 1878: 349-78). The example of Hamlin provides a hint of the coming "emergence of a non-Evangelical modernist Protestant perspective on Islam, which did not necessarily denounce Islam or the prophet, but argued that Muslims primarily needed civilization, not spiritual conversion" (Kidd, 2009: 54). This modernist twist to missions equated civilization with Christianity. The need for missionaries to convert people to Christ was downplayed. Following in Hamlin's footsteps, George Herrick, a missionary to Turkey who had been strongly influenced by modernists, exhibited traces of universalist ecumenism when he suggested there was truth in Islam and there were Muslims who sought after God and "who, it is reasonable to hope, have found him" (Herrick, 1912: 17-18, 212-15). Hamlin and Herrick were the trailblazers of what would become by the mid-twentieth century the "liberal Protestant mainstream," which would embrace a more "relativistic view of religion, once the outlook only of some Deists and Unitarians" (Heyrman, 2015: 255).

Although fundamentalist Evangelicals protested against this type of non-conversionist developmental education, the modernist approach was influential, and mainline denominations mostly abandoned conversion ministry. Meanwhile, fundamentalists founded new missionary agencies, resulting in a permanent divide over missions—a divide that still exists today.

The Postwar Era: Evangelical Renewal and the Rise of the Religious Right

Though they had been largely pushed to the margins of American society after the Scopes Trial, Evangelicals' cultural influence was back on the rise in the post–Second World War era (discussed here). However, they also faced an array of new threats in this period. For one, changing cultural attitudes on issues like family, sexuality, and religion in the public sphere posed challenges to Evangelical values; meanwhile, communism became a new enemy on the world stage, and this ideology increasingly appeared alongside Catholicism and Islam in Evangelical prophecies about end times. In addition to addressing these external threats, Evangelicals were also occupied with intra-Evangelical conflict, as those who sought a more moderate form of Evangelicalism increasingly distanced themselves from fundamentalist Evangelicals.

An early sign of the renewal and resurgence of Evangelicalism came in the form of the 1942 formation of the National Association of Evangelicals (NAE). In contrast to many fundamentalists, who were busy separating themselves as much as possible from mainstream culture, the NAE was formed by more moderate-leaning Evangelicals, who adopted a relatively positive and engaging approach to the wider culture, hoping that this strategy would offer Evangelicals greater potential to mold American culture. The NAE leaders distanced themselves from the term "fundamentalist" and instead advocated the label "New Evangelical." Although they did not agree on all theological points, moderate Evangelicals recognized the lack of cohesion of the Evangelical body in the United States and felt the need to bring some unity. They also recognized that since Evangelicals were scattered across many denominations rather than being united under a single umbrella, they were inherently weaker and less influential in matters of politics and media. The Evangelical ministers who joined the NAE felt that they should exercise righteous influence in the government, and the formation of this new organization was intended to increase their potential for influence (Sutton, 2013: 7).

A second sign of the reemergence of Evangelicalism as a significant cultural force was the popularity in the 1950s of crusading evangelists such as Billy Graham and Oral Roberts. Graham, the most famous representative of the NAE's "New Evangelicalism" in the post–Second World War era, had a simple Christian message for all who would hear and "embodied a dynamic Christianity that was unbound by the constraints of denominational difference" (Guest, 2017: 43). He packed out enormous stadiums in the nation's biggest cities preaching about the need for conversion to Christianity. His far-reaching influence is illustrated by the fact that he advised many US presidents, beginning with Harry Truman and including Barack Obama (Sutton, 2013: 8). By 1976, Evangelicalism had enjoyed such resurgence that Jimmy Carter, a confessing, "born-again" Baptist, was able to win election to the presidency of the United States. *Newsweek* magazine, recognizing the momentousness of that event and the wider renewal of Evangelicalism, dubbed it the "Year of the Evangelicals" (Marsden, 2006: 242).

But even as Evangelicalism was undergoing a resurgence, cultural changes beginning in the 1960s were challenging many cherished Evangelical values. Education about sex was increasingly considered the job of public schools; meanwhile, the Supreme Court ruled against teacher-led prayer and Bible reading. Outside of schools, the "cultural revolution" brought challenges to traditional values regarding sexuality and the family. The legalization of abortion, the growing explicitness of movies, and the gay rights movement were all signs of the change, and the commercial culture and the media reinforced these new social mores.

As distress over the possible secularizing trends of the 1970s grew, Evangelicals became "ripe for political mobilization" (Marsden, 2006: 241). As they sought to protect conservative values on issues like family, sexuality, and religion in public life, Evangelicals began to be more involved with conservative politics, creating organizations like the "Moral Majority" and "Focus on the Family," which were bastions of what came to be known as the "Religious Right." In the later twentieth century, the Religious Right enjoyed substantial political clout. Personalities such as Pat Robertson, Jim Bakker, Jerry Falwell, and Charles Colson became prominent spokesmen who talked about their faith and their politics and had no trouble mixing the two (Woodberry and Smith, 1998). These personalities made use of mass media and publicly backed specific political candidates, often Republicans, who typically supported the continuation of school prayer, pro-life policies, small government, and fiscal conservatism. These leaders helped bring some cohesion to the Evangelical movement, and they successfully mobilized Evangelical voters to vote for presidents such as Ronald Reagan and George W. Bush.

That is not to say that all Evangelicals embraced political conservativism or the Religious Right. Illustrating the ever-present variety in Evangelicalism, some Evangelical leaders such as Ronald Sider, Jim Wallis, and Clarence Hilliard began to mobilize in a more progressive direction. Criticizing conservative Evangelical politics for its lack of attention to social justice, these figures began to focus heavily on perceived issues of injustice like race and poverty. They also formulated a new, all-encompassing pro-life stance, which spoke out not only against abortion but also against war, the death penalty, and nuclear weaponry. Other Evangelicals, meanwhile, rejected the combination of faith and politics altogether, preferring to focus solely on faith. Even today, many theologically conservative Protestant ministers are apolitical; among Southern Baptist ministers in particular, "about half think political activism usually hurts the church, and half think some Southern Baptist leaders have gone too far in mixing religion and politics" (Woodberry and Smith, 1998: 47; see also Guth, 1997). These apolitical Evangelicals tend to fear that politics might water down the gospel message and true Evangelicalism.

At the same time that some Evangelicals were mobilizing politically for various causes, they continued to monitor rival religious and philosophical systems and to consider their place in end-time events. Evangelicals of this period continued to interpret Islam as an enemy of the people of God, and their speculations about the end times reflected that view. When Israel was reestablished in 1948, then won the Six-Day War in 1967, some explained the violence that ensued between Israelis and Muslims as a prophetic inevitability, one foretold in ancient scriptural references to Isaac (father of the Jews) and Ishmael (father of the Muslims). Descendants of Ishmael, they said, would always seek the annihilation of God's people Israel. This view of Islam was promoted by Evangelist Hal Lindsey, whose 1970 book *The Late Great Planet Earth* became America's most popular book on prophesy ever.

In addition to Islam, a new enemy, communism, also appeared in eschatological predictions of the second half of the twentieth century. In his book *Israel: Key to*

Prophecy (1957), William Hull, a Pentecostal missionary in Israel, predicted that communist Russia would join with Egypt, Iran, and Iraq and that these Muslim-majority lands would eventually be ruled by communists. God's judgment, however, would eventually eliminate the "Communist hordes" and Russia from the global stage (Kidd, 2009: 89), paving the way for a one-world antichrist government led by a Catholic American president. In the vein of previous American Protestants, Hull combined anti-Islamic and anti-Catholic thought, now adding in anti-communist thought as well.

Although Islam was viewed as an adversary, it is worth noting that not all Evangelical thinking about Muslims was focused on end-times scenarios. One example of a softer approach is the campus ministries to Muslims that emerged after the immigration reforms of 1965. In the wake of the reforms, more Muslims began immigrating to the United States, and Evangelicals realized that it was important to look inward as well as outward with their missionary efforts to Muslims. During this period, many of the parachurch organizations that existed on American college campuses, including Campus Crusade for Christ, InterVarsity, and the Navigators, formed new student ministry programs specifically focused on ministering to Muslims, typically using a relatively mild dialogical approach that discouraged Christian students from discussing foreign policy (Kidd, 2009).

As they pondered external threats, Evangelicals were simultaneously critiquing themselves from within. In particular, they debated one another on how much they could accommodate the increasingly secularized culture around them while maintaining adherence to Scripture. Was it possible to be virtuous while engaging with (or worse, blending into) wider American culture? Were the perils of separatism more sinful? As discussed, a new wave of moderate Evangelicals that emerged in the 1940s set out to pursue greater engagement with "modern" culture and to disassociate themselves with old labels that might turn outsiders off. Leaving the term "fundamentalist" behind, they preferred to be called "New Evangelicals" or simply "Evangelicals," and they hoped that the modifications to their identity could make Christianity more appealing to society (Marsden, 2006: 234–5). However, some Evangelicals were happy to label themselves as fundamentalist and accept the limitations that label placed on their ability to witness to others. Those Evangelicals who maintained a fundamentalist mindset tended to separate themselves as much as possible from mainstream culture, rejecting much of mainstream entertainment media as sinful (as did the early English Puritans) and choosing home schools or private Christian education for their children rather than enrolling them in public schools (Daniels, 1996). Like the fundamentalists of the 1920s, fundamentalists of the 1960s and 1970s felt that America had forsaken its Christian identity.

Contemporary Evangelicalism

Despite Evangelical fears that America is becoming less Christian, the United States today remains strongly religious (Hutchinson and Wolffe, 2012; see also

Oliver-Dee, 2015). Although American courts have been busy with cases brought by secularist groups—such as the American Humanist Association and Freedom From Religion Foundation—for decades, the fact that secularists are able to find areas of public Christianity and then file suit attests to the continued importance of religion in public life. In fact, Kidd believes that "America is more religious and Evangelical now than it was in the revolutionary era" (2010: 255). Hutchinson and Wolffe agree, suggesting that America is becoming even "more Christian" because of "the proximity to Latin America and the predominance of Catholic and Charismatic/Pentecostal practice among migrants" (2012: 212). Among the various faith groups in the United States, Evangelicals are still the largest, with Pew data suggesting they comprise 25 percent of the American population (Pew, 2014). But although Americans may still be religious in the sense that the majority of the population believes in God, research by the Pew Research Center finds that Americans are increasingly less attracted to *institutional* religion (Pew, 2014). According to Pew, this is particularly evident in growth among the "nones"—the "minority of Americans, particularly in the Millennial generation, who say they do not belong to any organized faith" (Pew, 2015b).

While Evangelicals are still apprehensive about many of their traditional enemies, such as Catholicism, communism, and secularism, the enemy that looms largest in the post-9/11 era is Islam. Aversion to Islam, and the desire to maintain religious liberty, has consequently meant that Evangelicals in general are strong supporters of the so-called war on terror, and the existence of that war has in turn worsened the relationship between Evangelicals and Muslims. Meanwhile, postmodernism is another enemy and has put more pressure on Evangelicals to soften their staunch doctrines. More Evangelicals are attending secular universities, and aspirations of affluence—rather than self-sacrifice—are on the rise. This chapter briefly considers Evangelicals' diverse perspectives on postmodernism and politics before concentrating on what seems to be Evangelicalism's chief enemy: Islam.

In the contemporary world, Evangelicals are increasingly having to confront the challenge of postmodernism. The skepticism and relativism characteristic of postmodernism have put pressure on Evangelicals to soften their staunch doctrines. Postmodernism is "on the left rather than the right . . . it is certain of its uncertainty, and often claims that it has seen through the sustaining illusions of others, and so has grasped the 'real' nature of the cultural and political institutions which surround us" (Butler, 2002: 2–3). Postmodernists can be within the Christian fold or outside of it, and for a number of reasons they tend to look down on traditional forms of Christianity and those who adhere to its doctrines. Evangelicals of today live in what Brian McLaren calls an "emerging culture" in which they have to grapple with the cultural shift from the modern world to the postmodern world, with increased diversity and immigration, and the fallout in the wider culture that results from the strong associations between Evangelicals and the Republican Party (McLaren, 2012: 3–5). While many Evangelicals have resisted postmodernist relativism and postcolonial theology some have opted to embrace both and work to change their more traditional churches from within

(Yancey and Quosigk, 2021; Quosigk, 2016). Others left their traditional churches and formed a new movement known as the Emerging Church which is connected to progressive Christianity and liberation theology. Those who identify with the Emerging Church see themselves as being in a process of "deconstructing their previous, personal faith," and they "maintain an orientation that is intellectually open and focused on relationships rather than concentrated on pinning down a correct set of specific beliefs and practices" (Marti and Ganiel, 2014: 59, 40). Conservative Evangelicals have critiqued the "Emerging Church," a movement whose primary origins are from within Evangelicalism (Marti and Ganiel, 2014: 42). Conservative Evangelicals typically see the Emerging Church and progressive Christianity as being too relativistic, postmodern, and baseless.

With the rise of postmodernism, American media have become increasingly prone to attacking various forms of "intolerance," leading many Evangelicals to become hyper sensitive about appearing narrow-minded (Lindsay, 2006: 215; see also Viola, 2016; Hafiz, 2014; Kown, 2013).[4] Evangelicals hope their faith seems "open and tolerant... while still faithful [to orthodox beliefs]" (Lindsay, 2006: 215). The fear of appearing intolerant has curtailed the dominant historical Evangelical impulses to proclaim what they perceive to be proper sexuality as between a man and a woman within the confines of marriage and to denounce homosexual practices as sinful due to the verses in the Bible historically perceived to broadly condemn them. Christians are struggling to be both "tolerant" and "orthodox." For example, Lauren Daigle, a popular singer and songwriter in the Evangelical world, publicly said she was unsure about whether or not homosexuality was sinful. She explained her uncertainty regarding the sinfulness of homosexuality, saying, "I have too many people that I love that are homosexual" and that she is also uncertain because she's "not God" (Merritt, 2018). Daigle's response of uncertainty allows her to appear more tolerant to those affirming of homosexual practices, while simultaneously not appearing to be overtly opposed to a traditional biblical understanding of sexuality. Despite her clear departure from the dominant historical Evangelical perception of proper sexuality, she remains embraced by much of conservative Evangelicalism; years after her remarks, she performed in a 2020 online Good Friday service alongside well-known Christian leaders such Max Lucado and Francis Chan (Longs, 2020).

Although Evangelicalism continues to thrive in America, the lifestyles of many Evangelicals have changed. There has been a shift away from an emphasis on self-sacrifice and toward a culture of self-fulfillment, a change Marsden attributes to the fact that Evangelicalism has been most attractive to people of the suburbs, areas that are characterized by both affluence and aspirations to influence (Marsden, 2006: 255). Mega-churches in these areas attest to the popular appeal and the consumer culture message. According to Woodberry and Smith (1998),

---

4. See Doyel (2013), Viola (2016), Kown (2013), Hafiz (2014), and Sieczkowski (2013, updated 2016) for online news stories and commentaries exemplifying the media's portrayal of portions of Evangelicalism or Evangelical responses to the media.

conservative Protestants have greater public visibility because they have increased their wealth and education.

As in the postwar period, Evangelicals continue to wrestle among themselves about how best to approach politics. While many Evangelicals still identify with the Religious Right, a number of movements have arisen to disrupt the stereotypical association of Evangelicalism with political conservativism. One alternative to the stereotypical association of Evangelicalism with the Religious Right include "Red Letter Christians," a movement led by Tony Campolo and Shane Claiborne. The name refers to the fact that the words of Jesus appear in red in many Bibles, and those involved with the Red Letter Christian movement claim to apply the teachings of Jesus foremost. Red Letter Christians are disapproving of the way many Evangelicals have participated in recent politics and aspire to "transcend partisan politics in a way that does not try to make Jesus into a Republican ... and not into a Democrat, either" (Campolo, 2008: 17).

Similarly, the New Evangelical Partnership for the Common Good (NEP), founded in January 2010 by Evangelical leaders Richard Cizik, Steven Martin, and David Gushee, has also challenged some of the political positions Evangelicals are commonly associated with. The NEP's vision is outlined in a book-length statement titled *A New Evangelical Manifesto: A Kingdom Vision for the Common Good* (2012). The book outlines concerns about certain views common among Evangelical Christians in areas like religion, race, gender, wealth, abortion, global warming, capital punishment, war, torture, and consumerism. Many of the book's contributors identify as Evangelicals and consider themselves to be theologically conservative, yet the political positions they espouse are relatively liberal.[5] These examples point to the findings of Guest, namely, that "Evangelical Christianity is less united, less a vehicle for right-wing politics and less dominant in the USA than it once was" (2012: 479).

While Islam has long figured in Evangelical consciousness, the religion of Islam has loomed especially large in the minds of Evangelicals in the post-9/11 world. According to Ahktar, "Almost all Evangelical denominations" depict Islam as the "enemy of Christianity and the embodiment of evil" (2011). The term "Evangelical Islamophobia" has been used to describe the perceived Evangelical Christian attitude of fear with respect to Muslims (McLaren, 2012). Scholars, as well as Christians who sympathize with postmodernism and liberal theology, are also busy connecting the historically negative Evangelical views of Islam with the "Islamophobic" views of many Americans today (Johnston, 2016; Nigel, 2016; Heyrman, 2015). The negative perceptions of Islam among some Evangelicals mirror the negative perceptions among Americans in general: Islam is widely regarded as the most resistant religion to Western, democratic principles, with

---

5. While most claim to be Evangelicals, some, especially the younger authors, are not sure about attaching the term "Evangelical" to themselves. Gushee notes that these apprehensive contributors "agreed to write for this collection maybe because they see NEP as 'all right' despite the 'E' in our name" (2012: xiii).

over half the population believing that relations between Muslims and Westerners are "generally bad" (Pew, 2006).

Cimino (2005) and Akhtar (2011) argue that Evangelicals are Muslims' strongest critics, as evidenced by Evangelical books and articles that have been published in the last decade by Evangelical leaders. Prominent Evangelical leader Jerry Falwell has called Muhammad a "terrorist," and Jerry Vines, another leading figure in Evangelicalism, has referred to Muhammad as a "demon-possessed pedophile" (Akhtar, 2011; Cimino, 2005). Some Evangelicals have become famous for their outspoken stances in regard to Islam. Terry Jones, pastor of Dove World Outreach Center in Florida, rose to fame in 2010 by organizing an "International Burn-a-Koran Day," which sparked condemnation from some US Evangelicals and additional Muslim violence against Westerners in the Middle East and Indonesia (Sheridan, 2012).

A significant factor that has worsened relations between Evangelicals and Muslims is the so-called war on terror. The war on terror broadly encompasses a series of military activities begun by the United States and its allies after 9/11, including the war in Afghanistan, the war in Iraq, and the more recent war against the Islamic State of Iraq and al-Sham (ISIS) caliphate in Iraq and Syria (Rockmore, 2006). Those with an unfavorable view of Islam, many being Evangelicals, were more likely to support the United States' entrance into both of these conflicts (Sides and Gross, 2013). Historically, Evangelicals have tended to identify strongly with the American nation and, at times, have been accused of conflating the enemies of America with the enemies of Christianity, as conservative Evangelicals view America as a safe-haven for Christians and a land that allows for its proliferation (Bean, 2014). Thus, in this age of terror, some Evangelicals perceive enemies of America to be enemies of Christianity. In a chapter entitled "Is War Normal for American Evangelical Religion?" Wellman ponders the association between southern Evangelical Christianity and war after walking past First Baptist Church in Venice, Florida, and seeing signs that read "God Bless America," "Jesus, the Supreme Commander," and "Pray for our Troops" (2007: 195). Wellman reports that Evangelicals are willing to back the state, and war, when the state battles to suppress evil, spread religious and political freedom, and/or maintain societal order to preserve the preaching of the gospel (2007: 195–208). A survey conducted by the Institute for Religious Research in 2013 found that white Evangelicals hold the most intense patriotic feelings and are more likely than any other religious group surveyed to believe God has granted the United States a special role in history. The *American's Patriot Bible*, published in 2009, targets the spiritual needs of these patriots. In this version of the Scriptures, "The story of the United States is wonderfully woven into the teachings of the Bible," and the edition includes "memorable images from our nation's history and hundreds of enlightening articles which complement the New King James Version Bible text" (Thomas Nelson). Underscoring the connection between faith and nationalism is the fact that this Bible is available in a pocket-sized camouflage version.

Variation among Evangelicals is also evident in the wide range of attitudes Evangelicals hold toward Islam and Muslims, illustrated by diverse perspectives on the "war on terror," the "A Common Word" (ACW) document, the assassination of Osama Bin Laden, and President Donald Trump's travel ban. After the terrorist attacks of September 11, 2001, which has been interpreted as sparking the "war on terror," there was an upswing in books and articles dealing with Islam published by Evangelicals or by traditionally Evangelical publishing houses (Jackson, 2020). My own examination of Evangelical works published in the United States after 9/11 has revealed at least five distinct genres of literature. The first is autobiographical literature, which are books written by Muslim converts to Christianity that offer Christians insider knowledge of Islam (e.g., Qureshi's *Seeking Allah, Finding Jesus: A Devout Muslim Encounters Christianity*, 2013). Qureshi's (2013) *New York Times* best-selling autobiographical book details his life as a Muslim and the difficulties, friendships, investigations, and supernatural happenings that were a part of his journey out of Islam and into Christianity. For example, Qureshi shares personal insights into "the offensiveness of Christianity to Muslim eyes" and "the historical facts . . . and visions and dreams that gave [him] the spiritual confidence [he] needed to approach the Bible as the Word of God" (2016: 17). Autobiographical literature tends to be among the most sought-after material on the topic of Islam. The second genre is missional literature, which is oriented toward evangelizing Muslim neighbors (e.g., Janosik's *The Guide to Answering Islam: What Every Christian Needs to Know About Islam and the Rise of Radical Islam*, 2019, and Medearis's *Muslims, Christians, and Jesus*, 2011). For example, Janosik hopes to help Christian readers to "defend the truth of Christianity and refute the errors of Islam, not in a spirit of fear, hatred or condemnation, but in the spirit of love and respect" (2019: 10). The third genre is terrorism literature, which points out the connections between Islam and terrorism (e.g., Youssef's *The Third Jihad: Overcoming Radical Islam's Plan for the West*, 2019, and Gabriel's *Islam and Terrorism*, 2002). Youssef, an Egyptian Coptic Christian and pastor of a megachurch in America, argues that he has an important perspective and appreciation for the ability of radical Islamists to Islamicize nations and encourages Western Christians to not ignore or belittle the calls for the Islamization of the United States, but rather to use their free speech to share the Christian gospel with Muslims (2019). The fourth genre is critiquing literature, which promises ways to overcome divisions with Muslims and which also incorporates intra-Evangelical literature aimed at critiquing Evangelical perceptions of Islam and Muslims (e.g., Gushee's *Evangelical Peacemakers: Gospel Engagement in a War-Torn World*, 2013, and Camp's *Who Is My Enemy: Questions American Christians Must Face about Islam—and Themselves*, 2011). Camp's critiquing book criticizes Christians for displaying what he believes to be an ethic more representative of Muhammad's militant approach than of Jesus's peaceful one. He also highlights past Christian involvement in war as a means to expose perceived hypocrisy. The fifth genre is eschatological literature, which focuses on how Islam is connected to the last days and to prophetic Scriptures (e.g., Lindsey's *The Everlasting Hatred: The Roots of Jihad*, 2011). Lindsey (2011) argues that the Bible predicted that the conflict among the descendants of the biblical patriarch Abraham (the sons of Isaac and Jacob against the sons of Ishmael and Esau) would continue to persist and the entire world would eventually be involved, igniting the war of Armageddon. There are also books on Islam by Evangelicals that attempt to incorporate all of these genres more holistically, such as *Answering Islam: The Crescent in Light of the Cross* (Geisler and Saleeb, 2002).[6] Within these five categories one can find a variety of attitudes toward Islam, ranging from appreciation to disdain. This variety of attitudes is also reflected among Evangelicals themselves, and all can be seen within Evangelicalism. Some Evangelicals are attempting to reshape Evangelical churches as places where alternatives to traditional Christian ideologies are imagined and discussed. Perhaps the majority are focused on proselytizing to Muslims. Still others take a more standoffish position, believing that many Muslims have a hegemonic agenda and that dialoguing with them is therefore mostly futile.

While many Evangelicals tend to have a negative view of Islam, there is nevertheless significant diversity in Evangelical attitudes regarding Islam, as evident in the fact that some Evangelicals are actively engaged in interfaith peace initiatives with Muslims. The largest of these interfaith initiatives has been ACW, launched in 2007 when 128 Muslims sent an invitation to Christian leaders calling on them to recognize what the authors suggested were shared fundamentals between Islam and Christianity.[7] Numerous prominent Evangelicals, notably Rick Love and Rick Warren, signed the document. Evangelicals who signed ACW tend to focus on finding commonalities between the faiths, such as love for God and neighbor, and building dialogue from that shared common ground. However, not all Evangelicals are in agreement that common ground exists. In his address concerning the Common Word initiative, Evangelical pastor and theologian John Piper strongly disagreed with the assumption that "common ground for Christian-Muslim dialogue is a shared love for the one true God and for our neighbor," further stating "that this absence of such common ground must be made explicit—not to destroy dialogue or to undermine peace, but (from the Christian side) for the sake of forthright, honest, biblically faithful, Christ-exalting, trust-preserving dialogue, and for the sake of truth-based, durable peace" (Piper, 2009; see also McCallum, 2012). Piper is not alone. Albert Mohler, while happy to engage in "respectful dialogue," has articulated his belief that Christians and Muslims share "no mere monotheism," as Christian monotheism is "deeply, inescapably, irreducibly, Christological" (2007). Reconciliation initiatives are controversial within the Evangelical community, as many are concerned and skeptical about interfaith movements that seem to them to downplay the uniqueness of Christ. Although some Evangelicals signed the ACW initiative, many did not, and some who initially signed later asked to have their names removed.

Another illustration of the variety of views on Islam is the range of opinions expressed by Evangelicals after former President Barack Obama announced the

---

6. While I did not conduct an exhaustive literature review of Evangelical publications after 9/11, my reading has been broad enough that I can identify these distinct genres with confidence.

7. The letter's full text is available at http://www.acommonword.com.

assassination of Osama Bin Laden. Some felt it was useful to celebrate his death as a form of victory over evil. Steven Furtick of Elevation Church, for example, encouraged people to "celebrate the sacrifice and victory" of the US troops (2011, as cited in Vu, 2011). Others, however, believed the scriptural command to "not rejoice when your enemies fall" applied to Bin Laden, and these adopted a more tempered view. John Piper wrote a blog answering the question "Is God Glad Osama Bin Laden's Dead?" where he outlined his belief that "God approves and disapproves the death of Osama bin Laden" at the same time (2011). Meanwhile, progressive emergent church leader Brian McLaren was critical of celebrating the death of Bin Laden, as that seemed to him to be adding to the cycle of violence (2011, as cited in Vu, 2011).

The diversity in Evangelical attitudes is also evident in the reaction to policies put forward by the administration of Donald Trump, who was elected the 45th president of the United States in 2016. As of this writing, white Evangelicals have been mostly supportive of Trump's presidency (Pew, 2017a). In particular, they supported Trump's push for implementation of a travel ban from certain Muslim-majority countries, which became commonly known as the "Muslim ban." Indeed, Pew found white Evangelicals to be more approving than other groups of the restrictive travel policies Trump proposed (Pew, 2017b). This is partly due to fears of terrorist attacks by Muslims after mass shootings by Muslims in 2015 in San Bernardino, California, and in 2016 in Orlando, Florida, as well as in numerous places abroad, especially in Western Europe (Pew, 2019; Nagel, 2016). However, some Evangelicals have loudly criticized the travel ban, and Nagel found that "evangelical pastors are among the small group of community leaders who are currently advocating for refugee resettlement on humanitarian grounds" (2016: 187). These leaders see welcoming Muslim refugees as an essential part of their Christian faith. Included in this group are leaders of World Relief, the humanitarian branch of the NAE, which created a petition addressed to President Trump and Vice President Pence expressing their opposition to the travel ban. The petition was signed by 100+ Evangelical leaders and was published in a full-page ad in *The Washington Post*. Taking a middle-of-the-road perspective, Lyman Stone has argued that Christians taking "a literal reading of scripture" must accept their "special duty of compassion to refugees" (2017). While Stone believes that Evangelicals should be accepting of refugees, he has also argued that the tendency among Evangelicals to oppose refugee resettlement in the United States has not been motivated by "racism" or "Islamophobia" but rather by their "globalized worldviews," fed especially by a multitude of missionary accounts about real persecution of Christians in Muslim-majority countries and, in some cases, Evangelicals' first-hand experiences of missionary work abroad. Stone argues that Evangelicals are genuinely (though in his view, unwarrantedly) concerned about possible refugee links to terrorism and that in spite of this they must "leap toward empathy faster" and "work to unlearn the fearfulness that has dominated so many." Stone ends with optimism, arguing that with "more complete information, my people, conservative evangelicals, will come around on this issue" (2017).

Divided on Missiology: Chrislam

Evangelicals continue to attempt to take the Christian gospel to Muslims, but as in previous eras, Evangelicals remain divided on missiological approaches to Islam. In the contemporary world, some Evangelicals have begun to argue that it is possible to be both an orthodox follower of Jesus and a Muslim at the same time, and they do not attempt to convert Muslims out of their religion. These Evangelicals encourage the existence of what have been termed "insider movements" (IMs). Generally speaking, IMs are groups of people from non-Christian backgrounds who have come to believe in Jesus as savior and consider themselves followers of Jesus, but nevertheless maintain their former non-Christian identity. However, defining the movement can be difficult due to the numerous voices working to define it and the fluid use of terminology used in doing so. As defined by Rebecca Lewis, an IM is "any movement to faith in Christ where a) the Gospel flows through pre-existing communities and social networks, and where b) believing families, as valid expressions of the Body of Christ, remain inside their socioreligious communities, retaining their identity as members of that community while living under the Lordship of Jesus Christ and the authority of the Bible" (Talman and Travis, 2015: 226; see also Lewis, 2009). With respect to Islam in particular, then, an IM is a group of individuals from Muslim backgrounds who believe in Christ as savior and consider themselves followers of Jesus, yet who still maintain their Muslim identity and remain (and are encouraged to remain) "inside" Islam.

Other Evangelicals have criticized this strategy, saying it promotes "Chrislam." As the term implies, Chrislam refers to a syncretism or blending of Christianity with Islam. The term was coined by Evangelicals in response to the growth of a philosophy within Christianity that held that it is possible to be both an orthodox follower of Jesus and a Muslim at the same time (IM ideology). The term was originally employed in a derogatory sense to deride what critics believed to be a heretical hybrid of the two religions. Debate centers around the following question: to what degree, if at all, can a follower of Jesus who comes from a Muslim background properly maintain his or her prior social identity as a Muslim?

The term became popularized with the 2011 publication of the book *Chrislam: How Missionaries Are Promoting an Islamized Gospel* (Lingel, Morton, and Nikides, 2011). The book, written in a self-labeled "forthright, unapologetic" tone, was composed by a number of Evangelical leaders, mostly missionaries, who were concerned about the rising popularity among Evangelicals of missiological methods that encourage IMs.

The *Chrislam* book solidified a rift between Evangelicals on how to think about Islam and Muslims. The book's authors argue that advocates of Chrislam are failing to make the proper distinctions between Islam and Christianity and rather are creating something extra-Christian that is far too sympathetic to Islam theologically, and is therefore heretical. Proponents of IMs, however, argue that Evangelicals holding views most aligned with the dominant historical Evangelical perspective—those who would demand a more evident conversion to Christianity and a rejection of the "false" religion of Islam—are expecting too much out of believers from Muslim backgrounds. Some IM proponents argue that an orthodox understanding of the Christian faith, including Trinitarian theology, will take more than one generation for Muslims to achieve.

Conclusion

Conflict with outgroups has been a continuous feature of Evangelicalism from the very origins of the movement. Beginning with Evangelicalism's first external foe—the Catholic Church—and ending with the enemy that looms largest for Evangelicals in the post-9/11 world—Islam—Evangelical identity has always been constructed at least partly in opposition to an "other." But if conflict with outgroups is one key theme of Evangelical history, another key theme is the *internal* conflict Evangelicals have experienced throughout their existence as they struggle to determine right from wrong. As demonstrated throughout this chapter, there is an enduring individualism in Evangelicalism that has led to divergent perspectives on topics such as war, the nature of "true" conversion, bodily manifestations of the Holy Spirit, the place of Islam in eschatology, the legitimacy of revolution and slavery, accommodation of cultural changes, nationalism, missiology, politics, and more. Reviewing the internal division that Evangelicals experienced in a number of major eras of Evangelical history provides evidence that Evangelicals have always passionately debated among themselves about how to respond to perceived enemies. Clearly, Evangelicals are not uniform in their understandings of the implications of their faith and certainly not in unanimous agreement on the implications of their faith with respect to Islam. The next issue to be addressed is *why* this intra-Evangelical division occurs. The next chapter draws on theoretical approaches from identity studies and sociology to explore how (Evangelical) identities are constructed in order to understand the social dynamics not only of why Evangelicals band together against a common enemy but also of why they engage in perpetual internal critique and why they are characterized by persistent diversity and conflict.

Chapter 3

THE GREAT DIVIDE

EVANGELICAL IDENTITY AND CONFLICTING MORAL AUTHORITIES

> What is ultimately at issue, then, are not just disagreements about "values" or "opinions." Such language misconstrues the nature of moral commitments. Such language in the end reduces morality to preferences and cultural whim. What is ultimately at issue are deeply rooted and fundamentally different understandings of being and purpose.
>
> —James Davison Hunter

Introduction

What inspires the internal diversity that exists among Evangelicals? Why is it that Evangelicals are prone to internal critique and disagreement and to construct their identity in opposition to outgroups? This chapter will identify important theoretical approaches that shed light on the social dynamics of these trends, thus helping to explain how Evangelicals can have such different approaches to Islam. It will also explore conceptual and methodological innovations I developed to improve the way these phenomena are studied.

The first part of this chapter explores the theoretical framework of "weak social constructionism" and then delves deeply into two specific theories of identity that have heavily influenced my research: (1) Christian Smith's subcultural identity theory; and (2) the moral authority argument of James Hunter's culture wars thesis. I analyze the strengths of Smith's theory (its explanation of Evangelical cohesion), as well as its weaknesses (a lack of explanation for Evangelicals' internal diversity). I also explore how Hunter's moral authority argument (that individuals usually lean progressivist or orthodox and that these two ideal types offer completely different understandings of being and purpose) explains internal diversity within Evangelicalism. Broadly, I argue that although Hunter's approach has limitations, it helps explain why contemporary US Evangelicals are dividing rather than uniting over Islam.

While Hunter analyzes how the orthodox-progressive divide applies to many different segments of Americans, I will be focusing on its application to and implications for Evangelicals in particular. Specifically, I will examine how Hunter's culture wars thesis and especially his moral authority argument help to explain why Evangelicals are so divided on the topic of Islam. I will also explore Hunter's more recent work that has built upon his popular culture wars thesis, such as *Is There a Culture War? A Dialogue on Values and American Public Life* (2006), *Before the Shooting Begins: Searching for Democracy in America's Culture War* (1994), and *Science and the Good: The Tragic Quest for the Foundations of Morality* (2018), as well as theoretical insights from his statements over the past two decades (Hunter and Nedelisky, 2020; Hunter, 2019; Hunter and Nedelisky, 2018; Hunter and Wolfe, 2006b).

In the final section of the chapter, I describe the methodological innovations that sprang from the theoretical considerations and empirical realities of the project. In other words, I present my refinements of Hunter's thesis and articulate two conceptual contributions my own research makes to his theory. The first is my creation of the two analyses—the stated moral authority analysis (the moral authority an individual *claims* to have) and the evidential moral authority analysis (the moral authority that the individual *actually* appeals to in reasoning about various subjects). I argue that the latter is the more reliable analytical tool. The evidential moral authority analysis is also innovative as it builds a bridge between quantitative and qualitative methods, and, as will be discussed, guards against researcher bias. The second refinement is my creation of the Progressive-Traditional spectrum with four categories, rather than simply two, with the two additional categories being "hybrid" categories that include those less polarized regarding moral authority. The impact of having the Progressive-Traditional spectrum is noteworthy, as it allows for a fuller understanding of the moral authority argument and the way moral authority works itself out in interactions. The last section also includes a broad overview detailing how I approached analysis of the following three chapters.

Weak Social Constructionism

This study benefited from certain aspects of social constructionism in the exploration of intra-Evangelical conflict using the aforementioned theories of both Smith and Hunter. Burr holds that social constructionism is an umbrella theoretical orientation that incorporates several different approaches for studying humans as social beings (e.g., discourse analysis, deconstructionism, instrumentalism, postmodernism) (2015). While some scholars disagree that social constructionists are closely associated with some of these orientations, what loosely links the approaches listed earlier is the acceptance of one or more of the following four beliefs (Burr, 2015; Weinberg, 2014; Gergen, 1985): First, social constructionism views human powers of observation with suspicion and invites us to question the accuracy of our assumptions about how the world seems to be. Second, social constructionism holds that the concepts and categories we employ to comprehend the world are "historically and culturally specific" and postulates that notions of specific societal norms undergo change over time (Burr, 2015: 1–5). Third, social constructionists argue that we develop our individual versions of social knowledge through social interactions with other people. Thus, within strong forms of social constructionism, truth as a mind-independent reality no longer exists, but rather is found via constant social interaction and engagement (Burr, 2015: 1–5). Finally, social constructionism allows for social engagement to produce a variety of possible social constructions and invites different kinds of action from human beings. In other words, social constructionists argue that individuals come to different social constructions as a result of their differing social experiences, and that their varying experiences, in turn, prompt them toward differing courses of action (Burr, 2015).

Because the theories of Smith and Hunter do reflect some elements of social constructionism, as described here, it is important to address the extent to which I believe social constructionism can be a helpful broad theoretical framework. There are various forms of social construction, including both weak forms and strong forms (Leeds-Hurwitz, 2009). One of the main aspects in which social constructionists differ relates to the questions of whether there exists a reality that is independent of our discourse about reality (Hermans, 2002). I am in disagreement with stronger forms of social constructionism, namely, those forms that hold our knowledge of reality to be *entirely* culturally relative (e.g., the "very concepts of real and unreal are socially created" [Leeds-Hurwitz, 2009]). For example, controversial strong forms of social constructionist orientation could result in readers dismissing the conclusions of this study as simply one construct that has no greater claim to truth than any other (Burr, 1998: 14; Mingerink, 2017; Boghossian, 2014; Williams, 2001). This critique of imbedded relativism and consequent meaninglessness within strong forms of social constructionism could lead to the undermining of the entire academic enterprise (Parton, 2012: 141; Boghossian, 2014; Williams, 2001; Edwards, Ashmore, and Potter, 1995). While I accept the assumption that human knowledge is at times conceptually mediated and can be influenced by sociocultural factors, I reject the suggestion, popular among some social constructionists, that humans have no access to reality and that we are trapped in epistemological and linguistic limits that do not allow us to verify whether our beliefs about reality are actually in harmony with externally objective reality. Therefore, I hold only a "weak" version of social constructionism (Smith, 2010). In my view, what is believed to be real is shaped, in varying degrees, both by objective reality and by sociocultural contexts (Yancey and Quosigk, 2021). This understanding allows one to view some aspects of human social life as flexible while still allowing for the existence of truth beyond one's perception of it. Although I am a "weak" social constructionist in the sense that I do not embrace strong forms of social constructionism, I still find certain aspects of social constructionism to be useful for my topic, because it explains how identity (in this case Evangelical identity) can be malleable and fluctuating rather than stagnant and unchanging. Features of social constructionism offer useful approaches for understanding group cohesion as well as ingroup variability. For this reason, elements of social constructionism underpin the approaches of both Smith and Hunter. Embedded within Smith's usage of the "ingroup/outgroup hypothesis" is an acceptance that part of how individuals may develop their versions of social knowledge is through social interactions with other people. And Smith's broader subcultural identity theory exists with the understanding that some of the concepts and categories adopted to comprehend the world are historically and culturally specific (e.g., Evangelicals thrive in modernity). Hunter's culture wars thesis also depends upon the analysis of public discourse, narratives, and symbols, thus necessarily exploring how people may jointly communicate their understandings of the world. In addition, according to Hunter, whether something is good or bad in many ways depends on the perspective of the observer. Taken together, these characteristics of the theories explored here can be viewed as tied to aspects of social constructionism.

Explaining Evangelical Cohesion: Smith's Subcultural Identity Theory

Sociologist of religion Christian Smith has undertaken the challenge of explaining why Evangelicalism continues to thrive in a pluralistic context. In his book *American Evangelicalism: Embattled and Thriving* (1998), Smith develops a subcultural identity theory, drawing from social identity theory, as an alternative theoretical perspective that allows for the viability of religions in modernity and explains why modern American Evangelicalism remains vibrant. Smith relies on cultural sociology and social psychology to support his subcultural identity theory.

The eight propositions included in Smith's subcultural identity theory of religious strength are as follows: (1) "Human drives for meaning and belonging are satisfied primarily by locating human selves within social groups that sustain distinctive morally oriented collective identities"; (2) "Social groups construct and maintain collective identities by drawing symbolic boundaries that create distinction between themselves and relevant outgroups"; (3) "Religious traditions have always strategically renegotiated their collective identities by continually reformulating the ways their constructed orthodoxies engage the changing sociocultural environments they confront"; (4) "Because the socially normative bases of identity legitimation are historically variable, modern religious believers can establish stronger religious identities and commitments on the basis of individual choice than through ascription"; (5) "Individuals and groups define their values and norms and evaluate their identities and actions in relation to specific, chosen reference groups; dissimilar and antagonistic outgroups may serve as negative reference groups"; (6) "Modern pluralism promotes the formation of strong subcultures and potentially 'deviant' identities, including religious subcultures and identities"; (7) "Intergroup conflict in a pluralistic society strengthens in-group identity, solidarity, resource mobilization, and membership retention"; (8) "Modernity can actually increase religion's appeal, by creating social conditions which intensify the kinds of felt needs and desires that religion is especially well-positioned to satisfy" (1998: 89–119).

Two aspects of Smith's theory are of particular relevance for my analysis of Evangelicals and their interactions with Muslims. First is his claim that Evangelicals have a style of "engaged orthodoxy" when encountering outside cultures—a claim that I engage only implicitly, but that provides important background for exploring intra-Evangelical diversity. Smith finds that Evangelicals have adapted quite well to modernity and have creatively responded to cultural, social, and political changes by using tools that modernity offers. Second is the claim that intergroup conflict strengthens the ingroup—a claim that I deal with explicitly and at length. While these two aspects help explain much about the social dynamics of Evangelicalism, they have their limitations, which I explore here.

Engaged Orthodoxy

Smith argues that Evangelicals have an "engaged orthodoxy" in the sense that they are committed to engaging the broader culture while simultaneously holding fast to their core religious beliefs (their orthodoxy). Thus Evangelicals are thriving by balancing between building cultural bridges with outsiders while at the same time protecting their beliefs—their "orthodoxy"—by highlighting their spiritual and moral differences with outsiders.

However, it is not clear that Evangelicals as a group are in fact emphasizing engagement and orthodoxy equally. For example, some sociological studies have found that Evangelicals are secularizing and shifting their arguments toward more humanistic and liberal explanations, away from traditional orthodoxy (Thomas, 2013; Thomas and Olson, 2012a; Chaves, 1993). My own analysis likewise suggests that various Evangelical groups reflect mostly one or the other half of Smith's concept of engaged orthodoxy. Specifically, some Evangelicals appear to focus primarily on engagement with Muslims and are not inclined to highlight differences between themselves and Muslims. Meanwhile, other Evangelicals focus largely on highlighting differences between Evangelicalism and Islam and tend to give less attention to interfaith forms of engagement. Thus, Evangelicals appear to be divided among themselves about how much engagement is appropriate and how important it is to protect orthodoxy.

The Ingroup/Outgroup Hypothesis

The seventh proposition of Smith's subcultural identity theory holds that "intergroup conflict in a pluralistic context typically strengthens ingroup identity, solidarity, resources, mobilization, and membership retention" (1998: 113). Smith explains:

> [C]onflict between groups often tends not to weaken but rather actually to strengthen groups internally. The disagreements and frictions that can arise between different social groups typically bolster their members' identification with, commitment to, and investment in their respective groups. Thus, "problems" for groups externally prove to be beneficial for groups internally. There is nothing quite like an outside threat or enemy to bring people together, make them set aside their internal differences, and increase their dedication and loyalty to the group. (1998: 114)

In order to better understand this hypothesis, it is worth briefly examining the historical background to Smith's ideas. The proposition that external conflict leads to internal cohesion is often communicated as the ingroup/outgroup hypothesis. The idea that groups might engage in conflict with outsiders in order to promote internal group cohesion was popularized initially by sociologists, several of whom are cited in Smith's work (Sumner, 1907; Simmel, 1955; Coser, 1956; Dahrendorf, 1964). These sociologists held that when the attention of a group is diverted toward an external menace, domestic strife will subside and the group will set aside internal differences in order to preserve the ambition of the group. Sociologist Ralph Dahrendorf, for example, wrote in his essay, "The New Germanies: Restoration, Revolution, Reconstruction," that it is generally true that "human groups react to external pressure by increased internal coherence" (1964: 58).

One of the significant early proponents of the ingroup/outgroup hypothesis was William Graham Sumner, whose 1906 study on the topic, titled *Folkways: A Study of the Sociological Importance of Usages, Manners, Customs, Mores, and Morals*, is discussed in Smith's work. Sumner argued that the amount of camaraderie and harmony in the ingroup and the amount of war and animosity toward the outgroups directly correlate to each other and that "the exigencies of war with outsiders are what make peace inside" (1907: 7). Sumner maintained that loyalty and sacrifice for the group plus disdain for outsiders "all grow together, common products of the same situation." For Sumner, this loyalty to the ingroup and antagonism toward those outside represented a social philosophy that "is sanctified by connection with religion" (1907: 7–8).

In 1908, two years after Sumner's *Folkways* was published, George Simmel wrote an essay on social conflict entitled "Conflict and the Web of Group-Affiliations," where he held that the sociological significance of conflict goes beyond "the reciprocal relation of the parties to it," to the point that it affects the inner structure of each party itself. Simmel argued that groups "in a state of peace can permit antagonistic members within to live with one another in an undecided situation because each of them can go his own way and avoid collision." However, a state of conflict "pulls the members so tightly together and subjects them to such a uniform impulse that they must either completely get along with, or completely repel, one another." Further, Simmel suggested that warfare with outsiders "is sometimes the last chance for a state ridden with inner antagonisms to overcome these antagonisms" because it forces the group to either band together or crumble completely (1955: 93).

In addition to relying on the work of Sumner and Simmel for support of his ingroup/outgroup hypothesis, Smith also made use of the work of Lewis Coser. In the latter's 1956 study titled *The Functions of Social Conflict*, Coser adopted many of the theories of social conflict that Simmel had previously proposed. Like Simmel, Coser did not have a purely "negative" view of social conflict but rather held that group conflict can have positive functions and can "contribute to the maintenance of group boundaries and prevent the withdrawal of members from a group" (Coser, 1956: 8).

In sum, the strength of the ingroup/outgroup hypothesis—and Smith's use of it to explain the social dynamics of Evangelicalism—is that it helps us understand how Evangelicals have constructed their identities in opposition to "others."

Limitations of the Ingroup/Outgroup Hypothesis

However, there are limitations to the ingroup/outgroup hypothesis: it does not always hold true in the real world. As we saw in the previous chapter, while Evangelicals may in part have banded together against external "enemies," they also have always harbored diversity within their ranks. Arthur Stein (1976) wrote explicitly about the limitations of the ingroup/outgroup hypothesis, arguing that external conflict may increase internal cohesion but only under specific conditions. In particular, the external threat must impact the entire group equally, and the situation must involve a potential solution. Stein also argued the group must "have been an ongoing one with pre-existing cohesion or consensus," must "have a leadership that can authoritatively enforce cohesion," must "be able to deal with the external conflict," and must be able to "provide emotional comfort and support to its members" (1976: 165). In other words, Stein believed the literature supports the ingroup/outgroup hypothesis but only under very limited conditions.

Coser likewise recognizes the limitations of the ingroup/outgroup hypothesis. Though generally a supporter of the hypothesis, he also presents a lengthy discussion of its qualifications and even offers a counter-hypothesis— namely, that external conflict does *not* always bring internal cohesion. The qualifications Coser articulates are important and helpful when exploring why Evangelicals do not always band together as one coherent unified group. For Coser, not every kind of group conflict is suitable to advance the structure of the group. Whether or not social conflict does in fact increase internal cohesion depends on the kind of issues at the center of the conflict as well as on the kind of societal form within which the conflict takes place. Internal conflicts over goals, values, and interests that don't contradict the foundational assumptions on which the group is built will generally draw the group together. These types of conflicts usually allow for "the readjustment of norms and power relations within groups in accordance with the felt needs of its individual members or subgroups" (1956: 151). By contrast, internal conflicts that *do* challenge those foundational assumptions—conflicts in which the parties no longer share the basic values on which their social system is built—will promote the group's fragmentation (1956: 151-2). Coser also warns that when a conflict arises, members within a group might seek to subvert the group, because of their lack of commitment. In sum, Coser sees conflict as sometimes leading to group cohesion and centralization.

For Coser, the "degree of group consensus prior to the outbreak of the conflict seems to be the most important factor affecting cohesion" (1956: 93). Thus, if the group is not in a "cohesive" state prior to the conflict, threats from outside the group will promote disintegration rather than cohesion. Coser uses the work of Robin

Williams to elucidate this point. Williams holds that, as a general rule, heightened internal cohesion will generally occur only under two specific conditions: "(a) the group must be a 'going concern,' i.e., there must be a minimal consensus among the constituent individuals that the aggregate is a group, and that its preservation as an entity is worthwhile; (b) there must be recognition of an outside threat which is thought to menace the group as a whole, not just some part of it" (Williams as cited in Coser, 1956: 93). Therefore, Coser, following Williams, suggests that conflict with an external entity will not increase internal cohesion in cases "where internal cohesion before the outbreak of the conflict is so low that the group members have ceased to regard preservation of the group as worthwhile" (1956: 93). The external threat will also fail to produce internal cohesion if parts of the group have come to "see the outside threat to concern 'them' rather than 'us'" (1956: 93). Coser argues that in these situations, "disintegration" rather than "cohesion" will be the fate of the group (1956: 93).

Sociologist Louis Kriesberg concurs with Coser, holding that involvement in external conflict, far from strengthening the ingroup, may aggravate existing internal divisions and cause greater internal group discord (Kriesberg, 1973: 249). For Kriesberg, social conflict is defined as a "relationship between two or more parties who (or whose spokesmen) believe they have incompatible goals" (1973: 17). Echoing Coser's belief that "the closer the group, the more intense the conflict" (1956: 152–3), Kriesberg notes that "the more groups have to do with each other, the more they have to quarrel about" (1973: 89). Kriesberg finds that under many circumstances, factors that contribute to the fragmentation of the group are factions and rivalries within groups and selective exits of less committed or militant members as well as the reaction of existing members to the new issues that arise from the confrontation.

If preexisting internal cohesion is key to a group remaining strong in the face of an external threat, the question then becomes, how cohesive has Evangelicalism been throughout its history and in recent years on matters aside from the subject of Islam? As demonstrated in the previous chapter, there has been a great deal of diversity that has existed within Evangelicalism from the beginning. Accordingly, there have been repeated episodes of intense internal conflict among Evangelicals over the centuries. Such internal conflicts continue today. Jeremy Thomas and Daniel Olsen (2012a), for example, have found that Evangelicals in the present are increasingly divided on the topic of homosexuality, and they hypothesize that the "increasing liberalization" of Evangelical beliefs on issues dealing with homosexuality "will likely cause substantial conflict within evangelicalism and could potentially lead to division and schism as more progressive evangelicals fall into increasing disfavor with more conservative evangelicals" (2012a: 269).

Homosexuality is just one topic of disagreement. Given the divisions that continue to plague Evangelicalism, it is not clear whether Evangelicals have a level of cohesiveness among themselves sufficient to preserve the group in the face of an external "threat" such as Islam. Coser's limitation is an important corrective when addressing Evangelicalism's continuing history of internal division.

The Potential for External Threats to Unite Disparate Groups

One other aspect of Simmel's and Coser's work deserves attention. While the bulk of Simmel's argument focuses on the point that conflict brings about internal unity as the hardships of conflict make it mandatory for groups to pursue conformity, Simmel suggests that outside conflict can sometimes join disparate groups together and "even cause enemies to join together against an outside foe" (Stein, 1976: 144). The apparent discrepancy in these two positions has led some to argue that Simmel is not fully consistent with himself (Stein, 1976). However, Coser agrees with Simmel that conflict in certain situations can unite previously antagonistic groups. Coser notes that conflicts with some will yield partnerships with others, and he argues that "conflicts through associations or coalitions, by providing a bond between the members, help to reduce social isolation or to unite individuals and groups otherwise unrelated or antagonistic to each other" (Coser, 1956: 155).

This hypothesis is useful for the present study because it may explain why some Evangelicals have reached out to accommodate Islam and even pursue partnerships with Muslims. As outlined in the previous chapter, there is a long history of internal antagonistic tendencies between various Evangelical groups. It is possible that this internal antagonism has been sufficient to alienate more progressive Evangelicals from their fellow Evangelicals and to prompt them to feel a greater sense of commonality with Muslim "outsiders" than with fellow Evangelicals. Further, this hypothesis foreshadows one of the key insights from Hunter: that progressives from different traditions are more likely to band together than progressives from within a tradition with orthodox from within that same tradition (and vice versa). The next part of the chapter explores how Hunter's culture wars thesis—in particular his moral authority argument—helps explain internal variation within Evangelicalism.

Explaining Internal Variation: Hunter's Culture Wars and the Moral Authority Argument

In a famous speech to the Republican National Convention in 1992, Patrick Buchanan passionately proclaimed that Americans were embattled in a culture war that amounted to a struggle for "the soul of America" (Buchanan, 1992). Just one year earlier, sociologist James Hunter had published *Culture Wars: The Struggle to Define America* (1991), which described a war waged between those with opposing worldviews—the orthodox, meaning those who are committed to a transcendent moral authority, versus the progressives, those who hold a moral authority that resides in personal experiences or scientific rationality. In this work, Hunter presents the culture wars as dividing Americans on topics such as abortion, homosexuality, affirmative action, childcare, values in public education, pornography, funding for the arts, and multiculturalism. He argues that the culture wars are the result of differing conceptions of moral authority in the two opposing camps, with the orthodox looking to a transcendental source for moral authority and the progressives looking to "the spirit of the modern age, a spirit of rationalism and subjectivism" (1991: 44).

Although other scholars have relied on Hunter's moral authority argument to examine other aspects of intra-Evangelical conflict, my application of Hunter's argument to intra-Evangelical divides specifically on the topic of Islam is new. I find the latter application appropriate, however, because debates within Evangelicalism on the topic of Islam concern matters of moral authority. Thus, the culture wars thesis should prove to be particularly well suited for exploring intra-Evangelical conflict on Islam.

Today, some discussion of a culture war with Islam is framed around the rhetoric of "radical Islam versus the West," but I argue that the reasoning some have for holding an unfavorable view of Islam is more deep-seated than a desire to simply protect the West, especially when it comes to US Evangelicals. Thus, Hunter's moral authority argument, which addresses the foundation from which individuals decide whether things are right or wrong, is a helpful analytic tool.

The remainder of this section and the following will explain Hunter's culture wars thesis in further detail, with particular attention to his moral authority argument and his discussion of the role of elites in promoting the culture war. Following that, I will survey the major sources from which Hunter's theory draws as well as look at the body of literature that has grown up around Hunter's work in the two decades since it was published, including some literature critical of his thesis. Finally, I will explain my own application of the culture wars thesis to the debates currently taking place between Evangelicals over the subject of Islam. I will argue that Hunter's approach to moral authority provides us with useful tools for explaining why there is variation within Evangelicalism; in particular, I will hypothesize that there may be overlap among those Evangelicals who are interested in validating aspects of Islam with the "Evangelical left" or "progressivism" and that there may be overlap among those who are more opposed to Islam with the "Evangelical right" or "orthodoxy."

Defining the Culture War

Using militant imagery, Hunter argues that the culture war is a cultural split that has now separated each major faith tradition and divided America into two distinct groups. On one side are the orthodox, those devoted to "external, definable, and transcendent sources of authority," and on the other side the progressivists, those who base their moral reasoning either on "self-grounded rational discourse" or in "personal experience" (1991: 120, 125). Importantly, this division over moral authority has created cleavages within each religious tradition, such that the divisions *within* each religious tradition are now more important than the differences *between* them. Hunter holds that conservative Catholics, Evangelicals, orthodox Jews, and Mormons are more inclined to partner with each other than with those from within their own traditions who hold progressive stances. Not surprisingly, given the date of his thesis, Hunter does not explore Muslims in depth; however, since 2001, other scholars have increasingly noted that Muslims, too, are prone to the same orthodox/progressive divide, and that conservative Muslims may find more commonalities with conservatives of other religious groups than with more liberal Muslims (Davis and Robinson, 2006a; Read, 2003; Bartkowski and Read, 2003).

According to Hunter, the cleavages between orthodox groups and progressive groups arise from differences in the moral authorities to which each side looks to develop its moral vision for life. Hunter also describes moral authority as the "basis by which people determine whether something is good or bad, right or wrong, acceptable or unacceptable" (1991: 42). He emphasizes the feeling of ultimacy attached to an individual's system of moral understanding, in contrast to more superficial attitudes that can easily change. Commitments to particular moral visions "provide a source of identity, purpose, and togetherness for the people who live by them" (1991: 42). Because of the fundamental nature of a person's moral framework, the divide between orthodox and progressives and their respective moral views is more powerful than divides created by class, race, politics, and even religion. Accordingly, the cultural conflicts resulting from differences in moral understanding are profound: they are "ultimately about the struggle for domination" and "the power to define reality" (1991: 42–52).

Hunter further postulates that today's political divisions are the result of fundamentally opposed worldviews, and that they involve conflicts about our most basic beliefs about how to structure our existence within society. Thus, Hunter argues that political disagreements in areas such as abortion, affirmative action, gay rights, and educational values "can be traced ultimately and finally to the matter of moral authority" (1991: 42).

Since the Second World War, the rise of parachurch and special agenda organizations—organizations created to propel a specific mission—has exacerbated the divide within denominations, because "most of these organizations coalesce fairly tightly around opposing ends of the new cultural axis: orthodoxy and progressivism" and have partisan agendas that offer a framework for new cultural allegiances to develop beyond the denomination (Hunter, 1991: 90).

Hunter on Moral Authority

The "orthodox" appeal to truths found in a particular "divinely revealed text"; or if not that, then at least they maintain a commitment to an "external, definable, and transcendent source of authority" (1991: 120). In sharp contrast, the broader progressivist alliance (including both the secular and the religious) appeal to authority based in part on "this-worldly" considerations and the conscious resymbolization of faiths and/or philosophical positions (1991: 122–4). Progressivists who distinguish themselves as religious usually hold a belief that "what is important in the scriptural accounts of God's dealings with His people is not whether they literally occurred but what they symbolize about human relationships today" and that moral and spiritual truth are "conditional and relative" (1991: 123–4). According to Hunter, these differing moral formulations are polarizing, and people are inevitably drawn to one or the other of the two impulses—either the orthodox or the progressivist. Hunter holds that "to speak of moral authority is to speak of the fundamental assumptions that guide our perceptions of the world" (1991: 119). These beliefs ground our understanding of right and wrong and serve as giving a standard for making moral decisions. According to Hunter, what "*divides* the orthodox and progressive *within* tradition are different formulations of moral authority" (1991: 120). While Hunter does acknowledge that all religious traditions, including those that are orthodox, "resymbolize" their traditions, he feels the "orthodox tend to do it unwittingly and as a defensive measure when they feel threatened," while "in the progressivists alliance" "resymbolization" is "accomplished more or less consciously, deliberately, and in a way that is compatible with the spirit of historical change" (1991: 123).

Though there are people in each extreme (particularly the leadership in each impulse), Hunter acknowledges that there are also "people somewhere in the middle," who draw from both the Enlightenment (progressive) and Biblical (orthodox) sources of moral understanding (1991: 132). Hunter acknowledges that "in social reality there is complexity and diversity"; he holds that "certain tendencies and commonalities exist on each side of the cultural divide" (1991: 120). Hunter also accepts that "the orthodox and progressivist conceptions of moral authority and the range of specific assumptions that follow from them are obviously more complex than the rough sketches" he presents (1991: 127).

Hunter holds a very broad definition of religion that encompasses essentially all Americans. Hunter argues that religion should encompass more than traditional theism, and that political philosophies should fall under the umbrella of the term "faith." In his definition, the traditional theistic belief systems of Protestantism, Catholicism, Judaism, and Islam would each be considered faiths, but secular ideologies and "comprehensive political philosophies" such as Marxism, fascism, and humanism would also be considered faiths (1991: 57). Though other theorists might use the less religious term "ideology" rather than "faith" to describe secular belief systems, Hunter argues that in the American context, even secular ideologies typically have a religious quality about them. Thus, for Hunter, in the American context, "the term 'faith'—even with its religious and sectarian connotations—seems more appropriate in capturing the essence of almost everything that passes for belief in America" (1991: 57). According to Hunter, these "faiths" offer different answers to deep questions of purpose (1991: 132).

Due to this Hunter does not see cultural conflict simply in terms of a political squabble, as Robert Wuthnow largely did in his book *The Restructuring of American Religion* (1988). Hunter asserts that to view cultural conflict simply as a political disagreement wrongly implies "that the new and opposing alliances in American public life operate on the same plane of moral discussion" and incorrectly assumes "that each side shares the same ideals of moral community and national life, but that they simply envision different strategies for getting there" (1991: 118). In reality, according to Hunter, those on the different sides of major cultural conflicts in America actually have fundamentally different moral frameworks. While Hunter believes that the orthodox and the progressives are drawn toward specific political perspectives (political conservatism and political liberalism, respectively), he asserts that these tendencies "are merely the *political manifestations of still deeper commitments*" and that more fundamental than any political disagreement is the fact that "orthodox and progressive alliances do not operate on the same moral discourse" (1991: 118). For Hunter, what is fundamentally at issue is not simply arguments about "values" or "opinions" but something rooted within the essence of moral commitment. He observes, "what is ultimately at issue are deeply rooted and fundamentally different understandings of being and purpose" (1991: 132).

Hunter on the Progressivist Appeal to Authority

The broad progressivist alliance includes both religious and secular progressives. While Hunter acknowledges that secular progressives might seem an odd group to include in a list with religious progressives, given that secular progressives are typically quite hostile to orthodox religious belief, he still perceives a deep affinity between the two groups—for example, viewing the cultural hermeneutics of liberal religious belief and of civic (or areligious) humanism as friendly. What unites all progressives, including liberal religious believers and civic humanists, is that they all "maintain the fundamental conviction that moral truth is perpetually unfolding; that moral truth is a human construct and, therefore, is both conditional and relative; and that moral truths should reflect ethical principles that have the human good as their highest end" (1991: 124).

According to Hunter, the moral authority of the progressivist emerges primarily within the context of "this-worldly" considerations. It can be based on two planes of moral reasoning: either "self-grounded rational discourse" or "personal experience" (1991: 124–5). Self-grounded rational discourse is in alignment with Enlightenment naturalism (e.g., that of Thomas Hobbes and the Enlightenment encyclopedists). The goal is to justify moral positions "solely on the grounds of evidence about the human condition," using rationality and the empirical method to evaluate moral claims (1991: 125). The second plane of moral reasoning is "personal experience" and is considered by Hunter to be the "dominant basis of moral reasoning" for religious progressivists (1991: 125). This basis is in alignment with Enlightenment subjectivism (e.g., that of "Kant, Existentialism, and Heidegger"). Using this basis, "experience is ordered and moral judgments are made according to a logic rooted in subjective intuition and understanding" (1991: 125). The moral logic of this basis has been described as liberal or expressive individualism (1991: 125). According to Hunter, "reason linked with a keen awareness of subjective orientation provides the ultimate crucible for determining what is right and wrong" (1991: 125–6). Although some scholars have argued that the progressivist wings of various religions have lost much of their clout in society because of their rejection of absolute moral authority, Hunter disagrees. He affirms that progressive "traditions still provide a powerful sense of continuity with the past, inform a style of communal worship and interpersonal solidarity, and guide their communities in the search for universal ethical principles—principles that have as their ultimate end the fulfillment of human needs and aspirations" (1991: 124).

Hunter on the Orthodox Appeal to Authority

In contrast to progressives, the orthodox are committed to transcendence, which is, according to Hunter, a type of "reality that is independent of, prior to, and more powerful than human experience" (1991: 120). For example, in the Christian tradition, believers hold that God communicates his authority through the "media" of "the spiritual prerogatives of the inerrant Scriptures, both Old and New Testaments," making the Scriptures a transcendent moral authority. Truth for orthodox individuals is believed to be divinely revealed "and not discovered through human endeavor or subjective experience" (1991: 120). The basis of transcendent authority for the orthodox is

> not just symbolic, but propositional; it is not just representational, but it has objective and concrete agency in human affairs. God, they would say, is real and makes Himself tangibly, directly, and even propositionally known in the everyday experience of individuals and communities. From this authority derives a measure of value, purpose, goodness, and identity that is consistent, definable, and even absolute. In matters of moral judgment, the unequivocal appeal of orthodoxy is to these uncompromisable standards. It is, then, an authority that is universally valid—adequate for every circumstance and context. (1991: 121)

The commitment of orthodox individuals to their respective "media of moral authority is so forceful and unwavering that believers in each would consider sources other than their own as heretical" (1991: 120). In this way, Hunter is able to explain why the orthodox branches of Evangelical Christianity hold the Qur'an to be heterodox and false, even while the more progressive branches of Evangelical Christianity are able to welcome the Qur'an.

Hunter sees some secularists on the side of the orthodox. While there are deep divisions between the secular orthodox and the religiously orthodox in terms of their philosophical commitments, some secularists still share with the religiously orthodox a commitment to a transcendent basis for morality. As an example of a secularist who falls on the orthodox side of the divide, Hunter cites Sidney Hook, a celebrated philosopher and conservative atheist. Hunter also suggests that some secular neoconservative intellectuals may be considered orthodox, as they feel religious argumentation holds "aesthetic value or even functional appeal," even if those arguments "are not personally or inwardly compelling" (1991: 121).

Hunter's discussion of the affinities between the religiously orthodox and orthodox secularists is an illustration of how "conservatives" of differing traditions have found more in common with each other than with "liberals" within their own tradition. Historically, as evident in my previous chapter, theological differences between various religious groups were of primary importance (Protestants were opposed to Catholics, etc.). But now, according to Hunter, the most important divisions in the United States are *within* particular religions (e.g., Episcopal conservatives split with Episcopal liberals over the issue of gay ordination). People seek out others who feel the same way about deep questions of meaning and feel strength of identity with those from other traditions who share those views.

The Role of Elites in the Culture War

According to Hunter, the culture war plays out largely among elites who lead institutions and organizations. This is an example of the elite social construction of identity, as elites and the institutions they lead, according to Hunter, construct the terminology used in general public discourse. For Hunter, elites are the ones who come to "create the concepts, supply the language, and explicate the logic of public discussion" (1991: 59). In Hunter's culture wars hypothesis, the realignment taking place in American public culture has been and remains enforced largely by organizations (such as religious denominations, political parties, foundations, and media outlets). Also institutionalizing the conflict are the elites whose "ideals, interests, and actions give all these organizations direction and leadership" (moderated discussion between Hunter and Wolfe, 2006a).

Jeremy Uecker and Glenn Lucke, authors of "Protestant Clergy and the Culture Wars: An Empirical Test of Hunter's Thesis" (2011), have tested Hunter's contention about the role of elites in culture wars and find that religious elites are indeed a key influence. Their study was concerned with whether or not religious leaders are involved in culture wars conflicts, the level of polarization among the clergy, and whether the cleavages between orthodox and progressives within religious groups are more important than the cleavages between those religious groups. Uecker and Lucke conclude that Protestant clergy are indeed participating in the culture wars, that polarization is related to moral authority issues (such as biblical inerrancy) more so than religious tradition, and that "polarization among clergy is somewhat more evident on culture wars issues than on other social and political issues" (2011: 692). Thus, in their view, explorations of Hunter's thesis should return "back where they were originally theorized to be waged: among elites" (2011: 692).

Hunter's position on the role of elites in cultural conflicts is widely shared by others. Michael Grillo, who has written specifically about anti-Muslim politics in the United States, focuses specifically on the way in which elites are able to influence internal conflicts by stoking emotion among their non-elite followers.

On the one hand, elites can and do draw on negative emotions like fear to encourage animosity among their members against outgroups (Grillo, 2014: 583; see also Petersen, 2002; Kaufman, 2001; Horowitz, 1985). At the same time, elites also encourage positive emotions—such as pride, confidence, and a feeling of energy—among their members regarding their own group. Political elites have an "ability to manipulate the emotions of the masses for the purposes of mobilizing and taking action against rival groups" (2014: 584). Adkins et al. (2013) also found that religious opinion leaders are able to impact how individuals process new ideas.

Predecessors of Hunter's Culture War Thesis

One of the figures on whose work Hunter builds is the French sociologist Emile Durkheim, who famously spoke of the division of society into the "sacred" and "profane." Preceding Hunter's moral authority argument, Durkheim interpreted the separation of the "sacred" as the collective expression of an ideal society, developed in relation to the lived experience of the "profane" society (1912: 50–1). Durkheim held that the "sacred" could be anything seen as "set apart" or anything that provides the "life-orienting principles of individuals and the larger community" (Hunter, 1991; see also Durkheim, 1912: 37–40). According to Durkheim (1912: 37), all religious beliefs

> presuppose a classification of all the things, real and ideal, of which men think, into two classes or opposed groups, generally designated by two distinct terms which are translated well enough by the words *profane* and *sacred* (*profane*, *sacré*). This division of the world into two domains, the one containing all that is sacred, the other all that is profane, is the distinctive trait of religious thought; the beliefs, myths, dogmas and legends are either representations or systems of representations which express the nature of sacred things, the virtues and powers which are attributed to them, or their relations with each other and with profane things.

For Durkheim, the two categories of "sacred" and "profane" are profoundly different and in opposition. The traditional divide between good and bad is not as deep as the divide between the sacred and profane, because while the former are part of the same world, the latter represent different worlds. As Durkheim explains, the good and the bad are "of the same class, namely morals, just as sickness and health are two different aspects of the same order of facts, life, while the sacred and the profane have always and everywhere been conceived by the human mind as two distinct classes, as two worlds between which there is nothing in common" (1912: 39). The two become "hostile and jealous rivals of each other" because "men cannot fully belong to one except on condition of leaving the other completely" (1912: 40).

Durkheim's idea of the "sacred" and "profane" lies behind Hunter's belief that the orthodox and progressivist impulses are warring due to "deeply rooted and fundamentally different understandings of being and purpose" (Hunter, 1991: 131). For Hunter and Durkheim, to understand what impassions and gives purpose to communities, one must understand the sacred or the guiding moral authorities. Hunter writes, "what is ultimately at issue are different conceptions of the sacred" (1991: 131). Agreeing with Durkheim, Hunter notes that "communities cannot and will not tolerate the desecration of the sacred" (1991: 131). The problem for Hunter is that "not only does each side of the cultural divide operate with a different conception of the sacred, but the mere existence of the one represents a certain desecration of the other" (1991: 131). In other words, the presence of progressive culture expresses irreverence for orthodox culture, and vice versa.

A second figure on whose work Hunter builds is Richard Merleman. In his book *Making Something of Ourselves: On Culture and Politics in the United States* (1984), Merleman proposes that American society can be broken into two types of moral community, one being the "tight-bounded" and the other being the "loose-bounded." In "tight-bounded" moral communities, moral obligations are fixed and are viewed by those within as an obvious truth of social life. In "loose-bounded" moral communities, moral commitments are individualistic and contingent, and it is the individual who offers moral judgment, rather than the group. Merleman's perspective is analogous to Hunter's distinction between the orthodox and progressive communities. Thus, Hunter's orthodox communities (which correspond to Merleman's "tightly bound" communities) "order themselves, live by, and build upon the substance of a shared commitment to transcendent truths and the moral traditions that uphold them," while progressivist communities (corresponding to Merleman's "loosely bound" communities) tend "not to be burdened by the weight of either 'natural law,' religious prerogative, or traditional community authority"; rather, their type of moral authority can be described as "uniquely shaped by and oriented toward legitimating the prevailing zeitgeist or spirit of the age" (Hunter, 1991: 127).

In addition to Merleman and Durkheim, about a century ago Gresham Machen articulated what he perceived to be foundational differences between "orthodox Christianity" and "liberal Christianity." Machen's work *Christianity and Liberalism* was based on theological analysis and first appeared in 1923. Machen argued that "Christianity is founded upon the Bible" and "it bases upon the Bible both its thinking and its life [this is tied to Hunter's commitment to a "transcendent basis" for morality]" (2009: 67). On the other hand, according to Machen, liberalism "is based upon the shifting emotions of sinful man" [Hunter terms this "personal experience"] (2009: 67). Machen noted that both groups share a common "traditional" phraseology but perceived "liberals" to make use of such language in order to transform it to "become the expression of totally alien ideas," completely reversing the original meaning (2009: 100). Thus, the divides Hunter argues are taking place within Christianity have been perceived by other scholars in various fields, even if termed differently.

Hunter's Culture Wars and the Moral Authority Argument: Strengths, Limits, and Significance

The relevance of Hunter's approach to explaining internal variation within Evangelicalism should by now be obvious. But given the influence that Hunter's culture wars paradigm has had over numerous fields of scholarship—not just the sociology of religion—it is worth considering the strengths, limits, and significance of his work in greater detail. This is important for understanding why I chose to employ Hunter's approach to moral authority in my own research and for explaining what my study adds to the ever-burgeoning body of literature that engages with the culture wars.

Strengths: Proponents of Hunter's Culture War Thesis

The scholarship that has incorporated and engaged with Hunter's culture wars thesis is vast, with authors from various disciplines recognizing the utility of his approach. I will offer a few examples to illustrate the approach's strengths. The first example (Wayne Baker) will focus on the application of the thesis to American culture in general, and the rest of the examples will concentrate on applications of the thesis to American Evangelicalism in particular.

Wayne Baker builds on Hunter in his work on the duality of moral visions in American culture. In "The Duality of American Moral Culture" (2010), Baker utilizes Durkheim's sacred/profane division and Hunter's polarization principle. The duality of moral visions that Baker describes overlaps significantly with Hunter's description of the divide between orthodox and progressive conceptions of moral authority, except that in Baker's analysis the two camps are termed "absolutists" and "relativists." Baker holds that "moral visions reside over attitudes or religious values" and "are fundamental beliefs about the location of moral authority" (2005: 9). Moral absolutists locate moral authority in the transcendental sphere. Most absolutists, according to Baker, see God as the transcendental source of moral authority, but some see moral authority as lying within pure ideas (i.e., Plato) or society itself (i.e., Durkheim). Similarly to how Hunter describes conceptions of moral authority among the orthodox, Baker describes the transcendental sphere as containing "absolute, eternal, and universal laws that always apply to everyone" (2010: 260). By contrast, for Baker's moral relativists—as for Hunter's progressives—"moral authority and judgment reside in the individual or in the local social situation," and it is the individual who decides between right and wrong (2010: 260). Baker believes that this duality shows itself in the form of a culture war where moral relativists and moral absolutists engage in battle (2005: 64–109). For evidence, Baker points to Thomson's analysis of the World Values Survey, which concluded that between 1981 and 1990 America became nearly evenly separated between "moral absolutists," who hold that there are simple definitive guidelines regarding good and evil, and "moral relativists," who decipher what is good or evil by depending on the specific circumstances (cited in Baker, 2005: 80). The same polarization continued through the 1995 and 2000 surveys (Baker, 2005: 79).

Coinciding dualities was an important theme during the second half of the twentieth century. Polarization in viewpoints occurs in various arenas, including the religious, political, and cultural spheres. It is not a strictly American phenomenon: systems of mutual opposites—dualities—have been found throughout the world and are deeply embedded in ancient narratives (e.g., Maybury-Lewis and Almagor, 1989; Jaspers, 1953). Still, polarization and division are well-known themes in American cultural discourse. A number of social scientists share the perception that America's cultural divisions have expanded unto polarization. In addition to Hunter, Os Guiness in *The American Hour: A Time of Reckoning and the Once and Future Role of Faith* (1993) articulates what he believes is a "cultural chasm" that began opening in the 1960s, and Margaret Wyszomirski in "From Accord to Discord: Arts Policy During and After the Culture Wars" (1994) notes a tendency toward ideological polarization in social and domestic matters. Echoing the aforesaid sentiments, Ellison and Musick in *Southern Intolerance: A Fundamentalist Effect* (1993) see an increase in the cultural polarization of American society since the 1970s.

There is a rich tradition of studies that have applied Hunter's work to Evangelicalism, in which my own work follows. During the George W. Bush era, Michael Lindsay noticed the "culture war" in his work with Evangelical leaders, pointing out how "President [George W.] Bush often speaks of the so-called war on terror as a Manichean struggle between forces of 'light' and forces of 'darkness'" (2007: 25). In addition, Lindsay noted why he believed Pat Buchanan's invocation of the "culture war" in his Republican National Convention speech (mentioned at the beginning of the chapter) was successful: because it was a "message that resonated with the conservative Evangelicals who believed they were engaged in an all-out 'culture war'" (2007: 21).

Jeremy Thomas and Daniel Olson have found great variety in Evangelical attitudes on culture war issues (2012a, 2012b). In their content analysis of the Evangelical magazine *Christianity Today* on the topic of homosexuality, Thomas and Olson found that there are indeed differences in moral authority among different segments of Christian society, and that these differences explain many of the cultural conflicts in which Christians are engaged, including conflicts over homosexuality. According to their analysis, Evangelical elites in the 1970s appealed primarily to Christian Scripture when constructing arguments about homosexuality and mostly came to positions opposing homosexuality. By contrast, however, Evangelical elites today are shifting from orthodox reasoning and toward more progressive reasoning when constructing arguments about homosexuality. In particular, Thomas and Olson find that Evangelical elites have been "reducing the frequency of their appeals to biblical sources of moral authority" and have relied more heavily instead on appeals to the natural order, science, and medicine. Simultaneously, these elites are also "reducing the frequency of their negative assessments of the personal morality of homosexuality" while also "demonstrating more tolerant and/or pluralistic attitudes both toward popular depictions of these debates and toward gay persons on the other sides of these debates" (2012a: 243). Further, in their qualitative study of one congregation of gay Evangelicals, Thomas and Olson explain that the form of Evangelicalism they have focused on is "the more progressive side of evangelicalism," the side that shows "a greater degree of flexibility in regard to some theological fine points and especially in regard to various social and political issues, most obviously those related to homosexuality" (2012b: 349–50). Thomas and Olson show how Grace Church, a congregation in the Midwest, has developed a new "approach to managing sexual relationships" that purposefully meshes "both gay and evangelical understandings of sexual and relational life," which are often thought to be fundamentally at odds with each other (2012b: 354).

Yancey and I found Hunter's moral authority argument to be useful in our mixed-methods study of US Christians entitled *One Faith No Longer: The Transformation of Christianity in Red and Blue America* (2021). We illuminate the stark differences between conservative Christians' commitment to what we term a "historic theology emphasizing biblical doctrines" (tied to Hunter's "orthodox" category) and the progressive Christians' commitment to what we call a "Humanistic Ethic of Social Justice" (tied to Hunter's "progressive" category). Ultimately, we argue that the divide between theologically progressive and conservative Christians is so great that one can realistically think of them as different religious groups (Yancey and Quosigk, 2021).

Justin Farrell in "The Young and the Restless? The Liberalization of Young Evangelicals" (2011) finds that differences regarding moral authority among Evangelicals are largely age-based. Farrell finds that younger Evangelicals are more likely to rely on their personal experiences to make moral decisions, whereas older Evangelicals are more prone to basing decisions on biblical teaching or "God's law." Thus, the younger Evangelicals in Farrell's study tend toward what Hunter would term a progressive sense of moral authority, whereas older generations tend toward an orthodox understanding. Beliefs surrounding moral authority are found to be mediating factors in age differences on issues like premarital sex, traditional marriage, pornography, and cohabitation (though not on abortion). According to Farrell, younger Evangelicals "know more unwed mothers, have more premarital sex, are more likely to live together before marriage, and have more homosexual friends" (2011: 520). Farrell attributes some of this difference in views to the effects of pluralistic modernity, which allows young Evangelicals, especially those who are unmarried, to pick and choose their identities, mixing and matching and changing, until they find something comfortable to them. Farrell holds that the dissension in views "about the basis of moral authority runs very deep and has widespread implications for the future of evangelicalism" (2011: 528). Accordingly, he suggests that "work on the causes and influences of this disagreement among evangelicals should be a high priority for scholars of religion" (2011: 528).

According to some sociologists, Evangelicals in general are moving from traditional sources of authority to progressive sources, and are increasingly undergoing a process of secularization, noticeable in the way that they articulate justifications for their positions. For example, Mark Chaves (1993, 1994) argues that Protestant leadership, which includes Evangelical leadership, is becoming less religious, which he refers to as a process of "internal secularization." Chaves argues that secularization should be thought of less in terms of declining rates of religious belief or participation and more in terms of declining scope of religious authority, by which he means the diminishing extent to which supernatural justifications are used to legitimize various manifestations of social control. Chaves finds that Protestant denominations, while having the outward appearances of being religious, are actually becoming less religious and supernaturally legitimated, especially in regard to their control of organizational resources such as money, property, publishing houses, and mission agencies.

In "Outsourcing Moral Authority: The Internal Secularization of Evangelicals' Anti-Pornography Narratives" (2013), Jeremy Thomas makes use of and furthers Chaves's "notion of internal secularization" to demonstrate how Evangelicals' anti-pornography narratives have become progressively secular (2013: 457). He argues that Evangelicals are actually involved in a process of "outsourcing" their moral authorities, meaning that Evangelicals are increasingly drawing from sources outside of their own explicitly religious tradition to inform their moral vision. Traditionally orthodox types of moral authority such as biblical restrictions regarding "God's will" for society are being used less frequently in Evangelical moral narratives. Instead, Evangelical narratives are increasingly demonstrating "secular forms of moral authority such as humanistic conceptions of individual rights and psychological health" (2013: 457).

Thomas illustrates this process by analyzing anti-pornography narratives current in Evangelical culture. According to Thomas, Evangelicals make use of three different anti-pornography narratives: the narrative of traditional values, the narrative of public-performer harm, and the narrative of personal-viewer harm. While the three anti-pornography narratives share the same moral goal of reducing or eliminating the production and/or the viewing of pornography, each of these moral narratives is legitimated by usage of a different moral authority. The latter two rely on a secular form of moral authority; the narrative of public-performer harm, for example, seeks the "humanistic goal of protecting individual rights through reducing violations of consent, reducing violence and abuse, and upholding sexual and gender equality," while the narrative of personal-viewer harm seeks the "humanistic goal of reducing personal harm through fostering psychological and relational health" (2013: 462). By contrast, the narrative of traditional values is legitimated through "scriptural prohibitions as well as derivative ideas about God's plan for society" (2013: 462). Thus, while the three narratives share the same moral goal, the moral authorities behind each narrative are noticeably different. Ultimately, Thomas finds that Evangelicals are increasingly basing their moral authority on secular sources.

Other researchers have argued specifically in support of Hunter's claim that the main conflicts between the dueling moral visions occur within denominations rather than between them. In "Culture Wars? Insights from Ethnographies of Two Protestant Seminaries" (1995), for example, Jackson Carroll and Penny

Marler find that Evangelicals were, at least in the mid-1990s, more at war with fellow Evangelicals than with outsiders, and that the same was true of mainline Protestants. Taking an ethnographic approach, Carroll and Marler present two case studies conducted over a three-year period in the 1990s at two theological schools—one liberal mainline Protestant and the other Evangelical. The two present evidence that the faculty at the conservative Evangelical theological seminary were engaged in a cultural war, but though the war was waged in part against "secular humanists" and modernist mainstream denominations, it was also waged in large part against fellow Evangelicals—those Evangelicals whom the conservatives thought had embraced modernity too uncritically and with an "a-theological accommodation of the culture" (1995: 7). Meanwhile, the two found that the liberal mainline seminary encouraged "intolerance of the intolerant, by which is meant conservatives or traditionalists" and "coming to terms with the anger of the oppressed, which typically includes everyone except white males (but especially Blacks and women)" (1995: 14). They also found that liberal mainliners were warring over the boundary lines regarding race and gender, unlike traditionalists.

Importantly, they found that conservatives held to the Bible authoritatively while liberals held to personal experiences authoritatively. For example, they found that the Evangelical school held Scripture to be the interpretive authority, while the mainline school held experience to be the interpretive authority (1995: 15). For Carroll and Marler, these contrasting visions of truth have a strong likeness to the moral authorities described in Hunter's culture wars thesis. They also agree with Hunter "that the two moral visions are grounded in religious or faith traditions that, in turn, make claims to truth about the world" (1995: 18). Carroll and Marler explicitly support Hunter's claim that the real battles are internal to each religious culture (rather than between them), with Evangelicals rallying "against the excesses who have sold out to the 'self' movement and to therapeutic and technocratic models of the church" (1995: 18–19). Notably, Carroll and Marler also draw attention to the common ground between the extremes and note that even Hunter "recognizes the existence of the middle," a statement they support by quoting Hunter as saying that "in truth, most Americans occupy a vast middle ground between the polarizing impulses of American culture" (1995: 19).

Scholars of moral cosmology theory explore the specific ways in which varying conceptions of moral authority affect politics (Starks and Robinson, 2009). Nancy Davis and Robert Robinson (2006a) argue that orthodox moral cosmology is "theologically communitarian in that it regards individuals as subsumed by a larger community of like-minded believers who are all subject to the laws and greater plan of God" (2006a: 169). Meanwhile, modernist (progressivist) cosmology is "theologically individualistic in that [it sees] individuals as largely responsible for their own moral decisions and fate" (2006a: 169). According to Davis and Robinson, "the theological communitarianism of the orthodox...inclines them to an authoritarian strand of cultural communitarianism, in which the community must enforce divinely mandated moral standards on abortion, sexuality, family, and gender" (2006a: 169). But theological communitarianism "also inclines the orthodox" toward what they call "economic communitarianism," "whereby wealth cannot be attained at the expense of others and whereby it is the community or state's responsibility to look out for those in need, reduce the gap between rich and poor, and intervene in the economy so that community needs are met" (2006a: 169). Robyn Ryle and Robert Robinson find in their study "Ideology, Moral Cosmology, and Community in the United States" (2006) that the religiously orthodox esteem "social ties with others as a source of community" more so than modernists (2006: 56). David Blouin and Robert Robinson (2007) likewise find that orthodoxy is a major factor in having compassionate feelings for those with lesser economic means and find these feelings typically render backing for government aid to those in poverty (Starks and Robinson, 2009: 652).

In "Two Approaches to Religion and Politics: Moral Cosmology and Subcultural Identity" (2009), Brian Starks and Robert Robinson also explore views on how religious identity may relate to political attitudes. They make use of Hunter's theory to explain the division between the religiously orthodox and modernists (Starks and Robinson choose to use "modernist" instead of Hunter's "progressivist" to avoid political connotations associated with the word "progressive"). Similar to how Hunter conceives of progressives, Starks and Robinson describe modernists as maintaining "that individuals are the ultimate judges of what constitutes moral action, that morality is an evolving, open quest that must be judged in its cultural context, and that individuals are largely independent from God in making their fates" (2009: 651). Starks and Robinson outline literature exploring moral cosmology and how researchers have found orthodoxy to compel tender feelings in their subjects toward those with less, while at the same time compelling them toward authoritarian cultural communitarianism (i.e., where the community enforces standards believed to be from the divine).

Judith Needham-Penrose and Harris Friedman, in their 2012 study of a fundamentalist group of Evangelical leaders, found a duality in American culture as well. Though their work is in the field of psychology and does not explicitly draw on Hunter, the two highlight two dueling ethics present in the American population that have striking similarity to Hunter's moral authority argument—that is, an "ethic of divinity" and an "ethic of humanity." Whereas some researchers have argued—based on how badly Evangelicals tend to fare in psychological studies—that Evangelicals are morally stunted, Needham-Penrose and Friedman note that a few researchers (e.g., Al-Shehab, 2002; Richards and Davison, 1992; Shweder, 1990; Lawrence, 1987) have argued that religious conservatives are not actually lacking in moral development; instead, they simply follow an alternative "set of moral values," namely, an "ethic of divinity" instead of an "ethic of humanity" (2012: 345). In this "ethic of divinity," religious conservatives "appear to conceptualize the self as a spiritual entity striving to attain holiness and sanctity in the eyes of the divine, instead of emphasizing the prevailing ethic in psychology of secular utilitarianism" (2012: 347). In contrast, progressives who emphasize an ethic of humanity are endorsing an "individual autonomy in which the self, rather than God, is placed as the center of ultimate value" (2012: 347). Needham-Penrose and Friedman address postmodernism as "one version of relativism that denigrates traditional values that are seen as absolute" and "which has been criticized for nihilistic undermining of all bases for ethics" (2012: 345). They further argue that scholarly study of morality is particularly susceptible to abuses since "unavoidably, morality is culturally defined" (2012: 360). In their study of Evangelical leaders, they found that "a different moral basis (e.g., orthodox, relational, and Biblical, rather than progressive or relativistic, using secular utilitarianism which values expediency) could be identified." Evangelical leaders in their sample focused on a divine ethic that is constant no matter the circumstances as opposed to what would be expedient for meeting human needs in the short term (2012: 356).

These studies illuminate some of the strengths of Hunter's approach in explaining the social dynamics of Evangelicalism. While I may be the first to apply his moral authority argument to Evangelical perspectives on Islam, I am building on a wider tradition of scholarship on Evangelicalism. But I also am aware of the perceived limitations in doing so.

The Progression of Hunter's Culture War

Since the publication of *Culture Wars*, Hunter's main reflections on the phenomenon have concerned both the saliency of the battle among people in the United States as well as within public discourse, and the moral nihilism he believes is embedded within the "new moral science" (which is linked to the moral authority of progressivists, who find a foundation in self-grounded rational discourse and Enlightenment naturalism).

Regarding how the culture war has progressed, Hunter has found some common ground that progressivists, the orthodox, and everyone in between share, namely their lack of well-reasoned apologetics when articulating their personal positions. In his follow-up book *Before the Shooting Begins: Searching for Democracy in America's Culture War* (1994), Hunter found that the actual statements of various organizations were indeed more polarized than many of the organizations' leaders themselves actually were. In other words, the rhetoric was more "over the top" and clearly either orthodox or progressive. Hunter found that many people were unable to argue a consistent well-reasoned position and rather allowed "transitory sentiment," or temporary emotion, to dominate in their debates regarding divisive issues. Hunter attributed much of this to the widely accepted multicultural movement which he argues offered an alleviating yet false belief in the uniformity, or "sameness" of people. In actuality, Hunter found that people within multicultural America held opposing moral ideals yet were unable to persuasively argue for them (2009, 1994). This inability to argue well does not indicate a lack of disagreement or conflict, however.

In various moderated discussions (Hunter and Wolfe, 2006a; Hunter and Wolfe dialogue, 2006b) Hunter upheld his view that there is indeed a culture war within the United States. Although he recognizes that there are some relatively ambivalent Americans, and though he acknowledges that it is only minorities within the general public who are polarized, he argues that these polarized minorities are more significant in number than commonly assumed. By his estimate, around 5 percent of the total American population gravitates to each polarized extreme (representing 10–12 million people on each side), and these individuals make up the grassroots groundwork for competing visions, forming the core of the combatants on the respective sides of the cultural partition (moderated discussion between Hunter and Wolfe, 2006a). Hunter argues that these core combatants "are motivated and active and influence constituencies that are not as motivated but are generally in agreement" (moderated discussion between Hunter and Wolfe, 2006a). Thus, he argues that it is hasty to dismiss the culture war simply due to the fact that the most polarized warriors are, represent only a small percentage of the whole.

Finally, another progression to the original theory involves Hunter's exploration of the extent to which science might contribute to morality. Acknowledging that religion has failed to provide a universally acceptable moral foundation for society, Hunter explored "science" and its ability to offer a basic morality from which the nation could find common moral ground, believing the relationship between science and morality to be critical in the larger culture war (2019, 2018: 9–10). In his coauthored book with Nedelisky, *Science and the Good: The Tragic Quest for the Foundations of Morality* (2018), he argues the new moral scientists (who share the idiom and sensibilities of the managerial elite of the dominant technocratic regime) look to science in order to find foundations of morality, or discover moral truths. However, according to Hunter and Nedelisky, they have failed. They contend that the scientific disciples within the new science of morality actually embrace "moral nihilism" in that morality (as a mind-independent reality) no longer exists. In other words, the moral scientists of today "no longer look to science to discover moral truths, for they believe there is nothing there to discover" (2018: 21). They note that science enthusiasts who "argue that science is or should be the foundation for morality are generally making an epistemological claim about the superiority of science over other forms of knowledge" (2018: 9). Their epistemological claim regarding the superiority of science is "in competition with perspectives that look to other, often nonscientific and nonempirical bases for truth, knowledge, understanding, and wisdom," for example, tradition, religion, and intuition (2018: 9). They note, despite the rhetoric around science as inherently unbiased and rational, that "irrationality, dogma, and fanaticism" are found within both sides of the culture war and "not least among those who claim the authority of autonomous reason and scientific partiality" (2018: 10). Ultimately, Hunter and Nedelisky argue that science cannot be the foundation for morality, offers no deep metaethical answers, and "tells us nothing about what moral conclusions we *should* draw" (2020, 2018: xiv).

The progression of Hunter's thought regarding the *Culture Wars* has involved both refining the strength of the polarity within the general population, as well as within public discourse, and delving into the ability, or lack of ability, of the "new moral science" (dependent on naturalism, realism, and scientific reductionism) to offer a meaningful foundation of morality (2020).

Limits: Criticism of Hunter's Culture Wars Thesis

Hunter's culture wars thesis has been criticized by a number of scholars. In particular, the degree to which everyday Americans have been polarized into warring sides has been and remains a point of academic disagreement. Most critics argue that Hunter gave too much attention to divisiveness in American culture and didn't give enough attention to moderating or unifying tendencies. They maintain that the religious divide between orthodox groups and progressive groups is not as wide as Hunter claims. For example, DiMaggio et al. (1996) argue that while there may be polarization on some social and cultural issues, there are many social issues on which attitudes have not become polarized. These would include such issues as women's rights and racial equality. Fischer and Hout, meanwhile, argue that although the divide between the "ideologically consistent liberals and conservatives may have widened a bit" there are actually fewer Americans in those strong ideological factions than there were in the 1960s (2006: 238). Taking one hot-button culture war topic as an example, Greeley and Hout argue that the distribution of conservative Protestants who reject abortion even when the mother's health is in danger is merely 3 percent of the whole (2006: 125), and that large majorities of the population favor abortion in cases where pregnancy resulted from rape or the health of the mother was in danger (2006: 121–3).

Some critics articulate a problem with the scope and totality of the implications of Hunter's moral authority argument. Davis and Robinson (1996a, 1996b, 1996c) argue that the majority of Americans are not bifurcated along the battle lines of the culture war. Rather, the orthodox are conservative on certain topics while simultaneously holding liberal stances on others. While Davis and Robinson agree with Hunter that religion can cause division, they argue that these divisions mostly affect "gender/family and sexuality issues" and do not embattle Americans on racial or economic issues (1996a: 782; see also Starks and Robinson, 2009). Billings and Scott challenge the idea that there are alliances across faiths by asserting that conservative Catholics and Fundamentalist Protestants do not share sociopolitical attitudes (1994: 180).

Opponents of the culture wars thesis also point to the similarities between the values and moral orientations of liberals and conservatives. For example, Wuthnow (1996) finds that both groups are often driven by self-interest and what feels good. He also argues that differences in sociopolitical views are more associated with people's religious participation than with their liberal or conservative religious beliefs (e.g., those who actively participate in religion, whether they be liberals or conservatives, typically agree on the majority of their worldviews) (1996: 326). Clydesdale (1997) also finds that strong religious beliefs do not always drive action and that family behaviors of religious conservatives are not different from those of religious progressives. Even Hunter acknowledges that the most conservative Evangelicals are not completely distinct from their surrounding culture but have rather "accommodated quite easily to contemporary American culture and are in many respects very, very comfortable" (moderated discussion between Hunter and Wolfe, 2006a).

Others dislike how religion has come to dominate most discussions about American culture wars. Whereas Hunter places greater importance on religious dimensions of culture than on political dimensions, these critics argue that politics is becoming more important than religion, rather than being influenced by religion. In a moderated discussion at Pew Forum's biannual Faith Angle Conference on religion, Hunter asserted that culture drives politics; but a strong critic of Hunter's thesis, Alan Wolfe argued instead that politics is driving culture and religion is taking a back seat altogether (moderated discussion between Hunter and Wolfe, 2006a). Thus, Wolfe holds that people's positions on a political issue determine their ideological and religious views, and not the other way around. Wolfe points to the flip-flopping of the Southern Baptist Convention (SBC) in reaction to *Roe v. Wade* (1973) as an example of the power of politics over religion. According to Wolfe, at first, because of the Baptist distrust of state-regulated mandates, the SBC supported the decision in favor of legalized abortions, but ten years later they ended their support and apologized. Wolfe believes this change of course toward an accommodation between state and church "reeked of political opportunism," as he perceived the SBC to not really have theological objections to abortion as they claimed, but rather to have simply changed their stance due to their allegiance to the Republican Party. For Wolfe, this demonstrated both that religion is in flux and that politics is increasingly becoming more paramount than religion (moderated discussion between Hunter and Wolfe, 2006a). In line with Wolfe, Wuthnow argues that religion is losing the power it once held to dictate nonreligious aspects of life, as it used to do in previous decades when individuals usually inherited a religious identity that then would influence their views on politics. Wuthnow perceives that American religion has been restructured and that individuals can now choose which religious subculture they want to mingle with, a choice they sometimes make based on preexisting political stances (1998, 1996, 1988, 1987). In agreement with Wuthnow, Bean found in her study of Evangelicals in the United States and Canada that political conflict can alter the content of religious morality. In her view, formulations of "Evangelical orthodoxy may be the outcome of power struggles, driven by the exigencies of partisan coalition-building rather than theological deliberation" (Bean, 2014: 8).

These critiques help us identify potential limits of Hunter's approach: while he may explain internal variation, it is possible that he overstates the degree of conflict and overemphasizes the importance of elites. As will be explored in later chapters, these limitations were considered, and in some ways confirmed in my own empirical research. However, these limits are found to refine rather than negate Hunter's main insights.

Refining the Theory: My Conceptual Contributions to Hunter's Moral Authority Argument

In the course of analyzing the data resulting from my interviews of Evangelical leaders and congregants, I discovered two areas in Hunter's conceptual framework relating to moral authority in which his work may have fallen short of fuller exposition. To address these issues, I developed new conceptual tools that further Hunter's argument. Here I present those two conceptual developments: the Progressive-Traditional spectrum as well as the evidential moral authority analysis, both of which are integral to the data analysis chapters that follow.

The Progressive-Traditional Spectrum with Four Categories

As I began analyzing the data from my interviews, I attempted to categorize each interviewee as either Traditional or Progressive based on their responses during our interview. However, I found that some interviewees did not conform to a strictly Traditional or strictly Progressive identity; some appealed to a mixture of both progressive *and* traditional sources of moral authority. In order to be as accurate as possible, and to allow for more complex descriptions of my interviewees, I felt the need to recognize a spectrum of identities rather than try to categorize interviewees according to a binary division. I opted to classify interviewees using four separate categories: "Progressive," "Progressive-Traditional," "Traditional-Progressive," and "Traditional." Hunter's two ideal types (the orthodox and the progressivist) have influenced my system of categorization; however, I have chosen to use the term "traditional" instead of "orthodox" to describe those who are committed to transcendence (according to Hunter, transcendence is a type of "reality that is independent of, prior to, and more powerful than human experience" [1991: 120]). "Traditional" was chosen because the term is more neutral in that it does not imply a "correct" position, as opposed to the "orthodox" label, which does imply a "correct" or "approved of" doctrine or conduct. The Progressive-Traditional spectrum is a new conceptual development in the sense that it advances beyond the way Hunter's theory has been conceived as simply being a dualistic division between progressives and traditionals, a dualism that has dominated discussions of the culture wars up to the present (see Figure 3.1). Further, the Progressive-Traditional spectrum allows for a more accurate and complex description of what I call "hybrid identities" (those categorized as "Progressive-Traditional" or "Traditional-Progressive").

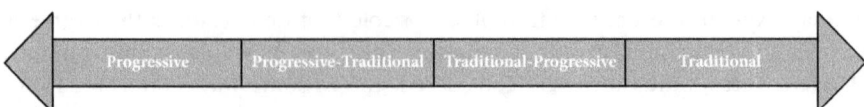

Figure 3.1 Progressive-Traditional Spectrum with Categories.

Evidential Moral Authority

As I analyzed the moral authority of each of my interviewees, it became clear that most if not all interviewees were using the same terminology to describe their moral authorities. At the same time, they were expressing genuinely different opinions on the topic of Islam. A question thus arose: If differing moral authorities really do play a substantive role in intra-Evangelical conflicts, as Hunter's thesis would suggest, why were Evangelical answers to questions about moral authority often so similar?

There are two obvious answers to this question. First, the similarity in views on moral authority (stated) is perhaps to be expected given that the vast majority of interviewees in my sample were Evangelicals, after all. And the agreement on moral authority might be comforting or relieving for Evangelicals, who may be consoled by the thought that they are mostly on the same page. But there is a second factor, perhaps disconcerting to some, that may also explain the high degree of similarity. While Evangelicalism is and always has been diverse, it makes sense that Evangelicals would respond to questions such as "How do you view the Bible?" with answers like "the Word of God" or "inspired," because these are conditioned responses in Evangelical communities. Thus, even those who have not thought about moral authority in depth might use the same terms to describe the Bible, simply because those are the terms they have heard repeated so frequently. The same is true with answers to the question, "Where do you get your idea of right and wrong?" Evangelicals such as those I spoke with might respond with a knee-jerk answer, such as "the Bible" or "Jesus," because these are the traditional authorities on which Evangelicals claim to rely. (Among Evangelicals, the word "Bible" is often treated as an acronym [Basic Instructions Before Leaving Earth], and mottos like WWJD [What Would Jesus Do?] are thoroughly ingrained in the community.) Thus, Evangelicals might respond to a question about the source of their ideas of right and wrong by appealing to traditional Evangelical authorities, even if they do not, in fact, look to these authorities when making decisions in day-to-day life about right and wrong, or when thinking about Muslims or the nature of Islam.

This potential for conditioned responses prompted me to develop the concept of evidential moral authority. Since it is possible for interviewees to claim one authority when asked directly but not to actually rely on that same authority when reasoning or making decisions in everyday life, I wanted to go beyond what interviewees stated their moral authority to be and look at how interviewees actually reasoned about questions not directly related to moral authority. Specifically, I decided to analyze how they answered questions about Islam and politics, and looked for the sources of moral authority to which they appealed in making their arguments. Thus, whereas Hunter spoke of moral authority as a single concept, I distinguish between what I am terming the "stated moral authority" and the "evidential moral authority" of each interviewee. It is important to emphasize that my conceptual developments—the Progressive-Traditional spectrum and evidential moral authority—are grounded in my empirical data analysis.

This double determination of moral authority has enabled me to offer thicker descriptions of the moral authority of each interviewee, which is advantageous in at least two senses. First, the indirect evidence of moral authority achieved through evidential analysis allows for more accuracy, in that an analysis of the way interviewees actually reason provides a truer reflection of interviewees' real moral authorities than their direct claims about their moral authorities. Second, because my analysis considers both stated moral authority and evidential moral authority, I am able to compare interviewees' *perceptions* of their own moral authorities, whether they be Progressive or Traditional, with the moral authorities to which interviewees *actually appeal* when they are discussing issues related to Islam, Muslims, and politics. One of my findings is that Evangelicals do not always appeal to traditional sources of moral authority (when answering questions about Islam and politics) as often as their direct statements about their own moral authorities might predict, which aligns with the findings of Thomas (2013) described earlier in this chapter, that some Evangelicals are actually involved in a process of "outsourcing" their moral authorities to secular sources.

Evaluation of Stated Moral Authority

To determine interviewees' stated moral authority, I relied on their answers to the following three questions: (1) Where do you get your idea of right and wrong? (2) What would you say is your highest moral authority? (3) How do you view the Bible? Thus, interviewees' stated moral authorities were derived from their answers to three questions directly related to moral authority. To categorize each interviewee on the Progressive-Traditional spectrum, I analyzed how often interviewees made reference to traditional Evangelical key words in their responses to each of these three questions (methods for coding responses found in Appendix 1). Interviewees who made regular mention of key words like "God," "Jesus," or "the Bible" to explain the source of their ideas about right and wrong were categorized as more traditional, as were interviewees who used phrases like "Word of God," "Inerrant," "Infallible," "God-inspired," "God-breathed," and "Authoritative" to describe their view of the Bible. By contrast, interviewees were categorized as more progressive if they mentioned terms like "Environment," "Innate," or referred to extra-Christian teachings to describe the source of their ideas about right and wrong; they were also categorized as more progressive if they avoided traditional descriptors to explain their view of the Bible or if they instead used terms like "humanly written" or "unique" (further details found in Appendix 1).

The bulk of interviewees, both leaders and congregants, answered direct moral authority questions in such a way as to place them on the more traditional end of the spectrum. With respect to leaders, only two were categorized as Progressive and only two additional leaders were categorized as Progressive-Traditional. With respect to congregants, there were no congregants categorized as Progressive and only one congregant was categorized as Progressive-Traditional. By contrast, ten leaders fell into the Traditional-Progressive category, and a majority (15) were categorized as straight Traditional. Similarly, eleven congregants fell into the

Traditional-Progressive category, and a majority (36) were categorized as straight Traditional.

Evaluation of Evidential Moral Authority

The questions from which I derived an individual's evidential moral authority included these: (1) Have you ever read the Qur'an? What do you think about it? (2) Do you think Muhammad was a prophet? What do you think about him? (3) What do you think of the term "Chrislam"? (4) What do you think about the ACW document? (5) What are your thoughts on interfaith dialogue? (6) How would you describe your political views? I chose these questions because they do not explicitly include traditional moral authority terminology in the question itself, as would a question like "Do Christians and Muslims worship the same God?"

To establish an individual's evidential moral authority, I analyzed interviewees' responses to the aforementioned questions for terminology reflecting a traditional Evangelical moral authority. Specifically, I looked for usage of the terms "God" (or any other term referring to God, for example, "Lord"), "Jesus" (or any other term referring to Jesus, for example, "Christ" or "Messiah"), "Holy Spirit" (or any other term referring to Holy Spirit, for example, "Holy Ghost" or simply "Spirit"), "Bible" (or any other term referring to the Bible, for example, "Word of God" or "Scripture" or "sword" [which is short for "the sword of the Spirit, which is the Word of God," a phrasing from the New Testament book of Ephesians that is sometimes used by Evangelicals to refer to the Bible], or any reference to a particular verse of Scripture, etc.). I took usage of these terms to be indicators of a more traditional evidential moral authority. While I didn't explicitly ask interviewees to back up their responses to the preceding set of questions using their moral authority, it does seem plausible that a traditional Evangelical would undergird their positions on Muhammad, interfaith dialogue, the Qur'an, syncretism, and politics with invocations of God, Jesus, the Holy Spirit, or Scripture. And it would also seem plausible that those more progressive-leaning Evangelicals would invoke God, Jesus, the Holy Spirit, or Scripture less frequently. After analyzing each answer for use of the aforementioned specific key words, I then categorized each interviewee on the Traditional-Progressive spectrum based on how frequently the interviewee made mention of traditional Evangelical moral authorities (further details found in Appendix 1).

A frequent criticism of qualitative research methods is that researchers can too easily select out only that data that support the researcher's presuppositions. However, my incorporation of an evidential analysis of moral authority in my study helps to avoid this pitfall, as the evidential analysis provides a way to corroborate or triangulate interviewees' self-perceptions. Specifically, the evidential analysis involves quantifying the number of times an individual employs traditional moral authority terminology in response to questions on Islam and politics. The quantitative aspect of this analysis improves the validity and reliability of my findings, as any other researcher familiar with traditional moral authority could analyze my data and arrive at the same results I did.

Confusion Regarding "Traditional" and "Progressive" Terms

As will be further explored in the following analysis chapters, interviewees sometimes had complicated understandings of moral authority. Specifically, some interviewees were categorized as Traditional on the Progressive-Traditional spectrum because they justified their perspectives on Islam and Muslims by appealing to such authorities as the "Bible," or "Jesus," or "God," or the "Holy Spirit" heavily (traditional Evangelical moral authority terminology); however, their views on Islam were very far removed from the specific set of beliefs associated with the earliest dominant Evangelical views of Muslims in the United States (e.g., the views of Jonathan Edwards) as detailed in Chapter 2. For example, such interviewees might believe that Muhammad is a prophet of God, or that God speaks truth through the Qur'an, or that Muslims and Christians are on equal footing in pursuit of the kingdom of God; thus, their beliefs on Islam are more progressive than the historical Evangelical perspective. Here, the predicament is that an Evangelical can heavily support his or her view of Islam with biblical support and/or references to one or more parts of the Trinity (which places them in the traditional category according to the Progressive-Traditional spectrum using the evidential moral authority analysis), but their actual views on Islam or Muslims can be progressive in that they differ from the historical tradition, or vice versa.

To avoid confusion, in the following three analysis chapters I have reserved the terms "traditional" and "progressive" for describing interviewees' moral authorities. Meanwhile, to characterize how an interviewee's views relate to the dominant historical perspective (i.e., that of Edwards and other early American Evangelicals), I describe their views as either "aligned with the dominant historical Evangelical perspective" or "dissenting from" or "out of step with the dominant historical Evangelical perspective."

Conclusion

The purpose of this chapter was to analyze theoretical approaches that not only explain how Evangelicals, whether traditionalist or progressivist, construct their identity in opposition to outgroups but also explain Evangelicals' tendency toward internal critique and diversity (intra-Evangelical battles between the traditional and the progressives). In particular, I engaged with the theoretical approaches of Christian Smith (ingroup/outgroup hypothesis) and James Hunter (the culture wars thesis and his argument about moral authority). I find Hunter's approaches to have significant explanatory power, but also to have limitations. The social dynamics of how Evangelicals construct their identities—and how they approach Islam—are perhaps more complicated than any one theory can suggest. Accordingly, I have refined Hunter's theory by proposing the existence of a Progressive-Traditional spectrum and by defending the need for an evidential moral authority analysis. The importance of a clear understanding of moral authority cannot be understated.

If one believes, as I do, that religious beliefs inspire action, and that those actions have consequences for society at large, one would conclude that studying moral authority and religious beliefs helps us better understand the world.

Now that I have outlined the theory behind my research and presented some of the conceptual tools I developed to analyze my data, the next task is to take a closer look at my sample of urban Southern Evangelicals to see how these ideas work themselves out in practice. Are Evangelicals reacting to Islam with increased internal cohesion? And do their highest moral authorities elucidate divergent Evangelical attitudes on topics such as interfaith dialogue with Muslims, politics, Muhammad, the Qur'an, missiology, and engagement with Muslims? In the following chapter I will specifically explore how Evangelical leaders are experiencing conflict within their community and how their moral authorities were aligned or unaligned with their views on Islam.

Chapter 4

EVANGELICAL LEADERS

CONFLICT AND DIVERSITY IN PLACES OF POWER

I think apart from Christ it's all meaningless. I don't see how you can combine the two [religions] because they contradict each other so much. Even if it's just the softest version of both, the heart of Christianity goes completely, completely against Islam.

—Tarifa, Evangelical author and former Muslim

Every morning I spend an hour and a half at this desk reading my Bible . . . and my Qur'an.

—Brad, Evangelical mega-church pastor

Introduction

In the post-9/11 era, the increasing amount of global attention focused on Islam has compelled Evangelical leaders in America to form responses to Islam. Leaders of various types—from professors to authors to mega-church pastors—have had to decide among a variety of approaches regarding how to think about Islam and how to interact with Muslims. Should they set themselves up in opposition to Muslims? Should they focus on common ground between themselves and Muslims? Should they band together with Muslims to work toward the perceived "common good" of their societies?

As it turns out, the way Evangelical leaders answer these questions varies dramatically. Thus, the first argument of this chapter is that there is considerable diversity and conflict among Evangelical leaders regarding Islam. Whereas Christian Smith's subcultural identity theory predicts that Evangelicals should band together and lay aside internal differences when confronted with a perceived external threat such as Islam, that does not appear to be happening. In fact, Evangelicals whose views deviate from the dominant historical Evangelical view of Islam appear to dislike Evangelicals whose views align with the dominant historical view more so than they dislike Muslims.

The second argument of this chapter is that the lens of moral authority is useful for understanding *why* Evangelicals hold diverse views on Islam. Consistent with

James Hunter's moral authority argument, the Evangelical leaders discussed in this chapter were drawn to one side or the other of the Progressive-Traditional spectrum. This means that some gravitated toward progressive moral authorities (such as personal experience, humanism, and self-grounded rational discourse) when forming their positions on various topics, whereas others tended to rely on traditional authorities (such as the transcendent and Scripture). Yet despite being drawn to one "pole" or the other, most Evangelical leaders relied on a mixture of progressive and traditional moral authorities when expressing their moral positions. Hunter theorized that cultural and religious leaders would be more likely than non-leaders to gravitate to extremes in terms of their moral authorities. Although it is true that leaders in my sample were more polarized than congregants, the majority of the Evangelical leaders were still relatively moderate. Most leaders fell in the Progressive-Traditional category or the Traditional-Progressive category when categorized based on their evidential moral authority (i.e., the authority an individual *actually* appeals to in reasoning about various subjects, as opposed to their stated moral authority).

In general, leaders' moral authority categories were predictive of whether their views deviated from or were consistent with the historical Evangelical perspective on Islam. Leaders in my sample who relied more on progressive moral authorities generally tended to have views of Islam that differ from historical Evangelical stances on Islam, whereas those with traditional moral authorities tended to uphold those historical Evangelical stances (those of early Evangelicals such as Jonathan Edwards and other early Evangelicals who saw Islam as being in opposition to Christianity and Muslims as being in dire need of conversion). But this was not always the case. Significantly, some Evangelical leaders with progressive moral authorities (according to the evidential moral authority analysis) held stances that are in line with the dominant historical Evangelical perspective on Islam, while others held to a relatively traditional moral authority but maintained stances that are out of step with historical Evangelical thinking on Islam. This shows that categories of moral authority are perhaps more fluid than Hunter imagined, at least in how leaders rationalize their positions, and that even leaders may be better viewed as representing a spectrum as opposed to two distinct camps.

A recurring theme throughout the chapter—one that is relevant to both the aforementioned arguments—is that Evangelical leaders' involvement (or lack thereof) with insider movements (IMs) is correlated with their opinions on key topics related to Islam and Muslims. As explored in Chapter 2, IMs are movements that encourage "believers in Christ" who come from Muslim backgrounds to remain culturally, and to varying degrees religiously, a part of their Muslim communities. Evangelical leaders who were affiliated with IMs were more likely to state an allegiance to traditional sources of moral authority than were Progressives, but at the same time, those affiliated with IMs were also more likely than some Progressives to hold stances out of step with dominant historical Evangelical thinking on Islam. In other words, close affiliation with IMs was a stronger predictor than a progressive moral authority categorization of a view divergent from the historical norm. These IM supporters were, for the most part, critical of Christianity and spoke highly of Islam.

In this chapter, I will begin by explaining why it is important to study the views of leaders and how I selected the sample of leaders that I interviewed. Next, I will give an overview of who these leaders are: What are their demographic characteristics? How involved are they with Muslims? What are their moral authorities, and what are their political views? I will then discuss what these Evangelical leaders say about the unity (or lack of unity) that exists among their fellow Evangelicals on the topic of Islam. Although Christian Smith predicted that Evangelicals should unite in the face of a threat like Islam, the leaders surveyed in this chapter agree that Evangelicals are in fact deeply *divided* over how to view Islam. Finally, the bulk of the chapter will explore leaders' varying perceptions on the topics of Chrislam (i.e., syncretism between Christianity and Islam), Muhammad, the Qur'an, interfaith dialogue, and initiatives such as "A Common Word" that emphasize what Muslims and Christians have in common. Throughout the chapter, I'll explain how these views are influenced by Evangelical interviewees' respective inclinations toward the traditional or progressive pole of moral authority according to the evidential moral authority analysis.

Why Leaders?

My inclusion of Evangelical leaders into my research design—and the decision to analyze their responses separately from congregants'—was theory driven. According to Hunter, the culture war plays out largely among elites who lead institutions and organizations. For Hunter, elites (leaders) are those who "create the concepts, supply the language, and explicate the logic of public discussion" (Hunter, 1991: 59). Other research also finds elites to be particularly influential in leading social change (Grillo, 2014; Uecker and Lucke, 2011; Peterson, 2002; Anderson, 1991). Accordingly, I conducted in-depth interviews with a total of twenty-nine Evangelical elites. Five of these elites were members of the two congregations that I observed as part of my field research; these congregations are discussed in detail in the next chapter. The other twenty-four Evangelical elites were from outside of these two congregations; these twenty-four individuals represented regions across the United States but were mostly located in the South.[1]

---

1. I use the terms "leader" and "elite" interchangeably. In this chapter, both terms refer to individuals who lead institutions or organizations, and/or individuals who have come to "create the concepts, supply the language, and explicate the logic of public discussion" (1991: 59) within Evangelicalism regarding Islam and Muslims. While some Evangelical leaders would likely struggle with being labeled an "elite," I use the term within my work (alongside "leader") because elite is the term Hunter used when describing those who play an important role in cultural battles.

Selecting the Sample

My main strategy for finding elite interviewees was to seek out individuals referenced in scholarly books and articles on the topic of Evangelical views of Muslims, as well as individuals referenced on that same topic in media outlets. However, some elites were also found through word of mouth or snowball sampling (which involves asking one interviewee for assistance in connecting with other individuals who would also be appropriate to interview). Snowball sampling in particular turned out to be a very useful technique for enlisting Evangelical elites in my research. Evangelical leaders tend to be difficult to reach, with some using pseudonyms on publications for security reasons, others having assistants culling through and responding to emails, and others with overcrowded schedules.

Leaders holding less amiable views of Islam were particularly hard to gain interviews with. I found that I usually needed to recruit the help of one well-respected leader who aligned closely with the dominant historical Evangelical perspective to put me in touch with a second leader holding similar views. For example, eighteen correspondence emails passed between one particular conservative leader (or one of his team members) and me before he chose to participate. In one email, the leader suggested I contact a different expert on Islam, giving me the alternate individual's name, a brief biography, and contact information. I ultimately decided to call the original individual even though I had almost given up hope, and to my surprise he answered and we conducted the interview later that afternoon. In another case, after sending a few emails to a leader who held views mostly aligned with the historical Evangelical perspective and getting no response, I recruited an acquaintance I had met during a conference on Islam who knew the individual I was trying to contact. I asked him to email her on my behalf. Using his name helped, and eventually I was able to schedule the interview.

In general, those leaders holding more left-leaning stances were easier to connect with, and many were willing to participate in my research without me needing to recruit a middleman. In several cases, leaders within liberal Evangelicalism were quick to connect me with others within liberal Evangelicalism, often unprompted. In part, the varying responses to my requests for interviews could be due to my status as a PhD student at a "secular" university. Within some Evangelical circles, it is believed that researchers from secular universities are more leftist and would be more likely to align themselves with liberal perspectives. This may explain why Evangelicals holding positions most aligned with the historical Evangelical perspective on Islam were more difficult to recruit. These Evangelicals who sympathize with historical Evangelical positions may distrust researchers from secular institutions, whom they may believe—from personal experience or anecdotal evidence—to be hostile to their worldview. They may therefore fear having their views misunderstood or misrepresented.

Who Are These Leaders?

My sample is not representative of Evangelicalism in the United States or even of elite Evangelicals in the United States. Rather, I tried to talk with Evangelicals who take very different approaches to interacting with Muslims, because I wanted in-depth insight on a variety of perspectives. I specifically hoped to capture a range of beliefs both on Islam and on various other topics that lend themselves to understanding how interviewees think about topics such as moral authority and interfaith dialogue with Muslims.

There were significantly more males than females represented in the twenty-nine leadership interviews (twenty interviewees were male and nine were female; all of the pastoral interviewees were men). My sample would have been even more dominated by male voices without my deliberate attempt to acquire a more gender-balanced sample. Although the majority of Evangelicals are usually "pragmatically egalitarian" (Gallagher, 2004), there is still a biblical understanding of men's headship (or authority) over women within conservative Evangelicalism, meaning that males are disproportionately represented in leadership positions. The leadership sample had an age range of twenty-three to eighty-three, with an average age of fifty-one. The entirety of my sample was either middle class or upper class, largely due to the fact that elites are by nature more likely to have advanced education (many of the elites I interviewed had postgraduate degrees) and represent a higher social class (demographics discussed further in Appendix 3).

In a study of Evangelical attitudes toward Islam, it is obviously relevant to understand how strongly participants identify with Evangelicalism as their personal religious perspective. Instead of requiring interviewees to fit a specific doctrinal rubric in order to be a part of the study, I chose to allow interviewees to tell me if they were comfortable being called an Evangelical. Thus, I allowed interviewees to self-identify. This method was used for both leaders and congregants. Unsurprisingly, the leaders I interviewed generally had a strong Evangelical identity. When I asked my sample of interviewees whether they were comfortable with being called an Evangelical, all but one answered "yes." Still, eight of the leaders added qualifiers, definitions, and additions in their responses. Of these eight leaders who added qualifiers, all but two leaned to the left on the Progressive-Traditional spectrum as positioned based on their evidential moral authority. However, only one leaned to the left on the spectrum based on stated moral authority. Some of these leaders whose views deviate from the dominant historical Evangelical perspectives on Islam stated that they intentionally remain inside Evangelicalism in order to change it from within. One interviewee, Andrew, a former Evangelical pastor, was included in the sample even though he no longer saw himself as an Evangelical at the time of our interview. Andrew was classified in the "Progressive" category for both stated and evidential moral authority. I chose to include his perspective because of his ample past involvement and his current connections with Evangelicalism, and because his books and his blog are both popular among Evangelicals. Some of the Evangelical leaders I interviewed (who held views regarding Islam out of step with the historically dominant Evangelical views) also considered him a spiritual companion. When asked if he identified with the term "Evangelical," he said that he has changed with age, whereas "a lot of Evangelicals don't [change]." He added that Evangelicalism "is my background, it is my heritage, and I care about Evangelicals a lot, whether or not I'm considered one."

Over half of the leaders I interviewed (16) were highly engaged with Muslims. About one-third of the sample was moderately engaged with Muslims, and a minority (3) fell into the category of low engagement. (These designations were determined by whether interviewees had Muslim friends and by the amount of contact they were having with Muslims on a regular basis. Details regarding how I calculated each individual's level of engagement are presented in Appendix 3.) Interviewees' levels of engagement with Muslims did not correlate with their position on the Progressive-Traditional spectrum. In other words, Progressives were not more engaged with Muslims than Traditionals, or vice versa. This is not surprising regarding the leadership specifically; however, because I chose leaders based on their engagement with the topic of Islam, it makes sense that most would also be engaged with Muslims.

A Broad Spectrum of Moral Authorities

Whereas Hunter spoke of moral authority as a single category, I distinguish between evidential moral authority (i.e., the moral authority that an individual actually demonstrates as he or she reasons about various topics) and stated moral authority (interviewees' self-reporting of their moral authority when asked directly). I have also argued that evidential moral authority is the more reliable indicator of an individual's actual position on the Progressive-Traditional spectrum. (Details about how I analyzed both stated and evidential moral authority are described in Chapter 3.)

When I asked direct questions about moral authority for the purpose of determining each individual's stated moral authority, most claimed relatively traditional Evangelical sources of authority. The majority of interviewees (23), for example, explicitly listed "the Bible" as their moral authority, and a majority (17) also mentioned "God" as a moral authority. In explaining how they viewed the Bible, interviewees tended to describe the Bible using relatively traditional language, such as by saying the Bible was the "Word of God" (used by sixteen), "God-inspired" (used by fourteen), or "inspired" (also used by fourteen). Thus, a majority of my interviewees were categorized as straight "Traditional" and another ten fell into the "Traditional-Progressive" category. Only two interviewees were categorized as "Progressive-Traditional" (Jim and Heather), and only two were categorized as straight "Progressive" (Hayden and Andrew).

When I switched from analyzing interviewees' claims about their moral authority (stated moral authority) to analyzing the moral authorities they appealed to in the course of discussing other topics (evidential moral authority), the outcomes proved quite different. In the analysis of evidential moral authority, just ten were in the Traditional-Progressive category and only five were categorized as Traditional. Seven proved to be Progressives and seven others were categorized as Progressive-Traditional (see Table 4.1). Thus, there is a discrepancy between my interviewees' stated and evidential moral authorities. Most leaders claimed to have relatively traditional moral authorities, but when answering questions not directly related to moral authority (such as questions on Islam and politics), many interviewees failed to reference traditional Evangelical moral authorities as they articulated their rationale and positions. Close analysis of how they actually used

Table 4.1 Leadership: Stated Moral Authority and Evidential Moral Authority with Demographics

Name	Occupation	Education	Political Views	Age Range	Stated MA	Evidential MA
Andrew	Author and Speaker	G	L	51–65	P	P
Brad	Pastor and Author	G	LL	51–65	TP	P
Emma	Nonprofit Employee	G	LL	Under 35	TP	P
Heather	Pastor and Artist	B	LL	Under 35	PT	P
Joseph	Professor and Author	G	L	35–50	TP	P
Marianne	Lecturer and Nonprofit Leader	G	RL	35–50	TP	P
Paul	Professor and Author	G	RL	35–50	T	P
James	Professor and Author	G	RL	Over 65	T	PT
Leah	Professor	G	RL	35–50	T	PT
Luke	Professor and Speaker	G	RL	51–65	TP	PT
Elizabeth	Apologist and Professor	G	RL	35–50	T	PT
Hayden	Author and Nonprofit Employee	G	LL	51–65	P	PT
Parker*	Pastor	B	RL	51–65	T	PT
Samuel	Apologist and Nonprofit Leader	G	RL	35–50	T	PT
Hakim	Pastor and Nonprofit Leader	G	RL	51–65	T	TP
Jane	Speaker and Nonprofit Leader	SC	R	51–65	T	TP
George	Professor and Author	G	R	35–50	T	TP
Tarifa	Student and Author	B	R	Under 35	T	TP
Ahmad	Apologist and Consultant	G	RL	35–50	TP	TP
Kevin*	Apologist and Author	G	RL	51–65	T	TP
Mark*	Pastor and Speaker	G	RL	Under 35	TP	TP
Oliver	Student and Nonprofit Leader	G	RL	35–50	TP	TP
Robbie	Professor and Author	G	RL	Over 65	TP	TP
Rose	Speaker and Nonprofit Leader	SC	RL	35–50	TP	TP
Gabriel	Apologist and Author	G	R	51–65	T	T
Jakob	Apologist and Author	G	R	Over 65	T	T
Jim	Author and Nonprofit Leader	G	LL	51–65	PT	T
Maria*	Speaker and Nonprofit Leader	G	LL	35–50	T	T
Navid*	Speaker and Nonprofit Leader	B	RL	Over 65	T	T

* Denotes the individuals that are included in this chapter as well as in Chapter 5. These interviewees are both national Evangelical leaders on Islam and members of the congregations examined in the following chapter.
SC = Some College, B = Bachelor, G = Graduate, L = Left, LL = Left Leaning, RL = Right Leaning, R = Right, MA = Moral Authority, P = Progressive, PT = Progressive-Traditional, TP = Traditional-Progressive, T = Traditional.

moral authority in their reasoning processes demonstrates that some leaders in my sample were actually relatively progressive in terms of moral authority—perhaps more progressive than they themselves realized.

Those who shifted the farthest left (meaning those who claimed to have a Traditional moral authority but whose evidential moral authority proved to be Progressive or Progressive-Traditional) were six in total. These six were generally highly educated; four were professors at universities, and two were well-known Christian apologists. Twelve interviewees fell into either the extreme left or the extreme right category based on analysis of their evidential moral authorities. Because of this fact, I concur with Hunter that there are indeed "polarizing impulses" (i.e., an "orthodox/traditional" impulse and a "progressive" impulse) at work in Evangelicalism. However, my findings show that there is a prevalent group within elite American Evangelicalism that appeals to a mixture of both progressive and traditional sources of moral authority. These hybrids (who were categorized as either Progressive-Traditionals or Traditional-Progressives) differ from those in the Traditional category in that they are not as likely to appeal to the Bible or divine sources of knowledge when explaining their positions on Islam. This shows they are not bashing people on the heads with their Bibles, nor rigid biblicists, when articulating their thinking with respect to Islam (as the monolithic stereotype portrays). Rather, hybrids demonstrate an awareness of and usage of progressive and humanistic forms of moral authority in addition to traditional sources. The fact that most individuals in my sample had a hybrid identity indicates that these leaders' moral authorities are more moderate than Hunter's thesis would have suggested leaders to be.

Interviewees' moral authorities usually—but not always—predicted their views on Islam. In general, individuals who relied on traditional sources of moral authority tended to have views on Islam that were consistent with historically dominant Evangelical perspectives on Islam. Likewise, individuals who relied on more progressive sources of moral authority were more likely to break from historically dominant Evangelical views regarding Islam. However, there were outliers—interviewees who had a progressive moral authority but held views aligned with the dominant historical Evangelical perspective on certain issues, or vice versa. Among these outliers were three interviewees categorized as Progressives or Progressive-Traditionals based on their evidential moral authorities. Two—Samuel and Elizabeth—were popular apologists within Evangelical circles at the time of interview and were known for debating top atheists and Muslims. The third—Paul—seemed to identify most strongly with his academic role as professor and author. Paul acknowledged the role the "academy" had played in influencing his life and his communication style. He said, "I'm an academic, so I can't answer anything without caveats." What these three progressive-leaning leaders had in common is that their professional activities all required them to primarily frame their positions without using biblical or existential reasoning. That may explain why they failed to use traditional Evangelical moral authority terminology to back up their perspectives in our interviews (i.e., they are out of the habit). But though they relied on progressive sources in their reasoning, all three still held views that were relatively consistent with historically dominant Evangelical perspectives on Islam.

At the opposite end of the spectrum were four outliers (Maria, Jim, Mark, and Oliver) who were categorized as Traditional or Traditional-Progressive but who held stances that dissented from the dominant historical Evangelical perspective on the subjects of politics or Islam/Muslims. Generally, these individuals were supportive of IMs. They were careful not to make negative judgments about Muhammad or the Qur'an, and they spoke about Islamic ideas with utmost reverence. In fact, when discussing Islamic beliefs, they rather ended up critiquing Evangelicals who held dominant historical Evangelical perspectives on Islam. For example, when I asked Mark if he considered Muhammad a prophet, he said that Muhammad likely would meet the New Testament criteria for a prophet; however, the idea of Muhammad as a prophet "is such an offensive idea [in Evangelical circles] because they don't even have a grip to understand it." He also said that he "kind of hate[s] these dichotomous either/or questions." Oliver also expressed difficulty with black-and-white responses, and when I asked him for his thoughts on Islam, he said, "The truth of the matter is some days I wake up, and I think one thing about Islam, and some days I wake up, and I think the opposite. [. . .] My personal beliefs about Islam are, it's a religion; it's a worldview; it's a culture." All four of these Evangelicals were accepting of certain Islamic beliefs that have not been historically accepted within Evangelicalism. They were more likely to see Islam as a cultural form, rather than a religion that is either right or wrong, and they saw ample room for negotiating aspects of Islam with aspects of Christianity. All spoke relatively positively about Islam and relatively critically about Evangelical Christianity. But these individuals were also traditional in the sense that they used the Bible and terms like "Jesus," "God," and "Holy Spirit" to justify their views (Jesus most often) and in the sense that their language portrayed a focus on the mission of being Christ-followers and talking about Jesus. However, it should be clarified these Evangelicals whose views deviate from the dominant historical Evangelical view of Islam are not simply making a conscious choice to emphasize similarities rather than differences between Christianity and Islam. My findings show that they genuinely perceive the two belief systems as having considerably more in common than do Christians whose views align with the dominant historical positions on Islam. As pointed out, they were much more comfortable downplaying the differences between Islam and Christianity and between Christians and Muslims, and were less willing to make black-and-white judgments about Islam.

Varying Views on Politics

I asked all the leaders to describe their political views, and I then asked several questions dealing with specific political issues. A third of my interviewees leaned politically liberal and about two-thirds leaned politically conservative. The majority who leaned toward the progressive end of the spectrum according to their evidential moral authority were also to the left in their political views. Likewise, the majority of those who leaned traditional according to their evidential moral authority were also to the right in their political views. Still, there were a few "crossovers," such as one or two interviewees who had "soft" traditional views in terms of moral authority (namely, those in the Traditional-Progressive category) but were politically liberal, and vice versa.

Interestingly, although interviewees generally leaned politically conservative or politically liberal, the majority (20) avoided portraying extremes in their political perspectives. This majority expressed pros and cons relating to both the Democratic and Republican Party positions on various social and economic issues. For example, Maria said, "I believe that both groups get some parts right and some wrong." Ahmad said he was conservative on some points and gave some examples, but then later said he leaned liberal on other issues and gave other examples. Such views were common. Emma described herself as fiscally conservative but not especially socially conservative, saying that she abandoned the party system after growing wiser and realizing that "nothing's as black and white as you maybe would like it to be." Generally, Samuel found more commonalities with the Republican side, but on certain social issues, such as prison reform, he sided with the Democrats.

Many leaders were cautious about discussing politics and wanted to minimize their political stances. Heather said she was "not a very political person" and identified herself as a political moderate. She acknowledged that she leaned to the left on social issues, but when I asked her about what particular issues, she told me that she was very uncomfortable with the question. Heather feared expressing her more leftist political perspectives because she held an important position for a large church made up mostly of conservatives, and she feared fellow congregants would find her political perspectives unorthodox. Maria likewise tried to minimize her political opinions and move the conversation beyond the seemingly uncomfortable realm of politics. She said, "I have political views, but they are not very critical for me, because I don't feel that they shape my thinking." She said if she had to pick, she would be a Democrat, because she believed in giving people choices even if she did not personally agree with how they exercised that power of choice. She then brought up homosexuality, saying, "I don't agree that a marriage can be defined as two men or two women living together. That goes against my understanding. But then I look at the bigger picture, that if God gives us that freedom, who are we to remove it?" Then, turning the conversation to interfaith issues, she argued for a vision beyond politics, saying, "I don't believe the Democratic version; I don't believe the Republican version. I believe that what God is saying is He loves, [and] that He's pouring His Spirit." Maria, as others, desired to appear tolerant and politically unaligned.

Evangelical Conflict on Islam

While most research suggests that Evangelicals are largely unified on Islam, one of the main arguments of my work as a whole has been that there is significant diversity among Evangelicals regarding Islam. When I asked interviewees what *they* perceived regarding Evangelical unity, they largely agreed that there are significant internal divisions within Evangelicalism on Islam. Specifically, when I asked, "Do you feel Evangelicals are unified on the topic of Islam?" most leaders responded with a clear "No." Marianne said, "Most definitely not," and Oliver said, "No way, exclamation point!" Often interviewees laughed when answering the question, as if to suggest the absurdity of the idea that Evangelicals would be united. According to Joseph, the most basic intra-Evangelical conflict on Islam concerns the question of what goal Evangelicals should have in their interactions with Muslims. For some Evangelicals, he said, the priority is evangelism, whereas other Evangelicals are more interested in dialogue. Ultimately, he told me, "there's no uniformity or unanimity in the Evangelical community on Islam."

Whereas Joseph described a binary division among Evangelicals, a number of other interviewees answered my question about disagreements among Evangelicals by describing a continuum or spectrum of views. Hayden, for example, divided Evangelicals into four categories based on how each category views the nature of the Islamic religion and what each category asks of converts. In the first category, he said, are those who hold the dominant historical Evangelical perspective that Islam is "demonic" because it is outside of Christianity. Those in the second category "have a more modern view," namely, that the Islamic religion contains a significant amount of truth, but that it is still fundamentally flawed, and thus Muslims should leave Islam in order to follow Christ. The third category included those, like Hayden himself, who believe that it is permissible for Muslims to remain socially, culturally, and politically a part of the Islamic religion; they can retain many Islamic teachings but simply need to "strengthen what they believe about Jesus and come to the traditional belief [of Evangelicals] that there is no salvation outside of Christ." The fourth category (a minority view, according to Hayden) was that to be born Muslim is "just a sociological phenomenon and the majority of people are nominal," in the sense of not taking their religion seriously.

Other interviewees likewise described a continuum of views among Evangelicals regarding the nature of Islam. Oliver, for example, told me, "You've got the whole spectrum from 'it's satanic' to 'there is some divine inspiration in it.' [. . .] In the middle, you've got the people who say it's a sociological phenomenon." The idea of a "spectrum" of Evangelical views regarding Islam also arose in my interview with Samuel, an outspoken Evangelical apologist, who categorized Evangelicals based on the feelings he perceived that they harbor toward Muslims. He held that some Evangelicals are so "loving that they'll lay down their lives to preach the Gospel [to Muslims]." Others, he said, harbor anger against Muslims because of the violence they perceive arising out of Islam. Still others are simply uninterested in Muslims, or they think evangelism is a waste of energy due to the supposed "hard-heartedness" of Muslims.

For Leah, a Jew who came to believe later in life that Jesus is the Messiah, Evangelical views were also on a spectrum, but in her perception the spectrum was primarily a spectrum of approaches to communication with Muslims. At one extreme, she said, are the "bridge builders," whom Leah viewed somewhat critically due to her perception that some bridge builders are too hesitant to openly and honestly identify themselves with Christ and do not focus sufficient energy on presenting the gospel. At the other extreme, she said, are apologists—those who focus primarily on debating Muslims and defending the Christian faith; this extreme she also associated with weaknesses, namely, the weakness that apologetics alone, without compassion, can "reinforce prejudice" against Muslims.

Although the notion of a spectrum of views was popular among my interviewees, not all leaders perceived diversity on Islam among Evangelicals. Seven leaders held that Evangelicals were mostly unified in their views of Islam, though most of them were not happy about the unity they perceived. Ahmad, himself a former Muslim, said he has found himself at times defending Islam to fellow Evangelicals, because Evangelicals can be "unified on stereotyping [Islam] and unified on exaggerating it." Brad, pastor of a mega-church in the South, believes Evangelicals are "Islamophobic." Brad claimed to have lost several hundred attendees after a number of Muslim Imams began coming to speak and teach introductory classes on Islam at his church. He said he thought "most Evangelicals do not like Muslims." He also said that Evangelicals are driven by "fear, [. . .] their own personal self-interest, and also a lot of misunderstanding," and as a result Evangelicals tend not to treat Muslims with enough respect. Andrew, the interviewee who no longer identifies as an Evangelical, believed that there are those around the margins of Evangelicalism who hold charitable views of Islam but said that the dominant view is "Evangelical Islamophobia." Thus, some saw a continuum of views among Evangelicals, where others saw general unity around an anti-Islamic view, but no one thought Evangelicals had generally positive views of Islam. Those holding the most critical views of Evangelicals regarding Islam came from Evangelicals that dissent from the traditional Evangelical perspective of Islam. These individuals were also the most likely to equate a negative view of the religion of Islam as a negative view of Muslims.

Many interviewees—including those who held Evangelicals to be divided and those who held them to be unified—brought up the same two issues as major hurdles that keep Evangelicals from engaging Muslims. The first is fear of Muslims (several interviewees told me that Evangelicals are afraid to talk to Muslims due to how Islam and violence have been interwoven in popular media) and the second, ignorance about Islam (interviewees said that many Evangelicals are afraid to talk to Muslims because they feel uneducated about Islam, leading to fear among Evangelicals that they would not be able to successfully persuade Muslims of the truth of their own Evangelical faith even if they were to try). Regarding ignorance among Evangelicals, Elizabeth told me it is unusual to find Evangelicals who have read the Qur'an, who know what the Hadith (a collection of traditions containing saying of Muhammad, which constitutes a major source of guidance for many Muslims alongside the Qur'an) are, or who are familiar with any of the practices of Islam. Luke mentioned that in his experience, ignorance about Islam keeps Evangelicals from engaging because they feel they have to engage doctrinally, rather than relationally. According to Luke, the Evangelicals who are willing to engage usually converse "on the level of doctrines" exclusively and fail to approach their Muslim neighbors on the "communal front"—a pattern he viewed as regrettable, given that "we all have the same problems and issues, and that should be a rallying point."

The Qur'an

Not only did Evangelical leaders perceive conflict within Evangelicalism about Islam—their perceptions were confirmed by the varying answers these leaders gave to questions about Muhammad, the Qur'an, and missiological strategies Evangelicals should use to engage with Muslims. Their responses attest to the diversity, disagreement, and division within Evangelicalism.

All but one of the leaders I interviewed said that they had read the Qur'an or at least parts of the Qur'an. The exception was Heather, whose primary interest with respect to Muslims was building friendly relationships and humanizing Muslims to those within the Evangelical community; her interest was not with what the Qur'an says, per se. Four interviewees (Joseph, Emma, Jane, and Paul) said that they had read sections of the Qur'an but not all of it; the rest indicated that they had read the book in its entirety. Progressives were the least likely to have read extensively from the Qur'an. Of the seven interviewees in the evidential Progressive category, only three had read the entire Qur'an; by comparison, all but one of the interviewees in the other categories had read the Qur'an in its entirety. Either the Progressives in my study were more willing to admit their limited knowledge of the Qur'an than those in other categories, or they genuinely had not read as much of the Qur'an as their counterparts to the right of the spectrum. Lack of compulsion to read the Qur'an could reflect the belief, held by some who hold dissenting views from the dominant historical Evangelical narrative, that cultural and socioeconomic forces dictate beliefs and actions more than a text like the Qur'an.

The majority of those on the progressive end of the Progressive-Traditional spectrum spoke positively or neutrally about the Qur'an, whereas the majority of those on the traditional end spoke negatively. This is consistent with Hunter's thesis, which suggests that Traditional individuals are sufficiently committed to their respective "media of moral authority" that they typically consider sources of moral authority other than their own to be heretical (1991: 120). In contrast to the Traditionals, the Progressives in my sample tended to elevate the Qur'an relatively highly, with some even going so far as to accept it as a God-breathed book (alongside the Tawrat, Zabur, and Injil).

Though Progressives in my sample tended toward positive views and Traditionals tended toward more negative views, the split was not a clean one. Although no one in the evidential Progressive category spoke negatively of the Qur'an, some who leaned traditional had remarkably elevated views of the Qur'an. This latter group was made up of those affiliated with IMs, and included Maria, who told me she read the Qur'an regularly because she saw the footprints of God within it; she also said that her reading had "been absolutely critical in gaining credibility in the Muslim community." She indicated that the Muslims in her circle "know that my supreme source of authority is the Bible," but she also said she made a point of using the language of the Qur'an in studies with Muslims.

Most interviewees, regardless of their position on the Progressive-Traditional spectrum, agreed that the teachings about Jesus in the Qur'an and the Bible have striking similarities. Some therefore felt that the Qur'an can be treated as a light that points to the divinity of Jesus. Parker, an evidential Progressive-Traditional and also an IM supporter, was one of those who held this view. In fact, he told me, the Qur'an is the best tract ever written to lead Muslims to Jesus. Parker was highly critical of historical Evangelical forms of evangelism, telling me that the Qur'an is like a small flame, and that older evangelistic approaches, which would reject the Qur'an, simply blow out that flame. Parker preferred instead to acknowledge that the Qur'an sheds light on Jesus. Brad, the southern mega-church pastor (also an IM supporter with a low view of Evangelicals aligned with the dominant historical perspective on Islam), held a similar view of the Qur'an as a useful "light." When I asked him if he had read the Qur'an, he said, "Yeah, many times. Every morning I spend an hour and a half at this desk reading my Bible . . . and my Qur'an." He did this, he told me, because he saw a lot of similarities between the scriptures of Islam and Christianity, including in the Qur'an's presentation of Jesus, which he said mirrors Christian beliefs about Jesus right up to the point of the crucifixion and the resurrection. These positive perceptions of the Qur'an coincide with a distrust of historical Christianity and a promotion of IM concepts.

Not all held such charitable views of the Qur'an, however. Robbie opposed attempts to "'Christianize' the Qur'an in sort of an ecumenical attempt to show that we all believe the same thing." Others pointed to verses in the Qur'an that violated their sense of human rights, especially verses regarding the treatment of women and the subjugation of unbelievers. Rose, for example, told me that the Qur'an requires believers to compel unbelievers to submit to Islam and said its advocacy of violence is clear. She opened her Qur'an and read to me suras (a sura is a chapter or section of the Qur'an) that she found disturbing; one of these suras spoke of cutting off the heads of unbelievers and burning them alive. Rose explained:

> I have been working in the Islamic world for over twelve years in Afghanistan, Palestine, and Iraq, and have spen[t] extensive amounts of time working directly with people who are under Sharia law . . . The thing is, you have to look at the Qur'an . . . if you take Islam literally from the teachings in the Qur'an, you're going to have what we're having today with Daesh [Islamic State of Iraq and al Sham] . . . We ask ourselves, where does this come from? Let's just look at an example here of surah 8:12-15. "God revealed his will to the angels saying, I shall be with you." This is talking about a battle that happened in 624, when Muhammad had planned to attack an unarmed caravan and he was only three hundred and nineteen strong, but he was able to gain the victory over a thousand and was giving God the glory for having helped him, saying, "You see, God has helped us" . . . This is the same thing we're hearing from the Islamic State. He says, "God revealed his will to the angels, saying I will be with you." He is talking about battle now, because this whole chapter is on the spoils of

battle, your booty. It says, "Give courage to the believers. I shall cast terror into the hearts of the infidels, strike off their heads, strike off the very tips of their fingers." That was because they defied God and his apostle. "He that defies God and his apostle [being Muhammad] shall be sternly punished by God. We say to them, taste this, the scourge of the fire awaits the unbelievers"... If you take the Qur'an literally and you believe you are mandated by God, Allah, to deal with unbelievers in this way... I just read to you why they are cutting people's heads off and burning them with fire. What I think about Islam is you have to look at what Islam teaches... this is the root of Islam that we have here [holds up Qur'an], in the Qur'an... I believe that the Qur'an does teach violence. It does teach them to cause anyone that is not a believer to submit and if not willing to submit, then you know some very strict rules of things they'll do... There is a chapter on women in the Qur'an. You want to go to surah 4, in the end of verse 34 it says, "Men have authority over women." I'm reading from the Qur'an. Be it English, but I am reading from a valid English translation. "Men have authority over women... As for those from whom you fear disobedience." This is talking about the man whose wife—he is afraid—is going to disobey. She hasn't done anything wrong. This is what the Qur'an tells them to do. "You should admonish them and forsake them in beds apart and beat them." You know, this is clear language. This is clear teaching. When I'm in Afghanistan, they are under Sharia law and they believe in the literal translation of the Qur'an. Saudi Arabia does too... You go anywhere alone, you get raped, it's your fault... women are treated so badly and cannot escape. If they run away, they are thrown in prison or they are killed. They have no rights whatsoever. A man can have up to four wives, as taught in the Qur'an. A woman cannot divorce. The man can divorce ... I actually know people who have worked in Afghanistan and come back to the United States of America to become educated in being able to counsel women because they've had to go and set up burn units in Afghanistan, because women are so desperate to get out of their situation that they commit suicide by burning themselves alive... These are just two small portions I've just read to you out of the Qur'an. If we don't take it literally, I'm not quite sure how we're going to take it, but let's say we're not going to take it literally, what about the fact that Saudi Arabia takes it literally? What about the fact that Pakistan takes it literally, and has blasphemy laws?... I feel it's a very serious matter and that it has the potential to... Certainly, this book has the potential, and those that take it literally, have the potential to have us soon plunged into a third world war ... This is how Muhammad lived and this is the faith, and this is what he taught. This is their most holy book. We can argue all day, but at the end of the day, it says what it says.

Jane expressed similar concerns about the Qur'an; in fact, she appealed to the Qur'an's treatment of women and its advocacy of violence to explain why she did not feel compelled to read the Qur'an in full. She did not understand why women in particular would remain Muslim, given that the Qur'an "says hell is populated mainly with women." Although she seemed somewhat torn about not reading more of the Qur'an, saying she knew that "understand[ing] it helps us to understand Muslims more," she ultimately indicated she had no desire to read further. The Qur'an, she said, "is filled with such hate and such violence, and it's led so many people astray. [. . .] I would rather focus my eyes and my heart on things that are good and lovely, pure and lovely [. . .], which would be the Word of God." Leaders who were not involved with IMs, yet were categorized as Traditional or Traditional-Progressive, were likely to have a negative view of the Qur'an and the perceived influence it has on Muslims regarding violence toward non-Muslims and treatment of Muslim women.

Muhammad

Interviewees were divided over how to view Muhammad. About half of the leaders spoke positively about Muhammad; the other half spoke comparatively negatively. Opinions ranged from Muhammad being a great ethical leader and possibly a prophet with a message from God, to being delusional and violent.

As with views of the Qur'an, the division in views of Muhammad was significantly related to whether or not an interviewee leaned progressive or traditional with respect to moral authority. The majority of Progressives and Progressive-Traditionals in my sample spoke positively about Muhammad, whereas the majority of Traditionals and Traditional-Progressives spoke negatively. However, the correlation between views of Muhammad and position on the Progressive-Traditional spectrum was far from perfect. Among evidential Progressives, no one expressed negative views of Muhammad, but a number of leaders in the Traditional and Traditional-Progressive categories spoke positively of Muhammad. In fact, a better predictor of an interviewee's view of Muhammad than his or her progressive or traditional leaning was his or her view of IMs.[2] Proponents of IMs usually found no value in criticizing Muhammad; some went so far as to say that the question of whether Muhammad was a prophet has no black-and-white answer.

One representative of a positive perspective was Luke, who saw Muhammad "as an inspirational leader," although short of being a divine guide. Jim similarly considered Muhammad to be "a great leader," partly on the grounds that Muhammad said many positive things about Jesus. On Muhammad's status as a prophet, Jim had a nuanced view—namely that although Muhammad was not a prophet, per se, he was nevertheless "'prophetic,' in that he turned idol worshipers away from their idols to worship the one almighty creator of heaven and earth."

Several interviewees expressed some uncertainty regarding Muhammad. Joseph, for example, said the framework of orthodox Christianity is exclusivist

---

2. Ten of my fourteen interviewees within the Progressive or Progressive-Traditional categories were fully supportive of or held sympathetic views toward insider movements, and four of the fifteen Traditionals or Traditional-Progressives were supportive of or sympathetic to insider movements.

and leaves little room for acknowledging other prophetic figures beyond those presented in the Bible, but said that he still respected the Muslim belief in Muhammad's prophetic status. In the end, he concluded, "I can't make an unequivocal yes [to the question of whether Muhammad was a prophet], but I don't want to be disrespectful to make it an unequivocal no, so God will tell us at the end." Parker also seemed unsure about Muhammad's prophetic status and expressed a discomfort in judging Muhammad's motivations:

> The reason the Qur'an exists, even in Muhammad's words, was that they had no book in their language. He was a caravan trader, he went to different places. He heard the [Biblical] stories. I think it's highly possible that he believed the stories and he tried to write them down so people that understood Arabic could understand the stories . . . some he got very right, some he didn't get quite as right. Eternity will only tell what his motivations were and it's not my job to judge him.

Parker's difficulty in judging Muhammad did not spill over into his view of Evangelicals whose views were more aligned with the dominant historical Evangelical perspective on Islam. For example, Parker was quick to judge well-known Evangelical author and pastor John Piper as "ignorant" regarding Islam.

Oliver likewise expressed uncertainty about Muhammad. When I asked him if he thought Muhammad was a prophet, he paused for a long moment and then gave a loud laugh. He seemed slightly uncomfortable and appeared to be searching for the right words. When he did finally respond, he told me that he did not believe Muhammad to be a prophet on par with the biblical prophets, but he said he nevertheless thought highly of Muhammad and felt that Muhammad "did an awful lot better than a lot of biblical prophets." Oliver went to some length to share what he believed Muhammad had done right, such as teaching monotheism, social justice, and equality; encouraging his followers to read the Old and New Testaments of the Bible; and advocating worship of the God of Jesus Christ. However, Oliver ended his response by saying, "I believe the devil masquerades as an angel of light," a comment that appeared to suggest Muhammad may have been inspired by something demonic rather than something holy.

Oliver's implication of possible demonic influence was a surprise twist, given that he was a proponent of IMs; no other IM proponents I spoke with referenced demonic influence on Muhammad. Usually, talk of Muhammad being influenced by ungodly forces came from Evangelicals whose views were more aligned with the dominant historical Evangelical perspective on Islam, such as Gabriel. Gabriel referenced the Islamic teaching that when Muhammad initially started receiving visions, he believed that he was being oppressed by a demon; Gabriel then questioned why one should not believe Muhammad's first impressions, since it was Muhammad himself who attributed his visions to demonic influence. Other interviewees made no reference to demonic influence on Muhammad, but they were unequivocal that Muhammad was not a legitimate prophet. Ahmad, for example, compared Muhammad to Joseph Smith, the founder of Mormonism.

Both men, according to Ahmad, thought they were prophets, but both were equally wrong. Robbie expressed similar certainty that Muhammad was not a prophet, although he showed more reserve in saying so: "I do not think of [Muhammad] as a divinely-inspired prophet in the biblical sense, but neither do I think of him as a demonized pedophile." He said that he did not see Muhammad "as an exceptionally evil person" and believed that "he was sinful like the rest of us."

Some highlighted the violent side of Muhammad. Samuel told me that Muhammad started off as a "good guy" teaching a message of peace, but that he acquired too much power too quickly, and his message changed over time. For this reason, according to Samuel, there are contradictory messages in Islam: Muslims can look to the sources of their religion and find messages of peace and tolerance, and they can claim that these messages represent Islamic teaching. However, according to Samuel, Muhammad became considerably more violent later in his career, and thus groups like ISIS that promote violence and subjugation can also look to the sources of Islam and find justification for their views. Leah also acknowledged the violence associated with Muhammad, although she framed his violence as comparable to that of famous Christian leaders, namely the Roman emperor Constantine.

Interestingly, both Oliver and Kevin, who disagreed on many other points, agreed that Christians should avoid negative talk about Muhammad when interacting with Muslims; they should rather focus on Jesus. Kevin spent considerable time detailing to me Muhammad's faults, but in the end, he told me, "the best thing to do is to avoid talking about Muhammed" with Muslims. "There's just no reason to get their backs up by attacking the man they regard as the Prophet," he said; instead, Christians should "focus on Jesus and who he was." Ultimately, those affiliated with IMs or those deemed as leaning progressive using the stated moral authority analysis refrained from negative statements about Muhammad, whereas Evangelicals whose views aligned with the dominant historical Evangelical perspective on Islam were more likely to offer a denunciation of Muhammad.

Chrislam

As discussed in Chapter 2, "Chrislam" is a derogatory term denoting the amalgamation of Christianity and Islam. The term arose in response to a series of Christian missiologists who began to promote IMs—that is, they argued that "believers in Christ" who are from Muslim backgrounds should be allowed and encouraged to remain culturally and even religiously a part of Muslim communities. Critics of the IM philosophy have accused its proponents of promoting "Chrislam" and thus undermining the uniqueness and truth of genuine Christian religion.

Slightly over half of my interviewees believed that Chrislamic approaches to missiology pose a threat to Evangelicalism. The majority of interviewees, however, showed nuanced opinions and seemed conflicted on the topic of Chrislam. For example, Rose was previously a missionary to the Middle East; she has helped Christian believers from Muslim backgrounds receive entry into the United States as refugees and then brought them to live with her and her husband in their home in the southern United States. She said she thought Evangelicals need to be careful "about finding Jesus in the Qur'an and trying to use the Qur'an as a bridge" because doing so creates a "danger of not presenting the true Jesus." She also felt, however, that it is unjust to completely rule out all concepts within the insider movement. "We have to be careful and use great wisdom, and be directed on an individual basis by the Holy Spirit of God," she told me, because in lands under Sharia law, "if you ask [believers from a Muslim background] to truly live out in public the Christian faith, fully, you've put a death penalty on them."

When I asked Samuel about his thoughts on Chrislam, he said he wanted to be careful in his response, because he realized that Muslims who convert to Christianity in countries practicing Sharia law (e.g., Pakistan and Saudi Arabia, et alibi) will be killed if they go out and proclaim the gospel. But he believed that some Christians go too far when they claim that believers can be both Christian and Muslim simultaneously, pretending there is no inconsistency in adhering to a Christian perspective while maintaining involvement in Muslim religious communities. For Samuel, Christianity and Islam *are* ultimately inconsistent with each other because of doctrinal differences on key subjects like the crucifixion of Jesus, his resurrection, and his atonement. In the end, he said, "You have to pick one [religion] or the other or reject them both."

When I asked Leah about Chrislam, she said she understood both sides, particularly since she came from a Jewish background and was personally familiar with the complexities of the process of conversion. She described herself as "a Jewish believer of Jesus," meaning that she considered herself to be following Jesus as a Christian but without having abandoned her Jewish identity. With respect to Chrislam, on the one hand she was concerned about Christians who do not actually call themselves by that name or who discourage others from overtly claiming the Christian label, because she sees this as dishonest and rendering their faith impotent. On the other hand, Leah, like other interviewees, referenced the danger converts face in proclaiming their Christianity in countries with majority Muslims populations and expressed concern for their plight. She understood that proponents of Chrislam are "trying to redeem the culture that we currently identify as Islam," and she believed that "God can redeem it."

About one-third of interviewees perceived no threat in so-called Chrislamist thinking and/or felt the term "Chrislam" has been applied incorrectly. For example, when I asked Brad, a proponent of IMs, if he had heard of the term "Chrislam," he said, sarcastically, "Yeah, I've heard of it. I helped start it. [The term 'Chrislam'] is just corny. It's just corny. I don't even take it serious[ly]." When I asked Hayden, another proponent of IMs, about Chrislam, he acknowledged being a supporter of IM thinking and said he felt that arguments against IMs are flawed and that use of the term "Chrislam" is unjustified. Critics of Chrislam, he said, try to say that whenever anyone seeks to adapt, make use of, or retain anything Muslim after becoming a Jesus follower, they are attempting to amalgamate two religions that are inherently not the same. He added, however, that "every single religious group on the planet evolved from or developed from something else." He noted the influence of European pagan religious forms on American Evangelicalism, such as in the use of Christmas trees, but said, "We don't call ourselves right now Europago Christians."

Mark said he is viewed as one of the founders of so-called Chrislamist thinking, but he believes the term to be illegitimate and denies actually promoting any amalgamation of the two religions. He believes fear is the motivating force behind Christian leaders' usage of the term. As Mark explained:

> I think that it's a clever phrase that can become a straw man for opponents to beat [and] along the way incite all kinds of fear among Christians. It still disturbs me how easily Christian leaders resort to fear-mongering . . . Yeah, we need to guard against heresy. I agree with that. I've read the pastoral epistles. I understand that. At the same time, living in fear like that, that seems to be the motivating influence behind the whole Chrislam thing. We're losing our faith. It just fits in with all these narratives that are low-hanging and probably unrighteous fruit for [us as] pastors to pick on and show our congregations and try to incite some sort of emotional response . . . It just strikes me as this weird fearful invention by Christian leaders . . . At the same time the people who are drumming up all the opposition to [insider movements] might have some good spiritual intentions, but they might also stand to benefit as those who are the true guardians of the faith . . . "now you should support me instead." So, there's a whole economy to this.

When I brought up the term "Chrislam" with Mark, I could sense significant emotion in his response, as had been the case with Brad and Hayden. All three seemed angry and sometimes sarcastic when they spoke of Christian leaders who use the term "Chrislam" as an accusation. By contrast, Maria, another supporter of IMs, was also emotional in her response, but the primary emotions she expressed were sadness and hurt rather than anger. She told me she had cried when she first watched "Half Devil, Half Child," a documentary about IMs in Bangladesh. The film is highly critical of IMs, questioning the depth of belief and conviction of Muslim followers of Jesus in Bangladesh, and their ability to contribute to, and understand, evangelism (e.g., they are able to maintain their status as a Muslim and are less likely to face martyrdom). Maria, who is directly involved in IM ministries in Bangladesh, felt misunderstood and labeled after viewing the film. She told me that what was shown in the film about Chrislam in Bangladesh was a distortion, and that she could tell me multiple stories of people who have been beaten because of choosing to follow Christ while remaining Muslim.

It is important to note that these four individuals (Mark, Hayden, Maria, and Brad) who held that the term "Chrislam" has been used unfairly came from all points on the Progressive-Traditional spectrum. But despite their differences with respect to moral authority, these IM proponents all shared commonalities, including their contemplative focus on cultural forms of living out faith, their expressed general dislike of many aspects of Western culture, and their suspicion of anything labeled "Christian" or "Christianity." All of the four were critics of Christianity from within the Evangelical fold.

About two-thirds of my interviewees felt, albeit to varying degrees, that the term "Chrislam" has utility and that the criticisms implied in the label are valid. Kevin, an apologist, used the term to describe the belief system of a Muslim scholar with whom he had debated many times over the years. Kevin's rationale for using the term to describe this individual's faith was that the man had made significant movement in the direction of Christian belief as a result of discussions between the two, but the man had not fully converted to Christianity and continued to espouse a "synchronistic view." Kevin described how he supports missionaries in countries such as Bangladesh, and how as a result he has entertained the question of whether or not it is possible to convert to Christ but continue living as a Muslim. On the one hand, Kevin acknowledged that he could not claim to fully understand the pressures of living in a Muslim-dominated culture where Christians experience real threats of persecution. Still, he said, he is inclined to believe "the Gospel calls upon us to confess Christ, and that to pretend to still be a Muslim when in fact you believe in Christ, and to worship in Muslim forms and so forth, is illegitimate."

Ahmad, a believer of Muslim background from the Middle East, told me he was one of the early critics of "insider movement tactics." Ahmad believed proponents of insider movements are "manipulating people to Christ," in the sense that their methods are "crafty" and trick people into becoming Muslims for Jesus. He said they push these questionable tactics simply because they want to be able to report high numbers of converts, and do so without thinking through what is lost in translation due to the perceived syncretism. He claimed that proponents of IM tactics are dishonorable to the Islamic communities because the proponents are concerned "about numbers" and "seeing results," which has led them to "do whatever [. . .] in order to see results so [they] could report them." Ahmad nuanced these harsh statements by saying that he believed the motives of IM proponents to be noble, and he specifically denied the claim made by some that proponents are interested in money. Still, he held that IMs "deceive people to Christ," in the sense that Christians corrupt Islam and try to deceive Muslims out of their religion by hiding their true identity and by using altered translations of the Bible that accommodate Muslim concepts of God.

When I asked Tarifa, another Christian from a Muslim background, about Chrislam, she said there were certain traits in Islam that she valued—specifically, the passion, discipline, and life of prayer characteristic of Muslims. But ultimately, she said, "I think apart from Christ it's all meaningless. I don't see how you can combine the two [religions] because they contradict each other so much. Even if it's just the softest version of both, the heart of Christianity goes completely, completely against Islam." Given the diametric opposition of the two, she explained, it is impossible to select out parts of Islam and try to fit them into Christianity. All three of these interviewees (Kevin, Ahmad, and Tarifa) who expressed concern about Islam were Traditional-Progressives. As can be seen, former Muslims were the most critical of IMs.

Significantly, interviewees were more likely to use traditional Evangelical moral authority terminology to justify their views on Chrislam than they were in their responses to other questions. Over half of all interviewees, regardless of their stance on Chrislam and regardless of how likely they were to use traditional moral terminology at other points in the interview, tended to rely heavily on traditional Evangelical moral authority terminology to justify their views on Chrislam. Also of interest is the fact that those who expressed concern about Chrislam tended to demonstrate relative comfort with being labeled Christians and being identified as a part of Christianity. By contrast, a number of the IM proponents I interviewed tended to avoid using the term "Christian" to describe themselves and instead preferred to be called "Jesus Followers," "Believers," "Christ Followers," or some similar term.

Interfaith Dialogue

So far, this chapter has demonstrated that Evangelical leaders represent considerable diversity in terms of their views on the character of Muhammad, the value of the Qur'an, and the appropriateness of missiological strategies that would allow Christian converts to remain part of their Muslim communities. But what of leaders' views on interfaith dialogue? How much agreement exists among Evangelical leaders on the question of whether people of different religions can and should engage in cooperative interactions?

To determine interviewees' views on interfaith dialogue, I first asked them directly about their thoughts on the topic. Then, later in the interview, I also asked about the ACW initiative—specifically, whether the interviewee was familiar with the initiative and what his or her views were regarding it. As will be shown in the remainder of the chapter, questions on both of these subjects revealed significant disagreement among Evangelical leaders.

The majority of leaders I spoke with (24) had a moderate view of interfaith dialogue and described both pros and cons related to it. Of these, fourteen were mostly skeptical, though still open to the benefits of interfaith dialogue. The other ten saw mostly benefits but were still able to critique the endeavor. Overall, the majority of my leaders described wanting to engage with Muslims but not in a "wishy-washy" or superficial kind of way. In terms of justifications for their views, only six leaders relied heavily on traditional Evangelical moral authority terminology, and about half of the interviewees made no mention at all of traditional Evangelical moral authority terminology in their responses. This was an unusually low rate of usage of traditional terminology compared to questions on other topics, and it suggests that interviewees may have felt less comfortable, or less coherent, attempting to marry their view of God or the Bible with their personal views on interfaith dialogue.

Oliver is an example of one leader with a moderate approach to formal interfaith dialogue. Specifically, he supported interfaith dialogue, but only in cases where such dialogue is "robust" and "honest." Oliver talked about the importance of having "humility" and "respect" in interfaith dialogue situations, and he held that all "should enter into inter-faith dialogue with the recognition that it is possible that we could be convinced of a new idea or a new way of understanding God, and vice versa." He also critiqued Evangelicals in his response, arguing, "We need to do a lot more listening." Then he brought up Jesus and the apostle Paul, saying these two figures focused less on preaching to people and more on reasoning and dialoguing with them. Oliver, like many other IM proponents, desired to approach Muslims humbly as a listener and learner, rather than as someone who has more correct answers than the Muslims they are dialoguing with.

Emma also expressed support for interfaith dialogue, but she noted that Christian participants must be willing to hear others' concerns, not just come to the table for the sake of expressing their own views. Indeed, she said, Evangelical participants might need to "throw [their] agenda out the window" and talk first about the issues on the agendas of other dialogue participants. Emma said, "It's kind of like Maslow's hierarchy of needs. You can't teach somebody philosophy if they're starving. If [something] is on the forefront of their mind, you have to be willing to sit and listen to whatever that is before you can maybe [. . .] circle around to your agenda." She invoked the Bible in her reasoning, mentioning that it speaks of "being quick to listen, slow to speak." Oliver and Emma represent the majority perspective among Evangelical leaders: they favored interfaith dialogue, and they favored listening to and learning from the Muslims involved, but hoped the dialogue would allow for truth claims from their Evangelical perspective as well, at least at some point within the exchange. According to these individuals, a number of boxes have to be checked before one is ready to discuss one's own personal Christian faith with another.

Those who expressed the most unqualified enthusiasm for interfaith dialogue were Andrew, Joseph, and Jim, all three of whom have been well known for critiquing Evangelicals whose views align with the dominant historical Evangelical positions on Islam and all of whom were comfortable with being labeled "Progressives" (a term they used to imply deviation from historical Evangelical views). Joseph described his involvement in interfaith initiatives with Muslims as being centered on collaborative efforts to try to curtail the United States' use of torture, which, he believed, had been almost exclusively applied to people of Muslim faith. He saw this involvement with Muslims, tackling human rights issues side by side, as a form of interfaith dialogue. He explained that he went into these collaborative events with the desire to understand "experientially" how Muslims felt about Americans using torture against Muslims. Joseph did not express a motivation to convert Muslims to Christianity, but he did express a desire to help Evangelicals that align with historical Evangelical perspectives to become more tolerant of other belief systems and mindful of the needs of those he perceived to have less access to power in Western culture. He was more concerned with issues of social justice—which for him include interfaith dialogue and listening to non-Christians—than with evangelism toward non-Christians.

The most negative views on public interfaith dialogue with Muslims came from Hakim, a Christian who had been previously persecuted in his home country in the Middle East, and Ahmad, a former Muslim, also from the Middle East. Their opinions reflected a distrust of formal dialogues between Christians and Muslims due to their belief that Christians lose more than they gain. Hakim acknowledged that communication is a good goal but said that most interfaith dialogue pushes the conclusion that "everybody is good" and all belief systems are ultimately similar. He added that he perceives Christians are typically not allowed to present truth as they see it. Of Muslim participation in particular, Hakim told me that Muslims typically only want to discuss interfaith peace if they live in cultures where Muslims lack power. However, according to Hakim, in cultures where Muslims do have power, most have no interest in dialogue and rather want Christians to submit to them under Dhimmi Status (the lower status of non-Muslims living under Islamic rule; see also Durie, 2010). Along the same lines, Ahmad brought up "Muslim craftiness" and said he believes Muslims do not really want to dialogue:

> It [interfaith dialogue] is just to polish the image of Islam . . . It's nothing but that. It's an attempt to make Islam look good, and that's fine, but when you participate in it, that's my problem, because I know Muslim craftiness . . . When you do it, they don't really want to dialogue with you . . . they know they are superior. They know they are right. There is nothing you're going to gain. They want you to submit to them under dhimmi status [the lower status of non-Muslims living under Islamic rule], if you are under them, or . . . if you are the dominant religion in that country, they want you to accept them as an equal religion. If you are a minority religion, as a Christian, you are a minority in their country, they want you to accept them as the leader religion. In a way, they just want to win. That's what the dialogue is. Is the dialogue about winning or about understanding? I don't think they want to understand the Christians. They think they understand them, because it [Christianity] exists in their scripture. Because of that attitude, they think they already know you, but they think you don't know them. Therefore, they want to have the dialogue so you know them, not for them to know you. That's a monologue, not a dialogue.

These individuals from the Middle East had a desire to communicate their Christian faith toward others in a manner of speech that was free and uninhibited, rather than with a mentality they perceived as dominant within interfaith dialogue, which is an oversensitivity to the Muslim that inevitably leaves the Christian as weak and impotent.

"A Common Word"

The largest Christian-Muslim interfaith peace initiative in existence at the time of my study was the "A Common Word" initiative, which was launched in 2007 when 128 Muslims sent a joint invitation to Christian leaders calling on them to recognize what the authors suggested were shared fundamentals between Islam and Christianity. Some Evangelical leaders signed the document, while others did not. Some signed it but then later asked to have their names removed. Due to its prominence as an interfaith initiative, I chose to explore interviewees' knowledge of and thoughts on ACW specifically.

All but seven interviewees had heard of ACW. However, even among interviewees who had heard of ACW, not all felt knowledgeable enough to make a judgment on it. A few said things like "I've heard of it, but I can't remember all of the details" or "I can't answer that one, because I haven't looked at the document." Thus, even though the majority had heard of ACW, not all interviewees had a strong opinion about it. In terms of their justifications, Rose, Elizabeth, Navid, Jakob, and Maria were the only five who justified their positions on the ACW initiative using traditional Evangelical moral authority terminology. The other leaders who knew enough about the initiative to comment (9) made no mention of traditional terminology.

In total, ten interviewees expressed a positive view of ACW. Although these ten represented all four categories of evidential moral authority, the group as a whole was relatively critical of dominant historical Evangelical perspectives on interfaith dialogue and relatively open to promoting interfaith dialogue focused on similarities between the two faith groups, rather than prioritizing theological differences between the faiths. Almost all were supportive of insider movements. Most saw imperfections in the ACW document but were willing to embrace it for the sake of bettering relationships and thus, in line with more humanistic principles, prioritized relationship over correct theology. Hayden acknowledged that the ACW wording was framed in such a way as to be thoroughly monotheistic, thus not recognizing the deity of Jesus. Still, he said, the document indicated an acceptance of the New Testament as divinely inspired, and he believed the document represented a genuine attempt from Muslim leaders to go as far as they could in establishing common ground with Christians. Thus, in spite of its failings from a Christian perspective, the initiative was one Hayden felt he could back as a "good first step." Maria likewise believed the ACW initiative was "a very good starting point" for promoting peaceful dialogue and understanding between Christians and Muslims. Although she did not agree with everything presented in the document, she was willing to compromise in spite of the theological shortcomings regarding Christianity. She believed the initiative shone a light on the more peaceful verses in the Qur'an and was therefore helpful in countering the Qur'anic narrative espoused by radicals:

> Now that doesn't mean that I agree with everything that is presented . . . You see, the Common Word happened because the Pope had gone to Germany . . . the previous Pope, and had a speech in which Muslims felt very offended. Well, some [Muslims] went into rampage, destroying, burning . . . But Prince Ghazi went under a tree and asked God to show him how he could engage the Christian world in a meaningful way to show them that that which the Pope said was wrong. So, he and 137 signatories came out with this notion that, if we can go back to a time where we can talk about being . . . worshiping . . . that we all

worship God, and we are to be good neighbors to each other, here we have some sort of common ground to start a conversation. That was very well received. And this idea of Common Word, it's actually rooted in the Qur'an that says that God is speaking through Muhammed telling him how to engage Christians. And he said, then, "Well, approach the people of the book in the best possible way, and call them to a common word, that 'Your God and our God [are] one.'" I believe that, yes, your God and our God [are] one, but we understand this God differently because of the biblical revelation through Jesus Christ that is unique and is not present in the Qur'an. The Common Word, for me, it's a very good starting point of showing that we can deal with differences by sitting [at] a table and at least giving each other the opportunity to bring the best of your understanding of the holy books, because right now everybody's listening to the Qur'an from the voices of the radicals: "Chop their heads, chop their hands," "Well, what about these verses in the Qur'an that say 'Approach the Christians' and 'There is no compulsion in religion'? Why do you wipe that off if it's in the same holy book? And how does this compare to these other verses?"

Eight interviewees expressed a negative view of ACW, and these individuals prioritized—in line with more rigid orthodoxy—theological correctness more than relational acceptance. Like those who supported the initiative, those expressing a negative view came from all points on the Progressive-Traditional spectrum. One interviewee (Marianne, the only evidential Progressive who criticized the initiative) felt the document didn't have enough women signatories. The others were generally critical because they perceived the initiative to downplay the uniqueness of Christ, and this perceived shortcoming was not something they could compromise on. Most of those who had unfavorable views tended to have a greater interest in apologetics and defense of truth than in relationship building or in interfaith dialogue from the posture of a listener/learner. For instance, Jakob (an evidential Traditional) acknowledged some similarities between Islam and Christianity (such as belief in one God, belief in prophets, and belief in the virgin birth, sinless life, and second coming of Jesus), but he considered these similarities to be in relatively non-essential areas, and he spent most of his time drawing attention to what he called "crucial differences." One key difference, according to Jakob, is that "Christians believe that Jesus died on the cross for the sins of the whole world and [was] raised again three days later. That's called the gospel. Islam rejects that." Other critical points of disagreement for Jakob were Muslims' rejection of the Trinity and their denial that Jesus was the Son of God. Because of differences on such "essential" doctrines, Jakob believed that "Christianity and Islam can never be, in their official orthodox forms, united."

As with those critical of interfaith dialogue, those most critical of the ACW initiative were former Muslims, namely Ahmad and Navid. Navid read me the verse from the Qur'an that is quoted in the ACW document as the basis of the initiative, giving commentary as he read. The verse begins, he explained, by calling the "people of the scripture" (i.e., Jews and Christians) to "come to a common word between us and you, that we shall worship none but Allah." Navid noted that the verse then specifically calls on readers to "ascribe no partner unto Him" and enjoins readers not to "take others for lords beside Allah." Such language, said Navid, explicitly denies the Christian doctrine of the Trinity and therefore declares Christianity to be false. Because this verse, which flies in the face of Christian belief, was the basis of the ACW document, Navid felt it was impossible for him to support the initiative. He went on to say that those Christians who signed the initiative have "convoluted minds," then lamented that "it has become a fashion if you agree with Islam and disagree with Christianity." Navid perceived the traditional form of Evangelicalism (that pits Christianity against Islam as two different religions) as discriminated against and the perpetrators as within the Christian fold.

Conclusion

While all interviewees in varying degrees usually shared the common goal of adding to the Muslim understanding of God an understanding of a divine view of Jesus, they still showed great diversity of opinion on Islam and on certain issues they even demonstrated outright opposition to one another. Far from being a monolithic block of far-right "Islamophobes," the twenty-nine Evangelical leaders featured in this chapter varied in both their religious and their political opinions about Islam and Muslims, with some even expressing more critique of traditional Evangelicalism than they did of Islam or Muslims.

My analysis confirms that many Evangelical leaders are engaged in the type of culture wars Hunter described, as evident by the divides in their views of Islam and Muslims, and the fact that leaders seemed to be drawn to one side of the Progressive-Traditional spectrum or the other. This accords with the argument of Hunter and other sociologists of religion who have claimed that divisions exist as much *within* religious groups as *between* them (Starks and Robinson, 2009; Wuthnow, 1998; Hunter, 1991). Thus, Hunter's conception of moral authorities proves to be a useful lens for understanding the views of Evangelical leaders, in that an individual's moral authority is usually indicative of whether his or her perspectives on Islam and Muslims will be relatively aligned with dominant historical Evangelical views or relatively out of step with those historical views.

Of course, there were some exceptions in my interviews where moral authority was *not* a good predictor of an individual's stances on Islam. In particular, supporters of insider movements tended to hold views regarding Islam that varied significantly from the dominant historical Evangelical perspective, but they still relied significantly on traditional Evangelical moral authority terminology to justify their views. Meanwhile, there were a few leaders whose professions require them to rely heavily on humanistic reason who held stances consistent with historical Evangelical perspectives but who often failed to use traditional moral authority terminology when explaining their views. Despite these exceptions, however, individuals who appealed to traditional moral authorities generally had views that aligned with the dominant historical Evangelical views on Islam, and those who appealed to progressive moral authorities generally had views that deviated from dominant historical Evangelical perspectives.

In the sense that leaders tended to gravitate to one pole of moral authority or the other, the findings of this chapter confirm Hunter's moral authority argument. In another sense, however, this chapter also challenges Hunter's argument. Hunter held that the culture wars are most pronounced among leaders, especially religious leaders. But among the leaders surveyed in this chapter, the evidence gathered from the evidential moral authority analysis does not indicate that Evangelical leaders can cleanly be bifurcated into two warring camps. Rather, the analysis shows there to be some messy inconsistencies in the way individuals defend their position and morally reason their perspectives (inconsistencies as well in their views of Islam and their approach to interactions with Muslims); for example, some held positions that deviate from the dominant historical perspective on Islam and yet often used traditional Evangelical moral authority to back up their deviant positions. Most leaders are moderate hybrids in terms of their moral authority, appealing to a mixture of both progressive and traditional moral authorities. Thus, I argue that there is a spectrum of beliefs among Evangelicals regarding Islam, and I advocate for recognition that Evangelical beliefs regarding moral authority may be quite complex, not always conforming strictly to a "Traditional" or "Progressive" view.

But are these findings unique to leaders? Would the same characteristics be found among Evangelical congregants? The following two chapters will address these questions. Chapter 5 will consider a sample of congregants, asking similar questions of them as this chapter has asked of Evangelical leaders: How unified are congregants on Islam? And how does their moral allegiance contribute to their views on Islam and Muslims? Chapter 6 will then continue this theme by making an explicit comparison of leaders and congregants, explaining how the two groups are similar as well as in what ways they diverge from each other.

Chapter 5

EVANGELICAL CONGREGANTS

STRIFE, VARIETY, AND MODERATION

Muhammed was a great guy. He was important for his people. He did amazing reform—for instance, for the rights of women. He helped his people turn from polytheism to serving the one true God. I think in the general term of a prophet, he's someone who came and proclaimed truth to his people.

—Gabriel, Mercy Church, ministry worker at Mercy

[Muhammad] was a man co-opted by the devil . . . a great imitator . . . That's why Islam is very close to the truth. That's what the devil masters . . . a lie close to the truth is very believable, and very easy to just roll off your tongue if you're not careful.

—Stuart, Adams River Baptist Church, retired salesman

Introduction

Like the Evangelical leaders interviewed in the previous chapter, Evangelical congregants in the urban southern United States have also been formulating opinions about Islam and Muslims. In part, their evaluations of Islam have been driven by increasing exposure to Islam in recent years, both in the form of more frequent in-person interactions with Muslims during their daily routines and in the form of frequent references to Islam in media outlets, including social media. This chapter addresses the same questions of the previous chapter, but this time with a focus on Evangelical congregants rather than on Evangelical leaders: To what extent are Evangelicals reacting to Islam with increased internal cohesion? And how might the moral authority of Evangelical congregants elucidate their attitudes on topics such as Chrislam, Muhammad, the Qur'an, interfaith dialogue, the A Common Word (ACW) initiative, and politics?

The argument of this chapter is threefold. First, I argue that there is considerable diversity among Evangelical congregants on Islam. As with the presence of diversity among Evangelical leaders, the presence of diversity among congregants poses a challenge to Christian Smith's subcultural identity theory (described in

Chapter 3), which predicts that Evangelicals tend to lay aside internal differences when confronted with a perceived external threat such as Islam.

Second, I argue that my data confirms Hunter's "culture wars" thesis (also described in Chapter 3). Consistent with Hunter, I find that Evangelical congregants are drawn to one side or the other of the Progressive-Traditional spectrum. As predicted by Hunter, this finding is less significant (not as strong) for the congregants than it was for the leaders. Further, my research confirms Hunter's thesis by suggesting that most congregants are not found on the extreme Evangelical right or the extreme Evangelical left, but rather have what I have termed "hybrid" identity, which is more moderate when categorized via the evidential moral authority analysis. Specifically, most fall in the Progressive-Traditional category or the Traditional-Progressive category. I also find that, similarly to the leaders, some Evangelical congregants hold stances on various topics relating to Islam that diverge from the dominant historical Evangelical perspective even while still maintaining a relatively traditional moral authority in terms of their usage of traditional terminology. This is particularly true of congregants sympathetic to IMs—that is, congregants sympathetic to missiological methods that encourage "believers in Christ" from Muslim backgrounds to remain culturally, relationally, and religiously (in ways that are perceived by IM leaders as compatible with following Christ) a part of their Islamic communities. Others, especially those who are less personally engaged with Muslims, have progressive moral authorities but still hold stances regarding Islam often associated with historical Evangelicalism. This shows that categories of moral authority are somewhat fluid. As Hunter predicted, Americans may be drawn toward either a progressive moral authority or a traditional one, and a vocal minority will pull to the extremes, but not all Evangelical Christians split into one of two radically divergent camps. This confirms my position that the moral authority of Evangelicals should be viewed less in terms of those on the extreme right or extreme left but rather as a spectrum.

Third, I find that the moral authority of congregants tends to correlate with their level of engagement with Muslims (engagement with Muslims is discussed further in Appendix 3). Specifically, those who were more engaged with Muslims and those who had spent more time learning about Islam tended to appeal to traditional moral authorities. This was the case even though highly engaged congregants came to very different opinions on topics such as Chrislam, Muhammad, the Qur'an, interfaith dialogue, ACW, and politics. By contrast, those who were less engaged with Muslims and knew less about Islam (most of those left of center had not heard of the ACW initiative or Chrislam) typically appealed to more progressive moral authorities, even though these less-engaged congregants also came to very different opinions on the same topics. An implication of this finding is that Evangelicals can reference the same authority yet still come to different conclusions on the topics they are reasoning about.

In this chapter, I begin by explaining the importance of interviewing congregants. Next, I describe the two congregations (Mercy in the City and Adams River Baptist Church) from which I recruited the interviewees who are included in this chapter, and I give an overview of the characteristics of the congregant interviews, including their moral authorities and demographic statistics (demographics discussed further in Appendix 3). I then move to discussing how the majority of congregants perceived significant divisions among Evangelicals on Islam, a finding that runs against Christian Smith's prediction in his subcultural identity theory that Evangelicals will abandon their differences and unify when confronted with an external "threat" (in this case, Islam). The bulk of the chapter then presents interviewees' varying perceptions on Muhammad, the Qur'an, interfaith dialogue, the ACW initiative, and Chrislam. I also analyze the extent to which interviewees' views on these various topics correlate with their inclinations toward either a traditional or a progressive source of moral authority, respectively.

As was the case with my leadership sample, a few of my congregational interviewees had complex moral authorities. Some appealed to traditional moral authorities like the "Bible," "Jesus," or "God" in their reasoning on various topics, and thus they were classified as Traditional in terms of their moral authority, but yet they held certain views on Islam that diverged significantly from the dominant historical Evangelical perspective. Others were the reverse: they appealed to progressive moral authorities, yet their views were quite well aligned with the dominant historical perspective. Again, as outlined in Chapter 3, it is important to clarify that the terms "traditional" and "progressive" refer only to interviewees' moral authorities as determined using the evidential moral authority analysis.

Why Congregations?

My inclusion of congregants from two Evangelical churches into my research design was theory driven. In Chapter 3, I challenged Smith's proposition that intergroup conflict strengthens the ingroup, arguing that Evangelicals appear to be experiencing intragroup divisions—rather than greater unity—in the face of the "threat" of Islam. It makes sense to look at congregations to explore the ingroup/outgroup hypothesis because congregational settings are environments where Evangelicals discuss the content of their faith, as well as issues they are confronted with due to intensifying pressures of an increasingly pluralistic society. Congregations also provide space for "people to give voice to their discontents, and organizations through which they can mobilize for action" (Ammerman, 1998: 8).

As Hunter predicted, culture war divisions have emerged not just within American culture broadly but also within Evangelicalism, both between and within the various Evangelical denominations. Thus, I chose congregations that represented more than one Evangelical denomination (one congregation is Baptist, the other nondenominational). The fact that I studied entire congregations allowed me to explore the variety of Evangelical thoughts on the topic of Islam within a particular congregation. Thus, I have been able to explore diversity on the topic of Islam not only *across* Evangelical congregations but also *within* them.

Who Are These Congregations?

Mercy in the City

The Mercy Family of Churches is an Evangelical but nondenominational cluster of multiple church campuses, most of which are located in and around the capital city of a southern US state. Each Mercy campus has its own leadership team, but they all fall within the same family of churches. While the church is technically nondenominational, the founding pastor's roots were in the Baptist denomination, and one leader for the church even called the church "foundationally Southern Baptist" in our interview.

To locate this congregation, I relied on my prior contacts within Southern Evangelicalism. I learned about Mercy through an Evangelical friend who told me that he and others from his Evangelical congregation go to a local mosque and pray to Jesus. Evangelicals praying to Jesus at the local mosque sounded fascinating to me, so my friend connected me with his pastor (i.e., the pastor of the Mercy in the City campus, which was at the time the most urban congregation of their campuses).

In my initial meeting with the pastor it became clear that the leadership was deeply involved with Muslims and was focused largely on building upon similarities between the faiths—a focus that was leading to pushback from others within Evangelicalism who disagreed with Mercy's approach. The catalyst for the Mercy leaders' special interest in Christian-Muslim relations was the 9/11 terrorist attacks. Following the attacks, a team from the multi-site church went to the site of the rubble in New York City to express their sorrow and confusion about the attacks. While in New York, the founding pastor felt called by God to engage the Muslim world and pursue peace and reconciliation with Muslims. Thus, after 9/11, the leaders of the Mercy churches received advice from a number of Evangelical groups and individuals already working with Muslims, but fostered a strong connection with one specific leader who had been actively reaching out to Muslims in the past and whose views Mercy found most appealing (adhering to ideas contrary to the dominant traditional historical Evangelical views on Islam). After actively pursuing friendships with Muslims in both the United States and abroad in the years directly following 9/11, the leaders at Mercy wanted to share, both with their own congregation and with any other Evangelicals willing to listen, what they had learned about building bridges with the Muslim community, about the connections between the Evangelical and Muslim communities, and about how to properly engage Muslims. It was in this atmosphere that their ongoing Qur'an and Christ (QAC) conference series was born. (As part of my research on Mercy, I attended a QAC conference held in February of 2015 at one of the Mercy campuses.)

In sermons and during interviews, many Mercy leaders talked extensively about "the kingdom" and how the kingdom must bring restoration to all areas of life, including their relationships with Muslims. In light of this, the church has implemented several programs focused on providing various forms of aid to the Muslim refugee population in the nearby town of Frankfort. In line with a more social justice focus similar to that form of theology fostered during the social gospel movement in American history, Mercy's leaders consider this type of social activism as much a part of God's mission as studying the Bible and thus are motivated by the idea of not simply personal conversion but also social reform. Mercy congregants were more optimistic regarding government as a force for positive change. Mercy put a large emphasis on serving and learning from those perceived to have unequal access to power in Western culture, such as racial and religious minorities.

Mercy leaders also spoke of the importance of having "conversations" with individuals outside the Mercy community regarding Jesus and the Kingdom, and they encouraged these "kingdom conversations" as an important key to sharing about Jesus in a pluralistic society. It seems they have been trying to balance the traditional Evangelical belief in the exclusivity of the gospel (*sola Christus*, salvation is obtained through Christ alone) with their very inclusive view of what it means to be "journeying toward the kingdom." The rhetoric of the congregation generally presents Christians and Muslims as being on equal footing in pursuing the kingdom of God, rather than presenting Christians as being a step ahead. Thus, their beliefs on Islam deviate from the historical Evangelical perspective that most conservatives espouse.

Within the Mercy congregations, there was variety in regard to the doctrines and beliefs of both congregants and leaders. For example, Daisy, an outreach leader who grew up in a non-Evangelical Methodist tradition, told me that when she first came to Mercy, she was confused by all of the "Christianese," but she said that, all in all, she has felt comfortable at Mercy. She did not indicate that she had become more Evangelical during her time at Mercy in the City; rather, she expressed concern over some of the interactions she'd had while working in the church's refugee ministry with other congregants whom she perceived to be more conservative: specifically, she was concerned that some Mercy congregants still seemed to want to "tell them [Muslim refugees] about Jesus." She said the leadership at Mercy has "trained [congregants] out of the word [conversion], but it's very much like they need Jesus . . . [and] let's change their whole religious structure entirely to ours." Daisy thought these Evangelicals whose views align with the dominant historical Evangelical view of Islam and missions were disingenuous, and she felt uncomfortable working alongside them. Daisy felt uneasy even saying the name "Jesus" to others, lest she come across as too preachy. She was critical of previous Christian missionary work, stating, "You may know that Christianity hasn't had a great track record in history with moving to different cultures and trying to share faith." In contrast, she described her own approach to interacting with Muslims as a better way to follow Jesus than attempting to change Muslims' beliefs and religious structures:

> In college, and the past couple of years, when I have conversation[s] with Muslims, it's just not that important to me to talk about [Jesus]. . . . We'll talk about other things. Then when I see myself working with them in the future, it's

more like how do we pursue a common goal of bringing the kingdom of God to the world in community development? How can we work together on these common projects? Which essentially is the following Jesus part rather than the Christology part.

Daisy had a strong desire to follow Jesus, but she clearly believed that she could follow him without talking about him. This belief suggests that many who focus primarily on social justice view it as more important than—and in fact not compatible with—converting others to Christianity. Christians who persist in such conversion efforts are not practicing true social justice, as Evangelicals such as Daisy define it.

Mercy's very detailed website did not contain a statement of faith as of the time of my research there, but the lack of such a statement is likely not an oversight. Rather, it is likely indicative of the church's desire to steer clear of such a document, which could come across as exclusive or alienating—both characteristics this group of congregations tries to avoid. The desire to refrain from appearing exclusivist lines up with recent developments in American media discussed in Chapter 2. In this sense, Mercy in the City has some commonalities with the "pluralist congregations" of the Emerging Church Movement (Marti and Ganiel, 2014), where "differences in belief, practice, and at times even doctrine are suspended or transcended so that the congregation functions as a whole" (Ganiel, 2016: 138).

In my time at Mercy in the City, it became clear that the church has a negative view of Evangelicals whose views align with the dominant historical position on Islam and was encouraging attendees to experience a "paradigm shift" with respect to Islam—that is, a shift away from historical Evangelical forms of interacting with Muslims and Islamic doctrine and toward forms that emphasize commonalities between the two groups and their adherents' mutual need for God. Mercy tries hard to approach Muslims "humbly," without having all the answers, and looks for ways to learn from Muslims, whom many Mercy leaders often speak of more highly than of other Evangelicals. My interviewees from Mercy spoke less about "Christianity," a term many frowned upon, and more about "following Jesus." Many interviewees also found major theological connections between Islam and Christianity, and would say that both groups worship the same God.

I observed a distinction between congregants who were involved in outreach to Muslims and those who were not. Many congregants had never attended QAC or visited Frankfort. I found invitations to these types of events/ministries in their bulletin, but they were not explicitly talked about in detail during the large Sunday services I attended. Further, while QAC teaches some very inclusive missiological concepts (such as the "kingdom circles," a diagram often used at QAC that places Christians and Muslims equally outside of the "kingdom of God"), such concepts were not brought up during the main services I attended, meaning many congregants attending Mercy in the City had likely not been exposed to them. Lay congregants who were not involved with Mercy's outreaches to Muslims and had never attended QAC, or had only recently attended, tended to hold perspectives about Muslims and Islam that aligned closer to the historical Evangelical perspective than did those who were highly involved. In other words, generally speaking, the higher up one is in leadership, the more unaligned one's views are to the dominant traditional Evangelical view of Islam. In terms of politics, congregants at Mercy held more leftist political stances than congregants at Adams River (all but six leaned, however grudgingly, toward the Democratic Party).

In the end, I spent three months with the Mercy congregation (from January to March, 2015). During this period, I not only conducted interviews with congregants but also attended Sunday morning services, church meetings, and a conference the church offered on Islam. In addition, I spent hours in the church's coffee shop. To locate interviewees, I initially relied on the assistance of the pastor. He connected me with one particular woman who became my first interviewee, and she then served as a gatekeeper who opened the way to interviewing others. As with my sample of leaders, I recruited many interviewees using the methods of "snowball sampling," meaning that existing participants recruited future participants from among their acquaintances. In addition, about one-fourth of the interviews arose out of my participant observation, during which I got to know people and then asked for interviews directly.

Adams River Baptist Church

Adams River Baptist Church is a mega-church located just outside a major city in the South. The church is a Southern Baptist congregation, therefore representing the largest Protestant denomination in the United States. I located this congregation through a friend, who has a colleague who attends Adams River. I was interested in Adams River because the church intentionally interacts with Muslims and teaches congregants about Islam; however, the leaders seemed to hold views that focused on differences (rather than commonalities) between Christianity and Islam, making this congregation different from Mercy in the City.

During my time there, Adams River's website had a statement of faith outlining the congregation's beliefs, as well as a separate document spelling out the congregation's core values. There was also a "Membership Expectations" document detailing how one could "Love the Lord your God with all your heart, soul, and mind" through actions like prayer, reading the Bible, and committing to be obedient to God's Word in Scripture. These documents could be indicative of the church leadership's desire to make clear their differentiating beliefs against what they perceive as a society increasingly moving away from exclusive truth claims. Here, Adams River, in contrast to the Mercy Family of Churches, appears to reflect an Evangelical posture Smith has described as "embattled yet thriving," a posture he attributes partly to Evangelicalism's desire to demonstrate a clear distinction from outgroups in pluralistic modernity (Smith, 1998).

Adams River first began its outreach to Muslims in the late 1980s through a partnership with the Foreign Mission Board (now International Mission Board). The Foreign Mission Board asked Adams River to "adopt" Muslims of a particular country in central Asia as a group of special focus for the church, which at first meant simply praying for the Muslim people from that area. After the fall of the

Soviet Union, the church's involvement became more hands-on, with multiple volunteer teams (business and medical) working alongside long-term missionaries on the ground in the region.

Like the Mercy congregations, Adams River is involved with refugee ministries. The congregation started helping Muslim refugees from Kosovo in the late 1990s, and since then the refugee ministries have expanded. Around 2010, congregants began working with Muslim refugees in Frankfort, the same refugee resettlement area in which the Mercy congregations work. In 2016, leaders at Adams River condemned the state leaders' attempt to stop the resettlement of mostly Muslim refugees into the state. The church has sponsored numerous Muslim families from abroad and provided them English tutoring, financial support, and assistance in finding jobs. They see their care for Muslim refugees as fulfilling the biblical mandate of Christians to minister to orphans, widows, and aliens. However, they are much more comfortable than Mercy with traditional terms such as "convert," "witness," and "missionary." Essentially—regarding these social justice activities—they hope they will be able to share their faith, and they are overt about their mission. This lines up with the more traditional historical Evangelical view of outsider faiths. In terms of politics, Adams River congregants held more conservative political stances than congregants at Mercy (all but two leaned, however grudgingly, toward more conservative parties).

The church periodically offers a class for members of the congregation titled "Islamic Awareness," taught by Navid, a former Muslim from a Muslim-majority country who is also a longtime member of Adams River. Navid, who I interviewed for my study, has taught classes on Islam at the church for over a decade and conducts frequent "mission trips" to Europe in which he offers pastoral care to former Muslims who have converted to Christianity. Overall, the goal of the class is to give attendees compassion for the Muslim people, a stronger knowledge of Islam, and a desire to build relationships that would ultimately enable them to tell Muslims about Christ and eventually convert them to Christianity. The particular course I took, which ran once a week from mid-August to mid-November in 2015, covered the history and beliefs of the Islamic faith; in addition, it focused on the fundamental differences between Islam and Christianity and how Christians should share their faith with Muslims. Part of the class also dealt with current events. Attendees were allowed to ask questions throughout, and there was also a designated Q&A portion of the class that brought up a wide range of issues that were on the minds of attendees. One attendee asked if Muslim men were really promised virgins in exchange for martyrdom. Some asked about things they had heard on the news recently, and others asked about what they had experienced with Muslims during their previous service in the military or in their day-to-day shopping, and so on. Some of these questions brought up political topics, prompting Navid to talk about what he perceived to be the dangers of political Islam to the West. Significantly, although the course began with close to 100 people, by the end there were closer to fifty attendees. Initially, there were younger attendees alongside the older attendees, but none of the younger attendees were attending any longer by the conclusion. While I did not ask the younger attendees why they stopped attending, it could be because of Navid's more antiquated and slower teaching style that relied largely on reading from books and lecturing.

The majority of individuals I interviewed at Adams River brought up the term "Christian" often and in positive ways. Rather than shying away from identifying as Christians, as did some leaders interviewed in the previous chapter and many congregants from the Mercy congregation, interviewees at Adams River generally felt that it was good and right to identify as Christians, and they tended to do so easily. When it came to missiology, interviewees talked about how to "reach Muslims" today, but they did not focus as much as Mercy interviewees had on addressing missiological mistakes Christians have made with Muslims in the past.

Although interviewees tended to focus on the needs of the present rather than errors in the past, some Adams River ministers disagreed with each other on issues related to certain missiological methods that are used today. For example, Navid thought it wrong to use the Qur'an in order to teach Muslims about Jesus or to allow Muslim followers of Jesus to continue to attend their mosque, whereas others at Adams River felt both to be acceptable and had tried to persuade Navid to their view. But despite the disagreement, interestingly, the church leadership had refrained from shutting down one side or the other and had instead allowed both types of approaches to be presented within the church simultaneously in different formats. I found this tolerance as countering the stereotype of more rigid Biblicist Evangelicalism.

Overall, the Adams River leaders viewed the Christian God as a different God from Allah, and they saw Muslims as in need of a right understanding of the "true God." Congregants were also, for the most part, not politically correct in sharing their very negative views about Muhammad. Most interviewees said they believed in helping Muslims and treating them as neighbors regardless of whether or not they ever became Christians, but the goal of sharing Christ was always undergirding their efforts. Interviewees from Adams River also talked about the importance of being able to defend their faith. The leadership was interested in promoting apologetics, and many of the interviewees had an interest in and esteemed the idea of apologetics, whether or not they were actively drawing from apologetic resources or had themselves undergone apologetics training in the past.

At Adams River, as with Mercy, I initially relied on one of the pastors to point me to congregants to interview. In addition, I began taking the church's "Islam Awareness" class, and the instructor of the class also helped me locate interviewees. As with my first study of congregants at Mercy, I recruited many interviewees using snowball sampling and word-of-mouth, and I also located some participants by talking with people and asking for interviews during my participant observations. As with Mercy, I spent three months with the Adams River congregation (from September to November, 2015). During this time, I conducted interviews and attended an array of church events, including Sunday morning services, Wednesday night fellowship meals, the sixteen-week "Islam Awareness" course mentioned earlier, and a separate conference the church offered with some speakers discussing Islam. I also spent many hours in the church's coffee shop.

Characteristics of the Congregants

The ratio of women to men in both congregational samples was relatively balanced; the Mercy in the City sample included twelve females and eleven males, and the Adams River sample included twelve females and thirteen males. The Mercy sample had an age range of eighteen to sixty-one, but the average age skewed relatively young, at just thirty-six. Mercy sits very close to two large universities, and many of the attendees were college students or recent graduates. For the most part, the leadership of the congregation was also young (the lead pastor, for example, was in his early thirties). In contrast, the majority of interviewees at Adams River were older. The Adams River sample had an age range of nineteen to eighty-nine, with an average age of fifty. After noticing that my sample at Adams River was skewing toward older individuals, I did try to contact younger interviewees and was successful to some degree, but older interviewees proved to be more interested and willing to participate. The entirety of my sample from both congregations was either middle class or upper class, a reflection of the fact that the congregations as a whole tended to be highly educated and were located in areas that had relatively high household incomes.

Both congregations were located in urban areas. This is because I was looking for congregations that were directly involved with Muslims, not just talking about Islam. I found that the rural churches I contemplated might hold a class or a special speaker would come in to speak on Islam, but the congregation itself was not directly involved with Muslims (perhaps because the majority of Muslims live in urban areas). This leads me to address the urban versus rural divide. Lindsay (2007) found there to be a substantial difference between the more urban "cosmopolitan" Evangelical and the more rural "populist" Evangelical. However, Dillon and Savage (2006) found "that religiosity trumps rural/non-rural location when it comes to social conservatism" and culture war issues. They found that highly religious individuals, whether they be rural or urban, are more likely to be against abortion and same-sex relations than those who are less religious. Given these two positions, it is wise to take a cautious stance on how much congruency exists between urban Evangelical views and rural Evangelical views. Since most of my interviewees were living in urban or suburban areas within the Bible Belt, the findings from my sample may or may not be applicable to rural Evangelical debates on Islam and Muslims. Including the rural Evangelical perspective would be an important area for further research.

The congregations as a whole tended to reflect some contrasting opinions and beliefs when the congregations were compared with each other, and members within each congregation held relatively similar beliefs (however, there were exceptions to this pattern). The relative agreement within my congregations is consistent with studies on "congregational cultures," which have found that congregants in a competitive religious marketplace often join congregations they believe share their own understandings about mission and identity (Finke and Stark, 1992; Becker, 1999; Ammerman, 2005). The relative agreement within the congregations also confirmed what I hoped my focused sample would provide—namely, two different congregations that offered different, often opposing, perspectives. Throughout the remainder of this chapter, interviewees from the two congregations are treated together as a single group. Each interviewee is identified as a congregant of either Adams River Baptist Church (denoted in parentheses after the name as "AR") or Mercy in the City (denoted as "M"). I have chosen to present the data from the two congregations together, rather than separately, for three reasons. Firstly, the joint analysis provides a more comprehensive picture of Evangelical diversity. Given that the congregational affiliation of each interviewee is identified throughout the chapter, the combined treatment of the two congregations allows the reader to see the diversity not only *within* congregations but also *across* congregations simultaneously. Secondly, the joint analysis also guards against the possibility that one congregation becomes pitted against another, which could stifle the individuality inherent in the moral authority argument that is being explored. Even as I explore group conflict within Evangelicalism, these conflicts are not necessarily confined to the congregational level. Thirdly, the data would eventually need to be combined in order to understand Evangelical diversity and conflict holistically, and I felt that combining the interviewees from both congregations in this chapter would allow this to happen most naturally and in the most comprehensive manner.

Comfort Level with the Term "Evangelical"

Of the forty-eight interviewees, forty-five answered "yes" when asked if they were comfortable with being called an Evangelical. Still, eight of the interviewees at Mercy and seven interviewees at Adams River added qualifiers, definitions, and additions in their responses. Of the fifteen interviewees who added qualifiers, all but five leaned to the left on the Progressive-Traditional spectrum based on their evidential moral authority. However, only one leaned to the left on the spectrum based on stated moral authority. Among those who said they were uncomfortable with the label, one (AR) preferred to be called a "Christ-follower," one (AR) preferred to be called a "Christian," and one (M) described herself as struggling with mild forms of proselytizing (e.g., she felt uncomfortable even saying the name Jesus, thinking it could be viewed as too preachy); this last congregant also described herself as taking a more liberal theological stance than most Evangelicals.

Level of Engagement with Muslims

Almost half of interviewees (23) were highly engaged with Muslims. About one-fourth of the sample (13) had a medium level of engagement with Muslims, and the same number (13) fell into the category of low engagement. (Details regarding how I calculated each individual's level of engagement are located in Appendix 3.) Interestingly, all nine interviewees who were categorized as Traditional on the Progressive-Traditional spectrum according to their evidential moral authority were also categorized as having high engagement with Muslims. On the other hand, the eight interviewees who were categorized as Progressive on the spectrum based on their evidential moral authority had mostly moderate or low levels of engagement with Muslims. Those with a hybrid identity according to their evidential moral authority (meaning those categorized as Progressive-Traditionals or Traditional-Progressives) also followed this trend, with those categorized as Traditional-Progressives on the Progressive-Traditional spectrum having higher engagement than those categorized as Progressive-Traditional on the spectrum. However, the Traditional-Progressive category included a more balanced number of individuals belonging to the low, medium, and high engagement categories. Thus, interviewees' levels of engagement with Muslims usually correlated with their position on the Progressive-Traditional spectrum, though this was most evident on the fringes of the spectrum.

Congregants' Stated and Evidential Moral Authorities

As with the leadership interviewees discussed in the previous chapter, I have distinguished between congregational interviewees' stated moral authorities and their evidential moral authorities, and I have argued that the latter offers a fuller indication of an individual's position on the Progressive-Traditional spectrum. To establish interviewees' stated moral authorities, I asked them direct questions about their moral authorities and the source of their understanding of right and wrong (as explained in Chapter 3). Based on their own claims about their moral authorities, no congregational interviewees were categorized as "Progressive" and only one (Daisy [M]) was categorized as "Progressive-Traditional." By contrast, eleven fell into the "Traditional-Progressive" category and a majority (36) were categorized as straight "Traditional." What this means is that most interviewees used traditional Evangelical terminology to talk about their moral authorities. Just over half of interviewees (25), for example, explicitly listed "God" as their moral authority, and many also listed "the Bible" (19), "Jesus" (15), and the "Holy Spirit" (7). In explaining how they viewed the Bible, interviewees tended to describe the Bible using relatively traditional language, such as with the phrases "God-inspired" (used by twenty-two), the "Word of God" (used by nineteen), or "inerrant" and/or "infallible" (used by nine).

Whereas most interviewees leaned traditional in the analysis of *stated* moral authority, they reflected far more progressivism in the analysis of *evidential* moral authority (also explained in Chapter 3). Eight interviewees were categorized as Progressives in the analysis of evidential moral authority and thirteen others were categorized as Progressive-Traditional. Eighteen were in the Traditional-Progressive category and only nine were categorized as Traditional. In total, thirty of the forty-eight interviewees moved one or more positions to the left on the Progressive-Traditional spectrum in the evidential analysis. Six shifted the farthest left (meaning those who *claimed* to have a Traditional moral authority but whose *evidential* moral authority proved to be Progressive). These six were generally highly educated, with four of them holding graduate degrees, but not in topics directly related to Islam or Christianity; most of the six lacked Muslim friends and were categorized as having only low or medium engagement with Muslims.

A side-by-side comparison of interviewees' stated and evidential moral authorities suggests that most interviewees were more progressive in terms of their moral authorities than they themselves may have realized. Most interviewees claimed to have traditional Evangelical moral authorities (such as God, Jesus, the Holy Spirit, the Bible, or some combination of them), but when answering questions not directly related to moral authority (such as on the topics of Islam and politics), many of these interviewees failed to reference such traditional moral authorities. This lines up with the findings of Guest from his study of Evangelicals attending St. Michael-le-Belfrey in the UK. According to Guest, "When asked about authority, they more often than not turn to scripture, but in terms of everyday practice, there is a discernable freedom with which human experience, in its mundane and spectacular forms, is attributed with spiritual meaning" (2007: 209).

Though most interviewees proved to be more progressive than they indicated at first, few in either congregation were pure extremists in their moral authority terminology, or lack thereof. Indeed, only seventeen interviewees fell on either the extreme left or the extreme right according to their evidential moral authorities. (Specifically, four Mercy congregants and four Adams River congregants were classified as Progressive, and four Mercy congregants and five Adams River congregants were Traditional.) As with the sample of leaders in the last chapter, most (31) of the congregational interviewees at both Mercy and Adams River had a hybrid identity, appealing to both progressive and traditional sources of moral authority when discussing their positions on Islam and politics (see Table 5.1). Thus, I conclude, as Hunter predicted, that the majority of interviewees' moral authorities are relatively moderate and not as extreme as the two opposing ideal types embedded in his moral authority argument, at least in how they use moral authority terminology to communicate their positions on Islam.

In most cases, interviewees' moral authorities correlated with their stances on issues related to Islam: interviewees with traditional moral authorities generally upheld the dominant historical Evangelical views on issues related to Islam, whereas interviewees with progressive moral authorities often broke from those dominant historical Evangelical views. Still, as noted at the outset of this chapter, a few interviewees were outliers in terms of moral authority, in the sense that they had a progressive moral authority but held views on issues related to Islam that largely aligned with the dominant historical Evangelical views on those issues, or vice versa. I found that these outlier positions were significantly correlated with the individual's level of engagement with Muslims and/or knowledge about Islam. Specifically, all those who had a traditional moral authority but who held views on issues related to Islam that dissented from the dominant historical Evangelical tradition had high engagement with Muslims. These individuals had Muslim friends and had read some or all of the Qur'an. Usually these individuals also supported IMs and avoided negative judgments about Muhammad and the Qur'an. They also spoke about Islamic ideas with reverence and were able to accept certain Islamic beliefs that have not been traditionally accepted. They could see room for negotiating aspects of Islam with aspects of Western Christianity. It was apparent that they had reflected upon social issues and differences within their

Table 5.1 Mercy and Adams River Congregants: Stated Moral Authority and Evidential Moral Authority with Demographics

Name	Occupation	Education	Political Views	Age Range	Stated MA	Evidential MA	Congregation
Henriette	For-profit Employee	SC	RL	Over 65	TP	P	Adams River
Nathaniel	Ministry	B	LL	Under 35	TP	P	Mercy
Erica	Nonprofit Employee	G	LL	Under 35	T	P	Mercy
Jackie	For-profit Employee	B	LL	Over 65	T	P	Adams River
Joel	For-profit Employee	G	RL	51–65	T	P	Adams River
Julia	Ministry	B	LL	Under 35	T	P	Mercy
Lauren	Ministry	G	LL	35–50	T	P	Mercy
Zachary	Engineer	G	RL	35–50	T	P	Adams River
Daisy	Ministry	G	L	Under 35	PT	PT	Mercy
Anna	For-profit Employee	G	R	51–65	TP	PT	Adams River
Bethany	Student	SC	LL	Under 35	T	PT	Adams River
Bobby	Student	SC	RL	Under 35	T	PT	Adams River
Esther	Ministry	B	RL	51–65	T	PT	Mercy
Gabriel	Ministry	G	LL	35–50	T	PT	Mercy
Michael	Student	SC	RL	Under 35	T	PT	Adams River
Parker*	Ministry	B	RL	51–65	T	PT	Mercy
Rita	Homemaker	SC	RL	Over 65	T	PT	Adams River
Scott	Ministry	G	RL	51–65	T	PT	Adams River
Tabitha	Homemaker	B	RL	Under 35	T	PT	Mercy
Tiffany	Student	G	LL	Under 35	T	PT	Mercy
Victoria	Nonprofit Employee	B	RL	35–50	T	PT	Adams River
Anja	Homemaker	SC	RL	35–50	TP	TP	Adams River
Ethan	Ministry	G	L	Under 35	TP	TP	Mercy
Mark*	Ministry and Speaker	G	RL	Under 35	TP	TP	Mercy

Name	Occupation	Education	Political	Age			Congregation
Meagan	Nonprofit Employee	G	R	Under 35	TP	TP	Adams River
Timothy	Ministry	G	LL	35–50	TP	TP	Mercy
Amanda	Nonprofit Employee	B	RL	Under 35	T	TP	Adams River
Bart	Ministry	B	RL	35–50	T	TP	Mercy
Danielle	Nonprofit Employee	G	LL	51–65	T	TP	Mercy
Kevin*	Apologist and Author	G	RL	51–65	T	TP	Adams River
Lacey	Nurse	B	RL	35–50	T	TP	Adams River
Matthew	Student	SC	LL	Under 35	T	TP	Mercy
Micah	Nurse	B	LL	Under 35	T	TP	Mercy
Patrick	IT Security	B	R	51–65	T	TP	Adams River
Phillip	For-profit Employee	G	RL	Over 65	T	TP	Adams River
Silas	Pharmacist	G	RL	Under 35	T	TP	Mercy
Simon	Student	B	RL	Under 35	T	TP	Adams River
Stuart	Retires Salesman	B	RL	Over 65	T	TP	Adams River
Valerie	Homemaker	B	LL	Under 35	T	TP	Mercy
Jesse	Ministry	G	LL	Under 35	TP	T	Mercy
Naomi	Ministry	B	L	Under 35	TP	T	Mercy
Camila	Ministry	SC	RL	51–65	T	T	Adams River
Celina	Homemaker	B	R	51–65	T	T	Adams River
Frank	Ministry	G	RL	35–50	T	T	Adams River
Judah	Physician Assistant	B	RL	Under 35	T	T	Adams River
Maria*	Nonprofit Leader	G	LL	35–50	T	T	Mercy
Navid*	Nonprofit Leader	B	RL	Over 65	T	T	Adams River
Teresa	Ministry	B	LL	Under 35	T	T	Mercy

* Denotes the individuals who are included in Chapter 4 as well as in this chapter. These interviewees are national Evangelical leaders on Islam and are also members of the congregations examined here.

SC = Some College, B = Bachelor, G = Graduate,
L = Left, LL = Left Leaning, RL = Right Leaning, R = Right,
MA = Moral Authority, P = Progressive, PT = Progressive-Traditional, TP = Traditional-Progressive, T = Traditional

own Christian community (intragroup conflict) and were usually highly critical of conservative Evangelicalism. These individuals had formulated clear opinions on Islam and conservative Evangelicalism. They were able to communicate their perspectives on Islam and politics in ways that made use of traditional moral authority terminology, such as using the Bible and invoking "Jesus" as they articulated their various positions. For some, this may have been deliberate in the sense that they hoped to influence those more traditional-leaning Evangelicals to experience a paradigm shift in how they think about Islam, Muslims, and politics, and were aware that in order to be heard by that particular type they must appeal to the Bible or God as their moral reference, whether or not they actually hold the Bible and God to be paramount.

In contrast, those outliers who had a progressive moral authority but held views more in line with historically dominant Evangelical views were more likely to have low or medium engagement with Muslims. These individuals were less likely to have Muslim friends, less likely to have read the Qur'an, and were for the most part unaware of terms such as "Chrislam" and "insider movements." For their part, these outliers—those who appealed to progressive moral authorities but held many views relatively similar to the dominant historical Evangelical perspective—may have been less inclined to bring up their faith in answering questions about Islam because they had not undergone a deep form of contemplation regarding their faith in general. Their restricted understanding of their own Evangelical beliefs and traditions coupled with ongoing remoteness from Muslims may have caused insecurity. These congregants tended to have low or medium engagement with Muslims and to have few (if any) Muslim friends. They were also less likely to have read the Qur'an or to have heard of terms such as "Chrislam" and "insider movements." They also spoke more negatively about Islam. It may be that they had not previously thought about or reflected upon the issues raised in my questions. This may have made them less likely to talk at length about their perspectives in a way that allowed them to articulate how their opinions related to their personal religious beliefs. This may have curtailed their use of terms like "Jesus," "God," "Holy Spirit," and "Bible" when justifying their views.

Varying Views on Politics

I asked all interviewees to describe their political views, and I then asked several questions dealing with specific political issues. About two-fifths (19) of my interviewees leaned politically liberal, and about three-fifths (29) leaned politically conservative. Those who leaned farthest toward the progressive end of the spectrum according to their evidential moral authority were also most likely to lean to the left in their political views. Likewise, those who leaned the most traditional according to their evidential moral authority tended to be right-leaning in their political views.

Although interviewees generally leaned politically conservative or politically liberal, the majority of congregational interviewees (41), like the majority of leadership interviewees, seemed to purposefully avoid extremes in their political perspectives, in order to appear more centrist. This majority expressed pros and cons relating to both the Democratic and Republican Party positions on various social and economic issues. It usually took a number of follow-up questions for interviewees to express a bias to the political left or the political right, and most interviewees appeared not to want to align themselves with one side or the other. Bethany (AR), for example, said she was a "moderate, probably" and was still trying to figure out her political beliefs. She was "definitely not either extreme" because "there's things that people on either side believe that I don't agree with." Amanda (AR) also described herself as a moderate, and she mentioned that she was "not well versed or active in politics." Timothy (M) said he leans left politically but that "you can't govern from extreme left and you can't govern from extreme right. There's balance in all of it." He then mentioned ways in which he thinks the right is correct, namely in areas of fiscal responsibility, and areas in which the left is correct, namely in "rais[ing] up the oppressed." Simon (AR) said he tends toward political conservatism because he broadly feels those views most align with Scripture, but he also indicated that he didn't feel party politics is the "right answer" and that the Republican stance on immigration, an issue very important to him, was unbiblical and wrong. This last view was common: many interviewees expressed disagreement with the conservative stance Republicans had taken on immigration.

Interviewees often expressed dissatisfaction with and distrust of politics and/or government in general. Patrick (AR), for example, said, "I'm not sure that the R[epublican]s and the D[emocrat]s don't go to the same locker room with the same agenda and just package it differently." And Bobby (AR), one of three interviewees (alongside Phillip [AR] and Judah [AR]) who expressed political stances that most align with the Libertarian Party, said, "I'm not an anarchist, because I think that a government is necessary . . . but ultimately, I think that the government screws up more than it helps."

Evangelical Conflict on Islam

When I asked interviewees at my two congregations whether they perceived Evangelicals to be unified on the topic of Islam, interviewees overwhelmingly answered, "No." Thus, most interviewees at the two congregations acknowledged intra-Evangelical conflict on Islam, with all but three perceiving clear divisions. Interestingly, congregational interviewees were just as inclined as the Evangelical leaders discussed in the previous chapter to point to fear and ignorance about Islam and/or Muslims as a significant contributor to division (twenty-five interviewees brought up issues of fear and/or ignorance). However, in contrast to the leaders discussed in the previous chapter, congregational interviewees generally did not use the language of a "continuum" or "spectrum" to describe views of Islam among Evangelicals. Unlike the leader interviewees, some congregational interviewees contrasted their views with those of their family members as they thought through the areas of disagreement between Evangelicals on Islam. Most interviewees who viewed Islam more positively saw themselves embattled against other Evangelicals who held a more negative view of Islam—more so than they saw themselves as embattled against Muslims. Even interviewees who viewed Islam more negatively were apt to contrast their mission-oriented perspectives with the perspectives of fellow Evangelicals whom they perceived to be "uninformed" about Islam. In general, congregational interviewees, especially those who viewed Islam more positively, were more likely to share negative perceptions about segments within Evangelicalism that they viewed as problematic than they were to share positive perceptions of Evangelical segments that they viewed as having an appropriate posture toward Islam.

Many interviewees spoke specifically of missiological disagreements among Evangelicals. Some of the missiological disagreements centered on what it means to be a true Christian; others were about how to share the gospel with Muslims. According to Gabriel (M), the divides within Evangelicalism regarding Islam run deep, affecting the very foundation of the Evangelical faith. Gabriel believed Evangelicals disagree among themselves about how to enter into a relationship with God, about how to enter the kingdom of God, and about who is "saved," and because they are not unified on these issues, the issue of contextualizing the gospel for Muslims is a divisive one within Evangelicalism. Echoing this sentiment, Mark (AR) held that Evangelical Christians are certainly not unified on Christianity, "let alone Islam." Ethan (M) likewise perceived tremendous diversity within Evangelicalism with respect to core beliefs and mission. He noted that even those who are distancing themselves from "Christianese" words and who advocate contextualizing the gospel for Muslims are not unified in their beliefs about Islam or about their "own status with God relative to those of Muslims." Jesse (M) also mentioned disagreement among Evangelicals regarding contextualization. He pointed out, for example, that some Evangelicals believe there to be truth in the Qur'an, such as in the Qur'anic words "God is most holy." Jesse personally shared this view of the Qur'an as containing some truth, telling me he believed "all truth is God's truth," but he noted that other Evangelicals would reject everything in the Qur'an as false. Lauren (M), Bart (M), and Valerie (M) all brought up dividing issues around contextualization, noting that there is disagreement among Evangelicals on questions regarding what a Muslim must do to correctly follow Jesus and how much of their Islamic culture they can retain. Jesse (M) saw a divide within Evangelicalism with respect to how and when Evangelicals should evangelize. Some, he said, focus inwardly and place emphasis on the church as a place to learn about God; the proper time to tell people about God, then, is when they come to church. Others focus outwardly and feel compelled to go out to places beyond the church to show others "the kingdom of God." Those most sympathetic to stronger forms of contextualization and more critical of traditional forms of missionary impulses came from the Mercy congregation.

Although the congregants I interviewed generally denied that Evangelicals are unified in their views about Islam, congregants often spoke about a general climate of fear and ignorance among Evangelicals regarding Islam. Micah (M), one of the only interviewees who said he saw Evangelicals as unified ("but in a bad way"), held that many Evangelicals had been indoctrinated with fear in their Evangelical congregations. Matthew (M) said Evangelicals are divided on how to interact with Muslims, but he, like Micah (M), drew attention to the groups of Evangelicals that are fearful due to 9/11 and more recent ISIS attacks. Esther (M) likewise believed fear to have caused conflict on the topic of Islam among Evangelicals, and she also referenced the problem of ignorance, mentioning that most Evangelicals do not read the Qur'an and do not even know how to converse with a Muslim. Jackie (AR) pointed to ignorance among Evangelicals as the major reason why some had come to the perceived wrong conclusion that Allah and the God of Christianity are the same and were thus deviating from the perceived true Christian stance regarding Allah. Naomi (M) mentioned how difficult it had been for her to talk about Muslims at family events, because she believed her family to have a limited understanding of Islam and Muslims. She blamed this lack of understanding on the politicization of the Evangelical church, which she believed had intermingled God and country. She saw the Christian worldview as depicting Islam as the enemy—a depiction she believed has caused Christians to react defensively to Islam. Rita (AR) agreed that some within the Evangelical fold have been hostile to Muslims since 9/11 and that they "paint all Muslims with the broad brush of terrorist." Julia (M) contrasted two groups within Evangelicalism, the first group being those Evangelicals who show "love and concern and care" for Muslims, and the second group being those who "have a lot of fears surrounding Islam and Muslims." Scott (AR) confessed that he used to be a part of the second group that Julia described. He said after 9/11 he knew little about Muslims and generally just avoided them. However, after taking a mission trip to Iraq, he softened his views of Muslims and "began to get a sense that Christ is the only answer for Muslims as well." Like Julia, Silas (M) contrasted those who "love Muslims" and show them "the love of Christ" with those who see Muslims as the "enemies of God" and feel justified in acts of war against Muslims. Naomi lamented the difficulty of helping Evangelicals overcome their fear due to the news cycles in mass media that routinely—and, in her mind, inappropriately—depict Muslims as terrorists; she was among the approximately one-quarter of interviewees who saw media outlets as presenting a biased view of Muslims and as pushing Evangelicals toward more negative perceptions of Islam. If Evangelicals are united on Islam in any way, the congregants I interviewed seemed to believe that the unity centers on ignorance about the true Islam.

The Qur'an

Nine interviewees had read the Qur'an in its entirety, and most others (33) had read at least some of the Qur'an. Of the six who indicated they had not read any of the Qur'an, five were to the left on the Progressive-Traditional spectrum based on evidential analysis. Thus, as with the leaders discussed in the last chapter, congregants who leaned progressive in their moral authority were less likely to have read the Qur'an than those leaning traditional. All six of the interviewees who had not read the Qur'an viewed the Qur'an either neutrally or positively, and most of the six were younger (between the ages of twenty and thirty-five). One example of an interviewee who had not read any of the Qur'an is Bethany (AR), a twenty-year-old college student and an evidential Progressive-Traditional. Bethany said she would "love" to study the Qur'an, but she questioned her ability to get her "hands on a real copy" because she had no trust in internet versions of the Qur'an that could have been altered. She also questioned her ability to understand the text correctly since she didn't speak Arabic and was suspicious about reading an English translation that would fail to capture the layers of meaning of the original language. Bethany was clearly immobilized by her distrust of language and belief that others are manipulating the true Qur'an, and also by her perceived deficiency, in that she was not able to speak Arabic and thus was unable to decipher the perceived sophisticated complexity of thought within the Qur'an.

The majority of congregants on the traditional end of the Progressive-Traditional spectrum spoke negatively about the Qur'an, consistent with Hunter's suggestion that traditional individuals usually will not consider sources of moral authority other than their own to be legitimate (1991: 120). By contrast, the Progressives in my sample tended to elevate the Qur'an relatively highly. But as with the leaders in the previous chapter, the split in views between Progressives and Traditionals was not perfect. In particular, some who leaned traditional had elevated views of the Qur'an, putting them out of step with the dominant historical Evangelical position on the Qur'an (such positive views were particularly likely among those sympathetic to IMs and those more highly engaged with Muslims). For example, Teresa (M), an evidential Traditional, said she believed there was "a lot of truth in the Qur'an" and that God could use the Qur'an to point to "the truth."

Some interviewees talked about reading the Qur'an in order to understand the common ground between the biblical and Qur'anic narratives about Jesus, often for the purpose of talking with Muslims about Jesus. Interviewees who read the Qur'an for these reasons generally were more engaged with Muslims and also tended to lean right of center with respect to their evidential moral authority. Esther (M), mirroring a statement from one of the leaders interviewed in the previous chapter, said that the Qur'an is the "best tract ever written for Muslims" to be led to Jesus. Danielle (M) told me the purpose of incorporating the Qur'an in conversations with Muslims was to "create a point of reference that you can then go to Jesus from." And Micah (M) said he often drew from the parallels between the two books in his discussions with Muslims by saying something like "Hey, let's look at the [Qur'an] and look at the Bible. Let me show you how similar they are and how similar our beliefs are." One commonality between Esther, Danielle, and Micah is that they were comfortable with IMs and they were interested in finding common ground between the Bible and the Qur'an. These three rarely, if ever, discussed points of diversion between the two texts, and all three generally spoke positively about the Qur'an. They also refrained from using missiological words reminiscent of historical Evangelicalism (e.g., "win the lost," "evangelism," "saved/unsaved," "witness," "missionary"). They were also highly critical of Evangelicals who hold views aligned with the dominant historical Evangelical view of Islam.

While Esther, Daniel, and Micah emphasized the commonalities between the Qur'an and the Bible, others held the belief that the Qur'an is more antagonistic to biblical truth than it is complementary. Frank (AR) acknowledged that the Qur'an has many stories similar to those in the Old Testament, but he said that the "closeness" Christians might perceive between the biblical and Qur'anic narratives was "by design to refute what [Christians] believe." He said he remembered reading a number of times in the text that the notion of God having a Son is blasphemy—a point Frank viewed as a problem, given that the belief that God had a Son is "the core of [Evangelical] faith." He added that Evangelicals should not overlook the Qur'an's refutation of that central doctrine in an effort to find common ground. Frank and others who held positions that closely aligned with the dominant historical Evangelical positions on Islam were keen to point out areas of divergence between the Qur'an and the Bible and tended to use words and phrases associated with historical Evangelicalism when speaking about the Qur'an. Interestingly, however, several of the Evangelicals who leaned toward the dominant historical Evangelical perspective and thus felt that the Qur'an was antagonistic to Evangelical truth still believed that Evangelicals should read it. For example, Simon (AR) told me, "I think it's a good thing for Christians to read the Qur'an to see what it says, to see what Muslims are looking to as their authority."

Some interviewees, particularly those who had low engagement with Muslims, expressed feeling conflicted about studying the Qur'an due to a sense that they should be reading the Bible instead. For example, Patrick (AR) said that he had read parts of the Qur'an but that he had not read more extensively due to lack of time; with the time he had, he wanted to read the Bible. Although Patrick explicitly clarified that he was "not afraid to read" the Qur'an, there were indications from others that fear could play a role in why some Evangelicals might not read the text. For instance, Micah (M), an evidential Traditional-Progressive who reads the Qur'an often, talked negatively about how decades ago his parents were taught in seminary that a demon would possess them if they even touched a Qur'an.

Some interviewees, particularly those who were left on the evidential Progressive-Traditional spectrum and who also held views on Islam that dissented from dominant historical Evangelical perspectives, questioned their own ability to comprehend the Qur'an and interpret it accurately. For example, Daisy (M) said she hadn't read much of the Qur'an because, similar to Bethany, she had a low view of her own ability to accurately interpret the Qur'an and because she had no proper commentary on it:

> I actually took a class at [university] called "Buddhism, Hinduism and Islam"... [The professor] was a Carmelite nun who was drawn to Hindu practices in India. She was a cool professor... she had a good perspective on Islam. I've read parts [of the Qur'an]. I read parts with that class. The stuff on Mary is fascinating. I have read parts like the creation. Basically, I've looked at parallels between the Bible and the Qur'an just to see what the Qur'an says about certain stories. How different is it really? I've not read the whole thing mostly because I haven't found, or in that class, I couldn't find a good commentary on it. It's just like reading

the Bible without a commentary. It's, "What are they talking about? What do people interpret this to mean because I am not interpreting this I'm sure the way that Muslims interpret it?" I think that's going to be an essential in the future to find a really good commentary so that I will be able to read other non-narrative parts of it.

Some interviewees brought up the ways in which the Qur'an has been linked with violence. Camila (AR) pointed out that the Qur'an allows Muslim men to beat their wives if the men fear their wives are disobedient or will become so. Although some appeared to believe that the Qur'an explicitly encourages violence, others felt that any Muslim reader who uses the text for violent ends has misinterpreted the meaning of the Qur'an to suit his or her goals. Michael (AR), an evidential Progressive-Traditional, said that he believed "fundamentalist and radical" Muslims of today "manipulate the Qur'an in order to serve [their] vision" and "inflict terror on Paris, or New York, or wherever." Parker (M) had a similar perspective, sharing with me that once, during a long discussion with a Muslim, Parker had asked the man, "Are you a Muslim that just uses your religion as an excuse to shoot people or do you actually believe your book?" Parker's question implies an acknowledgment that the Qur'an is sometimes used to hurt others, but it also implies Parker's belief that a violent interpretation of the Qur'an is a wrongful interpretation.

Muhammad

My sample of interviewees was very divided over how to view Muhammad. About half of the interviewees spoke positively or neutrally about Muhammad; the other half spoke comparatively negatively. To a certain extent, the division in views of Muhammad was related to whether or not an interviewee leaned progressive or traditional. The majority of Progressives and Progressive-Traditionals in my sample spoke positively about Muhammad, whereas the majority of Traditionals and Traditional-Progressives spoke negatively. However, a better predictor of an interviewee's view of Muhammad than his or her progressive or traditional leaning was his or her view of the kinds of missiological strategies reflected in IMs. Nineteen of my twenty-two interviewees who viewed Muhammad positively or neutrally were either fully supportive of or at least sympathetic toward the strategies promoted by IMs, although it is important to note that not all of these interviewees were actually aware of the term "insider movement" or were familiar with the Chrislam debate. Dynamic leaders within their church who were more immersed in IMs and were more engaged with Muslims, and usually held views more deviant regarding the dominant historical Evangelical view of Islam, usually influenced these interviewees.

Among those who saw Muhammad positively, several described him as a speaker of truth, with some even attributing to him the status of a prophet with a God-given message. Micah (M) told me that Muhammad "gave truth to the people" and that "that truth is from God because all truth is from God." Gabriel (M) also spoke positively about Muhammad, saying, "Muhammed was a great guy. He was important for his people. He did amazing reform—for instance, for the rights of women. He helped his people turn from polytheism to serving the one true God. I think in the general term of a prophet, he's someone who came and proclaimed truth to his people." Those individuals who spoke positively about Muhammad and his prophethood highly prioritized "honoring Muslims." Teresa (M) talked about it this way: "If the first thing you go in and say is, 'Muhammad is not a prophet and your book is full of lies,' then you're not going to have the conversation after that. If you go in honoring that they love this book and they respect the writer and you say, 'Let's look at it and see what he wrote,' [. . .] that's when God [can reveal] truth to them."

A number of interviewees conveyed mixed feelings about Muhammad. Naomi (M) was uncomfortable when I asked her about her thoughts on Muhammad and jokingly said, "Oh, what are we using this interview for?" as she did not want her view of Muhammad to be publicized in certain ways. Ultimately, she said that, yes, "Muhammad was a prophet in pointing people back to one God," but not everything he said was from God—although she acknowledged that "you could say the same for the Christian prophets as well." Jackie (AR) saw Muhammad as someone who may have "sincerely wanted to focus his people away from killing each other and worshiping hundreds of idols," but she also said he was not a figure to imitate given his brutality later in life and given his marriage to a nine-year-old girl. Then she ended by returning to the positive, saying, "I do think that at some point of his life he had a goal of trying to unify his people and one means of doing that was to try to focus them on this religion he came up with." Bart (M) started out by praising Muhammad and saying, "I think Muhammed is a great person; I think he did a lot of amazing things. I think he was a very dynamic leader and I think he did a great job of uniting the tribes that were on the fence over there back to the worship of one God." But he then questioned whether Muhammad was inspired by Satan or God, and said he did not know the answer. Jesse (M) went back and forth on whether or not Muhammad was a prophet. At first, he said he could see how Muhammad could have been a prophet, although he tried to minimize the importance of the label of prophet, saying, "We have to remember that prophets are humans, so all humans sin." But after this initial ambiguous response, he went on to categorically deny that Muhammad was a prophet. Ethan (M) believed Muhammad acted as a prophet and had a "prophetic call" from God in the first half of his ministry (the Meccan period), but that in the second half of Muhammad's ministry (the Medinan period), when Muhammad gained political power, he stopped acting prophetically. Regardless, Ethan said, "I would want to honor Muhammad in my conversations with Muslims." He also felt the need to defend his honoring of Muhammad as "real" and not simply a method to "try to get them to not hate me or kill me."

Others were not as interested in honoring Muhammad and rather spoke quite negatively about him. Although Celina (AR) was quick to praise Muhammad as having been "a very nice, kind, good person," she said that, eventually, "the devil got a hold of him and started playing with his mind." She lamented "Satan derail[ing] him" from the "truth" and from Jesus, and said, "I think he could have had a very profound influence for good, for Jesus, but he fell into deception and couldn't decipher what he was hearing as truth or deception." Stuart (AR) likewise believed Muhammad was "co-opted by the devil." Like other interviewees who held negative perceptions of Islam, he compared Muhammad to Joseph Smith, the founder of Mormonism, saying that both men were "phenomenal imitators." According to Stuart, such a close caricature of true religion is the kind of false belief system of which the devil is a master:

> [Muhammad] was a man co-opted by the devil and used by the devil. Just as God used his chosen vessels, the devil chose . . . a great imitator. The devil chose a man, and said, "We're gonna start our own religion." I mean, look at the Mormons. What a sad situation that is. So many good people. Almost righteous people. Of course, they're not righteous. But they're moral. They're good family people. Joseph Smith was not a Godly prophet, he was a devil's prophet . . . Like I said, he [Muhammad] is a phenomenal imitator. That's why Islam is very close to the truth. That's what the devil masters. Far-fetched lies . . . a lie close to the truth is very believable, and very easy to just roll off your tongue if you're not careful.

Patrick (AR) said that from all he knows about Muhammad, the latter was an "opportunist" who justified his lifestyle pursuits and hatred of people he felt had mistreated him by claiming religious justification. Bobby (AR) was blunt about his negative view of Muhammad, calling Muhammad a "greedy lunatic" and even comparing Muhammad to Hitler: "He was crazy. He was wrong. The fact that he led so many people down a path that he knew was completely wrong, that's really sick and disgusting and very sad. Just like Hitler, [Muhammad was] really talented, obviously, at persuading a lot of people to a very erroneous point of view." In spite of these comments, Bobby said he did not think it wise to focus on negativity about Muhammad in conversations with Muslims; it was better, he argued, to "focus on the positive apologetic of Jesus being who He said He was." The positive approach, he added, "will go a much longer way than trying to learn every little fault with Islam."

As seen in this section, most congregants held vastly different views on Muhammad. Those who sought to honor Muslims by honoring Muhammad usually refrained from negative judgments and viewed Evangelicals who spoke negatively about Muhammad as vilifying the religion of Islam and worsening relationships between Evangelicals and Muslims. Those who criticized Muhammad did so seemingly effortlessly and seemed less inhibited by what others thought of their opinion of Muhammad.

Chrislam

As explained in Chapter 2, the term "Chrislam" is considered inherently derogatory: critics employ it to decry the supposed syncretism of Christianity and

Islam that they perceive in certain missiological methods that encourage Christian believers from Muslim backgrounds to continue to participate in Muslim religious congregations and to retain aspects of their Muslim identity. Usage of the term is therefore controversial, with opponents of the term arguing that it represents a misunderstanding of the missiological methods in question and that such methods do not, in fact, represent a legitimate blending of Christianity with Islam.

Only half of the congregational interviewees (twenty-four of forty-eight) had heard the term "Chrislam" before. This is a considerably smaller ratio than among the leadership interviewees, where all but two had heard of the Chrislam debate. More congregants from Mercy were acquainted with the term than congregants at Adams River. This may be due to the fact that I interviewed more congregants who were involved with heading various ministries within the Mercy church than I did at Adams River; it may also be due to the fact that the Mercy congregation had been accused of supporting Chrislamic ideas (making congregants more likely to have been exposed to the term). In the two congregations together, those who leaned left on the Progressive-Traditional spectrum according to their evidential moral authority were less likely to be familiar with the term than those who leaned to the right (only five out of twenty-one progressive-leaning interviewees had heard the term, compared to nineteen out of twenty-seven traditional-leaning interviewees). This suggests that those more aware of intra-Evangelical debates on Islam are also more inclined toward using traditional Evangelical moral authority terminology.

Generally, interviewees with an awareness of the term "Chrislam" had higher levels of engagement with Muslims and were more aware of the intra-Evangelical missiological battles on Islam than interviewees who were not aware of the term. With such an awareness of the issues surrounding Chrislam comes a deeper understanding of the bitter intra-Evangelical disagreements about how to correctly be a "Christ-follower" and love Muslims. Most evidential Traditionals or Traditional-Progressives were aware of the Chrislam debate and thus had a keen awareness of what is often perceived to be at stake in the debate—namely, orthodoxy or heterodoxy.

Among my twenty-four interviewees who were familiar with the term "Chrislam," fourteen disapproved of the term, whereas the other ten believed it to have some utility. All those who leaned progressive on the Progressive-Traditional spectrum according to their evidential moral authority disapproved of the term. Interestingly, almost all interviewees with an opinion on Chrislam relied heavily on traditional Evangelical moral authority terminology to justify their reasoning on this particular issue. This was true regardless of whether or not they approved of the term "Chrislam" and regardless of how likely they were to appeal to traditional moral authorities on other issues.

Those interviewees who had heard of Chrislam but disapproved of the use of the term largely disapproved because they felt the term had been applied incorrectly, or because they were skeptical about the motives of those using the term, or simply because they knew they were uncomfortable with the label even though they were unsure of its origins and definition. An example of the latter was Lauren (M), who said one her best friends was incorrectly accused of "starting" Chrislam, but who said she personally had never studied the issue and didn't know anything about the debate. A few of the evidential Traditionals or Traditional-Progressives who expressed disapproval of the term had either been personally associated with so-called Chrislamist approaches to missiology in one way or another or else had had family members or friends accused of being Chrislamic. This group felt the term incorrectly implied that those to whom it was applied were universalists, postmodernists, or syncretists. They often pointed to Scripture, the words of Jesus, and stories of the early church to back up their missiological stances in an effort to show themselves to be as orthodox as—or possibly more orthodox than—those who had accused them or those close to them of being Chrislamic.

Representing one of those who disapproved of the term "Chrislam," Julia (M) felt the word was something that bloggers had fabricated to be divisive. She acknowledged that it was possible for Christians to fall into syncretism in their attempts to share Jesus with others, but ultimately, she said, she didn't know anyone who actually wanted to promote such syncretism. Simon (M) said he understood how people might mistake some of the things taught at the QAC conference his church puts on as heretical and might perceive the conference as promoting Chrislam, but he assured me that all of the content shared at the conference is "first and foremost biblical." He went on to share positive aspects of being accused of Chrislam, saying things like "I think it's a beautiful thing when we get attacked, because that means that people care about things being biblical. That helps us to make sure that we're being biblical."

When I asked Micah (M), who grew up in a predominantly Muslim country, what he thought about the term, he said the notion that some Evangelicals are promoting a syncretism between Christianity and Islam was "totally made up" and "a total lie." After this he said, "Jesus is the way to God, but there are many ways to Jesus." Micah (M) told me that some object to labels like "Muslim follower of Jesus" because they think that those who use the label just want to escape persecution. But Micah saw this accusation as false, claiming that much of the persecution that takes place in Muslim-majority countries has been not strictly on the basis of religion but has been targeted toward those converts to Christ who have also converted to "American or Western culture." Although he originally denied that persecution occurred primarily over religious differences, he then doubled back on himself by suggesting that conversion away from Islam must necessarily provoke a response in Arab shame-and-honor cultures: "If you shame your family by saying 'everything you believe is wrong, and I'm going to go live in America and be a Christian of the church because Islam is bad and the Qur'an is satanic' and all this stuff, you're just shaming your family and your culture, and so of course they're going to be upset."

In keeping with the postmodern propensity to distrust language, Evangelicals whose views deviated from the dominant historical Evangelical views on Islam tended to employ more flexibility in defining words. This flexibility has tremendous theological implications, as Chrislam becomes a difficult concept to appreciate. For example, some use this linguistic flexibility to support their belief that one can be both a Muslim and a follower of Jesus. By emphasizing the Arabic root of the word "Muslim" as "one who submits," instead of using the common dictionary definition of "Muslim" (an adherent of Islam), they allow the possibility that one can be a Muslim follower of Jesus. As mentioned before, these Evangelicals tended to frown on the terms "Christian" and "Christianity"; even though the concept of following Jesus is inherent in the dictionary definition of the word "Christian," they strove to avoid the term "Christian," believing that the word holds too much negative baggage. Some were skeptical of the term "Christian," pointing out that one can be a Christian while not being a true follower of God. After all, according to these Evangelicals, if someone called a Christian can be outside the kingdom of God and a Muslim can follow Jesus, it is quite possible that such a Muslim could be closer to God than many so-called Christians. Thus, whether from a linguistic perspective or otherwise, many Progressives affirmed that one could follow Jesus while being a Muslim. When I asked Naomi (M) about Chrislam, she said she understood why some people would fear syncretism and that she felt the concern among people who use the term "Chrislam" was that those who promote so-called Chrislamist approaches are undermining the uniqueness and significance of Jesus. In her mind, though, the fears were not justified:

> I don't even know exactly what that term is supposed to mean, unless it means basically universalism in a sense. I know I've certainly heard that term and . . . I don't know. I think the fear in people would be that Jesus doesn't matter as much as we thought he did, which I don't agree with. I think he's incredibly important, the most important. So, I don't know if I have a good comment on the fear of it. I understand why people would fear syncretism or that kind of thing. Do I think that someone could practice Islam—maybe not 100%, but a good portion—and follow Jesus at the same time? Yeah, I do.

The idea that both Muslims and Christians can genuinely seek God, taken with the belief that language fails to adequately define religious concepts, can beg the question of just who this "God" is to these more postmodern Evangelicals. In fact, most were comfortable agreeing that Allah is the same God as the one they claim. Naomi shared that she had felt close to her Muslim friends and to Islam for a long time, even more so after she took a world religions course in college and learned how Christians and Muslims have many similar beliefs about God. Then she attended a conference hosted by Christians whose views deviate from the dominant historical Evangelical view of Islam, which affirmed her notion that Allah of Islam and God of the Bible are actually the same:

> We're all worshiping the same God. . . . it was such a paradigm shift from doing a different religion to, "[W]e are all pursuing God," and just learning . . . I think I've always, just me personally, when I had some of those revelations, it was sort of like, "This is kind of what I've thought and sort of hoped. . . ." That's more of my tendency, is that God's bigger than what we paint him to be, especially in certain denominations and just Western Christianity in the South. . . . I think for me . . . rather than a hard transition. . . , it was more of, "This sounds like God to

me. Of course, he would be revealing himself to people all over the world in all kinds of different ways."

Evangelicals whose views deviate from the dominant historical Evangelical view of Islam are able, through their embrace of flexible language and boundaries, to view God and Allah as one and the same, and can accept the concept of a Christ-following Muslim.

Whereas many interviewees who had heard the term "Chrislam" felt the label was misleading or were suspicious of the term, about half felt the term had some utility and that the criticisms implied in the label were valid to varying degrees. This was a point of difference between congregations. The majority of those at Mercy who were familiar with the term felt it to be inappropriate, whereas the majority of those at Adams River who were familiar with the term felt it to have legitimacy. As with those who opposed usage of the term, interviewees who thought the term had some legitimacy often supported their positions using references to Scripture and the words of Jesus. Their frequent scriptural references may have been due to an awareness that their use of the "Chrislam" label implied a questioning of the orthodoxy of "Muslim followers of Jesus," and they may have been motivated to reason in such a way in order to protect themselves from seeming unnecessarily judgmental.

Even among those who believed the term "Chrislam" to have some legitimacy, most were relatively moderate in their thinking about the topic. Among these "moderates" were Frank (AR), who leaned toward skepticism of insider movements that allow converts from Muslim backgrounds to retain much of their Muslim identity, but who nonetheless said he had respect for some proponents of IMs. He also said that in his experience, even the strongest proponents of IMs with whom he had interacted had not been "flat out syncretistic." Frank mentioned a course his church offers titled "Perspectives on the World Christian Movement," saying the course has some "provocative stuff" and acknowledging that some would say the class had gone too far in its efforts to accommodate Muslims and contextualize the gospel for them. Still, Frank felt it was important and healthy to wrestle with various missiological methods that seek to "make Christ more palatable to a Muslim audience."

Meagan (AR) had heard the term "Chrislam" but was unsure of its definition. She brought up the C-scale, which describes various types of believers in Christ in terms of how much or how little they retain of Muslim religion and culture. She mentioned that the International Mission Board, the missionary-sending agency affiliated with the Southern Baptist Convention, is "C-4 No More"— meaning that the board encourages converts from Muslim backgrounds to retain Muslim forms and practices that are biblical (such as praying with raised hands or abstaining from pork), but stops short of the C-5 level, which would actually allow converts to continue referring to themselves as Muslims. Meagan then pulled out her "Perspectives on the World Christian Movement" textbook and let me take a picture of the scale she was referring to. She said she was uncomfortable with the C-5 level, but she said it can get "really messy" because "you can't really control whether [new believers] land on C-4 or C-5." She said most Evangelicals argue about the legitimacy of the C-4 versus C-5 levels. Meagan called herself a "black and white" person and said she really struggles with the idea of a hybrid identity that combines both Muslim and Christian elements, as exists among those who claim to be Muslim followers of Jesus. She said the danger of C-5 believers is that they can rightly believe that Jesus Christ is their Savior but also say that they are Muslims. Meagan believed this dichotomy allows Muhammad, the Qur'an, and Islamic prayers to play a contradictory role in the believer's life.

Like Meagan, Michael (AR) also had a problem with the idea of a "Muslim follower of Jesus." He said that he did not believe Christ would have intended Muslims to retain the "Muslim" identification. He believed full transformation must take place, wherein a believer is "truly committed to Jesus" and thus must "renounce the tenets of Islam and Muhammad as being false, as being not true." Still, he cautioned American Christians like himself to "stay away from cultural and political associations with Christianity that we've built, especially here in the new south over the last few decades." He said, "You do not have to be a Southern Baptist Christian who lives two miles from a golf course to be saved. I think it's important that we recognize that."

When I asked Simon (AR) about Chrislam, he said that it was possible that some Muslims could "come into a saving knowledge of Jesus" through the methods promoted by insider movements, but he also believed that such methods were confusing to Muslims because they promoted a separation between identity and behavior. When I asked him to explain further, he responded:

> For Christians, our identity is with Jesus Christ. When we identify with Jesus, we have to distance ourselves from certain things. For example, it would be very difficult for me to be a prostitute and identify with Jesus. Those lifestyles contradict. The lines are getting fuzzy when you talk about Chrislam. Can you identify with Jesus and still be associated with a religious system that denies all the most important things about who He is and what He says?

Simon believed those comfortable with IMs were usually Westerners, and he felt postmodernism may have impacted their opinions. He acknowledged that new believers do not necessarily need to become Westerners, but he still felt that believers from Muslim backgrounds should be prepared to distance themselves from Muslim culture, saying, "Ultimately, when we follow Christ, we are becoming aliens within our own culture, whatever culture we're coming from."

The term "Chrislam" helps one to understand the vast differences between Evangelicals who lean left on the Progressive-Traditional spectrum and those who lean right. Ultimately, traditional-leaning Evangelicals are far less open than those leaning progressive to the philosophy that it is possible to be both an orthodox follower of Jesus and a Muslim at the same time. Clearly the debate is birthed from the macro philosophical differences on religion and culture between those who are aligned with the historical Evangelical stances and those who are not.

Interfaith Dialogue

To determine interviewees' views on interfaith dialogue, I followed the same procedure as with leadership interviewees. I first asked directly about the topic, and then later I also asked whether the interviewee was familiar with the ACW initiative and what his or her views were regarding it. As with the leaders in the last chapter, the majority (43) of congregants I spoke with had a moderate view of interfaith dialogue, perceiving both pros and cons. Twenty-seven of these forty-three were mostly skeptical, though were still open to the idea that it might have benefits. The other fifteen emphasized mostly benefits but were still able to critique interfaith dialogue. In terms of justifications for their views, only twelve of my interviewees relied heavily on traditional Evangelical moral authority terminology. As with the leaders, interviewees were significantly less likely to use traditional moral authority terminology when speaking about interfaith dialogue than they were when speaking about other topics (such as Muhammad, the Qur'an, and Chrislam). This suggests that interviewees were either less willing or less able to articulate how their view of God impacted their views on interfaith dialogue.

Gabriel (M) is an example of one congregant with a moderate approach to formal interfaith dialogue, though he leaned more toward optimism on the topic than some others categorized as moderate. Specifically, Gabriel said he goes into interfaith dialogue situations with an open mind and as a learner, even though he said he had "some pretty strong opinions about what I believe." Although participants often enter interfaith forums "with the American mindset that we kind of know everything and are the best at everything," he suggested this was the wrong approach. If participants go in proud, he argued, it stifles their ability to really interact well with and listen to the other person from a different culture. He saw interfaith dialogue more as a positive exercise of cross-cultural understanding than one of cross-religious understanding, saying, "I think interfaith dialogue is really important because it's culture. It helps you understand culture." Thus, Gabriel perceived Islam as a cultural form more than as a religion that is either right or wrong. In addition, he and others affiliated with Mercy tended to relay the belief that to impose the claims of a dominant culture onto a marginalized culture was a violation of their sense of social justice. In suggesting that, he reflected a perspective that is shared by some other Evangelicals but that is out of step with the dominant historical Evangelical perspective on Islam. Another example of a moderate approach, albeit one that leaned more toward skepticism of interfaith dialogue and one that aligned more closely with the traditional Evangelical stance, came from Frank (AR). Frank saw value in Christian and Muslim leaders coming together to talk about points of agreement and points of disagreement, saying, "maybe it's something I'd be involved in some day." But he also said that participants in interfaith dialogue should "not just be content with, 'let's all get along.' You know, like the 'co-exist' bumper sticker. If that's the highest ideal, I feel that that is a tragedy." He contrasted that unbeneficial type of interfaith dialogue with one that he saw as correct, namely, "interfaith dialogue to build trust and friendship [so] that Muslims will truly see the love of Christ in us" and so that Evangelicals might have an "opportunity in a loving, respectful way to share our faith." Amanda (AR), a nonprofit employee who relocated to Frankfort (the local refugee community) in order to work alongside Muslims, was similar to Frank, in that she also held a moderate, albeit slightly skeptical, view of interfaith dialogue. When I asked her what she thought of interfaith dialogue, Amanda responded:

> That's something that I have recently encountered and I'm still not quite sure what I think about it. There was a prayer vigil here for the Naphtali earthquake victims several months ago, which actually turned out to be an interfaith sort of thing. It was very odd to me. Interesting. I can see pros and cons to it. One obvious pro is that it's kind of amazing to see a peaceful gathering of people from so many religions that do not agree with each other ... During Ramadan, when I went to see Muslim women, I encountered one who was a leader of an interfaith movement in her county between Christians, Jews, and Muslims. Interfaith dialogue is what they have and so I love the idea of coming together to speak peaceably and learn and exchange ideas from one another. My hesitation comes up whenever that may stray into saying we are all the same ... as if everything is all one truth because I really don't believe that.

Those who expressed the most enthusiasm for interfaith dialogue were usually supportive of or at least sympathetic toward the missiological approaches encouraged by IMs. They tended to be critical of traditional Evangelicalism, and many of them knew their views deviated from historical Evangelical views regarding Islam and Muslims. These individuals usually placed a high priority on honoring Muslims and their beliefs. For example, Lauren (M) said she approaches interfaith dialogue "as a learner." She said, "For me, that's not just rhetoric ... I can honestly go in as a learner and as a listener and just [ask] respectful questions." Ethan (M) had a similar perspective, saying that the concept of "mission" as connected with interfaith dialogue should be abandoned and replaced with ideas more oriented toward peacemaking and mutuality. He gave labels that he liked better than mission, such as "interfaith dialogue for peacemaking" and "transformative dialogue for peacemaking," and he also said that his "expectation and hope" was that "a generation or two from now ... Christian ministry will be ... more mutual interaction trying to pursue God's Kingdom with a deeper level of humility" toward members of other religions. In Ethan's view, interfaith dialogue should consist of a "mutual witness" wherein participants are able to share their faith with each other in such a manner as to motivate each other toward "heart transformation"—a transformation that he suggested should promote, among other things, "mutual action to caring for the poor." With this last comment, Ethan seemed to elevate a social gospel motivated not simply by the idea of personal conversion but also social reform.

The most negative views on public interfaith dialogue came from those who associated the exercise with "universalism" (which usually carries a negative connotation for Evangelicals whose views align with the dominant historical Evangelical view on Islam) and/or from those who felt involvement in interfaith dialogue necessarily meant participants would have to make compromises in their faith. Evangelicals in this camp were usually older (but not always), were more closely aligned with historical Evangelicalism, and had lower engagement with Muslims. For example, Zachary (AR) said, "To me, interfaith dialogue means universalism. I'm generally suspicious of anything labeled interfaith." And Stuart (AR) said, "I'm against it. The Bible doesn't associate with [interfaith dialogue], and I'm glad our pastor doesn't either . . . I think that's devil-inspired." He also used the story of Elijah and the prophets of Baal from the Old Testament (I Kings 18:27) to suggest that Christians do not have to accommodate others' religious views, and that in certain instances it is appropriate for Christians to actually mock other religions, as Elijah mocked those who worshiped Baal. Here, Stuart's reasoning referenced the Old Testament, a reflection of the fact that he and other interviewees with opinions more closely associated with historical Evangelicalism tended to view the Bible more holistically, incorporating both the Old and New Testaments into their reasoning as being both equally inspired by God. This contrasts with interviewees holding views deviating from historically dominant Evangelical views, who were more likely to focus on the words of Jesus in the New Testament over the words of the Old Testament (some explicitly stated that they hold the words of Jesus to override other portions of the biblical text).

"A Common Word"

As outlined in the previous chapter, the ACW initiative of 2007 was the largest Christian-Muslim interfaith peace initiative in existence at the time of my study. Among my interviewees, one of the critiques of it was that it was a top-level initiative. For example, though Maria (M) saw the effort as positive, she criticized it as "a conversation of the scholars up in their ivory towers" that was unlikely to make a practical difference. Perhaps this is why only about one-quarter (thirteen out of forty-eight) of my interviewees had heard of ACW—a considerably smaller ratio than among the leadership interviewees, where all but seven had heard of ACW. No congregational interviewee placed in the Progressive category according to his or her evidential moral authority had heard of the ACW, supporting the idea that those who appealed to traditional Evangelical moral authority terminology the least were also those least involved in Christian-Muslim relations. Even among interviewees who had heard of ACW, only six of the thirteen felt knowledgeable enough to make a judgment on it. A few said things like "I've heard of it, but I don't know much about it," or "I think I have the 'Common Word' document on my computer somewhere, but I actually don't remember," or "I can't remember, it was so long ago that I read it." Thus, even among the few who had heard of ACW, not all interviewees had a strong opinion about it.

In total, four interviewees expressed a positive view of ACW. Although these four represented three different categories of evidential moral authority, all were supportive of IMs, and the group as a whole was relatively critical of traditional forms of Christianity and relatively open to promoting interfaith dialogue focused on similarities between the two faith groups. Ethan (M) supported the initiative even while pointing out that other Christians view it negatively, saying, "a lot of Christians are afraid of [ACW]" because they have interpreted it as a form of interfaith dialogue that has characteristics of universalism. Parker (M) likewise said, "It's a great document." When I asked him what he thought about some of the criticisms of the initiative, specifically those voiced by Evangelical pastor and author John Piper (outlined in Chapter 2), he said, "I love Piper, but when it comes to the issue of Islam, he's just [. . .] completely ignorant, and by that I mean uninformed." Mark (M) felt the ACW document was "a really helpful start" and should be discussed more often in the context of questions regarding whether Islam is a religion of peace or a religion of violence. He said he felt ACW was a great example of Muslims initiating and pursuing more peaceful relations with Jews and Christians and added that he was "frustrated that a number of conservative, Evangelical voices criticized it for not going far enough rather than lauding it for being a good start. I don't think anybody ever intended 'A Common Word' to be the final word." He criticized those who just want to believe that Islam is "a religion of violence . . . so we can hate Muslims. I think that's [how] a lot of people want to live."

Two interviewees, both of whom were to the right on the Progressive-Traditional spectrum, expressed a more negative view of ACW. They held views that more closely aligned with the historical Evangelical views on topics related to Islam and usually were quick to highlight differences between the beliefs of Muslims and the beliefs of Christians. Both were over the age of sixty. They were critical mostly because they perceived the initiative to downplay the uniqueness of Christ. Kevin (AR) felt the document was not something that a Christian should sign because it simply affirmed the central truths proclaimed by the Islamic religion while ignoring truths central to the Christian religion. That, according to Kevin, is "just fatally compromising." He said, "They were willing to affirm that there's only one God, and then they were willing to affirm that Muhammed is the prophet of God. That just is Islam, that makes you a Muslim." For the most part, those who had a positive view of the ACW initiative held positions on Islam and Muslims that deviated from the dominant historical Evangelical view. In contrast, those who perceived the document to be too compromising to sign were those whose views align with the dominant historical Evangelical view on Islam and Muslims.

Conclusion

As with the leaders, in varying degrees, almost all congregants interviewed had a common desire to influence the Muslim understanding of God by communicating their view of Jesus. But despite this commonality, the forty-eight congregants still showed great diversity of opinion on both religious and political topics related to Islam, some holding positions that aligned with the dominant historical Evangelical perspective and others holding positions that dissented from that historical perspective. While these congregants were not as informed about the terms "Chrislam" or ACW as leaders, most understood the fundamental issues at play in these topics. This was evident in their detailed comments about interfaith dialogue and about the similarities and differences between Christianity and Islam.

The preceding analysis confirms Hunter's culture wars thesis in two ways. First, it demonstrates that congregants are engaged in just the type of culture war Hunter described. This is evident from the divides in their views on Islam and Muslims and from the fact that congregants seemed to be drawn to one side of the Progressive-Traditional spectrum or the other. As before, Hunter's conception of moral authorities proved to be a useful lens for understanding interviewees' views, in that interviewees' moral authorities were typically predictive of whether their perspectives on Islam and Muslims would be relatively progressive or relatively traditional. (This is true overall despite the fact that there were exceptions— even more so among congregants than among leaders—where moral authority was *not* always a seamless predictor of an individual's stances on Islam.) Second, my congregational data supports Hunter's prediction that the most polarized conceptions of moral authority will be more dominant among leaders, and the moral authorities of the people in the pews will be comparatively less extreme. In the sample, when using their positioning via the evidential moral authority analysis, most interviewees had a hybrid perspective on moral authority that reflected some aspects of progressivism but also some aspects of traditionalism. Given their somewhat complicated perspectives on moral authority, interviewees' views on Islam were at times also complicated, reflecting a spectrum of views rather than a clean bifurcation into two distinct camps.

This chapter and the preceding chapter have offered a detailed examination of the views of Evangelical leaders and Evangelical congregants, respectively. So far, the two groups have been considered largely independently. The following chapter, however, will take a comparative approach, exploring how leaders and congregants are similar to each other but also how they are different. In addition to comparing congregants with leaders, the chapter will also compare the different categories on the Progressive-Traditional spectrum. Aside from the question of how frequently they reference traditional moral authorities, what are the characteristics that distinguish Progressives from Traditionals? And how do these characteristics differ from the characteristics of those in the hybrid categories of moral authority?

Chapter 6

COMPLEXITIES OF EVANGELICAL VIEWS ON ISLAM

COMPARATIVE PERSPECTIVES OF LEADERS AND CONGREGANTS

There's no uniformity or unanimity in the Evangelical community on Islam.

—Joseph, Evangelical professor and author

Introduction

Having examined leaders and congregants separately in Chapters 6 and 7, I now turn to comparing the two groups with the goal of providing an overall sense of how leaders and congregants are different and how they are similar. I also analyze each of the four categories of moral authority on the Progressive-Traditional spectrum separately, discussing the characteristics of the interviewees who fell into each category and identifying the key shared views that united the leaders and congregants in each category. This is a useful endeavor since many scholars have pondered the level to which elites and everyday people in the pews have views that align with each other.

As previously demonstrated, both Evangelical leaders and Evangelical congregants proved to be more progressive on the Progressive-Traditional spectrum of moral authority when evaluated evidentially than when evaluated based on their stated moral authorities. But most still remained in the hybrid categories of moral authority (i.e., the Progressive-Traditional or Traditional-Progressive categories) when categorized using the evidential moral authority analysis. Interestingly, that seems to put many leaders and congregants broadly into the same moral universe in the sense that most appeal to both progressive and traditional sources of moral authority when talking about Islam, Muslims, and politics. Still, there was a substantial minority in each group who were on the fringes of the Progressive-Traditional spectrum and held views on topics related to Islam more strongly oppositional (in terms of how they substantiated their positions) to fellow Evangelicals on the other end of the spectrum. It is important to note that many of these oppositional views were also held by some Evangelicals holding hybrid identities, but they failed to undergird their positions with strong moral authority terminology. Overall, it is still safe to say that the hybrid categories of moral authority incorporated more Evangelicals who had more nuanced perspectives within Evangelicalism; and some of these individuals, particularly the ones in the hybrid category of Progressive-Traditional, held more moderate views on Islam.

This chapter is organized as follows. First, I establish the context by briefly reviewing the objectives and major findings of the leadership analysis (Chapter 4) and congregational analysis (Chapter 5). Second, I compare leaders' and congregants' stated moral authorities and their evidential moral authorities. I also compare leaders' and congregants' tendency to fall farther to the left on the Progressive-Traditional spectrum based on evidential analysis than when they are categorized based on their own statements about themselves. Next, I describe interviewees within the categories on the Progressive-Traditional spectrum and point out some interesting comparisons between these categories. Finally, I compare leaders' and congregants' views on a series of topics relating to Islam, including a specific comparison of how the two groups differ in their views of IMs. I have largely avoided comparisons between the two congregations, since such comparisons were discussed in Chapter 5. Certain details related to demographics or comparison between the two congregations can be found in this chapter but only when deemed key to understanding the findings.

Review of Leadership and Congregational Analysis

My chapter on Evangelical leaders examined two key questions: (1) To what extent are Evangelicals reacting to Islam with increased internal cohesion? and (2) How might the moral authority of interviewees elucidate Evangelical attitudes on topics such as Chrislam, Muhammad, the Qur'an, interfaith dialogue, the ACW initiative, and politics? My first finding from my exploration of these questions was that there is considerable diversity and conflict within Evangelical leadership on Islam, and my data suggest that Evangelical leaders are not banding together or laying aside internal differences in response to the threat of Islam. My second finding was that my data confirm Hunter's moral authority argument. Consistent with Hunter, I find that Evangelical leaders are drawn to either a progressive or a traditional pole of moral authority. However, my research makes use of a conceptual tool that I developed through my engagement with the data, the Progressive-Traditional spectrum. In contrast to Hunter's binary division between Progressives and Traditionals, this spectrum furthers Hunter's thesis by arguing that, yes, leaders are leading the culture wars; but the majority of Evangelical leaders in my sample have moderate hybrid identities with respect to moral authority. My third and final finding in the chapter was that an interviewee's involvement (or lack thereof) with IMs was correlated with his or her opinions on key topics related to Islam and Muslims. I found affiliation with IMs to be an important predictor that the interviewee would hold stances out of step with dominant historical Evangelical thinking on Islam while still maintaining a right-leaning stated and evidential moral authority.

My chapter on the two congregations empirically examined the same two questions asked of the leadership. As with the leadership, my first finding was that there is considerable diversity among Evangelical congregants with respect to Islam. Congregants did not appear to be banding together or laying aside internal differences in response to the threat of Islam any more than did leaders. The most animosity directed toward fellow Evangelicals came from those who held opinions on Islam that did not align with the dominant historical Evangelical perspective. My second finding was that my data on congregants, similarly to my data on leadership, confirm Hunter's moral authority argument. I found that Evangelical congregants are drawn to one side or the other of the Progressive-Traditional spectrum, but as predicted by Hunter, the inclination toward one pole or the other is less significant (not as strong) for the congregants as it was with the leadership. This finding suggests that most congregants, like most Evangelical leaders—but to an even greater degree than those leaders—are not found on the extreme Evangelical right or the extreme Evangelical left, but rather have a moderate hybrid identity. This finding lines up with what Hunter calls the "people somewhere in the middle," who draw from both the Enlightenment (i.e., progressive sources) and biblical sources (i.e., traditional sources) of moral understanding (1991: 132).

Comparison of Stated to Evidential Moral Authority, and Existence of Hybrid Identities

As outlined previously, whereas Hunter spoke of moral authority as a single category, I have distinguished between an individual's stated moral authority and his or her evidential moral authority. I found a substantial difference between interviewees' stated moral authorities and their evidential moral authorities, and I have argued that the evidential moral authority offers a fuller indication of an individual's true position on the Progressive-Traditional spectrum (as explained in Chapter 3).

With respect to stated moral authority, I found that the bulk of interviewees, whether leaders or congregants, answered direct questions about their moral authority in a way that placed them on the more traditional end of the spectrum. Among leaders specifically, only six fell on the progressive side of the spectrum according to their stated moral authority, whereas twenty-five fell on the traditional side. My analysis of congregants' stated moral authorities gave even more traditional-leaning results. Only one congregant fell on the progressive side of the spectrum, whereas forty-seven fell on the traditional side. The fact that congregants were even more likely than leaders to claim traditional Evangelical moral authorities may be due a greater tendency within congregants to fall victim to "Conditioned Responses," a problem I addressed by developing the idea of evidential moral authority, as explained in Chapter 3. Congregants may be more likely to respond to a question about the source of their ideas of right and wrong by appealing to traditional Evangelical authorities due to conditioning, even if they do not, in fact, look to these authorities when making decisions in day-to-day life about right and wrong, or when thinking about the nature of Islam or Muslims. Congregants are perhaps even more susceptible to this knee-jerk problem than leaders, as leaders are likely to have had more practice discussing the topic of moral authority and to have received more challenges to their moral authorities. Therefore, leaders may have been slightly more prone to nuance and moderation in their claims about their own moral authorities. Although both leaders and congregants were very likely to claim traditional Evangelical moral authorities, they differed as to which specific authorities they were most likely to reference. Leaders listed "the Bible" (twenty-three out of twenty-nine) as their moral authority significantly more often than did congregants (nineteen out of forty-eight); congregants, in turn, were slightly more likely to list "God" as a moral authority than were the leadership. In explaining how they viewed the Bible, however, both groups tended to use relatively traditional language such as the "Word of God," "God-inspired," "inerrant," or "infallible."

Though both leaders and congregants claimed traditional moral authorities when asked directly about the topic, both groups reflected far more progressivism in the analysis of evidential moral authority. In this second "evidential" analysis, the majority of leaders (21) fell on the progressive side of the spectrum and just fifteen fell on the traditional side of the spectrum. My analysis of congregants' evidential moral authorities gave similar results: twenty-one congregants fell on the progressive side of the spectrum and just twenty-seven—a much smaller number than in the stated analysis—fell on the traditional side of the spectrum. Thus, when asked directly about their personal moral authorities, most leaders and congregants claimed to have traditional moral authorities (including God, Jesus, Holy Spirit, the Bible, or some combination of these). However, when answering questions not directly related to moral authority (questions on Islam and politics), many interviewees failed to reference traditional Evangelical moral authorities as they articulated their reasoning and positions, suggesting their moral authorities were more progressive than they themselves believed or realized.

Although both leaders and congregants demonstrated more progressivism in general in the evidential analysis, both groups still tended to appeal to a mixture of traditional Evangelical moral authorities and progressive authorities, with the result that the majority in both groups fell into the hybrid categories of moral authority in the evidential analysis. The most populous category for both leaders and congregants was the hybrid "Traditional-Progressive" category, and the second most common category for both groups was the other hybrid category, the "Progressive-Traditional" category. As for the extreme ends of the spectrum, a higher ratio of leaders fell into the extreme "Progressive" or "Traditional" categories than did congregants. This is consistent with Hunter's moral authority argument, which holds that leaders are the ones to lead the culture wars and therefore are the figures most likely to show polarization. However, though leaders were more likely to be in the extreme categories than were congregants, the fact that the majority of the leaders gravitated to the hybrid categories suggests that leaders may not be as extreme as stereotypically thought or even as Hunter and other theorists have held. At the very least, it shows that some Evangelical

Comparison of Four Categories of Moral Authority

This section analyzes each of the four categories of moral authority on the Progressive-Traditional spectrum separately, discussing the demographic characteristics of the interviewees that fell in each category and identifying the key shared views that united the leaders and congregants in each category.

Progressive

Fifteen interviewees (out of seventy-two total) were categorized as Progressive on the Progressive-Traditional spectrum. The average age of the Progressives was forty-six, and their average engagement level was medium, rather than high or low. The average political stance was "left-leaning," which is situated between "straight left" and "right-leaning." There were more women in this category than men. Interestingly, females outweighed males in both the Progressive and Progressive-Traditional categories, whereas males outweighed females in the Traditional and Traditional-Progressive categories. Progressives were also the most highly educated, with two-thirds having graduate degrees. (The Evangelicals in the extreme categories were the most highly educated, making those in the hybrid categories the least educated. However, the sample as a whole was highly educated, and so "less educated" does not equal "uneducated.")

For the most part, the Progressives in my sample were innovators within Evangelicalism, in the sense that they were traveling a different road of belief from that of the dominant historical Evangelical beliefs, and held views on Islam and Muslims that deviated from the dominant historical Evangelical perspective on Islam. For example, many saw Islam more as a cultural form than a religion that was either right or wrong. They advocated caring for Muslims as neighbors, but they were, for the most part, uninterested in proselytizing as the word is commonly understood. Instead, individuals in this group were likely to endorse issues of social justice, such as community projects and working together side by side with Muslims. They were also likely to see interfaith dialogue and the ACW as mostly beneficial. The majority held surprisingly elevated views of the Qur'an, even though they were the least likely to have read it. (Because some who hold dissenting views from the dominant historical Evangelical narrative believe that cultural and socioeconomic forces tend to determine beliefs and actions more strongly than a text like the Qur'an, it is understandable that these individuals would feel no obligation to read the Qur'an.) On the whole, this group also had elevated views of Muhammad, and they generally refrained from speaking negatively about either the Qur'an or Muhammad. These individuals seemed to have curiosity about Islam and a humility of belief, in the sense that they felt they could learn about God from Muslims (many shared stories of how Muslims have impacted their lives). They were also heavily involved with critiquing the dominant historical Evangelical perspective on Islam. Some of the Evangelicals in this group have dedicated large portions of their lives to combating what they see as "damage" done by Evangelicals who align themselves with the dominant historical Evangelical perspective on Islam. Many of the Progressives spoke of such Evangelicals as having an unjustified fear of Islamic culture or theology and/or Muslims.

However, there were several outliers (one leader and three congregants) who did not conform to many of these characteristics that unified the rest of the group. The leader was an outlier in the sense that he was politically conservative and held views on Islam that mostly aligned with the dominant historical Evangelical perspective. Thus, he had much in common with those on the traditional side of the Progressive-Traditional spectrum of moral authority, except for the fact that he did not use traditional Evangelical moral authority terminology to express his views. However, his failure to use such terminology—and thus his classification as a Progressive—could be explained by the fact that he was a professor, and some professors are not accustomed to using traditional Evangelical terminology in an academic setting. Like the single outlier in the leadership group, the three congregant outliers also held views that mostly aligned with the dominant historical Evangelical perspective on Islam. But these individuals also shared two other significant characteristics—namely, lower engagement with Muslims and lower level of knowledge about Islam. These individuals' avoidance of traditional Evangelical moral authority terminology and their consequent classification as Progressives may be due to their lack of engagement with Muslims and lack of fluency in talking about Islam, which may have curtailed usage of traditional moral authority terminology to express their views.

Hybrid Categories: Progressive-Traditional and Traditional-Progressive

By definition, the key commonality among all Evangelicals in the hybrid categories of Progressive-Traditional and Traditional-Progressive is that they reasoned using both traditional and progressive moral authorities. They were less progressive than the Progressives and less traditional than the Traditionals, placing them between the extremes on the Progressive-Traditional spectrum. Beyond that, the two groups were very diverse and embodied a variety of characteristics. Generally speaking, these categories were filled with Evangelicals who had more moderate tendencies with respect to their views on Islam.[1]

Out of the total sample of seventy-two interviewees, nineteen were categorized as Progressive-Traditional. Among this group, the average age was forty-six and

---

1. Because both groups were filled with such diversity, and because there were similar patterns of diversity in both hybrid categories, I have chosen to describe their characteristics together.

the average engagement level with Muslims was medium. The average political stance was "right-leaning," which is situated between "straight right" and "left-leaning." As with the Progressive category, there were more women in the Progressive-Traditional category than there were men. Progressive-Traditionals were less educated on average than either Progressives or Traditionals but slightly more educated on average than Traditional-Progressives.

As for the Traditional-Progressive category, twenty-six interviewees (out of the total of seventy-two) fell into this group. The average age was forty-three, making this the youngest group. The average engagement level was medium, and the average political stance was "right-leaning." There were more men in this category than women. Although Evangelicals in the "Traditional-Progressive" category were the least educated among all categories, that is not to say that the group as a whole was uneducated: half of Traditional-Progressives had obtained graduate degrees.

The Progressive-Traditionals and Traditional-Progressives were very diverse. One-third of the hybrids (fifteen of the forty-five) could be described as similar to the Progressives but with slightly more political diversity (many articulated their political views in such a way as to appear centrist politically). For the most part, they were similar to the Progressives in that they tended to be innovators within Evangelicalism and tended to hold views on Islam and Muslims that were out of step with the dominant historical Evangelical perspective on Islam (in particular, they held elevated views of Muhammad, the Qur'an, and interfaith dialogue). However, some were not sure how they felt about these topics, as opposed to the Progressives who tended to have clearer positions. The majority of the individuals in this subgroup were IM practitioners or sympathizers, but three were not. Two of these three were mostly uncomfortable with proselytizing altogether (unlike those affiliated with IMs, who usually, to varying degrees, were comfortable looking at the Qur'an and the Bible together and talking about Jesus with Muslims), and neither had ever heard of Chrislam. Ten of the fifteen had acquired well-rounded knowledge of Islam and had strong relationships with Muslims. The remaining five did not have a well-rounded knowledge of Islam and did not have Muslim friends but were very open to learning more about and from Muslims. Taken together, for the most part these individuals were critical of Evangelicals who hold views of Islam and Muslims that align with the dominant historical Evangelical positions.

Just under one-third (twelve of forty-five) tended toward middle-of-the-road positions. Some did not have strong opinions on various issues I asked about, while others had never thought about some of the topics I raised. Politically, they appeared centrist. Most were willing to make some compromises on their theological stances in certain areas that they saw fit. For example, some saw the relational benefits of endorsing the ACW interfaith initiative even though they perceived it to be deficient theologically. Broadly, their views on Islam were not as negative as those of the Traditionals described here, but they were not uncritical of Islam altogether, and thus differed from many in the Progressive category. Those in this subgroup were not necessarily supportive of IMs, but those who were aware of the movement were also not highly critical of it. They mostly spoke positively about the Muslims they knew and were optimistic about interfaith dialogue.

Just over one-third (eighteen of forty-five) had commonalities with those in the Traditional category but reasoned their views by referencing traditional Evangelical moral authority terminology less than the Traditionals. Thus, these Evangelicals demonstrate an awareness of and usage of progressive and humanistic forms of moral authority. Twelve of the eighteen in this subgroup had well-rounded knowledge of Islam, and the majority had relationships with Muslims. The remaining six were less knowledgeable about Islam and did not have Muslim friends but were very open to learning more about Islam through classes and personal study; however, none of the six were interested in acquiring religious truth from Muslims themselves, as they saw Islam largely as a false religion that has trapped Muslims. Taken together, these eighteen individuals held views that mostly aligned with the dominant historical Evangelical perspective on Islam. They were as a whole less willing than other subgroups in the hybrid categories to compromise theology in an effort to improve relationships, and some were suspicious of interfaith dialogue. A number of those in this subgroup were well known for their outspoken negative stances on Islam (this subgroup included three Evangelicals from Muslim-majority countries, who tended to hold the most critical views of Islam of any interviewees).

Traditional

Twelve interviewees (out of seventy-two) were categorized as Traditional on the Progressive-Traditional spectrum. The average age in this category was forty-nine, and the average engagement level was high, making the group both the oldest and the most engaged with Muslims. The average political stance was "right-leaning," which is situated between "straight right" and "left-leaning." As with the Traditional-Progressive category, there were more men in this category than women. Traditionals were also highly educated, second only to the Progressives.

By definition, Traditionals were those who reasoned their views by referencing traditional Evangelical moral authority terminology frequently—more so than those in any other category. For the most part, Traditionals held views on Islam and Muslims that aligned with the dominant historical Evangelical perspective on Islam. Many of these Traditionals saw Islam as a false religion, and they were generally interested in proselytizing. While this group advocated caring for Muslims as neighbors, they felt it would be wrong to stop at "peaceful coexistence," and most felt that it was important for Christians to tell Muslims about their Christian faith in one way or another. The majority were mostly skeptical about interfaith dialogue, though still open to the benefits of it. Traditionals were the most likely to have read extensively from the Qur'an, and this may be due to their belief that what Muslims believe to be a revelation from Allah is highly motivational for Muslims themselves and thus is worthy of study in order to proselytize. Unlike the Progressives, who generally refrained from speaking negatively about the Qur'an or Muhammad, the majority of Traditionals held negative views of the Qur'an, and many were quick to point out perceived flaws in the character of Muhammad. These individuals felt they had obtained knowledge of the objective truth of Jesus, and they felt that Muslims needed to hear about this truth. The majority of these individuals were uncompromising on theological stances. They tended to prioritize being in a right relationship with God and living according to what they held God's precepts to be, even if doing so might come at the expense of building accommodating relationships with Muslims (such prioritization explains, for example, why several in this category refused to sign the ACW document, and why several indicated a willingness to express criticism of Islam or Muhammad even in situations where doing so might cause offense). But although they were critical of Islam, these individuals were also for the most part intentional about maintaining consistent contact with Muslims. The leaders often had job titles directly related to their interactions with Muslims, and many of the congregants had developed a strong bond with Muslim refugee families and/or had purposefully studied with, eaten with, or worked alongside Muslims on an ongoing basis.

However, there were a few outliers in the Traditional category (two leaders and three congregants) who did not conform to many of these characteristics described earlier. These individuals were outliers for similar reasons: all were either IM leaders or IM supporters, and all held views that ran counter to the dominant historical Evangelical perspective on Islam (e.g., each of the five had elevated views of Muhammad and the Qur'an). Not only did their own views deviate from historical Evangelical thinking on Islam, but these outliers were highly critical of Evangelicals who continued to adhere to the dominant historical Evangelical perspective on Islam. Despite their differences from other Traditionals, however, these outliers still had several things in common with other Traditionals in that they were highly engaged with Muslims, had Muslim friends, had read the Qur'an, and felt that Jesus was of great importance.

Diversity and Conflict

Most interviewees—both leaders and congregants—were comfortable being labeled Evangelicals. However, as discussed previously, a few were not, and some also disliked even the label of Christian, citing the baggage associated with it. Surprisingly, congregants were less comfortable owning the Evangelical label than were leaders; congregants were more likely to supply qualifiers and clarifications regarding their acceptance of the Evangelical designation. Usually, congregants added such qualifiers because they were aware of the stereotypes associated with Evangelicalism and wanted to clarify their positions in light of these stereotypes. As for leaders, they may have been less likely to add qualifiers to their acceptance of the Evangelical label, but this did not mean they had no reservations about the term. Many leaders genuinely identified with Evangelicalism, but others stated explicitly that they had placed themselves within the Evangelical fold so as to influence, critique, and speak into the Evangelical community. In other words, these leaders were primarily calling themselves Evangelicals so as to deliberately place themselves among the group they most want to influence and proselytize, namely, Evangelicals who adhere to the dominant historical Evangelical perspective on Islam.

More leaders than congregants were engaged with Muslims. But this was not surprising, as I chose Evangelical leaders specifically based on their engagement with the topic of Islam. I also chose congregations that were engaged with Muslims, but my congregant interviewees represented a mix of people, including some who had never engaged with Muslims before. Although leaders' levels of engagement with Muslims did not correlate with their position on the Progressive-Traditional spectrum, congregants' levels of engagement with Muslims *did* correlate with their position on the spectrum.

Leaders and congregants agreed that there is significant internal division within Evangelicalism on the topic of Islam. Those involved with "missions" to Muslims seem to have perceived the depth of these differences more fully. Congregational interviewees and leaders alike pointed to fear and ignorance about Islam and/or Muslims as significant contributors to division. Unlike the leaders—who generally described conflicting views of Islam by stepping back, using a macro perspective, and speaking of a "continuum" or "spectrum" of views among Evangelicals— many congregants spoke at a micro level, contrasting their views with those of their family members or coworkers. In general, most congregants and leaders who perceived Islam more positively viewed themselves as more embattled against other Evangelicals who perceived Islam more negatively than they viewed themselves as embattled against Muslims. But leaders who saw Islam more negatively discussed differences regarding different methods of engaging Muslims with less combative rhetoric; and many viewed these differences positively as useful differences within the "body of Christ," as the different emphases could more effectively communicate the Gospel to Muslims.

Although congregants and leaders generally leaned politically conservative or politically liberal, the majority in both groups avoided extremes in their political perspectives. This majority expressed pros and cons relating to both the Democratic and Republican Party positions on various social and economic issues. It usually took a number of follow-up questions for both leaders and congregants to express a bias to the political left or the political right. Although a small number identified strongly with either the Democratic or Republican Party, most interviewees, especially leaders, appeared not to want to align themselves with one side or the other; most preferred to present themselves as "center" or "moderate." In this way, they were actively chipping away at the stereotype suggesting that Evangelicals have sold out to the Republican Party. Perhaps the heightened political tensions due to the 2016 presidential election caused interviewees to err on the side of toning down their political stances. Regardless of the reason, the overall tendency toward political moderation in my sample is a sign that Evangelicals in the urban southern United States, both leaders and congregants, are not bound to a political party and thus are not the clichéd unreflective right-wingers that the stereotype of Evangelicalism in the United States portrays.

In terms of awareness of the heated missiological debates that occur among Evangelicals, leaders were more knowledgeable than congregants. Specifically, only half of the congregational interviewees had heard the term "Chrislam" before—a considerably smaller ratio than among the leadership interviewees, where all but two had heard of the Chrislam debate. Among those familiar with the term, there was significant disagreement about its utility. About one-third of leaders felt the criticisms implied in the term were illegitimate and therefore opposed usage of the term, whereas just over half of congregants felt the same. This higher ratio among congregants is presumably due to the fact that Mercy congregants were aware that their own congregation has been accused of promoting Chrislam because of the teachings they incorporate into their QAC conference. (The QAC conference, discussed in Chapter 5, presents Christians and Muslims as being on equal footing in pursuing the Kingdom of God, rather than presenting Christians as being a step ahead in the journey toward the kingdom. This is a teaching that many Evangelicals who align with the dominant historical Evangelical position on Islam vehemently dispute.) Whereas the leaders generally opposed the usage of the term "Chrislam" either because they felt the term had been misapplied or because they were skeptical about the motives of those using the term, some of the congregants disagreed with the term because their leaders had been accused of promoting Chrislam, and the congregants knew this was not a compliment. However, congregants were as a whole less knowledgeable about what the term might mean or where it came from than were the leaders. Those who disagreed with the terms often ascribed ulterior motives and bad intentions to those who find the term to have important utility in guarding against heresy. As for those on the other side of the debate, half of the leaders believed that the criticisms implied in the term "Chrislam" are legitimate, that Chrislamic missiological approaches are a threat, and that the term therefore does have utility. Just under half of the congregants who were familiar with the term felt the same. The leaders who felt that the term "Chrislam" had utility were overall more passionate and less moderate about their views than were the congregants who took the same position. Specifically, although the congregants stated disagreements with the methods and ideas of the so-called promoters of Chrislam, they were even more likely than the leaders to nuance their statements by acknowledging the genuineness and good intentions of those Evangelicals who promote so-called Chrislamist ideas.

Twenty-four leaders (of twenty-nine) and nine congregants (of forty-eight) had read the Qur'an in its entirety. An additional four leaders and thirty-three congregants had read at least portions of the Qur'an. Only one leader and six congregants had not read any of the Qur'an. Thus, leaders had had more exposure to the Qur'an than congregants, who were less well-versed in the Islamic holy book. Most leaders, and some congregants, agreed that the teachings about Jesus in the Qur'an and the Bible have striking similarities (a finding perhaps surprising to those who view Evangelicals as uneducated about Islam). While these similarities led some leaders to feel that the Qur'an can be treated as a light pointing to the divinity of Jesus, others were not willing to even entertain the notion that the Qur'an could be used to share the true Christ. Leaders were more likely to bring up theological similarities and/or differences between the Qur'an and the Bible than were the congregants. Aside from divisions between leaders and congregants on views of the Qur'an, there was also at least one significant gender difference: women, whether leaders or congregants, were more likely to point to verses in the Qur'an that violated their sense of human rights, especially verses regarding the treatment of women, whereas men were more likely to highlight verses focused on theological differences between the two religions. Even some women who had not read the Qur'an talked about verses they had *heard* were unfair to women, and they shared their feelings that if such verses really were in the Qur'an, the implications would be horrible for Muslim women. In this way, the women seemed to highlight "ethical concerns" about the Qur'an, while men seemed more concerned with whether or not there was "truth" in the Qur'an.

Interviewees were divided over how to view Muhammad. About half of the leaders and half of the congregants spoke positively about Muhammad; the other half spoke comparatively negatively. Those with a positive view of Muhammad described him variously as a great ethical leader, a speaker of truth, or even a prophet with a message from God. Others with a more negative view described Muhammad as delusional, violent, greedy, or selfish, especially during the second part of his ministry, the Medinan period. Thus, Muhammad seemed to be a polarizing figure for Evangelicals. Among most interviewees who viewed Muhammad more positively (and who therefore deviated from the dominant historical Evangelical perspective), talking about Muhammad seemed to produce discomfort and short, guarded responses. These leaders were especially sensitive to the fact that expressing a positive view of Muhammad could be controversial. Some leaders expressed concern about their response to the question of Muhammad "getting out" to others (which may mean their response to the question of Muhammad is situational and possibly censored). Most congregants did not seem as aware of the debate on the prophethood of Muhammad and thus were less aware that their opinions about Muhammad might be controversial. But though a number of interviewees indicated discomfort about discussing the subject, there were those, both leaders and congregants, who were willing to express their honest opinion, uncensored, whether endorsing or criticizing (though most individuals in this category were critical of Muhammad).

The majority of leaders as well as the majority of congregants described both pros and cons related to interfaith dialogue, but most leaned toward skepticism. Specifically, fourteen leaders (of twenty-nine) and twenty-seven congregants (of forty-eight) were mostly skeptical, though still open to the benefits of interfaith dialogue. Ten leaders and fifteen congregants saw mostly benefits, but some were still able to critique the endeavor. Overall, the majority of leaders I interviewed described wanting to engage with Muslims, particularly those whose views aligned with the dominant historical view of Islam, but not in a "wishy-washy" or "superficial" kind of way. Although the majority expressed both pros and cons about interfaith dialogue, there were numerous influential leaders and congregants who had more one-sided opinions. Some of these leaders and congregants were enthusiastic about interfaith dialogue and expressed no skepticism of the endeavor.

These individuals talked about "listening and learning" from Muslims, and they spoke of the need to overcompensate for the damage that they perceived American Evangelicals have done by going into interfaith situations lacking humility and lacking a desire to understand either the Muslim culture or the truth that Muslims can offer for the Evangelical understanding of faith. Meanwhile, a few other leaders and congregants expressed wholly negative views of interfaith dialogue and were unable to see any positive aspects. Among leaders, the most negative views on public interfaith dialogue with Muslims came from leaders from the Middle East, whereas in the congregations, the most negative views came from congregants who were older, were more closely aligned with historical Evangelicalism, and had lower engagement with Muslims. This is certainly a curious mix of individuals who were critical of interfaith dialogue with Muslims: Middle Eastern Evangelical leaders (some former Muslims) who have spent most of their lives living among Muslims, combined with older Southern American Evangelical congregants who had low levels of personal engagement with Muslims.

All but seven leaders had heard of the ACW interfaith initiative, whereas only about one-quarter of congregational interviewees had heard of it. This demonstrates that even though the initiative was the largest Christian-Muslim interfaith peace initiative in existence at the time of my study, it was largely a top-level initiative that did not—for the most part—reach down to the congregational level. Even among the congregants who had heard of the ACW initiative, very few felt knowledgeable enough to comment on it. Moreover, some leaders did not recollect enough of the details of the initiative to feel comfortable making a judgment on it. In total, ten leaders expressed a positive view of ACW. These supporters felt that the document could improve relationships between members of the two faiths, in spite of what they saw as the document's theological imperfections. These individuals exemplify a more pluralistic and less rigid movement within Evangelicalism that is more willing to compromise, and less likely to find it necessary to let one or two issues interfere with nurturing multicultural relationships. In this way, even though they often used traditional Evangelical moral authority terminology when reflecting on the ACW, they ultimately appealed to a progressive form of moral authority that is situational and that overrode their theological disagreements and affirmed the initiative. By contrast, eight leaders expressed a negative view of ACW. Most of those who had unfavorable views tended to have a greater interest in apologetics and defense of truth than in relationship building or in participating in interfaith dialogue from the posture of a listener/learner. In this way, they confirm some of the stereotypes believed of Evangelicals, namely, that Evangelicals value right beliefs over an agreeable existence with others. As with those critical of interfaith dialogue, those most critical of the ACW initiative were former Muslims.

A recurring theme throughout the previous chapters is that interviewees' involvement with IMs is correlated with their opinions on key topics related to Islam and Muslims. As explored in Chapter 2, IMs are movements that encourage "believers in Christ" from Muslim backgrounds to remain a part of their Muslim communities in a cultural sense and sometimes even in a religious sense as well. I found affiliation with IMs to help explain the outliers on the

Progressive-Traditional spectrum who held stances out of step with dominant historical Evangelical thinking on Islam while still maintaining a traditional stated and evidential moral authority. All such outliers were supportive of IMs. They appealed to traditional Evangelical moral authorities, but unlike others in the traditional category on the Progressive-Traditional spectrum, these outliers were careful not to make unprompted negative judgments about Muhammad or the Qur'an, mostly steered clear of talk of terrorism, spoke about Islamic ideas with reverence, and strove not to make generalizations regarding Islam. In fact, when discussing Islamic beliefs, they ended up instead critiquing Evangelicals. This commonality appears to show that these IM supporters feel more embattled against Evangelicals than against Muslims. These individuals became strongly emotional in response to my questions about Chrislam, many even seeming angry and sometimes sarcastic when speaking of Christian leaders who find the term "Chrislam" useful. IM supporters also tended to have a mindful focus on living out one's faith in accordance with culture, criticized certain aspects of Western culture, and were suspicious of anything labeled "Christian" or "Christianity." In other words, these outlier individuals were critical of Christianity from within the fold of Evangelicalism (see also Yancey and Quosigk, 2021).

Conclusion

The findings I have presented in this chapter, like the findings presented in Chapters 4 and 5, illustrate the complexities of Evangelicalism and of Evangelical thought on Islam. On issues of moral authority, politics, and Islam, and on questions regarding moderate, compromising, or extremist tendencies among Evangelicals in my sample, I have detailed important variations within the different categories on the Progressive-Traditional spectrum, and between the leadership and congregational sample. The lack of internal cohesiveness I have described, and the moderate tendencies of some I have uncovered within the sample, shows that Evangelicalism is diverse. The intra-Evangelical conflicts I have highlighted demonstrate that talk of Evangelicalism as a monolithic bloc of Republican voters who hate Muslims should be corrected and the conversation broadened to include the wider range of beliefs and opinions that exist within the Evangelical fold. The implications of my empirical findings will be developed more fully in the following and final chapter.

Chapter 7

MAKING SENSE OF THE CONFLICT

WHERE DO WE GO FROM HERE?

I am a great advocate of the constitutional right to freedom of speech. This means that abusive or insulting speech, I think, needs to be protected speech. The court has ruled that over and over again. The Ku Klux Klan people, Nazis, American flag burners, have the right to freedom of expression even though we may not like what they say. Similarly, I think that people who say things that Muslims may find insulting or hateful, is protected free speech, even if one would condemn the person for saying such a thing.

—Kevin, Christian apologist

I believe there are limits to free speech, and I believe there is a difference between free speech and hate speech. . . . I think our country has to come to terms with the fact that just because we believe in free speech and the First Amendment doesn't mean that we allow all speech. Some free speech is actually hateful and hurtful, so I believe these things about the draw Muhammad contest [referencing the Muhammad Art Exhibit and Contest of 2015 in Texas] and stuff, I believe that is hate speech; I believe it needs to be prevented by the government. Yes, I do.

—Oliver, Evangelical nonprofit leader

Introduction

This study has made both empirical and conceptual contributions to understanding Evangelicalism in the United States, challenging common stereotypes and assumptions. Empirically, the data demonstrate the diversity and conflict Evangelicals are experiencing among themselves on a wide range of issues related to Islam. Conceptually, I have created a new Progressive-Traditional spectrum that pushes beyond a binary division between progressive and traditional moral authorities. This spectrum is an analytical tool that advances Hunter's culture wars distinction between progressivism and orthodoxy. It also enables more accurate and complex descriptions of what I call "hybrid identities"—that is, identities that appeal to a mixture of both progressive and traditional sources of moral authority. In addition, I have contributed methodologically to Hunter's approach to moral authority by developing a new analytical tool that distinguishes between an individual's stated moral authority and evidential moral authority—how they say they make moral decisions, and how they actually think while making moral decisions. Both of my advancements—my development of the Progressive-Traditional spectrum and my distinction between stated and evidential moral authority—help to explain the empirical richness and diversity I have uncovered within Evangelicalism.

Ultimately, this research affirms the utility of Hunter's moral authority argument embedded in his 1991 book *Culture Wars* and in his subsequent thought since its introduction (Hunter and Nedelisky, 2020; Hunter, 2019, 1994; Hunter and Fiorina, 2007; Hunter and Wolfe, 2006b). This project also found Evangelicals to be drawn to either a progressivist impulse that reasons with personal experience and subjective intuition or a traditionalist impulse that reasons with a commitment to divine revelation. This affirmation—demonstrated in this work—of Hunter's moral authority argument in contemporary Evangelicalism is useful and validates the appropriateness of using his theory, now four decades after its original appearance in US society. However, my research also refines his thesis by arguing that the majority of Evangelical leaders in my study—the figures Hunter and others predicted would be most polarized—are for the most part not congregating on the extreme Evangelical right or the extreme Evangelical left, but rather have a moderate hybrid identity, in the sense that they responded to question using both progressive and traditional reasoning. As a group, the leaders in my study demonstrated more polarization and less hybridization in their identities than did congregants, suggesting that, yes, leaders are more extreme than congregants. But as a group, leaders are still less extreme than generally believed.

Taken holistically, this research demonstrates that some Evangelical leaders and congregants are still working out how they should think about Islam and how their faith should compel them to act toward Muslims, particularly as they desire to appear tolerant and accepting due to intensifying pressures of an increasingly pluralistic society. My study also implies that there is greater potential for Evangelical engagement with Islam and Muslims than commonly supposed, as this form of engagement is already happening on the ground in various places. This research is relevant to Evangelicals, Muslims, policymakers, academics, interfaith practitioners, and other stakeholders concerned with understanding the changing religious landscape in the United States, wherein the number of people following the Islamic religion is expected to double by 2050 (Pew, 2016).

This chapter is organized as follows. First, I present my findings in relation to how they address my research objectives. I highlight five most significant findings: (1) Evangelicals hold diverse views on Islam; (2) Evangelicals are not unified in response to the "threat" of Islam; (3) Evangelicals are more progressive than they realize; (4) moral authority largely correlates with views on issues related to Islam; and (5) with respect to moral authority, most Evangelicals have hybrid identities. Throughout, I compare and contrast data from leaders and congregants. Next, I proceed addressing why this research is meaningful and important. I explain how my findings contribute to the academic study of moral authority and identity, to Evangelical-Muslim relations, and to methodologies for social scientists. I then consider the limitations of my study and directions for future research. Finally, I consider how this study might be helpful to policymakers, interfaith practitioners, Muslims, and Evangelicals themselves.

Findings

My research project was guided by three distinct objectives: (1) to answer the questions, "What are Evangelical attitudes on the topic of Islam?" and "How are Evangelicals dialoguing about Islam?"; (2) to determine the extent to which Evangelicals are reacting to Islam with increased internal cohesion (an objective meant as a test of Christian Smith's subcultural identity theory, which predicts that Evangelicals will band together against a perceived external threat); and (3) to determine the manner in which interviewees' descriptions of their highest moral authorities elucidate divergent Evangelical attitudes on topics such as interfaith dialogue with Muslims, politics, Muhammad, the Qur'an, missiology, and engagement with Muslims (an objective meant as a test of James Hunter's moral authority argument, which holds that individuals exhibit views of moral authority that align with one of two "polarizing impulses"—either toward orthodoxy or toward progressivism).

I addressed my research objectives by employing qualitative methods. I interviewed a range of Evangelical leaders who have prominent voices on Islam, and I also conducted interviews with Evangelical congregants from two different congregations that are actively engaged with the Muslim community, which left me with seventy-two rich interviews in total. These methods offered me the data I needed to gain a detailed understanding of my interviewees' moral authorities and to conduct an in-depth analysis of intra-Evangelical conflict on Islam. While my observer role during the fieldwork was supplementary to the interviewer role, the field notes I garnered provided useful information that was helpful in backing up or challenging participants' interview responses.

My analysis of the two groups (leaders and congregants) together produced five major findings. Before I list my findings, it is important to note that because my study was both small and relatively focused (mostly including Evangelicals who are engaged with Islam and/or Muslims), I am not able to determine of the extent to which my findings might be reflected in US Evangelicals as a whole. The five findings discussed here are specific to Evangelicals in my study. Thus, when I generalize, I am generalizing about the findings within my study of Evangelicals.

Finding One: Evangelicals Hold Diverse Views on Islam

The first objective of my research was to answer the questions, "What are Evangelical attitudes on the topic of Islam?" and "How are Evangelicals dialoguing about Islam?" The diversity of Evangelical views on Islam was important to explore because of the dominant stereotyping of Evangelicals as a narrow-minded, monolithic, and ignorant group who reject, judge, fear, or even hate Muslims.

In spite of that dominant popular narrative, I found Evangelicals' attitudes regarding Islam, among both leaders and congregants, to be incredibly diverse. I also found the ways in which Evangelicals talked about Islam to be extremely varied: some of my Evangelical interviewees talked about Islam with admiration while heavily critiquing Christianity (particularly those strongly affiliated with IMs as well as Progressives); others saw little to admire in Islam and outright condemned many of its core beliefs; still others fell between these two stances.

I found that some Evangelicals viewed Islamic beliefs as largely distinct from and not overlapping with Christian beliefs. These interviewees often felt their own beliefs were more trustworthy than the beliefs they considered Muslims to hold. This was an expected finding that in many ways confirms the stereotype that portrays Evangelicals as rigid biblicists—looking down on beliefs they believe to be heretical. However, unexpectedly, I also found a substantial number of interviewees who viewed Islamic beliefs as very closely connected to Christianity. While I knew there were some within the Evangelical fold who held more accommodating views toward Islamic beliefs (e.g., believing that both faith groups ultimately are praying to the same God), I was not aware of exactly how closely connected some Evangelicals feel to Islamic beliefs (e.g., in their acceptance of the Islamic belief in Muhammad's status as a prophet, in their view of the Qur'an as containing God's truth, in their perception that Christians and Muslims are on equal footing in pursuing the kingdom of God, in their condemnation of Christianity and their high view of Islam, etc.). Although I anticipated diversity in the interview responses, the extent of the diversity surpassed my expectations.

Finding Two: Evangelicals Are Not Unified in Response to the Islamic "Threat"

The seventh proposition of Christian Smith's subcultural identity theory holds that a group will lay aside their differences and become more strongly united in the presence of an external threat, and his view is shared by other theorists who promote a strong version of the ingroup/outgroup hypothesis. This brings me to the second objective of my project: to test the ingroup/outgroup hypothesis embedded in Smith's subcultural identity theory and determine the extent to which Evangelicals are banding together and reacting cohesively to the "threat" of Islam.

Addressing this objective, the second major finding from my project is that, contra Smith, Evangelicals are not reacting to Islam with cohesion; they are largely not banding together or laying aside differences in light of the threat of Islam. Rather, the Evangelicals in my study were in conflict with each other over the subject of Islam, a reality they themselves acknowledged. Almost all leaders and congregants in my sample spoke of deep divisions within the Evangelical fold regarding Islam. Leaders generally described conflicting views of Islam by stepping back, using a macro perspective, and speaking of a "continuum" or "spectrum" of views among Evangelicals, while congregants spoke at a micro level, contrasting their views with those of their family members or coworkers. This lack of cohesion within Evangelicalism was particularly evident in views around the nature of Islam (e.g., whether interviewees viewed Islam more as a cultural form or as a false and dangerous religion). Disunity was also reflected in missiological disagreements around contextualization (e.g., to what degree interviewees believed it was appropriate to maintain religious beliefs and practices associated with another religion and still follow Christ). Leaders were more knowledgeable of the heated missiological debates on Islam than were congregants. Surprisingly, I found that Evangelicals who deviated from the dominant historical Evangelical perception of Islam were more likely to critique rival Evangelicals who adhered to the dominant historical positions than they were to critique Muslims. Similarly, regardless of whether they viewed Islam positively or negatively, interviewees tended to perceive themselves—to varying degrees—as embattled against fellow Evangelicals who hold different perspectives on Islam. Among many interviewees who viewed Islam more favorably, the feeling of embattlement against fellow Evangelicals was stronger than any sense of embattlement against Muslims. In other words, some Evangelicals viewed other Evangelicals to be more of a threat than Muslims. These findings run completely contrary to the ingroup/outgroup theory: the presence of a Muslim "threat" appears to have resulted in more conflict than cohesion.

Finding Three: Evangelicals Are More Progressive than They Realize

Hunter's moral authority argument holds that individuals exhibit views of moral authority that align with one of two "polarizing impulses"—toward either orthodoxy (which I refer to instead as "traditionalism" and which reasons based on divine authority and revelation for moral authority) or progressivism (which draws moral authority from personal experience and subjective intuition). Thus, the third objective of my project was to determine the extent to which interviewees' highest moral authorities might explain divergent Evangelical attitudes on topics such as interfaith dialogue with Muslims, politics, Muhammad, the Qur'an, missiology, and engagement with Muslims.

My first step in pursuing this objective was to analyze interviewees' moral authorities using both stated analyses (based on where interviewees claim to draw moral authority for their beliefs) and evidential analyses (based on the types of moral authority interviewees actually appealed to when they explained their reasoning for their beliefs). I then used the evidential results to place all interviewees on a spectrum from progressive to traditional. I found that many interviewees showed a substantial difference between their stated moral authority and their evidential moral authority, resulting in quite different placements on the Progressive-Traditional spectrum than if placed based on stated moral authority alone. Specifically, I found that when I asked interviewees directly about their personal moral authorities, most leaders and congregants claimed to have traditional moral authorities, including God, Jesus, Holy Spirit, the Bible, or some combination of these. (Leaders listed "the Bible" as their moral authority significantly more often than did congregants. Congregants were slightly more likely to list "God" as a moral authority than were the leaders.) However, when answering questions not directly related to moral authority (questions on Islam and politics), many leaders and congregants failed to reference traditional Evangelical moral authorities as they articulated their reasoning and positions.

Thus, the third major finding of my study is that Evangelicals tend to fall farther to the left on the Progressive-Traditional spectrum based on evidential analysis than when they are categorized based on their own statements about themselves. This suggests that most interviewees' moral authorities are more progressive than they themselves realize or feel comfortable expressing outright. This finding lines up with the work of Aune (2006) who found Evangelical women claiming to shape their marriages according to the Bible were actually involved in practices reflective of their less religious peers, demonstrating that factors other than the Bible were exerting a significant influence on their marital habits, despite their statements to the contrary. In addition, this finding can also be connected to Stringer's "coping religion," which he defines as that which most people turn to in order to cope with life (related to "evidential" moral authority) and can be contrasted with "transforming religion" which is where there should be a change of lifestyle connected to religious belief where the theological belief is paramount (related to stated moral authority) (2011). The fact that most interviewees' moral authorities are more progressive than they themselves realize or feel comfortable expressing outright also lines up with the work of Thomas and Olson (2012a, 2012b), which found Evangelical elites today are shifting from orthodox reasoning and toward more progressive reasoning when constructing arguments about homosexuality, and the findings of Thomas, which similarly found Evangelicals are increasingly drawing from sources outside of their own explicitly religious tradition to inform their moral vision (Thomas, 2013). Even if this shift is occurring, my findings suggest that many Evangelicals prefer to portray themselves as more traditionally aligned than they are in practice.

Finding Four: Moral Authority Largely Correlates with Views on Issues Related to Islam

As reviewed earlier, my third objective was to determine the extent to which interviewees' highest moral authorities could account for divergent Evangelical attitudes on topics related to Islam. The first aspect of addressing this objective was to identify interviewees' moral authorities; the second aspect was to determine the extent to which interviewees' authorities correlated with their views on Islam. Regarding this latter aspect, I found that in the majority of cases, interviewees' highest moral authorities—as derived from the evidential analysis—were indeed often correlated with their views on Islam. Specifically, interviewees who were to the traditional side on the Progressive-Traditional spectrum of moral authority were more likely to hold views that were aligned with the dominant historical Evangelical perspective on Islam (in other words, they were more likely to view

Islam as a false and dangerous religion). Conversely, interviewees who leaned progressive on the Progressive-Traditional spectrum of moral authority were more likely to hold views that deviated from that dominant historical perspective (e.g., they were likely to have an elevated view of Islam, viewing it more as a cultural form than a false religion). In this way, my research affirms the utility of Hunter's moral authority argument: consistent with his theory, the Evangelicals in my sample were drawn either to a progressivist impulse that reasons based on personal experience and subjective intuition or to a traditionalist impulse that reasons with a commitment to divine revelation (see also Yancey and Quosigk, 2021). And in the majority of cases, interviewees' moral authority placement aligned with their views on Islam. This was true of both the leaders and congregants.

However, my analysis chapters gave considerable space to discussing outliers (cases when an individual's moral authority did not accurately correlate with his or her specific opinions on Islam). These outliers show that, in a minority of cases, Evangelical interviewees sometimes appealed to the same moral authority yet came to very different conclusions regarding issues related to Islam, and possible reasons for this are explored in the analysis chapters. Thus, I find Hunter's moral authority argument highly illuminative, but not always perfectly accurate when using the evidential moral authority analysis. My findings were conclusive enough, however, to state that moral authority is a helpful predictor of views on Islam.

Finding Five: Most Evangelicals Have Hybrid Identities with Respect to Moral Authority

The fifth major finding of my study is that most Evangelicals have hybrid identities with respect to moral authority. When I looked at Evangelical opinions about Islam through the lens of moral authority, I found the majority of the Evangelicals I interviewed had a hybrid identity in terms of their *evidential* moral authority. This means they appealed to a mixture of both traditional Evangelical moral authorities and progressive authorities. In fact, the number of individuals who fell into this hybrid category prompted me to create two new categories in addition to the binary options of traditional or progressive: the Progressive-Traditional category (those who primarily lean toward the progressive side but incorporate significant traditional authority) and the Traditional-Progressive category (those who lean toward the traditional side but regularly employ some progressive authority). A majority of interviewees were placed in either the Progressive-Traditional category or the Traditional-Progressive category. This tendency toward hybridization was evident among both the leadership and the congregants. However, as predicted by Hunter, leaders were more polarized than congregants.

Here it is important not to equate a hybrid moral authority with a hybrid view of Muslims. As just discussed, I found that an individual's moral authority was not always correlated with his or her view of Muslims. However, generally speaking, those with hybrid views of moral authority were in fact more likely to hold moderate views of Islam (seeing truth both in views that align with the dominant historical Evangelical perspective on Islam and in views that dissent from that dominant historical perspective).

Many of the discussions around US Muslim-Evangelical relations highlight the supposedly negative attitudes Evangelicals have toward Muslims (the debates are usually not sophisticated enough to differentiate between critiquing Islam and hating Muslims). But these debates seem to have obscured the very real impulses that some Evangelicals have toward a hybrid middle ground, somewhere between extreme traditionalism and extreme progressivism and toward moderate views on Islam, at least in how they express their reasoning for holding their various positions on issues relating to Islam and politics.

These five findings accomplished my three main research objectives by providing clear, substantial answers to all of the initial questions.

Value of the Data for Research Aim and Objectives

I have made both empirical and conceptual contributions to sociology that contribute to debates around conflict and identity studies on both the group and individual levels. Together these contributions fill gaps, further existing theories, and offer new conceptual tools and methodologies.

Conceptual Contributions

Conceptually, I have created a new Progressive-Traditional spectrum that pushes beyond the progressive/traditional binary typically used in moral authority discussions, allowing for more accurate and complex descriptions using what I call "hybrid identities"—that is, identities that appeal to a mixture of both progressive and traditional sources of moral authority. This new Progressive-Traditional spectrum has advanced conceptualizations of Evangelicalism in that it provides a tool that guards against the kind of simplistic stereotyping that has taken place in the past. Application of this tool in future studies could allow for more nuanced findings wherever the moral authority argument is employed.

My research has also provided an analytical tool (the "evidential moral authority analysis") that distinguishes between stated moral authority and evidential moral authority. Specifically, this tool can differentiate between the moral authority an individual *claims* to have versus the moral authority that the individual *actually* appeals to in reasoning about various subjects. This analytical tool could be applied both to previous qualitative projects concerned with understanding moral authority and to those forthcoming.

This "evidential moral authority analysis" has value in two senses. First, it builds a bridge between quantitative and qualitative methods, in that I established an individual's evidential moral authority by counting interviewees' usage of traditional moral authority terminology in their responses to questions regarding Islam and politics. Thus, the evidential moral authority analysis was quantifiable and could be analyzed by another researcher familiar with Evangelical references to the supernatural and yield the same results. Interviewees were then placed in evidential moral authority categories on the Progressive-Traditional spectrum based on these quantitative results and irrespective of their views on Islam. This process helped me guard against a common criticism of qualitative work, namely, that the researcher can simply select quotes that support their preferred conclusions.

Second, as discussed in Finding Three (*Evangelicals Are More Progressive than They Realize*), this evidential analysis allowed this study to transcend interviewees' self-characterizations. Had the study solely relied on interviewees' stated moral authorities, the results would show little variation. However, the use of evidential authority shows that when evaluating Evangelical perspectives, it is important to understand that the similarity found in Evangelicals' stated moral authorities does not mean that Evangelicals actually have similar moral authorities in practice. Although my interviewees *claimed* similar moral authorities, my evidential analysis revealed that interviewees' *actual* moral authorities varied considerably from one person to another. The variation in evidential moral authorities, in turn, helps to explain why there is significant variety in beliefs about Islam and approaches to Muslims.

In addition, in Chapter 2, I contribute to the broad conceptualization of Evangelical written matter by articulating at least five distinct genres of literature. In my examination of overtly Evangelical works published after 9/11 I categorized five distinct genres of literature: (1) autobiographical literature; (2) missional literature; (3) terrorism literature; (4) critiquing literature; and (5) eschatological literature. Within these five categories one can find a variety of attitudes toward Islam and this heterogeneity correlates with finding one, namely that "Evangelicals Hold Diverse Views on Islam."

Further, in Chapter 2, I also contribute a precise articulation of the historic, traditional Evangelical view of Muslims—that is, the view of Muslims that predominated among Evangelicals in Evangelicalism's earliest years. This serves as a benchmark from which to compare Evangelical perspectives. This is useful to historians and social scientists interested in how Evangelical views of Islam and Muslims have changed over time.

Contribution to Diversity Research

This work provides much-needed research in an area that previous scholarship has neglected. To date, the body of work on Evangelical Christianity and Islam within sociology is surprisingly limited. In particular, the internal variation among Evangelicals' viewpoints on Islam and Muslims has not been widely discussed in sociological literature. My study helps to fill this gap, adding to literature on Evangelicalism and diversity, Muslim-Evangelical relations, and perceptions of Islam in the West.

Dominant Western views of Evangelicalism often promote stereotypes of Evangelicalism, as acknowledged by a number of scholars (Shields and Dunn, 2016; Yancey, Reimer, and O'Connell, 2015; Bean, 2014; Guest et al., 2013;

Hutchinson and Wolffe, 2012; Needham-Penrose and Friedman, 2012; Elisha, 2011; Mitchell and Ganiel, 2011; Yancey, 2011; Hankins, 2009; Lindsay, 2007; Tobin and Weinberg, 2007; Marsden, 2006; Reimer, 2003; Smith, 1998; Noll, 1994). Evangelicals are often presented as a monolithic group with big, angry, unsubstantiated opinions, especially when it comes to Muslims. Some academic scholarship has even added to the narrative that depicts the views of Evangelicals to be uniquely less tolerant than other groups in the United States (Jung, 2012; Rhodes, 2012; Ahktar, 2011; Kalkan, Layman, and Uslander, 2009; Beyerlein and Hipp, 2005, 2006; Cimino, 2005; Putnam, 2000; Wilson and Janoski, 1995). This means that some view Evangelicals as having a wrongful fear or hatred of Islam and Muslims, adhering to a doctrine of "Islamophobia," stifling positive views of the Muslim community in America, and hindering Muslim progress in America.

My research helps to balance the academic literature by calling for a reassessment of these stereotyped perspectives on American Evangelicals. This reassessment is valuable for a number of reasons, but perhaps the most important reason is that the data clearly show that oversimplified portrayals of Evangelicals as monolithically hateful are simply false. The internal variation and discussion among Evangelicals about Islam and about the way that contemporary Evangelicals should relate to Muslims has been clearly articulated in this work. Acknowledgment of the complexity in Evangelical views of Islam in the United States is rarely, if ever, evident in popular and academic discourses. But my findings point to the need for a deeper and more complicated understanding of what self-proclaimed Evangelicals really think of Islam and how they really interact with Muslims. Recognition of the subtleties in the thinking of Evangelical leaders is especially important, because it can enable a more sophisticated cultural conversation about Evangelicals and their relationships to Muslims—particularly in light of the emphasis on leadership in the culture wars thesis.

Contribution to Ingroup/Outgroup Literature

This study's treatment of intra-Evangelical conflict on Islam adds to the body of literature related to Smith's subcultural identity theory, particularly Smith's formulation of the ingroup/outgroup hypothesis in his seventh proposition (Shkurko, 2015; Grillo, 2014; Jung, 2012; Rhodes, 2012; Merino, 2010; Kalkan, Layman, and Uslaner, 2009; Smidt, 2005; Duke, 1976; Stein, 1976; Kriesberg, 1973; Dahrendorf, 1964; Coser, 1956; Simmel, 1955; Sumner, 1907). In accordance with Smith's theory, it is likely the case that the Islamic "threat" is uniting some subcultures within Evangelicalism, and it may be that some previously separate intragroups are "banding together" and laying aside difference in pursuit of their goals; however, my research shows that the challenge of Islam has also spawned conflict among Evangelicals and created "us" and "them" tensions from within.

My research refines the ingroup/outgroup hypothesis by illustrating its limitations. In regard to group conflict, Smith holds that there is a common practice "among many religious (and secular) groups of rhetorically highlighting their disagreements and tensions with outgroups with whom they view themselves in conflict" (1998: 115). In other words, groups should frequently be calling attention to areas of differences with outgroups. But my findings demonstrate that Evangelicals in my sample who deviate from the dominant historical Evangelical perception of Islam are more likely to critique fellow Evangelicals who adhere to dominant historical Evangelical positions on Islam than they are to critique Muslims or Islam. As discussed in Chapters 4-6, Evangelicals in my sample who view Islam more positively are also more likely to praise Muslims or Islam than they are to praise Christianity or Evangelicalism. These findings do not reflect Smith's expected ingroup/outgroup rhetoric in relation to Islam; in fact, they suggest that internal differences between some Evangelicals are more significant than differences between some Evangelicals and Muslims.

Given these findings, I see value in the important work of Stein (1976), Kriesberg (1973), Coser (1956), and Simmel (1955), each of whom have articulated limitations of the ingroup/outgroup hypothesis. Of particular value are Coser's limitations, the first of which is that "the degree of group consensus prior to the outbreak of the conflict seems to be the most important factor affecting cohesion" (1956: 93). Coser also suggests that if changes within a "social system" bring contending parties within the system to hold different basic values (the basic values limitation), these types of conflicts will likely split the system itself, rather than bringing about greater unity in reaction to the external threat. These limitations of the ingroup/outgroup hypothesis, combined with an understanding of Hunter's culture wars thesis, prove fruitful in explaining the incohesive Evangelical response to Islam.

As outlined in Chapter 2, there is a long history of internal antagonistic tendencies between various Evangelical groups. This internal antagonism may have been sufficient to separate Evangelicals who hold beliefs that deviate from the dominant historical Evangelical perspective of Islam and to prompt the "deviants" to feel a greater sense of commonality with Muslim "outsiders" than with fellow Evangelicals. My research has demonstrated that the limitations of the ingroup/outgroup hypothesis are at work within Evangelicalism, and they can help explain why some Evangelicals have been able to reach out to accommodate a very disparate religion (Islam) and pursue partnerships with Muslims. These limitations of the ingroup/outgroup hypothesis, particularly Coser's "basic values" limitation, should continue to be explored. This limitation is of particular interest in the debate on how adaptation to outside cultures may or may not lead to a thriving "engaged orthodoxy" (i.e, a balance within the ingroup between engaging the broader culture while simultaneously holding fast to their core religious beliefs).

Contribution to Moral Authority Argument

My research also adds to the moral authority argument embedded within Hunter's culture wars hypothesis. Since the publication of *Culture Wars* four decades ago Hunter's main reflections on the phenomenon have concerned both the saliency of the battle among people in the United States as well as within public discourse and the ability, or lack of ability, of the "new moral science" (dependent on naturalism, realism, and scientific reductionism) to offer a meaningful foundation of morality

(2020). Hunter's continued thought regarding the culture war is substantial (Hunter and Nedelisky, 2020; Hunter, 2019, 1994; Hunter and Nedelisky, 2018; Hunter and Fiorina, 2007; Hunter and Wolfe, 2006b). My research affirms the contemporary utility of Hunter's moral authority argument by finding that Evangelicals are drawn either to a progressivist impulse (one that reasons with personal experience and subjective intuition) or to a traditionalist impulse (one that reasons with a commitment to divine revelation). In my sample, the majority of Evangelicals on the traditional end of the Progressive-Traditional spectrum held views of Islam and Muslims that largely aligned with the dominant historical Evangelical view of Islam. Likewise, the majority of Evangelicals on the progressive end of the Progressive-Traditional spectrum held views of Islam that mostly deviated from the dominant historical Evangelical view. Still, I found there to be a number of outliers: those who leaned progressive but who adhered to dominant historical Evangelical views of Islam or those who leaned traditional but who deviated from that dominant view.

Significantly, I found that most of the Evangelicals in my study were in fact not extreme in terms of their traditionalism or their progressivism. The fact that the majority of interviewees in my study held moderate identities—falling into hybrid categories—does not contradict Hunter's moral authority argument. First, although Hunter described a polarization between progressivism and orthodoxy (i.e., traditionalism), he also explicitly spoke of the "people somewhere in the middle," who draw from both the Enlightenment (i.e., progressive sources) and biblical sources (i.e., traditional sources) of moral understanding (1991: 132). In addition, Hunter acknowledged and addressed critics who claimed that he gave too much attention to divisiveness in American culture, did not give enough attention to moderating or unifying tendencies, or questioned the degree to which everyday Americans have polarized into warring sides (Adkins et al., 2013; Starks and Robinson, 2009; Thomson, 2010; Fiorina, Abrams, and Pope, 2008; Fischer and Hout, 2006; Greeley and Hout, 2006; Demerath, 2005; Clydesdale, 1997; Davis and Robinson, 1996a, 1996b, 1996c; DiMaggio et al., 1996; Wuthnow, 1996; Carroll and Marler, 1995; Billings and Scott, 1994). His response to these critics is of interest, as my findings bring up some concerns consistent with these critics' points.

Hunter, for his part, largely agreed with these critiques, noting that it is only minorities within the general public who are polarized. However, he posited that the presence of a moderate majority does not undermine his theory. Instead, he suggested that the polarized minority consists mostly of those in cultural leadership roles, and that it is among these elites who lead institutions and organizations that the culture war largely plays out. Still, he said, these polarized elites have significant influence on non-leaders. Thus, said Hunter, the polarized minority should not be underestimated in spite of the fact that their numbers are small.

Because my sample included both congregants and leaders, my research is able to shed light on the question of whether or not elites are indeed more polarized than the general population. In one way, my findings confirm the hypothesis that leaders are more polarized with respect to their moral authorities: I used the same analysis of stated and evidential moral authority on both leaders and congregants and found that the percentage of those who pulled toward the extreme ends of the spectrum was indeed greater among elites than among congregants. Still, the majority of leaders in my sample had moderate identities with respect to their moral authorities (meaning they fell in the category of Traditional-Progressive or Progressive-Traditional); less than half fell into the extreme categories of either Traditional or Progressive. Thus, my findings suggest that, yes, leaders are more extreme, but as a group they are perhaps less extreme than Hunter and others have suggested. This could also be due to the changing era in American history, an era in which university degrees are more achievable than ever and speaking without offense is a coveted quality. My elites were mostly highly educated and perhaps were prone to nuance, or even soften, their positions because of this, leaving them less staunch in opinion. Thus, leaders may be directing their discourse from positions that are not as staunchly extreme—in terms of their progressive or traditional views—as they once were. By identifying an example where a majority of elites demonstrate hybrid identities, this finding points to new directions for research looking at the role of elites in conflicts.

My use of the moral authority argument in exploring Evangelical views of Islam and Muslims also demonstrates the argument's advantage in transcending a study's political context. I was able to explore and analyze the root cause of differences between people—and in the fundamental assumptions that guide our perceptions of the world—through studying moral authority. One's moral authority matters and motivates, and directs how one views Islam, Muslims, interfaith dialogue, and politics, rather than vice versa. Therefore, the conclusions this book present should hold true even under different political circumstances.

My Findings in Consideration of Recent Arguments in the Study of Evangelicalism

This work shares some similarities with a number of recent works that have caught the attention of scholars of Evangelical Christianity. I explore some of these points of connections in the next few paragraphs, and in doing so, I articulate areas for further inquiry.

Steensland and Goff's *The New Evangelical Social Engagement* (2013) is a compilation of fourteen essays that ultimately argue that the US Evangelicals of today are more often viewed as tackling issues commonly associated with social justice—such as racial reconciliation and peacemaking—rather than refraining from these issues (the perception being that Evangelicals in the 1980s may have held back for fear of being labeled "liberals"). Ultimately, many of the contributors see this change positively; Stassen, for example, wrote in his final comments that Evangelicals are "recover[ing] a thicker Jesus" who will catalyze an increase in actions associated with social justice. My work affirms their findings in the sense that those whose views deviate from the dominant historical Evangelical positions on Islam are very likely to be actively engaged with issues of social justice in a way that does not necessitate them to push conversion to Christianity in order to better society. Those individuals are also more open to reasoning using social analysis derived from progressive sources of moral authority, such as material from non-Christian social scientists and humanists (rather than biblical hermeneutics). The movement toward progressive sources of moral authority is evident in my study, and even some individuals who held views that mostly align with the dominant historical Evangelical views on Islam were prone to incorporate progressive reasoning into their thinking. These findings comport with a greater willingness among Evangelicals to engage with social justice issues.

Steensland and Goff also argue that for Evangelicals, the decline of liberal mainline Protestantism has weakened the identity threat once associated with social justice–type concerns (e.g., the liberal Christians are no longer a threat because there are so few left). Thus, Evangelicals can more freely move into working toward specific social concerns that once were only promoted in liberal mainline Protestantism. I think this argument is quite interesting, although it leaves one to question how Evangelicals who are increasingly becoming preoccupied with the same sort of social concerns as mainline Protestants can manage not to end up in the same situation in which mainline Protestants find themselves now: in steep numeric decline and with little, if any, distinction between themselves and the non-Christian society at large. Steensland and Goff believe the answer "depends more on compelling voices, organizational infrastructure, and ideological innovation" of these new Evangelicals they describe. Interestingly, those factors are more related to "this-worldly" concerns, which reflect a progressivist source of moral authority. This is especially true of the notion of "ideological innovation," which holds that the understanding of truth (even biblical truth) and best practices is on an upward trajectory, and that the Christian faith is developing and flexible. This notion flows naturally into the views espoused by many in my study whose views on Islam deviate from the dominant historical Evangelical positions on Islam. In both cases, Evangelicals are able to embrace a departure from tradition because of their progressive moral authority and openness to a developing truth rather than a static one.

The New Evangelical Social Engagement also surveys how Evangelicalism has been influenced by its cultural context, a phenomenon that I articulate in Chapter 2 of this book. For instance, in the aftermath of desegregation and the sexual revolution, the cultural climate in the United States steadily shifted, as much of the elite—with the help of the media—dedicated significant energy to calling out perceived racism and bigotry. These accusations are usually leveled in such a way as to blur the lines between not agreeing with a specific belief and hating someone believing said belief. This means that an Evangelical critiquing Islam as an "evil and wicked religion"—as did Franklin Graham—is often equated to hating Muslims and being a racist. (Even though Muslim believers come from all parts of the world and make up various ethnicities, race and religion are not cleanly separated in the media.) Specifically, this work highlighted the ways in which some Evangelicals are softening their positions on Islam in order to appear tolerant and nonjudgmental when it comes to Muhammad, whom Muslims revere, and the Qur'an, which many Muslims believe to be the perfect words of Allah. Due to the increased cultural pressure to appear tolerant and accepting, for many Evangelicals "saving face" is not necessarily done solely in order to appear right before their God, but also to appear right before humanity, particularly those who would label them as intolerant, uncompassionate, or bigoted.

My work also lines up with that of Markofski in *New Monasticism and the Transformation of American Evangelicalism* (2015) in two important ways. First, we both draw attention to the inaccuracy of treating US Evangelicalism as a monolith. Markofski goes about this by arguing that Protestant neo-monasticism (which incorporates insights from Catholic, Eastern Orthodox, and Anabaptist communities into American Evangelicalism) is an important example of diversity within the Evangelical field. He finds neo-monasticism to be "dominated" within Evangelicalism, in the sense that it is less powerful than conservative Evangelicalism. Markofski argues that neo-monasticism fits alongside the Evangelical left and the emerging church in that all these groups are dominated within American Evangelicalism. He perceives the Christian right and mega-churches to make up conservatism and to be the more "dominant" wing of Evangelicalism. If there is sufficient variation within Evangelicalism to see dominating and dominated groups, the whole of Evangelicalism cannot be treated as a monolith, and in this rejection our works agree.

This leads to the second point of continuity between my work and that of Markofski: we find these "dominated" forms of Evangelicalism (in my work it is those whose views deviated from the dominant historical Evangelical views on Islam) to be insurgent, in that they intentionally work to be a voice of dissent within conservative Evangelicalism and position themselves in opposition to conservative Evangelicalism. Markofski found that by intentionally remaining involved with those they criticize, these dominated Evangelicals are able to preserve the parts of Evangelicalism they deem good while attempting to transform the parts they do not find favorable. This could be compared to how modernists worked within Evangelicalism during the Fundamentalist-Modernist divide of the nineteenth century. I have articulated many examples of how Evangelicals whose views deviated from the dominant historical Evangelical views on Islam found themselves more embattled with conservative Evangelicals than they did with Muslims. I also noted their desire to help conservative Evangelicals experience a paradigm shift away from "faulty thinking" about Islam and Muslims and toward the beliefs they themselves possess (a great example of this is the QAC conference put on by the Mercy congregation described in Chapter 5).

Hochschild's *Strangers in Their Own Land* (2018) is different from the other books explored in this section in that it is solely concerned with understanding a group, which, according to Hochschild, many social scientists do not: conservatives. The conservatives she studied have similarities with those Evangelicals in my study whose views on Islam were in alignment with the dominant historical positions. Hochschild, a self-described progressive sociologist from Berkeley, wanted to climb what she has termed the "empathy wall" in order to know the "other side"—specifically, the world of Tea Party Republicans and Conservative Evangelicalism in Louisiana. Her goal was to understand these people rather than explain them away as simply ignorant and malevolent. She found these Louisianans—even those who had personally suffered due to the environmental hazards associated with the oil and chemical companies in their area—to support the political right despite their understanding that more left-leaning political stances might help them by regulating these same companies that have had such a negative effect on their lives. Hochschild was surprised by this apparent contradiction and wanted to know why they would support these seemingly self-destructive policies. She found that their loyalty is given to the political right because they believe the policies of the right most closely align with the principles of God and support the traditional family. She shows how they choose to reject apparent material self-interest and instead opt for a sense of religious solidarity. They see the federal government as self-serving and condescending and would rather reject its benefits, remaining hopeful that their Christian Churches will help them. They would rather risk dying from cancer due to the negative environmental effects of these companies in their hometowns than vote for a political party they perceive to be godless.

In many ways, these individuals line up with those staunchly committed to traditional moral authority. Similar to my Evangelicals whose views align with the dominant historical positions on Islam (usually the Traditionals), they seem to hold a type of moral authority that does not equally value the flourishing of humanity and its environment, at least in the way usually understood by those leaning more left (e.g., the pollution and negative health effects caused by these companies are not the main concerns of these individuals). Rather, they hope to align their positions and votes with those they believe are most explicitly pro-God and pro-family. Both these individuals and my Evangelicals holding to the dominant historical views on Islam are willing to condone avoidable strife, suffering, or conflict on earth in order to remain faithful to the dictates of traditional moral authority, as they interpret them.

Jones's *The End of White Christian America* (2016) argues just that: white Christian Americans are losing their influence. His book was published mere months before the election of 2016, and Jones predicted that the Republican nominee would not claim the White House due to the perceived waning influence of white Christian Americans. He was wrong, and Donald Trump was elected to the presidency, which in some ways makes his argument less believable; however, the data set he uses does point to a steep decline in white Christians in America, suggesting that whites are projected to lose majority status by 2042. But more importantly for Evangelicals, he finds that white *Christians* are in decline, and he blames it on what he perceives to be Christianity's accommodation of slavery, apathy toward desegregation, political involvement in the closing decades of the twentieth century, and inadequacy in addressing issues such as lesbian, gay, bisexual, and transgender rights.

As evidence of this decline, he draws attention to the old Protestant structures in America, meant to be beacons of Christianity, now having completely different purposes from their founder's ambitions. For example, he references how the United Methodist building on Capitol Hill, once a strong Christian presence on Capitol Hill, began the mainline trajectory of decline, first by choosing to focus attention on peace and equality issues and now by renting part of its building to the Islamic Society of North America. I have also observed this shift in buildings during my time living abroad in Europe, specifically the conversion of churches into mosques, and it seems, according to Jones, there are trends of Christian real estate vanishing in the United States as well. This phenomenon is understandably perceived to be a sign of the decline of Christianity and its structures in America.

Here, Jones's *The End of White Christian America* and Steensland and Goff's *The New Evangelical Social Engagement*—taken together—lead me to continue asking whether or not progressive Christianity (represented by those in my study whose views deviate from the dominant historical view of Islam) has staying power. Steensland and Goff argue that the progressive Christianity's ability to survive depends on the success of the leadership of the Evangelical left, such as Brian McLaren, Shane Claiborne, David Gushee, Richard Cizik, Ronald Sider, and Jim Wallis. However, these are all white males, whose influence, Jones argues, is waning. If Jones's prediction is right, and white Christians are increasingly nearing extinction, then it is fair to ask whether or not Christianity will ultimately continue to bind these left-leaning individuals together, particularly considering their aversion to conservative Evangelicalism. Jones would likely argue that it will not. Perhaps progressives will deemphasize their affiliations with Christianity as a unifying cause (some already have) and rather overtly opt for something perceived to provide a more inclusive sense of purpose and community. A new study finds that those whose views deviate from the dominant historical Evangelical view of Islam (progressivists), particularly the leadership, rely on a more explicitly humanistic form of principles—a Humanistic Ethic of Social Justice—that positions itself in fierce opposition to conservative Christianity (Yancey and Quosigk, 2021).

Considering this book's connections to other recent publications on Evangelical Christianity places it into the context of the larger conversations taking place about the state of Evangelicalism. It demonstrates what larger trends this work may reflect and points out areas and questions that invite further exploration.

Limitations and Future Research

Though I am able to say that there was significant diversity within the group of Evangelicals with whom I spoke on the topic of Islam, the data set drawn was both small and relatively focused. In particular, I sought out Evangelicals who are engaged with Islam and/or Muslims. A limitation of my study is that I am not able to determine how much this diversity might be reflected in US Evangelicals as a whole. My research is a helpful basis for future research in that it suggests various possible positions that Evangelicals can take with respect to Islam, but additional quantitative and qualitative studies are needed to get a better idea of the prevalence of each of these various positions among US Evangelicals. However, it will be important to ask similar questions about Islam and Muslims as this study has and not to assume negative views based on their stated moral authority.

A second limitation of my study is that while I measured the degree to which interviewees made use of traditional Evangelical moral authority terminology, I was not able to know if and how my status as a researcher affected interviewees' frequency of use of such terminology. It is possible that some interviewees omitted certain references to their traditional Evangelical moral authority because they felt it might not be seen as credible by a researcher. While it would be difficult to conduct, a future study could compare Evangelical interviewees' usage of traditional Evangelical moral authority terminology when being interviewed by an academic from a secular institution with their usage when being interviewed by a popular, more traditional-leaning Evangelical magazine or media outlet.

Future research could more deeply explore how Evangelical relationships with Muslims vary depending on the specific form of Islam being practiced (Sunni, Shia, Sufi, Ahmadiyya, Ismaili, etc.). The term "Muslim" is used broadly in this research to encompass a vast variety of followers of Islam from different countries and cultures. It is possible that some of the disagreements within Evangelicalism on the topic of Islam and Muslims are disagreements based on the different forms of Islam Evangelicals are encountering (Azumah and Riddell, 2013). As McCallum recognized in his study of Evangelicals in the UK, when studying Evangelical views of Muslims and Islam one comes to find "that 'Muslims en masse' often serve as 'the Other' and thus is "utilized as it reflects what so often happens in real life" (2011: 35). Rasanayagam argued that one Muslim's "Islam" is different from every other Muslim's "Islam" and that when one tries to make Islam an object it automatically loses value and distorts reality (Quosigk, 2015). Clearly, there are multiple interpretations of Islam by Muslims. Thus, further research could examine Evangelicals' views of Islam and Muslims based on the type of Islam to which they have had the greatest exposure.

Another area for expansion would be to evaluate the validity of some of the most negative cultural impressions regarding Evangelical-Muslim relations. Devout Evangelicals are often categorized as extremists and/or fundamentalists within Western societies (Merritt, 2016; Gillum, 2013; Markay, 2013). These terms can insinuate that Evangelical Christians are committing acts of violence against Muslims in the United States today. It would be important to accurately measure this perception and pursue a qualitative study of the motivations and implications of Evangelical Christians who act violently toward Muslims, if indeed this is a problem in the United States. It is important to point out that I found no support for this during my research. A future study could examine how accurate this categorization of Evangelicals is. A case for reexamination of such characterizations may be furthered by my findings that show warmer views toward Muslims as a whole and many moderate and accommodating views of Islam within Evangelicalism.

The impact of race on Evangelicals' viewpoints on Islam could also be grounds for study. While I did interview Evangelicals from various ethnic backgrounds, I did not focus on the race of interviewees, for two reasons: first, because asking about race made me uneasy due to unpleasant personal experiences of being asked repeatedly by classmates "What are you?" (my "race" being perceptibly ambiguous) through my years in public education (personal reflexivity regarding race found in Appendix 2); and second, because the literature around moral authority does not highlight race as a factor that would push an individual toward one pole of moral authority or the other. However, the issue of how an Evangelical's "race" may affect his or her views of Islam and Muslims is certainly an area for further exploration. A number of academic and popular media outlets place much emphasis on studying race. A survey conducted by the Pew Research Center in 2014 found that "no other religious group is cooler toward Muslims than are white Evangelicals" (Pew, 2014). Race may be of even greater interest now than when the Pew survey was published, given the recent literature that has pointed to white Evangelicals, as opposed to Evangelicals of color, being the most supportive of President Donald Trump's policies—including policies that have significant implications for Muslims, such as Trump's ban on travel to the United States from certain Muslim-majority countries (Edgell, 2017). This encouraged sociologists to continue to explore the role of race in the 2016 election of Donald Trump. Marti postulated that the travel restrictions were tied to "racial bias" on the part of the Trump Administration and that Trump's views on terrorism and immigration are related to his acceptance of Christian nationalism, whose ideal type Marti characterizes as white (Marti, 2020). Whitehead and Perry also connect Christian nationalism with race and define it as a "cultural framework" that ties religious identity with race, nativity, citizenship, and political ideology, arguing that it was an important predictor of whether or not an Evangelical voted for Donald Trump in 2016 (2020: x). Edgell (2017) argues that the white Evangelical voters who supported Trump in the 2016 election were partially motivated by "racial resentment and xenophobia," and while I did not find evidence that this was the case with interviewees from my sample, it would be worthwhile to examine how the race of Evangelicals affects their views of Muslims. In addition, it would be insightful to examine the level to which Evangelicals perceive Muslims racially and/or by their religious beliefs, and which of the two factors most strongly informs their differentiation of Muslims from non-Muslims in America. Judging from my study, I would lean toward the latter being accurate (differentiating by religious beliefs rather than race).

Interestingly, I found the interviewees of color who were from Muslim-majority countries to hold the harshest views on Islam and Muslims. McCallum, in his study of Evangelicals and Muslims in the UK, also found the Christian participants who were from a Muslim background and "who report[ed] suffering to different degrees at the hands of their former co-religionists . . . tend[ed] to a more negative response" toward Islam (2011: 293). McCallum linked his finding with the work of historian Thomas Kidd highlighting that converts out of Islam provide "the inflammatory characterizations of Islam" (McCallum, 2011: 294; Kidd, 2009: 147). In relation to my study, a comparative study of white American Evangelicals and their views of Islam and Muslims with the views of Evangelicals from Muslim-majority countries would help elucidate this finding.

Implications of the Research: Sociological Considerations

The research in this book has meaningful implications for a number of different groups. One valuable insight is into the barriers that prevent some Evangelicals from working together in interfaith dialogue. Evangelicals who expressed the most unqualified enthusiasm for interfaith dialogue fell primarily on the left end of the Progressive-Traditional spectrum, and they were often critical of the dominant historical Evangelical positions regarding Islam that have tended to focus largely on differences between the two religions. This suggests that the interfaith movement has been most successful in bringing in support from more progressive Evangelicals who focus on similarities between Evangelicals and Muslims. However, many Evangelical leaders holding historically dominant traditional Evangelical beliefs are still in many ways alienated from interfaith movements. My research on this latter group of Evangelical leaders suggests that they are interested in engaging with Muslims and are trying in their own way to accommodate Muslims. For example, several reported having altered their tone and forcefulness to be more candid and expressive in their formal debates and in their personal encounters with Muslims. They claim these changes reflect their effort to better appeal to the Muslims with whom they are interacting by matching the more outspoken style typically appreciated by Muslims and by intentionally rejecting the cultural placidity of many Westerners that they understand Muslims to find off-putting or weak.

However, these types of Evangelicals, who fall mostly to the traditional end of the Progressive-Traditional spectrum, and who often perceive significant differences between Evangelicalism and Islam, typically do not feel that their views are appreciated in interfaith dialogue forums. The main reason for this feeling, they report, is that they see interfaith dialogue as largely refraining from honestly discussing differences between faith groups. Thus, there are two perspectives on how interfaith dialogue should be conducted, with one perspective emphasizing the need to discuss commonalities and the other emphasizing the need to acknowledge differences. In order to achieve more inclusive dialogue, it would be useful to bring in more Evangelicals who lean to the right on the Progressive-Traditional spectrum. Perhaps the best way to do this is to be more open to dialoguing about differences.

For Evangelical interfaith practitioners, this research points to a need to sharpen the Evangelical understanding of what interfaith dialogue is and to grow in their ability to articulate whether and how their Evangelical faith supports the various forms of interfaith dialogue. Since Evangelicals in my study were significantly less likely to use traditional moral authority terminology when speaking about interfaith dialogue than they were when speaking about other topics (such as Muhammad, the Qur'an, and the debate around Chrislam), this suggests that interviewees were either less willing or less able to articulate how their view of God impacted their views on interfaith dialogue. It is possible that their beliefs and philosophies surrounding interfaith dialogue were less established or refined than their other opinions, which may reinforce stereotypes about interfaith dialogue as "the preserve of an academic elite" (McCallum, 2011: 90). This should signal to active interfaith practitioners the importance of engagement regarding the purposes, value, and methods of interfaith dialogue.

For policymakers, my research points to the importance of understanding Evangelical views of Islam and Muslims rather than discounting such opinions as irrelevant. While the West generally appreciates the separation between church and state, large portions of the constituents in America hold religious beliefs. Actively engaging with these constituents on the topic of these beliefs could lead to better governance. When Evangelicals engage with Muslims, they often engage not only on a humanitarian level but also on a religious level, which is often important to Muslims (Pew, 2014). The importance of religion or faith can be ignored and/or difficult to understand by the nonreligious who often fail to see religious motivations as powerful (Quosigk, 2016; Berger, 2008). Because of the commonalities among some Muslims and Christians—not only in terms of religious links but also with respect to certain social issues—it could be beneficial for those involved with public policy to draw on the experiences of Evangelicals and Muslims in an effort to better understand religious motivations. Many in both groups lean toward being religiously devout and are both often categorized similarly as extremist and/or fundamentalist groups within the quickly evolving rubrics of Western societies (Merritt, 2016; Gillum, 2013; Markay, 2013). Policymakers who move beyond these generalities could benefit from a more accurate understanding of their religious constituents.

For Muslims, it is important to recognize that not all Evangelicals conform to the stereotypical image of angry, hateful, Islamophobes; indeed, none in my sample fit this image. I found that both among highly educated leaders and among ordinary Evangelicals at the congregational level there was a strong impulse to refrain from stereotyping Muslims. Many in my sample had Muslim friends and spoke highly of them. In addition, some of the Evangelicals with whom I spoke were passionately against any push for banning Muslim refugees into the United States. Moreover, these Evangelicals, both those who lean traditional and those who lean progressive, were an integral part of the support network that welcomes and provides ongoing support to Muslim refugees in the United States. This finding could be helpful for Muslims who fear Evangelicals are against them, in the sense that it could help Muslims to be more open to engaging Evangelicals and partnering with them. Evangelicals, particularly those on the traditional side of the Progressive-Traditional spectrum, will likely be interested in sharing their faith with Muslims and pointing out the perceived faults with Islamic doctrines. Evangelicals to the progressive side may do so as well. They will be less likely to point to perceived faults in Islamic doctrines, either due to seeing such acts as unhelpful or because they actually find little to no fault within Islam. It should be helpful to the Muslim community to understand the different ways Evangelicals perceive Islam and the variety of ways they go about engaging Muslims.

My research also has implications for Evangelicals with respect to how they should dialogue with each other and how they can bridge the divide that exists among Evangelicals with respect to Islam. In particular, those Evangelicals who hold relatively positive, accommodating views of Islam must be able to clearly articulate to fellow Evangelicals why they hold positive views of Muhammad and the Qur'an. They must be able to explain that these views are honest, deeply held beliefs and not simply a convenient pose when interacting with Muslims (e.g., due to a belief that Muslims are incapable of dialoguing with someone who disagrees with their faith) or the theological consequences of surrendering to relativism. They must also be able to explain to skeptical fellow Evangelicals that their views are not a form of radical accommodation that could eventually undermine the strength of the Evangelical religious tradition. This is an especially relevant consideration in light of the rapid decline of the mainline churches that similarly sought ecumenical visions that primarily focused on similarities between faith groups. Put differently, as Evangelicals who have positive views of Islam seek to break down the traditional boundaries that have historically existed between Christianity and Islam, it will be important for them to determine what truth claims of Christianity remain valid. It also will be important for them to determine what continues to distinguish their own religion from Islam and how best to protect these distinguishing beliefs within their own Evangelical communities. This is important both for the survival of their own faith and for the purpose of articulating their position convincingly to other Evangelicals. McCallum also found Evangelicals who lean toward a more confrontationalist approach (which shares some commonalities with those in this study that align close to the "dominant historical Evangelical positions on Islam") regarding Islam and Muslims are concerned that Evangelicals with a more conciliatory approach (linked with those in this study whose views deviated from the dominant historical Evangelical positions on Islam) are liberalizing the faith, which will "inevitably end with 'cognitive surrender' to Islam, secularism and ideological pluralism" (2011: 306). In addition, considering my finding that Evangelicals whose views deviate from the dominant historical position on Islam are more apt to critique Evangelicals whose views align with it than they are to critique Islam or Muslims, these deviating Evangelicals would perhaps find it helpful to pinpoint what exactly it is about the others they disdain so much and whether it is perhaps rooted in differences of moral authority.

By contrast, for those Evangelicals who hold views of Islam that *do* align with dominant historical Evangelical beliefs—in other words, for those Evangelicals who do not view Muhammad and the Qur'an in an elevated light and who do not find as much commonality between Evangelical Christianity and Islam—it will be increasingly important to engage in humanitarian work on behalf of Muslims. This is because one of the most unrelenting critiques of such Evangelicals who adhere to a less positive view of Islam is that they are not sympathetic to or engaged with Muslims. This lack of engagement is often attributed either to an unsubstantiated fear of Muslims or to a selfish interest in protecting their own "privileges." It will also be important for these Evangelicals who continue to stress the division between Christianity and Islam to clearly articulate to fellow Evangelicals how their frank and uncompromising speech can be Christlike and can coincide with a demonstration of caring for others. Otherwise they are vulnerable to charges from fellow Evangelicals that they are being divisive, harsh, and un-Christlike. Finally, the term "Islamophobic" has become popularized by much of the intelligentsia and elite media and is often attributed to Evangelicals aligning themselves with dominant historical Evangelical beliefs regarding Islam and Muslims (e.g., the views of Jonathan Edwards described in Chapter 2; see also Yancey and Quosigk, 2021). McCallum considered the difficulty researchers of Islamophobia face when trying to accurately "distinguish between 'legitimate criticism and disagreement' and a full-blown phobia" and also warns "confrontational Evangelicals" that "there is a very fine line between raising legitimate concerns and provoking fear" (2011: 302). Due to this, Evangelicals who hold to a critical, less accommodating view of Islam need to consider how to guard their form of Evangelicalism from being perceived as Islamophobia or hate speech, or, indeed, from descending to that level. However, since accusations of Islamophobia have widened and can include any criticism of or disagreement with Islam, and since Evangelicals whose views align with the dominant historical Evangelical views on Islam are the ones usually criticizing Islam, it will be crucial to contemplate the implications of the majority of traditionalist Evangelicals being stigmatized as phobic: in other words, of being labeled as sick and in need of a cure.

Conclusion

It is far easier to identify the variety of ways Evangelicals have come to view Islam and Muslims than it is to remedy the intra-Evangelical divides on Islam and create a clear path to optimal Muslim-Evangelical relations. However, I hope that this book, by exposing as myth the stereotype of Evangelicals as a monolithic group, can pave the way for alternative ways of thinking about Evangelicalism that expand beyond the confines of the generalizations so often perpetuated. It is to be hoped that these more accurate understandings of Evangelicalism in the United States can make room for relationships between conflicting groups to progress: between Evangelicals and Muslims, between those holding negative stereotypes of Evangelicals and Evangelicals themselves, and among the Evangelicals of entirely different beliefs that somehow still share a common name.

APPENDIX 1

QUALITATIVE APPROACHES: JUSTIFICATION OF METHODS AND DATA ANALYSIS

In order to accurately understand the diverse ways in which American Evangelicals approach the topic of Islam, researchers need honest and effective qualitative research that counters the dominant Western stereotyping of Evangelicalism (especially Southern Evangelicalism) as monolithically intolerant, rural, and anti-intellectual. This stereotyping has been acknowledged by many scholars of Evangelicalism (Bean, 2014; Guest et al., 2013; Hutchinson and Wolffe, 2012; Needham-Penrose and Friedman, 2012; Elisha, 2011; Mitchell and Ganiel, 2011; Yancey, 2011; Hankins, 2009; Tobin and Weinberg, 2007; Lindsay, 2007; Marsden, 2006; Reimer, 2003; Smith, 1998; Noll, 1994). There are, however, few studies that look at American Evangelical attitudes toward Islam, and even fewer that use qualitative methods. Most studies use survey data that is limited to rigidly definable variables, and most of these simply encourage the above typecast of Evangelicalism as monolithically antagonistic toward Muslims. Without thoughtful qualitative research on the diverse ways Evangelicals are thinking about and approaching Muslims and Islam, stereotypes are likely to persist, which hinders an accurate understanding of Evangelicalism.

Thus, I chose a qualitative "approach that stresses 'quality' not 'quantity,' that is, social meanings rather than the collection of numerate statistical data" (Miller and Brewer, 2003: 238). This approach emphasizes the importance of getting close to those being researched in order to depict participants' views of social reality more precisely. Qualitative research allows me to uncover issues and complexities that inevitably arise in answers to "how" and "why" questions but that would be missed in a quantitative approach.

The decision to adopt a qualitative approach for my research was motivated by my desire to understand the variety of ways those within an ingroup identify themselves and how those identities influence the ingroup's view of outsiders. In order to understand the variety of ways individuals perceive both themselves and outsiders, it is necessary to include an approach that allows people the freedom to share how they understand themselves, how they think about those around them, and how they justify their positions and actions (Ganiel, 2008; Neitz, 2004; Brewer, 2000; Ammerman, 1994). These "stories" are best obtained using qualitative approaches. In particular, I was inspired by ethnographic approaches to gathering data, which emphasize learning about people's social worlds through hearing their stories and observing their actions. Ethnography is, as defined by Brewer in his book *Ethnography*, "the study of people in naturally occurring settings or 'fields' by methods of data collection which capture their social meanings and ordinary activities, involving the researcher participating directly in the setting, if not also the activities, in order to collect data in a systematic manner but without meaning being imposed on them externally" (2000: 6). Thus, an ethnographic approach gives individuals the opportunity to tell their stories and express themselves without rigidly defined boundaries imposed by the researcher.

Most ethnographies involve an extended time period "in the field," interacting with research participants. Given the time and geographical constraints on my research, I cannot go so far as to claim that my approach was purely ethnographic, but I chose the methods most often employed in ethnographies. To best capture participants in their natural settings and to allow them to express themselves as freely as possible, the primary methods I used were participant observation and semi-structured interviews. Data gathered from these methods give insight into how "microlevel processes take place" (Ganiel, 2008: 157). It is advantageous to combine participant observation with interviews because the data from each can be helpful "to illuminate the other"; specifically, one's experience as a participant observer gives a fuller understanding when interpreting what people say in interviews (Atkinson and Hammersley, 1995: 131). These methods are fitting for gathering data that answers my questions about *how* identities are constructed and *how* individuals describe outsiders.

Participant observation allows the researcher to be exposed to "activities of participants" (Schensul, Schensul, and LeCompte, 1999). Semi-structured interviews have open-ended interview questions that allow interviewees to construct detailed narratives in which they can talk about what they find meaningful (Ganiel, 2008).

Semi-structured interviews also allow the researcher to better ascertain interviewees' perceptions of issues that may be complex or contradictory. For example, if a survey finds that a high percentage of Evangelicals do not fear Islam, the percentage does not explain why. In my own experience of semi-structured interviewing, I found that when I asked participants whether or not they feared Islam, many responded with a quick "no"; however, as they explained the answer in the minutes following, they would often express fear of Islam or Muslims. This seeming contradiction may be due to the awareness from either their personal studies or their church teaching of the biblical counsel not to fear anyone but God (Matthew 10:28). So the immediate response to my question may be "no," but the explanation to that response offers more insight and demonstrates more complexity in participants' thinking than the initial "yes" or "no" answer would suggest.

Participant observation is an important method for gaining trust in the community one is observing and "for building the sort of relationships that make the interview process both open and enjoyable" (Ganiel, 2008: 158). The field notes created during participant observation provide useful information that might not surface during interviews and that can be used to back up or challenge participants' interview responses. Participant observations are also useful for identifying further points to investigate in future research.

Qualitative approaches stress quality over quantity. Because my interviews were in-depth and time-intensive, my sample size was necessarily small. And because of the unique role of the researcher in qualitative studies, it is not possible to fully replicate the study. For these reasons, it is important not to make broad generalizations about my data (Ganiel, 2008; Miller and Brewer, 2003). The data are not representative of Evangelicalism, but such a wide representation is not the goal of my research.

Interview Design and Approach

My primary data-collection method was in-depth, semi-structured interviews, which allowed conversation to move beyond my prepared questions and into other relevant areas as well. In total, I conducted seventy-two interviews, most lasting from thirty minutes to three hours. The majority of interviews lasted over one hour and under two hours. Interviews began with general questions about the interviewee's background and then moved into more in-depth questions dealing with Islam, using an interview guide that I prepared. I used the same interview guide for my interviews with congregants and for most of my interviews with elites. However, five of the leadership interviews were preliminary interviews that I conducted prior to interviews with members of my first congregation. These five preliminary interviewees were asked a handful of broad questions about Evangelicalism and its relationship to Islam. The purpose of these preliminary interviews was to gather data on relevant themes from Evangelicals who write and/or speak on the topic of Islam, which formed the basis upon which I prepared the interview guide that I used in the remaining nineteen leadership interviews and with the congregant interviewees. Questions pertinent to my study that were not asked of these preliminary interviewees were asked and then answered via email.

In some cases, when interviewees were more concise, I was able to ask all of the questions on the guide. At other times, if interviewees had time constraints or lengthier answers, I had to skip certain unnecessary questions. I often asked at the beginning of the interview if interviewees had a specific time they needed the interview to end and then accommodated.

The questions for participants were constructed to produce data that was centered on identity in various areas: sociological, theological, and political. These questions explored how interviewees might describe features of their identity that permitted me to explore the ingroup/outgroup hypothesis and moral authority argument. Questions for participants were also designed to generate data on conflict and cohesion both among Evangelicals and between Evangelicals and Muslims. Many questions were designed to give interviewees freedom to respond. If a question was more restrictive or if a participant's answer was so concise that I could not understand *why* the interviewee believed this or that, I tried to follow up with a "why?" or "why not?" I did my best to appear fair-minded and unaligned. This was not usually difficult, as I went into interviews with the attitude of someone eager to learn, and participants appeared to appreciate my posture as a listener/learner.

In order to explore the ingroup/outgroup hypothesis, I asked questions such as, "Are you comfortable with being called an Evangelical?" and "Do you feel like Evangelicals are unified on the topic of Islam—why or why not?" Insight into this issue also came from the questions, "Do the Evangelicals you are close to share most of your sentiments about Islam?" and "What do you think of the term Chrislam?"

In order to explore interviewees' moral authority and to test Hunter's theory, some of my questions included, "Where do you get your idea of right and wrong?" and "What would you say is your highest moral authority?" I also asked, "How do you view the Bible?" and "What do you think of the idea of looking at the Bible literally?"

In order to draw connections between how interviewees describe their moral authorities and how they view Islam, I asked, "Do you think Muhammad was a prophet? What do you think about him?" and "Have you ever read the Qur'an? What do you think about it?" I also asked interviewees whether Christians and Muslims worship the same God and where interviewees learned the most about Islam. I also thought it was important to determine interviewees' views on interfaith dialogue. I first asked interviewees directly about their thoughts on the topic. Then, later in the interview, I asked about the "A Common Word" (ACW) initiative—specifically, whether the interviewee was familiar with the initiative and what his or her views were regarding it. These questions all allowed participants to give narratives that addressed important themes related to their personal belief systems and to how they view Muslims and Islam.

Data Analysis and Additional Details for Formulation of Evidential Moral Authority

There are numerous ways I could have analyzed my qualitative data. I opted for a thematic analysis focusing on identifiable themes and patterns found across my data sets; the themes I have focused on are those that are relevant to understanding Evangelical diversity and that are associated with my specific research questions (Benner, 1985; Leininger, 1985; Taylor and Bogdan, 1984).

I began my data analysis by having interviews transcribed. These are verbatim transcriptions with the exception of filler words such as "uhh" and "umm." Transcripts include both the questions and responses, and they capture incomplete sentences and repeated words. The data are detailed and context-rich.

Following the sociological tradition of thematic analysis, I next identified themes in the textual data and then coded the data by theme. Coding provided a framework for my analysis that allowed me to more easily compare issues, search for patterns, and describe the themes, patterns, and context more thoroughly. The coding included two phases. In the first phase, I selected about one-fourth of my study data and developed an initial list of codes to begin with. I intentionally chose transcripts that were diverse so as to analyze a wide spectrum of perspectives. The codes were identified by intense reading and organizing of the data (Saldaña, 2009: 32; Charmaz, 2006: 73). I created a codebook that listed all themes, identified when each particular theme was appropriate to use, and provided an example of each code, to afford clarity during this process. This codebook served as my central reference for all codes, and the clear descriptions of the codes in the book helped to ensure consistent application of codes.

The codebook included multiple types of codes. One type was inductive codes, which included repeated words or in vivo phrases such as "kingdom circles," "paradigm shift," or "lesser of two evils." Another type was conceptual codes, which captured more abstract issues or underlying concepts, such as "pressure to respond a certain way" or "self-perception." An additional type of code was deductive codes, which were topics elicited from my interview questions and concepts from my research literature such as "highest moral authority" and "Chrislam." Codes also developed around uncovering the variety of opinions Evangelicals have toward Muslims, their perceptions of unity (or lack thereof) with fellow Evangelicals, and the connection between their moral authorities and their views of Islam. I stopped coding the first one-fourth of data when I reached the point of saturation. In other words, when no new codes emerged, I felt comfortable moving forward with my list of codes.

Phase two of coding involved applying the codes developed in the first phase to all of my congregant interviews and leadership interviews. I also added and rearranged codes as needed. During the coding process, I remained intentional about inductively analyzing the data, allowing themes and issues from participant perspectives to emerge (Patton, 1990). In this process, I placed a high value on diversity and recognition of outliers.

I chose to use MAXQDA to facilitate my analysis of the textual data as it offered a straightforward way to search and retrieve data segments. I attended a training workshop to help me effectively use the MAXQDA software program, and I used the program for the entirety of both phases of analysis.

I methodically coded responses. Specifically, I assigned a value of one (1) for each Progressive response, a value of two (2) for each Progressive-Traditional response, a value of three (3) for each Traditional-Progressive response, and a value of four (4) for each Traditional response. I assigned the stated moral authority as Traditional for an average above 3.5. I assigned Traditional-Progressive for an average between 2.5 and 3.5. I assigned Progressive-Traditional for an average between 1.5 and 2.5. Finally, I assigned Progressive for an average below 1.5. The averages ranged from one (1) to four (4).

To arrive at a category for views of right and wrong, I used key words like "God," "Jesus," "Holy Spirit," or "Bible" to place an interviewee toward the traditional end of the spectrum. Lack of mention of any traditional terms or the mention of terms like "Environment," "Innate," or "extra-Christian teachings" led to placement on the more progressive end of the spectrum. Interestingly, all twenty-nine leaders used "Bible" in their response, and thirty-six of the forty-eight congregants did as well. Also interestingly, a majority of leaders used terms like "innate" or "conscience," but these were typically used in conjunction with the key term "Bible," and some interviewees spoke of God putting the conscience inside of the individual, implying a more traditional and less progressive view. Only twenty-one congregants mentioned terms like "innate" or "conscience," and, similarly to the leadership, the majority of them suggested that the human conscience was God-given.

To arrive at a category for views of the Bible, I analyzed the key words used by my interviewees and separated interviewees accordingly. Traditional phrases and combinations of phrases like "Word of God," "Inerrant," "Infallible," "God-inspired," "God-breathed," and "Authoritative" led to placement of an interviewee toward the traditional end of the spectrum. By contrast, use of key words or phrases like "humanly written" or "unique," especially in connection with the absence of traditional descriptors, prompted placement toward the progressive end of the spectrum. With respect to the Bible, my Evangelical leaders often, though not always, expressed very similar views. The most frequent descriptors were "Word of God" (used by sixteen interviewees), "God-inspired" (used by fourteen), or "inspired" (also used by fourteen). And my Evangelical congregants also tended to describe the Bible using relatively traditional language, such as by saying the Bible was "God-inspired" (used by twenty-two), the "Word of God" (used by nineteen), or "inerrant" and/or "infallible" (used by nine).

To arrive at a category for moral authority, I again analyzed the key words used by my interviewees. Traditional terms like "God," "Jesus," "Holy Spirit," and "Bible" placed an interviewee toward the traditional end of the spectrum, whereas mentions of terms like "the environment," "society," "conscience," or something "innate" (especially in connection with the absence of traditional descriptors) resulted in placement on the more progressive end. The majority of leaders (23) referenced the Bible as their moral authority. The majority of leaders (17) also mentioned "God," and fewer than ten said anything leaning progressive. Just over half of my congregants (25) explicitly listed "God" as their moral authority. Many congregants also listed "the Bible" (19), "Jesus" (15) and "the Holy Spirit" (7).

After analyzing each answer for use of the aforementioned specific key words, I then categorized the answers using the following classification system: answers that made no mention of traditional Evangelical moral authorities were given a code of zero (0); those that made some mention of traditional Evangelical moral authorities received a value of one (1); responses with heavy appeals to traditional Evangelical authorities received a value of two (2). The averages ranged from zero (0) to two (2). I assigned the evidential moral authority as Traditional for an average above 1.5. I assigned Traditional-Progressive for an average greater than 1 up to 1.5. I assigned Progressive-Traditional for an average greater than 0.5 up to 1. Finally, I assigned Progressive for an average of 0.5 or below.

APPENDIX 2

BIOGRAPHICAL REFLEXIVITY, RESEARCHER IDENTITY, AND ETHICAL CONSIDERATIONS

Today, social scientists are aware that researchers cannot offer complete objectivity, and it is no longer necessary for researchers to appear distant and unaware of those they are researching in order to seem "objective." Instead, it is now considered best practice to be reflective about how the researcher's identity affects processes of data collection, data analysis, and the entire production of information (Neitz, 2014; Ganiel, 2008: 166). Both the participants and the researcher "work together to produce the data and how they perceive each other impacts the data that is gathered" (Ganiel, 2008: 166). Previous literature discussing the insider/outsider balance has articulated the risks associated with a researcher being too attached to his or her subjects or too uncritical of them. This research guided my practice and helped me keep a critical distance during the data-gathering process (Kvale and Brinkmann, 2009; Ganiel, 2008; Ganiel and Mitchell, 2006; Brewer, 2000; Gomm, 2000; James, Hockey, and Dawson, 1997; Clifford and Marcus, 1986).

I consider myself to be an Evangelical and that makes me an insider. Insiders are those who in one way or another "belong" to Evangelicalism and likely share common beliefs and religious vocabulary (Ganiel, 2008: 167). There is a risk involved with being an insider, in that it could "be tempting for the insider to accept the participants' perceptions and conclusions at face value, or to slip into advocacy" (Ganiel, 2008: 170). Brewer warns that researchers "must attempt to maintain the balance between 'insider' and 'outsider' status; to identify with the people under study and get close to them, but maintaining a professional distance which permits adequate observation and data collection" (2000: 59–60). Because I had previously been exposed to a variety of cultures within Southern Evangelicalism, I tried to be careful not to overlook what might have seemed like knowledge to take for granted. This meant that participant observation was all the more crucial to incorporate as a research method. While observing, it was clear to me that I was there as a researcher, not simply as a participant; and my awareness of my research role as I attended events and reflected on what was taking place helped me to see the Evangelical church differently. I paid close attention to aspects of congregational life (such as gender roles, authors mentioned by speakers, media references, usages of the Bible) on which I normally would not focus if I were simply a participant.

In terms of advocacy, I tried hard to give a balanced analysis that would not advocate one type of perspective over another. This came most naturally, as I found myself empathizing with interviewees falling on all points of the Progressive-Traditional spectrum, and I tried intently to understand and grasp all perspectives. Various aspects of my background helped me to interact with and appreciate the perspectives of interviewees holding diverse, and often dissenting, opinions. I have had significant exposure to forms of Evangelicalism that align most closely with traditional Evangelical perspectives through attendance at an array of Evangelical churches (most of them Baptist, Methodist, Church of Christ, Church of God, or nondenominational). But I was also exposed to more leftist views, as I attended public school and have now spent the last eighteen years at five different universities where I have formed friendships with both conservatives and liberals representing a wide range of religious perspectives. These experiences have helped me relate to Evangelical participants holding a wide range of views, as I am able to understand the perspectives and language of both groups: those holding views that align with the traditional Evangelical perspective and those holding dissenting perspectives.

I believe my identity as an Evangelical helped me to enlist Evangelical participants (many interviewees knew of my Evangelical identity). Participants may have been more comfortable talking with someone like-minded. Specifically, Evangelicals who may have perceived themselves to be "embattled" with the outside world may have been more open with a religious "insider," whom they may have felt was battling alongside them (Smith, 1998). Many Evangelicals are keenly aware of the negative perception of Evangelicalism in academia. Thus, it is possible that some interviewees would have turned down an interview with an outsider for fear of the possibility of more bad press from a social scientist they could have perceived as biased against them. In addition, because I am an insider, I was not tempted to reduce what Evangelicals said about the divine to social phenomena, and I was interested in the "believing" aspects of life (Mitchell and Ganiel, 2011). This made it easier to take seriously what Evangelicals told me, and this can only have been helpful during my study of congregants. While it may be possible for empathetic outsiders to do the same, it came naturally as an insider. If people had felt that they were being looked down on, or that I as a researcher were uninterested in how God had intervened in their lives, the participants might have felt the need to censor their words, and I would not have obtained an understanding about how these experiences had shaped the participants' views on critical societal issues.

My Evangelical identity also helped me recognize potential knee-jerk responses and know when to look more deeply into participants' views. An example of this occurred in connection with a question I mentioned previously: "Do you fear Islam?" Being an insider, I knew the conditioned answer was no, so I knew to look beyond that first response and pay close attention to what interviewees said as they went into further detail. This doesn't mean that I saw the interviewee as lying or as really afraid. I am sure some interviewees have no fear of Islam. It just meant that I was careful not to take the first response as the definitive answer.

Although I am an insider in Evangelical circles, there were times in the course of my field research and interviews when my experience shaded into that of a religious outsider, a phenomenon other sociologists have also experienced (Mitchell and Ganiel, 2011; Neitz, 2002; Wilcox, 2002). For example, some leaders from Mercy in the City used vocabulary that I did not understand at first, and I had to ask for explanation of phrases like "kingdom circles" and "insider movements." I also remember a young interviewee from Adams River explaining to me what the "C-Scale" represents (see Chapter 5). I was an outsider in those moments.

Furthermore, the fact that I am an Evangelical did not mean that all interviewees would have viewed me as a like-minded individual. As has been well established in my previous chapters, Evangelicalism is diverse, and there is intra-Evangelical conflict on many issues. Thus, my Evangelical identity would not have automatically signified to interviewees that I was someone they could trust or someone who would agree with their opinions. In fact, the fact that I was not a part of either congregation was likely a reason for interviewees to approach me with some caution.

There are other ways in which I likely appeared as an outsider. To begin with, I was a PhD student at a university in Northern Ireland, which makes me an outsider both in terms of my occupation (only two female interviewees from Mercy and Adams River were pursuing a PhD) and in terms of my foothold in European culture. My Pakistani heritage also sets me apart. Many of the congregants asked where I was from and thus knew of my Pakistani background. Both congregations for my studies were predominately white, and the majority of my interviewees were white. The fact that I have a Pakistani background may have affected how participants talked to me. In particular, many would have known that Pakistan is a Muslim-majority country and the Evangelical congregants from my study at Mercy and Adams River may have perceived me as knowing more about Islam than they did; it is theoretically possible that they may have said less about what they "know" about Islam for fear of appearing incorrect in my eyes.

In one sense, my Pakistani heritage might have been greeted with disapproval because some interviewees may have perceptually tied Pakistan with state-sponsored terrorism. In addition, some may have viewed Pakistan as a Muslim-majority country that is becoming less tolerant of Christianity, perhaps due to their reading of Christian resources dedicated to the topic of the persecution of Christians in other countries (e.g., *Voice of the Martyrs* and *Open Doors USA*) (Lowry, 2019; McAlister, 2019; Ahmed and Tanveer, 2018). Pakistan is a Muslim-majority country that is increasingly becoming less tolerant of Christianity. But ironically, the fact that I am part of a stigmatized minority and yet also an Evangelical insider may simultaneously have made me appealing as a researcher. In his study of a southern Evangelical church, Marti (2016) found that the church's mostly white Evangelical congregants liked the foreignness of their pastor, Pastor Sameer, as his presence gave congregants a feeling of being both accepting and triumphing. It was meaningful to attend a church with a pastor who was from an Islamic culture and yet who chose Christianity over Islam.

At a postgraduate conference in 2015 where I presented some of my research on Evangelical views of Islam, one scholar asked me if it was difficult to work within American Evangelicalism, as a woman. She wanted to know if I felt disapproval from the Evangelicals I was studying because I was not relegating myself entirely to the home, and so forth. My answer was no. In fact, to my surprise, being a woman actually helped me gain access to people whom I might not have been able to access otherwise. I think my position as a female and an insider made me appear less threatening and kept me from being conflated with what Mitchell and Ganiel call a "muscular, politicized, male evangelicalism" that could be combative and/or politically driven (2011: 47). This warmth toward me as a woman and scholar lines up with the work of Neitz on religion and gender in sociology in that "religious groups" can be "places that we see women's agency, sometimes in ways that violate our expectations and contradict what we as sociologists think we know" (2014: 520–1).

When I began my initial study with Mercy congregants, my first son was a year old. My first interview was in the home of a young couple who was very involved in the church. They were extremely kind to me upon arrival. As I learned more about them before the interview began, we found that we had much in common. They already had a daughter a little older than my son. We found out we both appreciate natural remedies and hot tea. I believe that my being a woman and a mother only helped in the process of building trust.

I was in my third trimester of pregnancy with my second son during my second study with Adams River congregants. I conducted interviews right up to my due date. Adams River has a reputation of being more conservative, so members might be more inclined to believe women should adhere to exclusive domesticity (Gallagher, 2004). However, all of my interviewees were supportive of my research and were willing to help me by scheduling the interviews in a timely manner due to the fact that my baby was obviously coming soon. Many women congratulated me for pursuing my studies while being a mother. One interviewee told me to let her know when the baby came so she could organize the women in the class on Islam to bring me meals. She also offered to come to my house and take care of the baby so that I could rest. These are a few examples illustrating how I think being a woman and/or a mother helped me seem normal and unthreatening, and helped me garner the support of interviewees.

Choosing a place to conduct the interviews with men was sometimes a challenge. Some Evangelical men prefer to meet with women only when another woman is present, or only in a public place, in order to appear blameless and guard against any sexual misconduct. This is a special sensitivity that I was aware and appreciative of. With most male interviewees interviewed within the church walls (belonging to either congregation), I was able to conduct the interview in a quiet public area of the church in question, but twice at Adams River it was difficult to find an area that was quiet enough for recording purposes and yet not excessively private. The difficulty resulted in the interviews moving from one public area of the church to another, with some negative consequences for the quality of the recording. This gender issue was not a problem when interviews were conducted online.

As a social scientist, it was necessary for me to ask an array of demographic questions to enrich the analysis. I found that some of these demographic questions—such as "What is your highest level of education?" or "What do you do?"—were among the most difficult of all my questions for me to ask. The fact that

I asked the demographic questions at the beginning of the interview made me feel as if it might appear to interviewees that I was sizing them up and/or placing them into conceptual boxes based on characteristics like profession or level of education.

I did not consistently ask interviewees about their race as I found questions about race very uncomfortable to ask. This could be due to my acceptance of the popular, and controversial, narrative that holds that the best way to combat racism is to be "colorblind" and not draw attention to our racial differences or at least acknowledge a common racial fluidity (Saperstein and Penner, 2012). My uneasiness was also due to personal experiences of being asked repeatedly by classmates "What are you?" through my years in public education (my "race" being perceptibly ambiguous). Being asked about my race made me uneasy and I certainly did not want to inflict similar feelings on interviewees. Grier, Rambo, and Taylor conducted a study exploring others also considered racially ambiguous, entitled "What Are You?: Racial Ambiguity, Stigma, and the Racial Formation Project" (2014). My uncomfortability as a researcher asking interviewees to identify their race can be contrasted with other researchers which Grier, Rambo, and Taylor refer to as "only too comfortable with imposing their own racial formation projects on their research subjects or outright stigmatizing them" (2014: 1008). Throughout my life I have often resisted being put into racialized boxes. My personal experience lines up with the subjects of Grier, Rambo, and Taylor who self-identify as racially ambiguous and did not passively give into what they perceived to be the continued racialization of society, but rather "were active agents who interrupted or resisted the racial formation projects being imposed upon them" (2014: 1008).

After demographic questions, the second most difficult type of questions—from my perspective—were political questions. These included "How would you describe your political views?" and "Do you vote for a particular party?" These questions were difficult to ask because many interviewees seemed uncomfortable with the questions, and I do not like to make people uneasy. Often interviewees struggled to align with a particular party. I did not get the feeling that this was because they were evenly split between a Republican and a Democratic stance; rather, it seemed that they were uncomfortable voicing their alignment to me. This meant I had to press in order to uncover their real political views. I did not like "digging," but I thought it was important to give interviewees more time in order to articulate their thoughts. Some interviewees, particularly the elites, asked for specific policy issues to comment on rather than affirming general allegiance to one party or the other. One female leader even asked me to skip the political questions altogether because they made her uncomfortable. This could be because she considered herself a progressive and held more progressive political views that might not be favorable to those within her congregation.

While some of my demographic and political questions were difficult to ask, it was easy for me to ask "Where are you from?" and "Are you comfortable with being called an Evangelical?" and "Could you tell me your age or your age range?" These questions did not feel negatively reductive, most likely due to my personal experiences.

To understand the ethical practices I should implement for my project, I relied on literature dealing with the topics of qualitative research ethics and safety (Brewer,

2016, 2014, 2013, 2012a, 2012b, 2000; Ganiel, 2016; Marti and Ganiel, 2014, 2013, 2008; Mitchell and Ganiel, 2011; Ganiel and Mitchell, 2006). In addition, I benefited from the ethical guidelines given by the School of Religions, Peace Studies, and Theology at Trinity College Dublin and by the School of Social Science, Education and Social Work's Social Research Ethics Committee at Queen's University Belfast.

Data collection and interviews for the study of Mercy were all completed between January 2015 and March 2015. I provided a consent form that was signed by each interviewee prior to the interview. The consent form informed interviewees that if they wished, their confidentiality would be protected at all times, meaning their name would not be used in connection with any quotes. In addition, the consent form encouraged interviewees to contact me at any time if they had concerns. Data collection and interviews for Adams River were all completed between September 2015 and November 2015. I provided each interviewee with a participant information sheet and consent form. In some cases I offered the forms by email, in some cases I provided them in person before setting up the interview, and in some cases I brought them to the interview to be signed before the interview began.

For the leadership interviews, the majority of the interviews were conducted over the phone or online, and I followed the same ethical procedures and guidelines outlined for my study of congregants at Mercy. Risk to participants was very low. Still, Islam is sometimes a controversial topic in the United States, so I accounted for the possibility that some interviewees could become emotional during the interview and some could be reminded of trauma (for instance, if they knew of someone who was involved in 9/11, or a victim of the terror attacks in various parts of the United States since 9/11, or served in wars in the aftermath of the 9/11 attacks). Interestingly, even in my small sample, this was the case. Two interviewees from Adams River were deeply affected by 9/11. I let interviewees know that they should feel free to refrain from answering any questions should they feel uncomfortable.

For the protection of my interviewees, I chose to use pseudonyms for the interviewees as well as the churches. I guaranteed confidentiality to all interviewees within the law, and this information was included in the consent form they signed.

I audio recorded each interview and in fact double recorded each whenever possible. To ensure security of the data, my computer is password protected, and I have saved all the recordings/transcripts locally on an encrypted external hard drive.

All interviews that required travel took place within the same state, with the exception of one, which was located in a neighboring southern state. I traveled by car for interviews and to attend events. Some interviews were conducted over the phone or Skype if that was the preferred method of the interviewees or when distances were unreasonable to conduct the interview in person.

For permission to participate in certain meetings at Mercy in the City and Adams River, I sought approval from the gatekeepers at each site (the head pastor and the assistant pastor, respectively). However, not everyone in the various settings knew that I was researching or was aware of being observed. For example, in the large regular church services at each site, very few of the participants knew of my research. There was nothing about my appearance that made me so unusual or foreign that would make it obvious that I was observing. Also, the vocabulary and behaviors I had learned growing up in various Evangelical churches meant that I could usually blend in with little, if any, question as to "why" I might be there. However, if I engaged in conversation with attendees, I quickly made a point to mention my research and the fact that their church was under study. In some smaller group settings, such as the Wednesday night class I took on Islam at Adams River, I announced my research project to the class mid-way through the course and asked if anyone would like to participate in my research. I took a similar approach at a conference I attended at one Mercy branch, where conference attendees sat around various circular tables. As I got to know individuals from my table, I let them know that I was a researcher and that one of their fellow campuses, Mercy in the City, was under study. This openness allowed me to feel more at ease throughout the entire participant observation process. Being upfront about my status as a researcher was important to me. While I understand that covert unobtrusive observation is preferred for certain research projects, I am glad that I was able to be upfront about my role as a researcher, as I would struggle ethically with pretending to be someone I am not.

While I was able to be upfront about my role as a researcher, I was not necessarily forthcoming about the theoretical framework I would be using to analyze my data. Thus, I felt that interviewees did not know explicitly what kinds of connections might unfold during my analysis, particularly in regard to the question of moral authorities. Although I never lied, my lack of forthrightness about my theoretical perspective made me feel uneasy at times. However, I felt it was important to keep the theoretical framework unknown to the interviewees because I was not sure myself how the analysis would take shape, particularly during my first study of congregants at Mercy, before my theoretical chapter was fully complete. In addition, had I explicitly discussed my theoretical framework, I would risk interviewees knowingly or unknowingly altering their speech in order to position themselves in the portion of the moral authority spectrum (from progressive to traditional) they believed to be correct or that they felt pressure to be a part of. I wanted interviewees to speak freely, and for that reason I chose not to discuss the theoretical framework. Instead, I focused on communicating to interviewees that the purpose of my research was to gather the variety of opinions within Evangelicalism on the topic of Islam. Communication of that specific goal seemed to satisfy my ethical obligations as a researcher, and the interviewees seemed content with that goal as well.

Interviewees appeared content that my project was looking at variety within Evangelicalism. The majority of interviewees—both congregants and leaders—said Evangelicals are not unified on the topic of Islam, which came as a surprise to me, as I thought some within Evangelicalism would rather try to protect Evangelicalism from seeming fractured. Interviewees' comfort with variety in Evangelicalism may be linked with their acknowledgment of intra-Evangelical conflict on the topic of Islam and Evangelicalism's individualistic tendencies, which allow for different opinions and actions.

APPENDIX 3

ADDITIONAL DEMOGRAPHICS AND LEVEL OF ENGAGEMENT WITH MUSLIMS

My sample is not representative of Evangelicalism in the United States. Rather, I tried to talk with Evangelicals who take very different approaches to interacting with Muslims. My sample was focused (rather than representative) in that I wanted in-depth insight on a variety of perspectives. I specifically hoped to capture a range of beliefs—both on Islam and on various other topics—that lend themselves to understanding how interviewees think about topics such as moral authority and interfaith dialogue with Muslims. I used my participant observation periods during my study of congregants to obtain a purposeful and focused sample of people with diverse perspectives. Through my casual interactions with people in participant observation periods, I was able to evaluate who might be able to provide me with a slightly different perspective. In order to capture the diversity of the types of Evangelicals within the church, I specifically attempted to interview congregants and leaders who varied in age, sex, and ministry role or occupation. Still, I was able to achieve more diversity in terms of ministry role and occupation at Adams River than I was at Mercy in the City. This is because of the snowball sampling method that I used initially at Mercy, which seemed to point me toward one leader after another (there was also a "you have to talk to this person" element that encouraged me to keep interviewing those who held large and small ministry roles within the church). As I neared completion of my seventy-two interviews, I was able to confirm that I had reached a "saturation point" simply by the evidence of significant diversity found in my sample.

The subject of gender imbalance arose in a few interviews; one female leader, for example, told me she boycotts an influential Christian journal due to the relatively few female authors included in its pages, and she also condemned the Muslim-Christian "A Common Word" initiative as being "almost exclusively male." This particular female leader recruited two other female leaders to participate in my study. But the majority of female congregant and leadership interviewees focused more on gender imbalance within the Islamic community than they did on gender imbalance within the Evangelical community.

At Mercy in the City, the balanced ratio of males to females (twelve females and eleven males) came naturally, with little need to recruit one sex or the other. While no Mercy campuses have a woman as head pastor of any of their congregations, Mercy in the City does have women in various other leadership roles in the church, especially in areas of interest for my research, such as in their conferences on Islam and in their various refugee ministries. While the main speaker at the numerous conferences on Islam is a male, women do share the stage and teach as well.

About mid-way through my study of congregants at Adams River, I began to notice that I was interviewing more men than women. On the recommendation of my supervisors, I briefly presented my research at the beginning of the Wednesday night class I was attending at the church and invited class attendees to participate in my study. I explained that I wanted a balanced sample and was in need of female interviewees. This effort was successful, and before the end of class, I had obtained the names, email addresses, and phone numbers of about seven willing women. Some men also showed interest, but I eventually decided against interviewing more men in pursuit of a more balanced gender ratio of twelve females and thirteen males (see Table A.1).

Social class in this study is defined by educational level and occupation. Those with a bachelor's degree were defined as middle class. Those with graduate degrees were categorized in a higher social class. Those with educational levels beneath a bachelor's degree were assessed by occupation. In class categories, ten interviewees had attended some college without obtaining a degree or had obtained a technical degree, twenty-two had obtained a bachelor's degree, forty had obtained a graduate degree, and twenty-one of those with a graduate degree had gone on to obtain a PhD or DMin degree. None of my interviewees without bachelor's degrees could be categorized as members of the lower class, due either to their spouse's occupation (gathered during the interview) or to the fact that they were attending college and working toward a degree but had not obtained it yet. Thus, the entirety of my sample was either middle or upper class. These two class categories were overrepresented in my total sample because most of the Mercy in the City attendees were highly educated, situated as they were in close proximity to two large university campuses, because Adams River attendees were also highly educated (the church is located in an upper-middle-class city with a median income per household of over $70K), and because the sample included the additional twenty-four interviews with elites, many of whom had postgraduate degrees.

Table A.1 Leadership and Mercy and Adams River Congregants: Gender Ratio

	Male	Female	Total
Leadership	20	9	**29**
Congregations	25	23	**48**
Deduct Overlap*	−4	−1	-5
Total	**41**	**31**	**72**

* Denotes the individuals who are included in the leadership analysis (Chapter 4) as well as the congregational analysis (Chapter 5). These interviewees are both national Evangelical leaders on the topic of Islam and members of the congregations examined.

Engagement Levels

Some research on American Evangelicals not only sees Evangelicals as antagonistic and inhospitable to Muslims, but it also sees Evangelicals as lacking the necessary social capital that would allow them to build bridges with the Muslim community (Beyerlein and Hipp, 2005; Putnam, 2000; Wilson and Janoski, 1995). In light of this, I thought it was important to look at the level to which Evangelicals in my sample were actually engaged with Muslims. Level of engagement was determined by whether interviewees had Muslim friends and by the amount of contact they were having with Muslims on a regular basis (see Tables A.2 and A.3).

The majority of leaders (17) were highly engaged with Muslims. Likewise, just under half of congregants (22) were also highly engaged. Some had lived among Muslims in Muslim-majority countries for stints of time, some were working

Table A.2 Leadership: Demographics

Name	Gender	Education	Age Range	Engagement with Muslims
Ahmad	Male	G	35–50	High
Brad	Male	G	51–65	High
Emma	Female	G	Under 35	High
Hakim	Male	G	51–65	High
Hayden	Male	G	51–65	High
Jane	Female	SC	51–65	High
Jim	Male	G	51–65	High
Luke	Male	G	51–65	High
Maria*	Female	G	35–50	High
Marianne	Female	G	35–50	High
Mark*	Male	G	Under 35	High
Navid*	Male	B	Over 65	High
Oliver	Male	G	35–50	High
Parker*	Male	B	51–65	High
Robbie	Male	G	Over 65	High
Rose	Female	SC	35–50	High
Samuel	Male	G	35–50	High
Andrew	Male	G	51–65	Medium
Elizabeth	Female	G	35–50	Medium
Gabriel	Male	G	51–65	Medium
George	Male	G	35–50	Medium
Heather	Female	B	Under 35	Medium
Jakob	Male	G	Over 65	Medium
James	Male	G	Over 65	Medium
Kevin*	Male	G	51–65	Medium
Leah	Female	G	35–50	Medium
Joseph	Male	G	35–50	Low
Paul	Male	G	35–50	Low
Tarifa	Female	B	Under 35	Low

* Denotes the individuals who are included in the leadership analysis (Chapter 4) as well as the congregational analysis (Chapter 5). These interviewees are both national Evangelical leaders on the topic of Islam and members of the congregations examined.
SC = Some College, B = Bachelor, G = Graduate.

Table A.3 Mercy and Adams River Congregants: Demographics

Name	Gender	Education	Age Range	Engagement with Muslims
Amanda	Female	B	Under 35	High
Bart	Male	B	35–50	High
Bethany	Female	SC	Under 35	High
Camila	Female	SC	51–65	High
Celina	Female	B	51–65	High
Danielle	Female	G	51–65	High
Frank	Male	G	35–50	High
Gabriel	Male	G	35–50	High
Henriette	Female	SC	Over 65	High
Jesse	Male	G	Under 35	High
Judah	Male	B	Under 35	High
Julia	Female	B	Under 35	High
Maria*	Female	G	35–50	High
Mark*	Male	G	Under 35	High
Meagan	Female	G	Under 35	High
Micah	Male	B	Under 35	High
Naomi	Female	B	Under 35	High
Navid*	Male	B	Over 65	High
Parker*	Male	B	51–65	High
Scott	Male	G	51–65	High
Simon	Male	B	Under 35	High
Teresa	Female	B	Under 35	High
Erica	Female	G	Under 35	Medium
Esther	Female	B	51–65	Medium
Ethan	Male	G	Under 35	Medium
Jackie	Female	B	Over 65	Medium
Kevin*	Male	G	51–65	Medium
Michael	Male	SC	Under 35	Medium
Patrick	Male	B	51–65	Medium
Phillip	Male	G	Over 65	Medium
Silas	Male	G	Under 35	Medium
Tabitha	Female	B	Under 35	Medium
Timothy	Male	G	35–50	Medium
Valerie	Female	B	Under 35	Medium
Zachary	Male	G	35–50	Medium
Anja	Male	SC	35–50	Low
Anna	Female	G	51–65	Low
Bobby	Male	SC	Under 35	Low
Daisy	Female	G	Under 35	Low
Joel	Male	G	51–65	Low
Lacey	Female	B	35–50	Low
Lauren	Female	G	35–50	Low
Matthew	Male	SC	Under 35	Low
Nathaniel	Male	B	Under 35	Low
Rita	Female	SC	Over 65	Low
Stuart	Male	B	Over 65	Low
Tiffany	Female	G	Under 35	Low
Victoria	Female	B	35–50	Low

* Denotes the individuals who are included in the leadership analysis (Chapter 4) as well as the congregational analysis (Chapter 5). These interviewees are both national Evangelical leaders on the topic of Islam and members of the congregations examined.

SC = Some College, B = Bachelor, G = Graduate

hard at building relationships with and serving Muslims in cities in the United States with high Muslim populations, and some were leading or participating in interfaith ministries or nonprofits that were heavily engaged with Muslims. An example of a highly engaged individual is Mark (M), who was involved with leading missionary trips to Muslim-majority countries and visiting Muslims in the local mosque. He shared with me how he came to view Muslims differently from how the "Evangelical church" had previously taught him to view Muslims. He attributed this shift to his personal engagement with Muslims:

> My first exposure to Muslims was in London, and I was part of the aggressive Christian ministry that was targeting debate-oriented conversations with Muslims. Our job was to go out and argue with them at the point of contention. We got into fairly heated conversations, maybe even yelling matches. It didn't strike me [as] particularly productive for the Gospel . . . It seemed to be more about shame and honor and we're just fighting for who is smarter . . . Even in those conversations I remember meeting some of those Muslims who were there and they were surprisingly gracious and it rattled what I had heard and assumed stereotypes about Muslims to be. . . . How in the world has Satan convinced a large majority of the Evangelical church that they simply cannot believe anything a Muslim friend tells them because the Muslim friend is just lying to them? I had that conversation just two weeks ago with a pastor was saying, "Sure, they've been nice to you, but once they get the power then they're allowed to lie. They have the permission to lie." "So, you're telling me that every conversation I've had with a Muslim. It's really been authentic and deep and everything else, has just been a lie. They were just lying to me." . . . "Well," I said, "There's your problem. No wonder you can't reach them" . . . I had a lot of these preconceived notions from my training, from Evangelical sources . . . This Qur'an [holds up Qur'an to show me] was from one of the first guys I met in London. We had long and deep conversations about Abraham. He went to the central mosque and he bought me this Qur'an, gave it to me. I still have it today and it's a really sweet memory to me . . . We took another couple of trips to Lebanon and to Syria. I met some more Muslims there. They turned out be quite gracious and hospitable . . . Then we went to Jordan to learn about Muslims Followers of Jesus. We did some just relational stuff, meeting Muslims out and about. With that new mindset, I'm not trying to rip you out of your world, or even stop you from being Muslim. . . . I just want to talk about Jesus. That new mindset opened up everything. Suddenly conversations became much, much better . . . When we came home from that, we started to go and visit mosques. Not to attack but just to listen and learn. I attended a Friday night Qur'an class that taught the Qur'an verse by verse in the mosque. I remember knowing that the imam, he's still an imam here . . . He's a good man. I remember talking to him, visiting several mosques, getting to know some guys in the neighborhood. So, kind of began to develop from there. Probably my best friendships now are those that have come out of the work that was done in Frankfort [the local refugee community] . . . Anyway, my relationships with Muslims now have changed significantly [from what] they were originally.

All interviewees categorized as highly engaged said they had Muslim friends. These individuals were intentional about maintaining consistent contact with Muslims. In the case of leaders, they often had job titles directly related to their interactions with Muslims. In the case of congregants, they had often developed a strong bond with Muslim refugee families and/or purposefully studied, eaten, or worked alongside Muslims on an ongoing basis.

About one-third of the leaders (9) and about one-fourth of the congregants (13) had a medium level of engagement with Muslims. Those in the "medium" category were those who had at least one Muslim friend (not simply an acquaintance) and who were engaged with Muslims sporadically. For leaders, sporadic engagement often came in the form of debate formats or interfaith formats, and so on. Kevin, for example, had developed a relationship with Muhammad Ibrahim, a top Muslim debater, during his experiences in numerous formal debates. Kevin describes his sporadic engagement with Muslims this way:

> I had the privilege of debating probably the most important Islam apologists that are out there today, and I'm thinking of people like Usman Assad, whom I debated at Columbia University, and Muhammad Ibrahim, who has a dawah [proselytizing] center in New York, and has debated with me in, I think, five or six debates across the country . . . I've had a really good experience with these debates. My experience has been that when you approach the issues on a rational level, and avoid ad hominem sorts of attacks, that you can have a very interesting and good discussion. My other colleagues who have debated, particularly Muhammad Ibrahim, have had a similar experience. All the Christians I know love Muhammad Ibrahim. I've never heard anybody speak negatively about him. Even though we disagree with one another, everybody likes him. These debates [with Muhammad] have been a really great experience for me, and we've debated the whole gamut of issues such as the concept of God in Islam and Christianity, who was Jesus, the historicity of the resurrection of Jesus, even had a debate with Muhammad on what must I do to be saved, which was extremely interesting.

As with Kevin, many individuals in this category were committed to other ministry or work that made consistent interaction with Muslims more difficult. For congregants, sporadic engagement often came in the form of various forms of mission trips that interviewees intentionally took to interact with Muslims (though not all interviewees were comfortable with the term "mission") and/or in their engagement with their Muslim friend/s.

The category of low engagement encompassed those who had no Muslim friends and who had little or no personal interaction with Muslims. A minority of the leaders (3) fell into this category. However, about one-quarter of the congregants (13) were categorized as having low engagement. Some of these, particularly in the case of the leaders, were engaged with Muslims academically but not relationally (e.g., by publishing a book on the topic). Some interviewees noted their knowledge of Islam was "all second hand." Some of these, particularly the congregants, had been in the process of taking a class on Islam, or had recently attended a conference on Islam, and had very limited knowledge of Islam or Muslims coming into these settings. One interviewee in the category of low engagement, however, represented a very different case. She was a college student who left Islam and became a Christian, and in the process had to leave her family home for fear of death. When I asked her if she had any Muslim friends, she said:

> I don't. Not right now. I did at one point. [. . .] I'm not one that can really have personal contact because there is such a physical threat . . .Yeah, aside from really hurting for them [Muslims] and having compassion and praying for them, I really can't have interaction that's on a personal level because of who I am and what I stand for.

Leaders' levels of engagement with Muslims did not correlate with their position on the Progressive-Traditional spectrum. In other words, Progressives were not more engaged with Muslims than Traditionals, or vice versa. This is not surprising, however, because I chose leaders based on their engagement with the topic of Islam, and it makes sense that most would also be engaged with Muslims.

In contrast, congregants' levels of engagement with Muslims did correlate with their position on the Progressive-Traditional spectrum. Evidential Traditionals were more engaged with Muslims than Progressives. Interestingly, though evidential Traditionals all shared the same "high" level of engagement with Muslims, they came to very different conclusions on various issues related to Islam and Muslims.

REFERENCES

Adkins, T., Layman, G., Campbell, D. and Green, J. (2013), "Religious Group Cues and Citizen Policy Attitudes in the United States," *Politics and Religion*, 6 (2): 235–63.

Ahmed, M. and Tanveer, A. (2018), *Protests in Pakistan Delay Release of Christian Women*. Available at: https://www.foxnews.com/world/protests-in-pakistan-delay-release-of-christian-woman (Accessed August 27, 2020).

Akhtar, I. (2011), "Race and Religion in the Political Problematization of the American Muslim," *Political Science and Politics*, 44 (4): 768–74.

Akhtar, S. (2008), *The Qur'an and the Secular Mind*. New York: Routledge.

Akhtar, S. (2010), *Islam as Political Religion: The Future of an Imperial Faith*. London: Taylor and Francis.

Al-Shehab, A. J. (2002), "A Cross-sectional Examination of Levels of Moral Reasoning in a Sample of Kuwait University Faculty Members," *Social Behavior & Personality: An International Journal*, 30 (8): 813–20.

Ammerman, N. T. (1990), *Baptist Battles: Social Change and Religious Conflict in the Southern Baptist Convention*. New Brunswick: Rutgers University Press.

Ammerman, N. T. (1994), "Telling Congregational Stories," *Review of Religious Research*, 35 (4): 289–301.

Ammerman, N. T. (1998), *Bible Believers: Fundamentalists in the Modern World*. New Brunswick: Rutgers University Press.

Ammerman, N. T. (2005), *Pillars of Faith: American Congregations and Their Partners*. Berkeley: University of California Press.

Ammerman, N., Carroll, J., Dudley, C. and McKinney, W., eds. (1998), *Studying Congregations: A New Handbook*. Nashville: Abingdon Press.

Anderson, A. (2014), *An Introduction to Pentecostalism*. Cambridge: Cambridge University Press.

Anderson, B. R. (1991), *Imagined Communities: Reflections on the Origin and Spread of Nationalism*. Rev. and extended edn. London: Verso.

Atkinson, P. and Hammersley, M. (1995), *Ethnography: Principles in Practice*. Madison: Routledge.

Aukst-Margetić, B. and Margetić, B. (2005), "Religiosity and Health Outcomes: Review of Literature," *Collegium Antropologicum*, 29 (1): 365–71.

Aune, K. (2006), "Marriage in a British Evangelical Congregation: Practising Post-feminist Partnership?," *The Sociological Review*, 54 (4): 638–57.

Austin, D., Doolittle, A., Bellamy, J. and Edwards, J. (1794), *The Millennium; or, the Thousand Years of Prosperity, Promised to the Church of God, in the Old Testament and in the New, Shortly to Commence, and to be Carried on to Perfection, Under the Auspices of Him, Who, in the Vision, Was Presented to St. John* [Six lines of Scripture texts]. Elizabeth Town.

Backus, I. and Weston, D. (1871), *A History of New England*. 2 vols. Newton: The Backus Historical Society.

Bainton, R. H. (1950), *Here I Stand; A Life of Martin Luther*. New York: Hendrickson Publishers Marketing.

Bainton, R. H. (1960), *Christian Attitudes Toward War and Peace; A Historical Survey and Critical Re-evaluation*. New York: Abingdon Press.
Baker, W. (2005), *America's Crisis of Values: Reality and Perception*. Princeton: Princeton University Press.
Baker, W. (2010), "The Duality of American Moral Culture," in S. Hitlin and S. Vaisey (eds.), *Handbook of the Sociology of Morality*, 255–74. New York: Springer.
Balmer, R. H. (2006), *Mine Eyes Have Seen the Glory: A Journey into the Evangelical Subculture in America*, 4th edn. Oxford: Oxford University Press.
Bartkowski, J. P. and Read, J. G. (2003), "Veiled Submission: Gender, Power, and Identity Among Evangelical and Muslim Women in the United States," *Qualitative Sociology*, 26 (1): 71–92.
Baylor, M. (2012), *The German Reformation and the Peasants' War: A Brief History with Documents*. Boston: Bedford/St. Martin's.
Bean, L. (2014), *The Politics of Evangelical Identity: Local Churches and Partisan Divides in the United States and Canada*. Princeton: Princeton University Press.
Bebbington, D. W. (1989), *Evangelicalism in Modern Britain: A History from the 1730s to the 1980s*. London: Unwin Hyman.
Becker, P. (1999), *Congregations in Conflict: Cultural Models of Local Religious Life*. Cambridge: Cambridge University Press.
Bellah, R. N. and Greenspahn, F. E. (1987), *Uncivil Religion: Interreligious Hostility in America*. New York: Crossroad.
Benedict, D. (1813), *A General History of the Baptist Denomination in America, and Other Parts of the World*. 2 vols. Boston: Lincoln & Edmands.
Benner, P. (1985), "Quality of Life: A Phenomenological Perspective on Explanation, Prediction, and Understanding in Nursing Science," *Advances in Nursing Science*, 8 (1): 1–14.
Berger, P. (1967), *The Sacred Canopy: Elements of a Sociological Theory of Religion*. New York: Anchor.
Berger, P. (1999), "The Desecularization of the World: A Global Overview," in P. Berger (ed.), *The Desecularization of the World: Essays on the Resurgence of Religion in World Politics*. Grand Rapides: Eerdmans.
Berger, P. (2006), *Religion in a Globalizing World*. Available at: http://www.pewforum.org/2006/12/04/religion-in-a-globalizing-world2/ (Accessed July 30, 2017).
Berger, P. (2008), *Secularization Falsified*. Available at: https://www.firstthings.com/article/2008/02/ secularization-falsified (Accessed July 18, 2017).
Berger, P. (2010), *Rethinking Secularization*. Available at: http://www.albertmohler.com/2010/10/11/rethinking-secularization-a-conversation-with-peter-berger/ (Accessed August 18, 2017).
Berger, P. and Huntington, S. (2002), *Many Globalizations: Cultural Diversity in the Contemporary World*. New York: Oxford University Press.
Berger, P. and Luckmann, T. (1966), *The Social Construction of Reality: A Treatise in the Sociology of Knowledge*. Garden City: Doubleday.
Beyerlein, K. and Hipp, J. (2005), "Social Capital, Too Much of a Good Thing? American Religious Traditions and Community Crime," *Social Forces*, 84 (2): 995–1013.
Beyerlein, K. and Hipp, J. (2006), "From Pews to Participation: The Effect of Congregation Activity and Context on Bridging Civic Engagement," *Social Problems*, 53 (1): 97–117.
Bhatia, A. (2015), *Perspectives, Attitudes, and Practice of American Evangelicals Towards Muslims in the U.S.* PhD dissertation, Trinity International University, USA. ProQuest, UMI Dissertations Publishing, 3720946.

Bhatia, A. (2016), "American Evangelicals and Islam: Their Perspectives, Attitudes and Practices Towards Muslims in the US," *Transformation: An International Journal of Holistic Studies*, 34 (1): 26–37.

Billings, D. B. and Scott, S. L. (1994), "Religion and Political Legitimation," *Annual Review of Sociology*, 20: 173–202.

Bloomfield, D. (1997), *Peacemaking Strategies in Northern Ireland: Building Complementarity in Conflict Management*. Hampshire: Palgrave MacMillan.

Blouin, D. and Robinson, R. V. (2007), "What Makes People Good? The Social Basis of Compassion in the United States," presented at the joint meetings of the Midwest Sociological Society and the North Central Sociological Association in Chicago, Illinois.

Boghossian, P. (2014), *Fear of Knowledge: Against Relativism and Constructivism*. Oxford: Clarendon.

Bok, J. (2014), "Symbolic Filtering: Selectively Permeable Evangelical Boundaries in an Age of Religious Pluralism," *Journal for the Scientific Study of Religion*, 53 (4): 808–25.

Bray, T. W. (1780), *A Dissertation on the Sixth Vial; In Five Parts: With an Introduction Upon the Design of Prophecy in General, and the Book of Revelation in Particular*. Hartford: Hudson & Goodwin.

Brewer, J. (1993), "Sensitivity as a Problem in Field Research," in C. Renzetti and R. Lee (eds.), *Sensitive Research Topics*. London: SAGE.

Brewer, J. (2000), *Ethnography: Understanding Social Research*. Buckingham: Open University Press.

Brewer, J. (2012a), "Inescapable Burden of 'Guilty Knowledge,'" *Times Higher Education*. Available at: https://www.timeshighereducation.com/comment/letters/inescapable-burden-of-guilty-knowledge/418834.article (Accessed July 9, 2017).

Brewer, J. (2012b), "Researching Sensitive Topics," in S. Becker, A. Bryma and H. Ferguson (eds.), *Understanding Research for Social Policy and Social Work*, 69–73. Bristol: Policy Press.

Brewer, J. (2013), *The Public Value of the Social Sciences*. London: Bloomsbury.

Brewer, J. (2014), "Society as a Vocation: Renewing Social Science for Social Renewal," *Irish Journal of Sociology*, 22 (2): 127–37.

Brewer, J. (2016), "The Ethics of Ethical Debates in Peace and Conflict Research: Notes Towards the Development of a Research Covenant," *Methodological Innovations*, 9: 1–11.

Bridges, E. (2014), *Pastor David Platt Succeeds Ton Elliff as IMB President*. Available at: http://www.bpnews.net/43237/platt-succeeds-elliff-as-imb-president (Accessed June 15, 2017).

Bromley, A. E. (2019), Culture Wars *Author James D. Hunter Takes on New Science of Morality*. Available at: https://news.virginia.edu/content/culture-wars-author-james-d-hunter-takes-new-science-morality (Accessed August 27, 2020).

Brown, M. (2020), *Is NY Times Right? Are (White) Evangelicals Responsible for Spread of COVID-19?* Available at: https://www.christianpost.com/voices/is-ny-times-right-are-white-evangelicals-responsible-for-spread-of-covid-19.html (Accessed April 17, 2020).

Buchanan, P. J. (1992), *Republican National Convention Speech*. Available at: http://buchanan.org/blog/1992-republican-national-convention-speech-148 (Accessed July 29, 2015).

Burge, R. (2020), *Atheists are the Most Politically Active Group in the United States*. Religion in Public. Available at: https://religioninpublic.blog/2020/04/13/atheists-are-the-most-politically-active-group-in-the-united-states/?fbclid=IwAR0nY12gK8rPl-ZhHdiZbKqDQDFzWNo-E6a2egJRob90keXT6vDFv23wAj0 (Accessed April 22, 2020).

Burr, V. (1998), "Realism, Relativism, Social Constructionism and Discourse," in I. Parker (ed.), *Social Constructionism, Discourse and Realism*. London: Sage.

Burr, V. (2015), *Social Constructionism*, 3rd edn. Hove: Routledge.

Butler, C. (2002), *Postmodernism: A Very Short Introduction*. Oxford: Oxford University Press.

Camp, L. (2011), *Who Is My Enemy: Questions American Christians Must Face About Islam—and Themselves*. Grand Rapids: Brazos Press.

Campolo, T. (2008), *Red Letter Christians: A Citizen's Guide to Faith and Politics*. Ventura: Regal.

Carroll, J. W. and Marler, P. L. (1995), "Culture Wars? Insights from Ethnographies of Two Protestant Seminaries," *Sociology of Religion*, 56 (1): 1–20.

Charmaz, K. (2006), *Constructing Grounded Theory: A Practical Guide Through Qualitative Analysis*. London: SAGE.

Chaves, M. (1993), "Intraorganizational Power and Internal Secularization in Protestant Denominations," *American Journal of Sociology*, 99 (1): 1–48.

Chaves, M. (1994), "Secularization as Declining Religious Authority," *Social Forces*, 72 (3): 749–74.

Cimino, R. (2005), "No God in Common: American Evangelical Discourse on Islam After 9/11," *Review of Religious Research*, 47 (2): 162–74.

Clifford, J. and Marcus, G. (1986), *Writing Culture: The Poetics and Politics of Ethnography*. Berkeley: University of California Press.

Clydesdale, T. T. (1997), "Family Behaviors among Early U.S. Baby Boomers: Exploring the Effects of Religion and Income Change, 1965–1982," *Social Forces*, 76 (2): 605–35.

Community Relations Council (n.d.), "Community Relations: A Brief Guide." Belfast.

Conti, J. A. and O'Neil, M. (2007), "Studying Power: Qualitative Methods and the Global Elite," *Qualitative Research*, 7 (1): 63–82.

Coser, L. A. (1956), *The Functions of Social Conflict*. Glencoe: Free Press.

Cox, D., Jones, R. P. and Navarro-Rivera, J. (2013), *Most are Proud to be American, Republicans More Likely to Engage in Patriotic Activities*. Available at: http://www.prri.org/research/july-2013-prri-rns/ (Accessed October 20, 2016).

Dahrendorf, R. (1964), "The New Germanies: Restoration, Revolution, Reconstruction," *Encounter*, 22: 50–8.

Daniels, B. (1996), *Puritans at Play: Leisure and Recreation in Colonial New England*. New York: Palgrave Macmillan.

Davie, G. (2013), *The Sociology of Religion: A Critical Agenda*, 2nd edn. Los Angeles: SAGE.

Davis, N. J. and Robinson, R. V. (1996a), "Are the Rumors of War Exaggerated? Religious Orthodoxy and Moral Progressivism in America," *American Journal of Sociology*, 102 (3): 756–87.

Davis, N. J. and Robinson, R. V. (1996b), "Religious Orthodoxy in American Society: The Myth of a Monolithic Camp," *Journal for the Scientific Study of Religion*, 35 (3): 229–45.

Davis, N. J. and Robinson, R. V. (1996c), "Rejoinder to Hunter: Religious Orthodoxy— An Army Without Foot Soldiers?," *Journal for the Scientific Study of Religion*, 35 (3): 249–51.

Davis, N. J. and Robinson, R. V. (2006a), "The Egalitarian Face of Islamic Orthodoxy: Support for Islamic Law and Economic Justice in Seven Muslim-Majority Nations," *American Sociological Review*, 71 (2): 167–90.

Davis, N. J. and Robinson, R. V. (2006b), "Using a Research Article to Foster Moral Reflection and Global Awareness in Teaching about Religion and Politics, Theory Testing, and Democracy in the Muslim World," *Teaching Sociology*, 34 (3): 296–312.

Demerath, N. J. (2002), "A Sinner Among the Saints: Confessions of a Sociologist of Culture and Religion," *Sociological Forum*, 17 (1): 1–19.

Demerath, N. J. (2005), "The Battle Over a U.S. Culture War: A Note on Inflated Rhetoric Versus Inflamed Politics," *The Forum*, 3 (2), Article 6.

Dickerson, J. (2012), *The Decline of Evangelical America*. Available at: http://www.nytimes.com/2012/12/16/opinion/sunday/the-decline-of-evangelical-america.html (Accessed June 15, 2017).

Dillon, M. and Savage, S. (2006), *Values and Religion in Rural America: Attitudes Toward Abortion and Same-Sex Marriage* (Carsey Institute Policy Brief). Durham: University of New Hampshire.

Dillon, M. and Wink, P. (2007), *In the Course of a Lifetime: Tracing Religious Belief, Practice, and Change*. Berkeley: University of California Press.

DiMaggio, P., Evans, J. and Bryson, B. (1996), "Have Americans' Social Attitudes Become More Polarized?," *American Journal of Sociology*, 102 (3): 690–755.

Dix-Richardson, F. (2002), "Resistance to Conversion to Islam Among African American Women Inmates," *Journal of Offender Rehabilitation*, 35 (3): 107–24.

Dixon, J. (1849), *Personal Narrative of a Tour Through a Part of the United States and Canada: With Notices of the History and Institutions of Methodism in America*. New York: Lane & Scott.

Doyle, G. (2013), *Agreeing to Speak at Intolerant Church Is Tebow's Greatest Sin*. Available at: https://chicago.cbslocal.com/2013/02/19/gregg-doyle-agreeing-to-speak-at-intolerant-church-is-tebows-greatest-sin/ (Accessed October 17, 2016).

Duke, J. T. (1976), *Conflict and Power in Social Life*. Provo: Brigham Young University Press.

Durie, M. (2010), *The Third Choice: Islam, Dhimmitude and Freedom*. Melbourne: Deror Books.

Durkheim, E. (1912), *The Elementary Forms of the Religious Life*. London: George Allen & Unwin Ltd. Available at: http://www.gutenberg.org/files/41360/41360-h/41360-h.htm#Page_36 (Accessed August 31, 2015).

Dwight, T. (1798), *The Duty of Americans at the Present Crisis, Illustrated in a Discourse, Preached on the Fourth of July, 1798*. New Haven: Thomas and Samuel Green.

Dwight, T. (1812), *A Discourse in Two Parts Delivered July 23, 1812, on the Public Fast, in the Chapel of Yale College*. New Haven: Howe and Deforest.

Ecklund, E., Park, J. and Veliz, P. (2008), "Secularization and Religious Change among Elite Scientists," *Social Forces*, 86 (4): 1805–40.

Edgell, P. (2017), "An Agenda for Research on American Religion in Light of the 2016 Election," *Sociology of Religion*, 78 (1): 1–8.

Edwards, D., Ashmore, M. and Potter, J. (1995), "Death and Furniture: The Rhetoric, Politics and Theology of Bottom Line Arguments Against Relativism," *History of Human Sciences*, 8 (2): 25–49.

Edwards, J., Austin D. and Doolittle, A. (1793), *History of Redemption, on a Plan Entirely Original: Exhibiting the Gradual Discovery and Accomplishment of the Divine Purposes in the Salvation of Man; Including a Comprehensive View of Church History, and the Fulfilment of Scripture Prophecies*. New York: T. and J. Swords.

Elisha, O. (2011), *Moral Ambition: Mobilization and Social Outreach in Evangelical Megachurches*. Berkeley: University of California Press.

Ellison, C. G. and Musick, M. A. (1993), "Southern Intolerance: A Fundamentalist Effect?," *Social Forces*, 72 (2): 379–98.

Ernst, D. (2020), *Trump, Christians Ripped in NYTs op-ed: "The Road to Coronavirus Hell was Paved by Evangelicals"*. Available at: https://www.washingtontimes.com/news/

2020/mar/27/trump-christians-ripped-in-nyts-op-ed-the-road-to-/ (Accessed January 5, 2021).

Farrell, J. (2011), "The Young and the Restless? The Liberalization of Young Evangelicals," *The Journal for the Scientific Study of Religion*, 50 (3): 517–32.

Fea, J. (2018), *Believe Me: The Evangelical Road to Donald Trump*. Grand Rapids: Wm. B. Eerdmans Publishing.

Finke, R. and Stark, R. (1992), *The Churching of America 1776–1990*. New Brunswick: Rutgers University Press.

Fiorina, M. P., Abrams, S. A. and Pope, J. C. (2008), "Polarization in the American Public: Misconceptions and Misreadings," *The Journal of Politics*, 70 (2): 556–60.

Fischer, C. S. and Hout, M. (2006), *Century of Difference: How America Changed in the Last One Hundred Years*. New York: Russell Sage Foundation.

Fowler, J. W. (1981), *Stages of Faith: The Psychology of Human Development and the Quest for Meaning*. San Francisco: Harper & Row.

Friedman, H. (2002), "Psychological Nescience in a Postmodern Context," *American Psychologist*, 57 (6–7): 462–3.

Gabriel, M. (2002), *Islam and Terrorism: What the Quran Really Teaches About Christianity, Violence and the Goals of the Islamic Jihad*. Lake Mary: Frontline.

Gallagher, S. (2004), "Where Are the Antifeminist Evangelicals? Evangelicals Identity, Subcultural Location, and Attitudes Toward Feminism," *Gender and Society*, 18 (4): 451–72.

Ganiel, G. (2008), *Evangelicalism and Conflict in Northern Ireland*, 1st edn. Contemporary Anthropology of Religion. New York: Palgrave Macmillan.

Ganiel, G. (2016), *Transforming Post-Catholic Ireland: Religious Practice in Late Modernity*. Oxford: Oxford University Press.

Ganiel, G. (2013), "Research Ethics in Divided and Violent Societies: Seizing the Ethical Opportunity," in C. Russell, L. Hogan and M. Junker-Kenny (eds.), *Ethics for Graduate Researchers*, 167–81. Amsterdam: Elsevier.

Ganiel, G. and Mitchell, C. (2006), "Turning the Categories Inside-Out: Complex Identifications and Multiple Interactions in Religious Ethnography," *Sociology of Religion*, 67 (1): 3–21.

Geisler, N. and Saleeb, A. (2002), *Answering Islam: The Crescent in Light of the Cross*. Grand Rapids: Baker Books.

Gergen, K. J. (1985), "The Social Constructionist Movement in Modern Psychology," *American Psychologist*, 40 (3): 266–75.

Gillum, R. (2013), *No Difference in Religious Fundamentalism between American Muslims and Christians*. Available at: https://www.washingtonpost.com/news/monkeycage/wp/2013/12/16/no-difference-in-religious-fundamentalism-between-american-muslims-and-christians/?utm_term=.e9515db0b5f5 (Accessed July 17, 2017).

Gomm, R., Hammersley, M. and Foster, P. (2000), *Case Study Method: Key Issues, Key Texts*. London: SAGE.

Greeley, A. M. and Hout, M. (2006), *The Truth About Conservative Christians: What They Think and What They Believe*. Chicago: University of Chicago Press.

Grier, T., Rambo, C. and Taylor, M. (2014), "'What Are You?': Racial Ambiguity, Stigma, and the Racial Formation Project," *Deviant Behavior*, 35 (12): 6–22.

Grillo, M. C. (2014), "The Role of Emotions in Discriminatory Ethno-Religious Politics: An Experimental Study of Anti-Muslim Politics in the United States," *Politics, Religion & Ideology*, 15 (4): 583–603.

Guest, M. (2007), *Evangelical Identity and Contemporary Culture: A Congregational Study in Innovation*. Studies in Evangelical History and Thought. Eugene: Wipf and Stock Publishers.
Guest, M. (2012), "Keeping the End in Mind: Left Behind, the Apocalypse and the Evangelical Imagination," *Literature and Theology*, 26 (4): 474–88.
Guest, M. (2017), "The Emerging Church in Transatlantic Perspective," *Journal for the Scientific Study of Religion*, 56 (1): 41–51.
Guest, M., Aune, K., Sharma, S. and Warner, R. (2013), *Christianity and the University Experience: Understanding Student Faith*. London: Bloomsbury Academic.
Guiness, O. (1993), *The American Hour: A Time of Reckoning and the Once and Future Role of Faith*. New York: Free Press.
Gushee, D. P., ed. (2012), *A New Evangelical Manifesto: A Kingdom Vision for the Common Good*. St. Louis: Chalice Press.
Gushee, D. P., ed. (2013), *Evangelical Peacemakers: Gospel Engagement in a War Torn World*. Eugene: Wipf and Stock Publishers.
Guth, J. L. (1997), *The Bully Pulpit: The Politics of Protestant Clergy Studies in Government and Public Policy*. Lawrence: University Press of Kansas.
Hackling, I. (2000), *The Social Construction of What?* Cambridge: Harvard University Press.
Haddad, Y. Y. and Smith, J. I. (2009), "The Quest for 'a Common Word': Initial Christian Responses to a Muslim Initiative," *Islam & Christian-Muslim Relations*, 20 (4): 369–88.
Hafiz, Y. (2014), *Christian Activists Rally Behind Benham Brothers Following Cancellation of HGTV Show*. Available at: http://www.huffingtonpost.com/2014/05/09/christian-acti vists-benham-brothers-hgtv_n_5289625.html (Accessed October 17, 2016).
Hamlin, C. (1878), *Among the Turks*. New York: R. Carter & Brothers.
Hamm, M. (2007), *Terrorist Recruitment in American Correctional Institutions: An Exploratory Study of Non-Traditional Faith Groups*. Washington, DC: Department of Justice.
Hammersley, M. (1995), *The Politics of Social Research*. London: SAGE.
Hankins, B. (2009), *American Evangelicals: A Contemporary History of a Mainstream Religious Movement*. Lanham: Rowman & Littlefield.
Hansbury, L. (2011), "In the World But Not of It: Negotiating Evangelical Tradition and Gendered Identity in Contemporary Family Life," *Undergraduate Research Journal*, 5 (1): 11–23.
Hatch, N. (1989), *The Democratization of American Christianity*. New Haven: Yale University Press.
Haykin, M. A. G., Stewart, K. G. and George, T., eds. (2008), *The Emergence of Evangelicalism: Exploring Historical Continuities*. Nashville B & H Academic.
Hermans, C. (2002), "Social Constructionism and Practical Theology: An Introduction," in C. Hermans, G. Immink, A. de Jong and V. Lans (eds.), *Social Constructionism and Theology*. Leiden: Brill
Herrick, G. F. (1912), *Christian and Mohammedan: A Plea for Bridging the Chasm*. New York: Fleming H. Revell.
Hewstone, M. and Brown, R. (1986), "Contact Is Not Enough: An Intergroup Perspective on the 'Contact Hypothesis,'" in M. Hewstone and R. Brown (eds.), *Contact and Conflict in Intergroup Encounters*, 1–44. Oxford: Basil Blackwell.
Heyrman, C. (2015), *American Apostles: When Evangelicals Entered the World of Islam*. New York: Hill and Wang.
Himmelfarb, G. (1999), *One Nation, Two Cultures*. New York: A.A. Knopf.

Hirsi Ali, A. (2015), *America's Academies for Jihad*. Available at: https://www.wsj.com/articles/ayaan-hirsi-ali-americas-academies-for-jihad-1427843597 (Accessed April 18, 2020).

Hochschild, A. (2018), *Strangers in Their Own Land: Anger and Mourning on the American Right*. New York: New Press.

Holly, I. (1774), *God Brings About His Holy and Wise Purpose or Decree, Concerning Many Particular Events, by Using and Improving the Wicked Dispositions of Mankind in Order Thereto; and Often Improves the Present Corruptions of Sinners, as the Means to Chastise and Punish Them for Former Wickedness; Briefly Illustrated in a Sermon, Preached at Suffield, December 27, 1773, the Next Sabbath after the Report Arrived, that the People at Boston had Destroyed a Large Quantity of Tea, Belonging to the East-India Company, Rather Than to Submit to Parliament-acts, Which They Looked Upon Unconstitutional, Tyrannical, and Tending To Enslave America*. Hartford: Ebenezer Watson.

Holmes, D. L., Reddish, M. and Marty, M. (2012), *The Faiths of the Postwar Presidents from Truman to Obama*. George H Shriver Lecture Series in Religion in American History, No 5. Athens: University of Georgia Press.

Hoover, D. (2004), "Is Evangelicalism Itching for a Civilization Fight?," *The Brandywine Review of Faith and International Affairs*, 2 (1): 11–16.

Hopwood, D. (2020), "Egypt." *Encyclopedia Britannica*. Available at: https://www.britannica.com/place/Egypt/Rural-settlement (Accessed August 27, 2020).

Horowitz, D. (1985), *Ethnic Groups in Conflict*. Berkeley: University of California Press.

Hughes, J. and Donnelly, C. (1998), *Single Identity Community Relations*. Jordanstown: University of Ulster.

Hull, W. (1957), *Israel: Key to Prophecy*. Grand Rapids: Zondervan.

Hunter, J. D. (1983), *American Evangelicalism: Conservative Religion and the Quandary of Modernity*. New Brunswick: Rutgers University Press.

Hunter, J. D. (1987), *Evangelicalism: The Coming Generation*. Chicago: University of Chicago Press.

Hunter, J. D. (1991), *Culture Wars: The Struggle to Define America*. New York: Basic Books.

Hunter, J. D. (1994), *Before the Shooting Begins: Searching for Democracy in America's Culture War*. New York: Free Press.

Hunter, J. D. and Fiorina, M. P. (2007), *Ideological Culture Wars in America*. Available at: http://www.c-span.org/video/?202596-1/ideological-culture-wars-america (Accessed July 31, 2015).

Hunter, J. D. and Nedelisky, P. (2018), *Science and the Good: The Tragic Quest for the Foundations of Morality*. New Haven: Yale.

Hunter, J. D. and Nedelisky, P. (2020), Discussion Moderated by Teti, S. "The Interview: James Davidson Hunter and Paul Nedelisky Discuss Science and the Good: The Tragic Quest for the Foundations of Morality". Available at: https://bioethicsjournal.hms.harvard.edu/winter-2020/interview-james-davison-hunter-and-paul-nedelisky (Accessed August 27, 2020).

Hunter, J. D. and Wolfe, A. (2006a), Discussion Moderated by Cromartie, M. "Is There a Culture War?". Available at: http://www.pewforum.org/2006/05/23/is-there-a-culture-war/ (Accessed August 3, 2015).

Hunter, J. D. and Wolfe, A. (2006b), *Is There a Culture War? A Dialogue on Values and American Public Life*. Pew Forum Dialogues on Religion and Public Life. Washington, DC: Brookings Institution Press.

Hutchinson, M. and Wolffe, J. (2012), *A Short History of Global Evangelicalism*. Cambridge: Cambridge University Press.

Hutchison, W. R. (1987), *Errand to the World: American Protestant Thought and Foreign Missions*. Chicago: University of Chicago Press.
Inglehart, R. and Baker, W. E. (2000), "Modernization, Cultural Change, and the Persistence of Traditional Values," *American Sociological Review*, 65 (1): 19–51.
Isaac, R. (1982), *The Transformation of Virginia, 1740–1790*. Chapel Hill: University of North Carolina Press for The Institute of Early American History and Culture.
Jackson, R. (2020), "War on Terrorism: Unites States History." *Encyclopedia Britannica*. Available at: https://www.britannica.com/topic/war-on-terrorism (Accessed August 27, 2020).
Jacobsen, D. G. and Jacobsen, R. H. (2008), *The American University in a Postsecular Age*. Oxford: Oxford University Press.
James, A., Hockey, J. and Dawson, A. (1997), *After Writing Culture: Epistemology and Praxis in Contemporary Anthropology*. London: Routledge.
James, C. F. (1971), *Documentary History of the Struggle for Religious Liberty in Virginia*. Civil Liberties in American History. New York: Da Capo Press.
Janosik, D. (2019), *The Guide to Answering Islam: What Every Christian Needs to Know About Islam and the Rise of Radical Islam*. Cambridge: Christian Publishing House.
Jaspers, K. (1953), *The Origin and Goal of History*. New Haven: Yale University Press.
Jensen, D. (1981), *Reformation Europe: Age of Reform and Revolution*. Lexington: D.C. Heath and Company.
Jensen, L. A. (1998), "Different Habits, Different Hearts: The Moral Languages of the Culture War," *The American Sociologist*, 29 (1): 83–101.
Johnston, D. (2016), "American Evangelical Islamophobia: A History of Continuity with a Hope for Change," *Journal of Ecumenical Studies*, 51 (2): 224–35.
Jones, R. (2016), *The End of White Christian America*. New York: Simon & Schuster.
Jung, J. H. (2012), "Islamophobia? Religion, Contact with Muslims, and the Respect for Islam," *Review of Religious Research*, 54 (1): 113–26.
Kalkan, K. O., Layman, G. C. and Uslaner, E. M. (2009), "'Bands of Others'? Attitudes Toward Muslims in Contemporary American Society," *Journal of Politics*, 71 (3): 847–62.
Kaufman, S. (2001), *Modern Hatreds: The Symbolic Politics of Ethnic War*. Ithaca: Cornell University Press.
Kidd, T. S. (2007), *The Great Awakening: The Roots of Evangelical Christianity in Colonial America*. New Haven: Yale University Press.
Kidd, T. S. (2008), *The Great Awakening: A Brief History with Documents*. Boston: Bedford/ St. Martin's.
Kidd, T. S. (2009), *American Christians and Islam: Evangelical Culture and Muslims from the Colonial Period to the Age of Terrorism*. Princeton: Princeton University Press.
Kidd, T. S. (2010), *God of Liberty: A Religious History of the American Revolution*. New York: Basic Books.
Kown, L. (2013), *Christians Respond to Giglio's Withdrawal: New Era of Religious Intolerance in America?* Available at: http://www.christianpost.com/news/christians-respond-to-giglios-withdrawal-new-era-of-religious-intolerance-in-america-88068/ (Accessed October 17, 2016).
Kriesberg, L. (1973), *The Sociology of Social Conflicts*. Englewood Cliffs: Prentice-Hall.
Kvale, S. and Brinkmann, S. (2009), *Interviews: Learning the Craft of Qualitative Interviewing*. London: SAGE.
Kymlicka, W. (1995), *Multicultural Citizenship: A Liberal Theory of Minority Rights*. Oxford: Clarendon Press.

Lawler-Row, K. (2010), "Forgiveness as a Mediator of the Religiosity—Health Relationship," *Psychology of Religion and Spirituality*, 2 (1): 1.

Lawrence, J. A. (1987), "Verbal Processing of the Defining Issues Test by Principled and Non-Principled Moral Reasoners," *Journal of Moral Education*, 16 (2): 117–30.

Leeds-Hurwitz, W. (2009), "Social Construction of Reality," in S. Littlejohn and K. Foss (eds.), *Encyclopedia of Communication Theory*. Thousand Oaks: SAGE.

Leininger, M. M. (1985), *Qualitative Research Methods in Nursing*. Orlando: Grune & Stratton.

Leland, J. (1791), *The Rights of Conscience Inalienable, and therefore Religious Opinions not Cognizable by Law: Or, the High-Flying Churchman, Stript of His Legal Robe, Appears a Yaho*. New London: T. Green & Son.

Levin, J., Chatters, L. and Taylor, R. (1995), "Religious Effects on Health Status and Life Satisfaction Among Black Americans," *The Journals of Gerontology Series B: Psychological Sciences and Social Sciences*, 50 (3): S154–63.

Lewis, R. (2009), "Insider Movements: Honoring God-given Identity and Community," *International Journal of Frontier Missiology*, 26 (1): 16–19.

Lincoln, A., Gates, H. L. and Yacovone, D. (2009), *Lincoln on Race and Slavery*. Princeton: Princeton University Press.

Lindsay, D. M. (2006), "Elite Power: Social Networks Within American Evangelicalism," *Sociology of Religion*, 67 (3): 207–27.

Lindsay, D. M. (2007), *Faith in the Halls of Power: How Evangelicals Joined the American Elite*. Oxford: Oxford University Press.

Lindsey, H. (2011), *The Everlasting Hatred: The Roots of Jihad*. Washington, DC: WND Books.

Lindsey, H. and Carlson, C. C. (1970), *The Late Great Planet Earth*. Grand Rapids: Zondervan.

Lingel, J., Morton, J. and Nikides, B. (2011), *Chrislam: How Missionaries Are Promoting an Islamized Gospel*. Garden Grove: i2 Ministries Publishing.

Lipset, S. M. (1996), *American Exceptionalism: A Double-edged Sword*. New York: W.W. Norton.

Livingstone, D. N. (1984), *Darwin's Forgotten Defenders: The Encounter between Evangelical Theology and Evolutionary Thought*. Vancouver: Regent College Publishing.

Livingstone, D. N., Hart, D. and Noll, M., eds. (1999), *Evangelicals and Science in Historical Perspective*. Oxford: Oxford University Press.

Longs, H. (2020), *Lauren Daigle, Nick Hall & More to Bring you Streaming "Good Friday Service"*. Available at: https://www.thechristianbeat.org/index.php/news/7464-lauren-daigle-nick-hall-more-to-bring-you-streaming-good-friday-service (Accessed April 20, 2020).

Lowry, L. (2019), *Breaking: Asia Bibi Leaves Pakistan, Safe in Canada*. Available at: https://www.opendoorsusa.org/christian-persecution/stories/breaking-asia-bibi-leaves-pakistan-safe-in-canada/ (Accessed August 27, 2020).

Luther, M. (2014), *On the Jews and Their Lies*. Austin: RiverCrest Pub.

Luther, M. and Helfferich, T. (2013), *On the Freedom of a Christian: With Related Texts*. Indianapolis: Hackett Publishing Co.

Luther, M. and Nichols, S. J. (2002), *Martin Luther's Ninety-Five Theses*. Phillipsburg: P & R Pub.

MacCulloch, D. (2003), *The Reformation: A History*. New York: Penguin Group.

Machen, J. Gresham (2009), *Christianity and Liberalism*. Grand Rapids: Eerdmans.

Mark, J. (2009), "Ancient Egypt." *Ancient History Encyclopedia*. Available at: https://www.ancient.eu/egypt/ (Accessed August 27, 2020).

Markay, L. (2013), *Defense Department Classifies Catholics, Evangelicals as Extremists*. Available at: http://www.washingtontimes.com/news/2013/apr/5/dod-presentation-classifies-catholics-evangelicals/ (Accessed July 17, 2017).

Markofski, W. (2015), *New Monasticism and the Transformation of American Evangelicalism*. Oxford: Oxford University Press.

Marsden, G. M. (2006), *Fundamentalism and American Culture*. Oxford: Oxford University Press.

Mason, J. (2011), *At Prayer Breakfast, Obama Calls Jesus "My Lord and Savior"*. Available at: http://blogs.reuters.com/talesfromthetrail/2011/02/03/at-prayer-breakfast-obama-calls-jesus-my-lord-and-savior/ (Accessed June 15, 2017).

Marti, G. (2016), "'I Was a Muslim, But Now I Am a Christian': Preaching, Legitimation, and Identity Management in a Southern Evangelical Church," *The Journal for the Scientific Study of Religion*, 55 (2): 250–71.

Marti, G. (2020), *American Blindspot: Race, Class, Religion, and the Trump Presidency*. Lanham: Rowan & Littlefield Publishers.

Marti, G. and Ganiel, G. (2014), *The Deconstructed Church: Understanding Emerging Christianity*. Oxford: Oxford University Press.

Mather, C. (1699), *Decennium Luctuosum an History of Remarkable Occurrences, in the Long War, Which New-England Hath had with the Indian Savages, from the year, 1688. To the year 1698*. Boston: B. Green, and J. Allen.

Mather, I. (1677), *A Relation of the Troubles Which have Hapned [Sic] in New-England by Reason of the Indians there from the Year 1614 to the Year 1675 Wherein the Frequent Conspiracys of the Indians to Cutt Off the English, and the Wonderfull Providence of God in Disappointing Their Devices is Declared: Together with an Historical Discourse Concerning the Prevalency of Prayer Shewing that New Englands Late Deliverance from the Rage of the Heathen is an Eminent Answer of Prayer*. Boston: John Foster.

Maybury-Lewis, D. and Almagor, U. (1989), *The Attraction of Opposites: Thought and Society in the Dualistic Mode*. Ann Arbor: University of Michigan Press.

McAlister, M. (2019), "Evangelical Populist Internationalism and the Politics of Persecution," *The Review of Faith and International Affairs*, 17 (3): 105–17.

McCallum, R. (2011), *A Sociological Approach to Christian-Muslim Relations: British Evangelicals, Muslims, and the Public Sphere*. Exeter: University of Exeter.

McCallum, R. (2012), "Love: A Common Word Between Evangelicals and Muslims?," *Political Theology*, 13 (4): 400–13.

McDermott, G. (2000), *Jonathan Edwards Confronts the Gods: Christian Theology, Enlightenment Religion, and Non-Christian Faiths*. Oxford: Oxford University Press.

McLaren, B. D. (2012), "The Church in America Today," in D. Gushee (ed.), *A New Evangelical Manifesto: A Kingdom Vision for the Common Good*. St. Louis: Chalice Press.

McLaren, B. D. (2012), *My Take: It's Time for Islamophobic Evangelicals to Choose*. Available at: http://religion.blogs.cnn.com/2012/09/15/my-take-its-time-for-islamophobic-evangelicals-to-choose/ (Accessed April 18, 2013).

McMillan, W. (2013), "Contextualization, Big Apple Style: Breaking Evangelical Stereotypes in Modern-Day Manhattan," *Symposia*, 5: 1–16.

Medearis, C. (2011), *Muslims, Christians, and Jesus*. Grand Rapids: Zondervan.

Merelman, R. M. (1984), *Making Something of Ourselves: On Culture and Politics in the United States*. Berkeley: University of California Press.

Merino, S. M. (2010), "Religious Diversity in a 'Christian Nation': The Effects of Theological Exclusivity and Interreligious Contact on the Acceptance of Religious Diversity," *The Journal for the Scientific Study of Religion*, 49 (2): 231–46.

Merritt, J. (2016), *Are Conservative Christians "Religious Extremists?"*. Available at: https://www.theatlantic.com/politics/archive/2016/03/are-conservative-christians-religious-extremists/473187/ (Accessed July 17, 2017).

Merritt, J. (2018), *Lauren Daigle and the Lost Art of Discernment*. Available at: https://www.theatlantic.com/ideas/archive/2018/12/let-lauren-daigle-be-unsure-about-lgbt-relationships/577651/ (Accessed April 17, 2020).

Miller, R. and Brewer, J., eds. (2003), *The A-Z of Social Research*. London: SAGE.

Mingerink, R. (2017), *Social Constructionism: What Is It? Reformed Free Publishing Association*. Available at: https://rfpa.org/blogs/news/social-constructionism-5-what-is-it (Accessed August 27, 2020).

Mitchell, C. and Ganiel, G. (2011), *Evangelical Journeys: Choice and Change in a Northern Irish Religious Subculture*. Dublin: University College Dublin Press.

Mitchell, C. and Todd, J. (2007), "Between the Devil and the Deep Blue Sea: Nationality, Power and Symbolic Trade-Offs Among Evangelical Protestants in Contemporary Northern Ireland," *Nations and Nationalism*, 13 (4): 637–55.

Mohler, H. (2007), *A Christian Response to a Common Word Between Us and You*. Available at: http://www.desiringgod.org/messages/evangelicals-and-a-common-word (Accessed June 15, 2017).

Mulcahy, K. V. and Wyszomirski, M. J. (1995), *America's Commitment to Culture: Government and the Arts*. Boulder: Westview Press.

Nagel, C. (2016), "Southern Hospitality? Islamophobia and the Politicization of Refugees in South Carolina during the 2016 Election Season," *Southeastern Geographer*, 56 (3): 283–91.

Needham-Penrose, J. and Friedman, H. L. (2012), "Moral Identity Versus Moral Reasoning In Religious Conservatives: Do Christian Evangelical Leaders Really Lack Moral Maturity?," *The Humanistic Psychologist*, 40 (4): 343–63.

Neitz, M. J. (1987), *Charisma and Community: A Study of Religious Commitment Within the Charismatic Renewal*. New Observations. New Brunswick: Transaction Books.

Neitz, M. J. (2002), "Walking Between the Worlds: Permeable Boundaries, Ambiguous Identities," in J. Spickard, J. Landres and M. McGuire (eds.), *Personal Knowledge and Beyond: Reshaping the Ethnography of Religion*. New York: New York University Press.

Neitz, M. J. (2004), "Gender and Culture: Challenges to the Sociology of Religion," *Sociology of Religion*, 65 (4): 391–402.

Neitz, M. J. (2014), "Becoming Visible: Religion and Gender in Sociology," *Sociology of Religion*, 75 (4): 511–23.

Nigel, C. (2016), "Southern Hospitality? Islamophobia and the Politicization of Refugees in South Carolina during the 2016 Election Season," *Southeastern Geographer*, 56 (3): 283–7.

Noll, M. A. (1994), *The Scandal of the Evangelical Mind*. Grand Rapids: W.B. Eerdmans.

Noll, M. A. (2002), *God and Mammon: Protestants, Money, and the Market, 1790–1860*. Oxford: Oxford University Press.

Noll, M. A. (2002), *The Work We Have To Do: A History of Protestants in America*. Oxford: Oxford University Press.

Noll, M. A. (2006), *The Civil War as a Theological Crisis*. The Steven and Janice Brose Lectures in the Civil War Era. Chapel Hill: University of North Carolina Press.

Oberman, H. A. (1989), *Luther: Man between God and the Devil*. New Haven: Yale University Press.

Okeley, W. (1676), *Eben-Ezer, or, a Small Monument of Great Mercy Appearing in the Miraculous Deliverance of William Okeley, William Adams, John Anthony, John Jephs, John Carpenter from the Miserable Slavery of Algiers: With the Wonderful Means Of Their Escape in a Boat of Canvas, the Great Distress and Utmost Extremities Which They Endured At Sea For Six Days . . . and the Following Providences of God Which Brought Them Safe from England*. London: Printed for Nat. Ponder.

Oliver-Dee, S. (2015), *God's Unwelcome Recovery: Why the New Establishment Wants to Proclaim the Death of Faith*. Oxford: Monarch Books.

Parekh, B. (2000), *Rethinking Multiculturalism: Cultural Diversity and Political Theory*. London: Palgrave MacMillan.

Parton, N. (2012), "Thinking and Acting Constructively in Child Protection," in S. Witkin (ed.), *Social Construction and Social Work Practice*. New York: Columbia University Press.

Patton, M. (1990), *Qualitative Evaluation and Research Methods*. Beverly Hills: SAGE.

Petersen, R. (2002), *Understanding Ethnic Violence: Fear, Hatred, and Resentment in Twentieth-Century Eastern Europe*. New York: Cambridge University Press.

Pew Forum (2010), *Growing Number of Americans Say Obama Is Muslim*. Available at: http://www. pewforum.org/2010/08/18/growing-number-of-americans-say-obama-is-a-muslim/ (Accessed October 19, 2014).

Pew Research Center (2001), *Post 9/11 Attitudes*. Available at: http://www.people-press.org/2001/12/06/post-september-11-attitudes/ (Accessed April 18, 2013).

Pew Research Center (2003), *Survey on American Attitudes Toward Islam*. Available at: http://www.people-press.org/files/legacy-pdf/189.pdf (Accessed April 18, 2013).

Pew Research Center (2006), *The Great Divide: How Westerners and Muslims View Each Other*. Available at: http://www.pewglobal.org/2006/06/22/the-great-divide-how-westerners-and-muslims-view-each-other/ (Accessed June 13, 2017).

Pew Research Center (2007), *Converts to Islam*. Available at: http://www.pewresearch.org/fact-tank/2007/07/21/converts-to-islam/ (Accessed July 30, 2017).

Pew Research Center (2014), *Religious Landscape Survey*. Available at: http://www.pewforum.org /religious-landscape-study/ (Accessed June 13, 2017).

Pew Research Center (2015a), *Religious "Nones" Are Not Only Growing, They're Becoming More Secular*. Available at: http://www.pewresearch.org/fact-tank/2015/11/11/religious-nones-are-not-only-growing-theyre-becoming-more-secular/ (Accessed June 13, 2017).

Pew Research Center (2015b), *U.S. Public Becoming Less Religious*. Available at: http://www.pewforum.org/2015/11/03/u-s-public-becoming-less-religious/ (Accessed June 15, 2017).

Pew Research Center (2016), *A New Estimate of the U.S. Muslim Population*. Available at: http://www. pewresearch.org/fact-tank/2016/01/06/a-new-estimate-of-the-u-s-muslim-population/ (Accessed June 18, 2017).

Pew Research Center (2017a), *Among White Evangelicals, Regular Churchgoers Are the Most Supportive of Trump*. Available at: http://www.pewresearch.org/fact-tank/2017/04/26/among-white-evangelicals-regular-churchgoers-are-the-most-supportive-of-trump/ (Accessed June 15, 2017).

Pew Research Center (2017b), *Most White Evangelicals Approve of Trump Travel Prohibition and Express Concerns About Extremism*. Available at: http://www.pewresearch.org/fact-tank/2017/02/27/most-white-evangelicals-approve-of-trump-travel-prohibition-and-express-concerns-about-extremism/ (Accessed June 15, 2017).

Pew Research Center (2017c), *The Changing Global Religious Landscape*. Available at: http://www.pewforum.org/2017/04/05/the-changing-global-religious-landscape/ (Accessed June 15, 2017).

Pew Research Center (2017d), *Americans Express Increasingly Warm Feelings Toward Religious Groups*. Available at: http://www.pewforum.org/2017/02/15/americans-express-increasingly-warm-feelings-toward-religious-groups/ (Accessed August 14, 2017).

Pew Research Center (2017e), *God or the Divine Is Referenced in Every State Constitution*. Available at: http://www.pewresearch.org/fact-tank/2017/08/17/god-or-the-divine-is-referenced-in-every-state-constitution/?utm_source=Pew+Research+Center&utm_campaign=af58cf2f8f-EMAIL_CAMPAIGN_2017_08_23&utm_medium=email&utm_term=0_3e953b9b70-af58cf2f8f-3999726 (Accessed August 27, 2017).

Pew Research Center (2018), *Disagreements about Trump Widely Seen as Reflecting Divides Over "Other Values And Goals."* Available at: http://www.pewresearch.org/fact-tank/2018/03/15/disagreements-about-trump-widely-seen-as-reflecting-divides-over-other-values-and-goals/ (Accessed December 14, 2018).

Pew Research Center (2019), *Around the World, More Say Immigrants Are a Strength Than a Burden*. Available at: https://www.pewresearch.org/global/2019/03/14/around-the-world-more-say-immigrants-are-a-strength-than-a-burden/ (Accessed January 5, 2021).

Piper, J. (2007), *A Christian Response to a Common Word Between Us and You*. Available at: http://www.desiringgod.org/messages/evangelicals-and-a-common-word (Accessed June 15, 2017).

Piper, J. (2009), *Evangelicals and "A Common Word."* Available at: https://www.desiringgod.org/messages/evangelicals-and-a-common-word (Accessed January 5, 2021).

Piper, J. (2011), *Is God Glad Osama Bin Laden's Dead?* Available at: http://www.desiringgod.org/articles/is-god-glad-osama-bin-ladens-dead (Accessed June 15, 2017).

Prescott, B. and Gee, J. (1743), *A Letter to the Reverend Mr. Joshua Gee, in Answer to His of June 3. 1743. Address'd to the Reverend Mr. Nathanael Eells, Moderator of the Late Convention of Pastors in Boston*. Boston: Green, Bushell, and Allen.

Putnam, R. (2000), *Bowling Alone: The Collapse and Revival of American Community*. New York: Simon & Schuster.

Quosigk, A. (2015), *Conference Report: Rethinking Boundaries in the Study of Religion and Politics*. Available at: https://www.religiousstudiesproject.com/response/conference-report-rethinking-boundaries-in-the-study-of-religion-and-politics/ (Accessed August 27, 2020).

Quosigk, A. (2016), *Conference Report: "Religious Pluralisation—A Challenge for Modern Societies"*. Available at: https://www.religiousstudiesproject.com/response/conference-report-religious-pluralisation-a-challenge-for-modern-societies/ (Accessed August 27, 2020).

Quosigk, A. (2017), "The German Peasants' War (1524–1525)," in J. Shaw and T. Demy (eds.), *War and Religion: An Encyclopedia of Faith and Conflict*. Santa Barbara: ABC-CLIO.

Qureshi, N. (2016), *Seeking Allah, Finding Jesus: A Devout Muslim Encounters Christianity*. Grand Rapids: Zondervan.

Read, J. G. (2003), "The Sources of Gender Role Attitudes Among Christian and Muslim Arab-American Women," *Sociology of Religion*, 64 (2): 207–22.

Regnerus, M., Christian, S. and Sikkink, D. (1998), "Who Gives to the Poor? The Influence of Religious Tradition and Political Location on the Personal Generosity of Americans Toward the Poor," *Journal for the Scientific Study of Religion*, 37 (3): 481–93.

Reimer, S. H. (2003), *Evangelicals and the Continental Divide: The Conservative Protestant Subculture in Canada and the United States*. McGill-Queen's Studies in the History of Religion, Series Two. Montreal: McGill-Queen's University Press.

Rhodes, J. (2012), "The Ties That Divide: Bonding Social Capital, Religious Friendship Networks, and Political Tolerance Among Evangelicals," *Sociological Inquiry*, 82 (2): 163–86.

Rich, E. (1775), *The Number of the Beast Found Out by Spiritual Arithmetic: Or the Art of Heavenly Arithmetic, Learned Only in Christ's School. By Which Is Plainly Discover'd, Some of the Secret Depths of Satan*. Chelmsford: Nathaniel Coverly.

Richards, P. S. and Davison, M. L. (1992), "Religious Bias in Moral Development Research: A Psychometric Investigation," *Journal for the Scientific Study of Religion*, 31 (4): 467–85.

Riddell, P. (2013), "Poles Apart: Diverse Muslim Perspectives on 'True' Islam," in J. Azumah and P. Riddell (eds.), *Islam and Christianity on the Edge: Talking Points in Christian-Muslim Relations into the 21st Century*. Victoria: Acorn Press.

Rockmore, T. (2006), "Hegel on History, 9/11, and the War on Terror, or Reason In History," *Cultural Politics*, 2 (3): 281–98.

Ryle, R. R. and Robinson, R. V. (2006), "Ideology, Moral Cosmology, and Community in the United States," *City & Community*, 5 (1): 53–69.

Saldaña, J. (2009), *The Coding Manual for Qualitative Researchers*. London: SAGE.

Saperstein, A. and Penner, Andrew M. (2012), "Racial Fluidity and Inequality in the United States1," *American Journal of Sociology*, 118: 676–727.

Scala, J. (2020), "Polls and Elections: The Skeptical Faithful: How Trump Gained Momentum Among Evangelicals," *Presidential Studies Quarterly*, 50 (4): 927–47.

Schensul, S., Schensul, J. and LeCompte, M. (1999), *Essential Ethnographic Methods: Observations, Interviews, and Questionnaires*. Oxford: Rowman Altamira.

Scribner, B. and Benecke, G. (1979), *The German Peasant War of 1525: New Viewpoints*. London: George Allen & Unwin.

Sheridan, M. (2012), *Florida Pastor Terry Jones Burns Copies of Koran Outside Church*. Available at: http://www.nydailynews.com/news/national/florida-pastor-terry-jones-burns-copies-koran-church-article-1.1069458 (Accessed October 19, 2016).

Shields, A. and Dunn, J. (2016), *Passing on the Right: Conservative Professors in the Progressive University*. New York: Oxford University Press.

Shkurko, A. (2015), "Cognitive Mechanisms of Ingroup/Outgroup Distinction," *Journal for the Theory of Social Behaviour*, 45 (2): 188–214.

Shumack, R. (2014), *The Wisdom of Islam and the Foolishness of Christianity*. Melbourne: Island View Publishing.

Shweder, R. A. (1990), "In Defense of Moral Realism: Reply to Gabennesch," *Child Development*, 61 (6): 2060–7.

Sider, R. (2012), "Back Cover Recommendation," in D. Gushee (ed.), *A New Evangelical Manifesto: A Kingdom Vision For The Common Good*. St. Louis: Chalice Press.

Sides, J. and Gross, K. (2013), *Stereotypes of Muslims and Support for the War on Terror*. Available at: http://home.gwu.edu/~jsides/muslims.pdf (Accessed October 19, 2016).

Sieczkowski, C. (2013, updated 2016), Duck Dynasty *Star Phil Robertson Makes Anti-Gay Remarks, Says Being Gay Is a Sin [Updated]*. Available at: http://www.huffingtonpost.com/2013/12/18/duck-dynasty-phil-robertson-gay_n_4465564.html (Accessed October 17, 2016).

Silverman, D. (2000), *Doing Qualitative Research: A Practical Handbook*. London: SAGE.

Simmel, G. (1955), *Conflict*. Glencoe: Free Press.

Smidt, C. E. (2005), "Religion and American Attitudes Toward Islam and An Invasion of Iraq," *Sociology of Religion*, 66 (3): 243–61.

Smith, A. D. (1991), *National Identity: Ethnonationalism in Comparative Perspective*. Reno: University of Nevada Press.

Smith, C. (1998), *American Evangelicalism: Embattled and Thriving*. Chicago: University of Chicago Press.

Smith, C. (2003), *The Secular Revolution: Power, Interests, and Conflict in the Secularization of American Public Life*. Berkeley: University of California Press.

Smith, C. (2010). *What Is a Person?* Chicago: University of Chicago Press.

Smith, C. and Denton, M. (2009), *Soul Searching: The Religious and Spiritual Lives of American Teenagers*. New York: Oxford University Press.

Smith, L. (2012), *The First Great Awakening in Colonial American Newspapers: A Shifting Story*. Lanham: Lexington Books.

Sokolove, M. (2019), *Why Is There So Much Saudi Money in American Universities?* Available at: https://www.nytimes.com/2019/07/03/magazine/saudi-arabia-american-universities.html (Accessed March 15, 2017).

Sommers-Flanagan, J. and Sommers-Flanagan, R. (2012), *Counseling and Psychotherapy Theories in Context and Practice: Skills, Strategies, and Techniques*. Hoboken: John Wiley and Sons.

SpearIt (2012), "Raza Islamica: Prisons, Hip Hop & Converting Converts," *Berkeley La Raza Law Journal*, 22 (1): 175–201.

Starks, B. and Robinson, R. V. (2009), "Two Approaches to Religion and Politics: Moral Cosmology and Subcultural Identity," *The Journal for the Scientific Study of Religion*, 48 (4): 650–69.

Steensland, B. and Goff, P. (2013), *The New Evangelical Social Engagement*. New York: Oxford University Press.

Stein, A. A. (1976), "Conflict and Cohesion: A Review of the Literature," *The Journal of Conflict Resolution*, 20 (1): 143–72.

Stewart, K. (2020), *The Religious Right's Hostility to Science Is Crippling Our Coronavirus Response*. Available at: https://www.nytimes.com/2020/03/27/opinion/coronavirus-trump-evangelicals.html?action=click&module=Opinion&pgtype=Homepage (Accessed January 5, 2021).

Stone, L. (2017), *Conservative Christians are Divided on Trump's Stance on Refugees—But They Can be Convinced*. Available at: http://www.salon.com/2017/02/06/the-left-needs-the-religious-right-conservative-christians-are-divided-on-the-refugee-ban-but-they-can-be-convinced/ (Accessed June 15, 2017).

Stringer, M. (2011), *Contemporary Western Ethnography and the Definition of Religion*. London: Bloomsbury Academic.

Sumner, W. G. (1907), *Folkways: A Study of the Sociological Importance of Usages, Manners, Customs, Mores, and Morals*. Boston: Ginn.

Sutton, M. A. (2013), *Jerry Falwell and the Rise of the Religious Right: A Brief History with Documents*. The Bedford Series in History and Culture. Boston: Bedford/St. Martin's.

Talman, H. and Travis, J., eds. (2015), *Understanding Insider Movements: Disciples of Jesus Within Diverse Religious Communities*. Pasadena: William Carey Library.

Taylor, S. J. and Bogdan, B. (1984), *Introduction to Qualitative Research Methods: The Search for Meanings*, 2nd edn. New York: Wiley.

The Bible English Standard Version (2007), Wheaton: Crossway Bibles.

Thomas, J. N. (2013), "Outsourcing Moral Authority: The Internal Secularization of Evangelicals' Anti-Pornography Narratives," *Journal for the Scientific Study of Religion*, 52 (3): 457–75.

Thomas, J. N. and Olson, D. V. A. (2012a), "Evangelical Elites' Changing Responses to Homosexuality 1960–2009," *Sociology of Religion*, 73 (3): 239–72.

Thomas, J. N. and Olson, D. V. A. (2012b), "Beyond the Culture War: Managing Sexual Relationships Inside a Congregation of Gay Evangelicals," *Review of Religious Research*, 54 (3): 349–70.

Thomas Nelson (n.d.), *The NKJV, American's Patriot Bible, Hardcover*. Available at: http://www.thomasnelson.com/the-american-patriot-s-bible-1 (Accessed October 18, 2016).

Thomson, I. T. (2010), *Culture Wars and Warring About Culture*. Contemporary Political and Social Issues. Ann Arbor: University of Michigan Press.

Thompson, M., Ellis, R. and Wildavsky, A. B. (1990), *Cultural Theory*. Political Cultures. Boulder: Westview Press.

Thumma, S. (1991), "Negotiating a Religious Identity: The Case of the Gay Evangelical," *Sociology of Religion*, 52 (4): 333–47.

Tobin, G. and Weinberg, A. (2007), *Profiles of the American University, Volume II: Religious Beliefs and Behavior of College Faculty*. San Francisco: Institute for Jewish and Community Research.

Tocqueville, A. and Reeve, H. (1835), *Democracy in America*. 4 vols. London: Saunders and Otley.

Uecker, J. E. and Lucke, G. (2011), "Protestant Clergy and the Culture Wars: An Empirical Test of Hunter's Thesis," *Journal for the Scientific Study of Religion*, 50 (4): 692–706.

Urdank, A. M. (1991), "Evangelicalism in Modern England," *Journal of British Studies*, 30 (3): 333–44.

Vander Werff, L. L. (1977), *Christian Mission to Muslims: The Record: Anglican and Reformed Approaches in India and the Near East, 1800–1938*. The William Carey Library Series on Islamic Studies. South Pasadena: William Carey Library.

Viola, F. (2016), *9 Lies the Media Likes to Tell About Evangelical Christians*. Available at: http://www.patheos.com/blogs/frankviola/media/ (Accessed October 17, 2016).

Vu, M. (2011), *Piper: God has Mixed Emotions on Osama Bin Laden's Death*. Available at: http://www.christianpost.com/news/piper-god-has-mixed-emotions-on-osama-bin-ladens-death-50097/ (Accessed June 15, 2017).

Waller, J. (2003, October 14), *Statement of J. Waller Before the Subcommittee on Terrorism, Technology and Homeland Security Senate Committee on the Judiciary*. Available at: https://www.judiciary.senate.gov/imo/media/doc/waller_testimony_10_14_03.pdf (Accessed August 17, 2017).

Watt, J., ed. (2006), *The Long Reformation*. Boston: Houghton Mifflin Company.

Weinberg, D. (2014), *Contemporary Social Constructionism: Key Themes*. Philadelphia: Temple University Press.

Wellman, J. (2007), "Is War Normal for American Evangelical Religion?," in J. Wellman (ed.), *Belief and Bloodshed: Religion and Violence Across Time and Tradition*. Boulder: Rowman and Littlefield Publishers.

Whitehead, A. and Perry, S. (2020), *Taking America Back for God: Christian Nationalism in the United States*. New York: Oxford University Press.

Wilcox, M. (2002), "Dancing on the Fence: Researching Lesbian, Gay, Bisexual, and Transgender Christians," in J. Green, M. Rozell and C. Wilcox (eds.), *Personal Knowledge and Beyond: Reshaping the Ethnography of Religion*. New York: New York University Press.

Wilcox, W. (1999), "American Evangelicalism: Embattled and Thriving, Christian Smith," *Review of Religious Research*, 41 (2): 281–83.

Wilkinson, K. (2012), *Between God and Green: How Evangelicals Are Cultivating a Middle Ground on Climate Change*. New York: Oxford University Press.

Williams, J. R. (2012), "Trusting Doctors: The Decline of Moral Authority in American Medicine," *The Heythrop Journal*, 53 (5): 879–80.

Williams, R. (1676), *George Fox digg'd Out of His Burrovves, Or, An Offer of Disputation on Fourteen Proposalls Made This Last Summer 1672 (so call'd) unto G. Fox Then Present on Rode-Island in New-England*. Boston: John Foster.

Williams, R. H. (1997), *Cultural Wars in American Politics: Critical Reviews of a Popular Myth*. Social Problems and Social Issues. New York: Aldine de Gruyter.

Williams, R. M. (1947), *The Reduction of Intergroup Tensions: A Survey of Research on Problems of Ethnic, Racial, and Religious Group Relations*. Social Science Research Council Bulletin 57. New York: Social Science Research Council.

Williams, S. (2001), "Sociological Imperialism and the Profession of Medicine Revisited: Where Are We Now?," *Sociology of Heath and Illness*, 23 (2): 135–58.

Wilson, J. and Janoski, T. (1995), "The Contribution of Religion to Volunteer Work," *Sociology of Religion*, 56 (2): 137–52.

Woodberry, R. D. and Smith, C. S. (1998), "Fundamentalism et al: Conservative Protestants in America," *Annual Review of Sociology*, 24 (1.25): 25.

Wuthnow, R. (1987), *Meaning and Moral Order: Explorations in Cultural Analysis*. Berkeley: University of California Press.

Wuthnow, R. (1988), *The Restructuring of American Religion: Society and Faith Since World War II*. Studies in Church and State. Princeton: Princeton University Press.

Wuthnow, R. (1996), *Christianity and Civil Society: The Contemporary Debate*. The Rockwell Lecture Series. Valley Forge: Trinity Press International.

Wuthnow, R. (1998), *After Heaven: Spirituality in America since the 1950s*. Berkeley: University of California Press.

Yancey, G. (2011), *Compromising Scholarship: Religious and Political Bias in American Higher Education*. Waco: Baylor University Press.

Yancey, G. and Quosigk, A. (2021), *One Faith No Longer: The Transformation of Christianity in Red and Blue America*. New York: New York University Press.

Yancey, G., Reimer, S. and O'Connell, J. (2015), "How Academics View Conservative Protestants," *Sociology of Religion*, 76 (3): 315–36.

Young, R. (2003), "Introduction: Constructivism and Social Constructionism in the Career Field," *Journal of Vocational Behavior*, 64 (3): 373–88.

Youssef, M. (2019), *The Third Jihad: Overcoming Radical Islam's Plan for the West*. Carol Stream: Tyndale Momentum.

Zwemer, S. M. (1907), *Islam, a Challenge to Faith*. New York: Student Volunteer Movement for Foreign Missions.

Zylstra, S. (2015), *Pew: Evangelicals Stay Strong as Christianity Crumbles in America*. Available at: http://www.christianitytoday.com/news/2015/may/pew-evangelicals-stay-strong-us-religious-landscape-study.html (Accessed June 15, 2017).

INDEX

abolitionism 27
abortion 2, 6, 32–3, 37, 53, 55, 64, 67, 70, 71, 116
Abraham (patriarch) 39–40, 196
absolutism 62–3
"A Common Word" (ACW) 39, 40, 81, 102–5, 107, 138–9, 182, 192
activism 9, 17 n.2, 33, 111
affinity 57
affluence 35, 36
Afghan war 38, 92, 93
Afganistan 38
agnosticism 4
Ahktar, Iqbal 37
Ahmadiyya 172
à Kempis, Thomas 17
Allah 39, 93, 104–5, 115, 125, 133–4, 148, 168
Allahu Akbar 1
American Board of Commissioners for Foreign Missions (ABCFM) 28, 31
American Evangelicalism: Embattled and Thriving (Smith) 48
American Hour (Guiness) 63
American Humanist Association 35
American Revolution 21, 22
American's Patriot Bible (Nelson) 38
Anabaptists 19, 169
Analytical tool 46, 54, 155–6, 162
Anglicanism, formal prayers 22
animism 30
Answering Islam (Geisler and Saleeb) 40
anti-intellectual 2, 30, 179
antichrist 16, 20, 25, 34
apologetics 68, 90, 104, 115, 130, 153
apostasy ix
Armageddon 40
Arminius, Jacob 23
Asbury, Francis 26
Asia (region) 1, 113

aspirations 35, 36, 58
atheism/atheists xi, 4, 58, 86
atonement 9, 29, 97
Augsburg Confession 26
Augustine 17
Austin, David 24
autobiographical literature 39, 163

Baal (object of worship) 138
Backus, Isaac 22, 25–6
Baker, Wayne 62
Bakker, Jim 33
Bangladesh 98–9
Baptists 12, 22, 25, 26, 27, 32, 33, 38, 109, 110, 113–15, 117, 134, 135, 169, 186
Barbary pirates 20–1
Bebbington, David 9–10, 17
Bebbington quadrilateral 9–10
Before the Shooting Begins (Hunter) 46, 68–9
belonging 48
Berger, Peter 1, 4
Bible
    battle against superiority of 25, 28–30, 32, 36, 66, 160
    as confusing 127–8
    holistic view of 138
    as the inspired word of God 9, 25, 27, 29, 39, 61, 73–6, 84, 113, 118
    marriage according to 36, 160
    moral authority of 30, 42, 61, 66, 74, 76, 84, 92, 109, 118, 122, 144, 159–60
    and prayer at school 28, 32–3
    prophecies 26, 39–40, 95
    and Qur'an/Islam, commonalities between 92, 95, 126–8, 133, 147, 151–2, 182
    reading/studying the 15, 27, 79, 95, 98, 111, 113, 127, 138

as source of divine knowledge 61, 86
  translation of 18, 99
  usage of 84–7, 101, 109, 118–19, 122, 138, 144, 159–60
"Bible Belt" 2, 8, 22, 116
Biden, Joe *xii*
Bin Laden, Osama 39, 41
blasphemy 127
blasphemy laws ix, 93
Blouin, David 67
Body of Christ 42, 150
book burnings 23, 38
"born-again" 8, 9, 32
boundaries
  between groups 48, 50
  as flexible to progressives 134, 176
  researcher 180
Bray, Thomas Wells 24
Bryan, William Jennings 30
Buchanan, Patrick 53, 63
Buddhism 127
Burr, Vivien 46–7
Bush, George W. 33, 63
Butler Act 30

C-scale 134–5, 187
Cairo conference 30–1
California (San Bernardino) 41
Calvin, John 18, 19, 27
Camp, Lee 39
Campolo, Tony 37
Campus Crusade for Christ 34
capital punishment 37
captivity narratives 19–20
Carter, Jimmy 32
Catholic Church/Catholicism
  abuses in 17, 18–19
  and the British crown 24–6
  comparison to Islam 19–21
  criticism of 16
  and the culture war 54, 56, 59, 70, 169
  less suspicion toward 16
  and *The New World* 19–21, 23–5
  predominance of 35
  protest against 16–26
  school *ix*
Chan, Francis 36
Charismatics 10, 35

Chauncey, Charles 23
Chaves, Mark 65
childcare 53–4
children xv, 34
Chrislam 42–3, 75, 81, 96–100, 107, 108, 109, 122, 128, 130–5, 139, 142, 147, 151, 154, 174, 182, 183
Chrislam: How Missionaries Are Promoting an Islamized Gospel (Lingel, Morton, and Nikides) 42
Christ-follower 87, 100, 117, 131, 135
Christian fold/Evangelical fold 10, 35, 99, 105, 125, 149, 154, 158
Christian Fundamentalism 2, 10, 28–32, 34, 67, 70, 128, 169, 172, 175
Christian nation
Christian nationalism 4, 16, 38, 43, 173
Christian-Muslim relations 3, 5–6, 11, 35, 38, 103–4, 110, 114, 124, 130, 138–9, 148–9, 153, 157, 163, 172, 197
Christianese 111, 124
Christianize 92
Christianity and Liberalism (Machen) 61. *See also* traditional phraseology (progressivist usage of); resymbolization (of Progressives)
Christianity Today magazine 63
Church of England 21, 24–5
church-state separation 21–6, 29, 38, 71, 175, 187
city on a hill (as biblical description given to the "New World") 19
Civil War 26–8
Cizik, Richard 37, 171
Claiborne, Shane 37, 171
class 26, 55, 60, 83, 116, 193
clergy 25, 59
clothes burning 23
coexist 13, 148
cognitive surrender (to Islam) 176. *See also* pluralism
cohabitation 64
Coleman, Benjamin 23
colonial America 18–26
colonialism 18–26, 30, 35–6, 111
Colossians (book of) *xvi*

Colson, Charles 33
communitarianism 66–7
compassion 41, 67, 90, 114, 198
compromise (in beliefs) 103–4, 138, 147–8, 153. *See also* progressivism
conceptual tool 72, 77, 142, 162
conflict, definition 10–11
"Conflict and the Web of Group-Affiliations" (Simmel) 50
confrontational/confrontationalist 176–7
Congregation 8, 12, 21, 23, 25–7, 31, 64, 81, 85, 98, 108–19, 121–5, 131, 134, 138, 140, 142–3, 150–4, 157, 169, 175, 181, 185, 187–9, 193–5, 199–200, 204, 215
Congregational church 21, 31. *See also* Congregationalists
Congregationalists 25, 27
conservative Christians/Evangelicals xi, xii, xiii, 27, 30, 36–8, 41, 63–4, 87, 111, 114, 139, 171. *See also* dominant historical Evangelical perspective on Islam
consumer culture 36–7
consumerism 37
contextualization 124, 134, 159. *See also* Chrislam
conversion ix, xii, 9, 15, 20, 21, 24, 27–8, 30–2, 42–3, 80, 97, 111–12, 132, 137, 167, 171. *See also* Evangelicalism; proselytization
cooperation 9, 24, 100
"coping religion" 160
Corinthians (book of) xvi
Coser, Lewis 50–3, 165
counterterrorism 4
Covid-19 1. *See also* Media
Crescent in Light of the Cross, The (Geisler and Saleeb) 40
critique
    of Evangelicalism/Christianity 39, 81, 87, 92, 95, 99, 101, 103–5, 111, 124, 138, 154, 158–9, 165, 176
    of interfaith dialogue 104, 138
    lack of toward Islam 81, 94, 105, 111, 138, 154, 159, 165, 176

of progressive Christianity 36, 96, 99, 105
critiquing literature 39, 163
Culture Wars (Hunter) 54–5, 60–72, 156, 165
"Culture Wars? Insights from Ethnographies of Two Protestant Seminaries" (Carroll and Marler) 66
culture wars
    and the Bible 36, 61, 66, 76, 87, 101, 109, 111, 116, 144, 185
    and Christianity 31–2, 34–6, 61, 63, 81, 87, 105, 140, 165
    and *Christianity and Liberalism* (Machen) 61
    contributions to 72–6, 165–7
    criticism of 70–1
    and ethic of divinity *vs.* ethic of humanity 67–8
    definition 5–8, 11–3, 53–60
    and humanistic ethic of social justice 64, 171
    and Hunter 6–13, 45–6, 48, 53–4, 59–72, 76, 81, 105–9, 140, 142, 144, 155–6, 165–6
    and orthodoxy 6–8, 36, 45, 48–9, 53–4, 59, 61–3, 65–72, 132, 134, 155, 165–6
    and politics 33, 35, 49, 59–61, 63, 66–71, 81, 87, 105, 108, 142, 144
    and sexuality 6, 20, 32–3, 36, 53, 63, 65, 67, 70, 116

Daesh 92. *See also* Islamic State of Iraq and al-Sham (ISIS)
Dahrendorf, Ralph 50
Daigle, Lauren 36
Darwin, Charles 29
Darwinism 28–30
Davenport, James 23
Davis, Nancy 66–7, 70
dawah 197
death penalty 2, 33, 97
deconstruction (of faith) 36
deconstructionism 46
democracy 46, 68
Democratic Party 37, 88, 113, 123, 150, 189

Deism 19, 31
Deity (of Jesus) 103
delirium 23
devil 5, 20, 25, 95, 98, 107, 129-30, 138. *See also* Satan
dhimmitude 102
disciple (scientific) 69
discourse analysis 46, 48, 63, 80, 167
diversity
 contribution to research of 163-4
 within Evangelicalism vii, 2-3, 5, 10, 12-13, 15-18, 35, 40-1, 43, 45, 49, 51-2, 56, 76, 79, 89, 90-1, 100, 105, 107, 109, 117, 124, 139, 142-3, 146-7, 149, 155-6, 158, 163, 169, 171, 182-3, 192
divine 6, 19, 55, 58, 67-8, 86, 89, 94, 96, 103, 105, 156, 159, 161, 166, 186
Dixon, James 27
doctrine xii, 17-18, 24-5, 27, 29, 35, 64, 72, 90, 104-5, 111-12, 127, 164, 175
"doctrine of evolution" 29
dominant historical Evangelical perspective on Islam
 traditional holding to 10-12, 16, 19, 36-7, 42, 76, 79-80, 82-4, 86-7, 89, 91-2, 95-6, 101, 103, 105-6, 108-12, 119, 122, 126-8, 132-9, 142-3, 145-54, 159-62, 165-71, 174-7. *See also* Edwards, Jonathan
 deviation from 48, 79-80, 83, 87, 106, 111, 128, 132, 133-4, 137, 139, 145, 149, 152, 159, 161, 165-69, 171, 176
doubt 27, 29
Dove World Outreach Center 38
dreams 23, 39
dualism 72
"Duality of American Moral Culture, The" (Baker) 62
Durie, Mark 102
Durkheim, Emile 60-2
Dwight, Timothy 24

early church 17, 132
ecumenism 27, 31, 92, 176

education
 Christian 34
 and culture war 53, 55
 higher education 2, 29, 83, 193
 deemphasis upon 23, 30
 liberal takeover 30
 and missionary work 31
 public 30, 32, 34, 53, 172, 189
 secularization of 29, 32, 37
educational values 55
Edwards, Jonathan 19-20, 24, 76, 80, 176
 beliefs as definition of dominant historical traditional Evangelical beliefs on Islam 19-20, 76, 80, 176
egalitarianism 26, 83
Egypt
 colonization of 30
 eschatological predictions about 34
election (presidential) 4, 32, 150, 170, 173
Elevation Church 41
Elijah (biblical prophet) 138
elite
 academic/educational 2, 4, 69, 169, 174, 176
 and the culture war 30, 54, 59-60, 63, 69, 71, 81, 141, 160, 166-8
 evangelical sample 82-3, 86, 141, 160, 181, 189, 193
embattled 19, 48, 53, 113, 124, 150, 154, 159, 169, 186
Emerging Church Movement/Emergent 36, 41, 112
empathy wall 169
End of White Christian America, The (Jones) 170-1
end times/end-time events 23-5, 32-4
enemy x, 15-16, 18-19, 21, 25-6, 32-3, 35, 37, 39, 43, 49, 125
engaged orthodoxy 48-51, 165. *See also* subcultural identity theory
Enlightenment 17, 56-7, 68, 143, 166
environmentalism xii, 170
Episcopal Church 59
equality issues 27, 65, 70, 95, 170
Esau (Isaac's son) 39
eschatological literature 20, 23, 39-40, 163
eschatology 20, 21, 23-4, 33-4, 43

eternal
  life 29, 95
  and moral absolutists 62
  salvation 29
"ethic of divinity" 67-8
"ethic of humanity" 67
Euphrates 24
Evangelical congregants, unified/diverse views of Islam 107-40
  on ACW initiative 138-9
  Adams River Baptist Church, case study 113-15
  characteristics of 116-22
  on Chrislam 130-5
  on interfaith dialogue 136-8
  Mercy church, case study 110-13
  on Muhammad 128-30
  on politics 122-3
  on the Qur'an 125-8
Evangelicalism
  and Baptists 12, 19-20, 22, 25-7, 32-3, 38, 71, 107-10, 113, 117, 134-5, 169, 186
  and conversion from Islam to Christianity ix, xii, 3, 4, 5, 20, 22, 31, 29, 42, 89, 97, 99, 100-1, 112, 114, 132, 134, 173
  core (orthodox) values/beliefs 32-3, 35-6, 37, 48-51
  definition (Bebbington quadrilateral) 9-10
  and education 32-3, 34, 35, 37, 53-4
  and media 32-3, 36
  and progressivism 54, 155, 159, 162
  and traditional moral authority 7-13, 29, 56, 60-8, 72-109, 117-26, 131, 140-8, 153-6, 159-63, 166-76, 183-4, 191
  NEP's vision 37
  origins and history 15-43
    communism as enemy 16, 32-5
    contemporary 34-43
    "enemies" of 15-19, 33-4, 35
    First Great Awakening 21-4
    internal conflict 21-6, 32, 34
    Islam as enemy 19-21, 27-8, 33, 35, 42-3
    modernism 28-31
    postmodernism 35
    postwar renewal and resurgence 31-4
    Protestant Reformation 16-19
    Revolutionary War 24-6
    secularism 35
  and politics 4, 25, 32-3, 37, 55
  and wealth 34, 36-7
Evangelicalism in Modern Britain (Bebbington) 17
Evangelical leaders, unified/diverse views of Islam
  on ACW initiative 102-5
  on Chrislam 96-100
  evangelism as priority 89
  on interfaith dialogue 89, 100-5
  on moral authorities 84-7
  on Muhammad 94-6
  on politics 87-8
  on the Qur'an 91-4
Evangelical leadership and congregational analysis, unified/diverse views of Islam 141-54
  on ACW initiative 153
  Chrislamist ideas 151-4
  on interfaith dialogue 152-3
  moral authority 143-54
  on Muhammad 145, 147, 148-9
  political perspectives 150
  on the Qur'an 142, 145, 147, 151-2, 154
Evangelical Peacemakers (Gushee) 39
Evangelicals
  as "bridge builders" 89-90
  comfort level with identity/label 117
  and Covid-19 pandemic 1
  criticism of leaders/ministers 23-4
  duty/mission to evangelize 15
  fear of Muslims/Islam among 90-1, 124-5
  ignorance of Islam among 90-1, 124-5, 139
  modernist 48-9
  persecution of 22, 26
Evangelicals and Islam tension
  Evangelical literature on 39-40, 163
  historical review 15-43
  IM ideology 42-3
  interfaith dialogue 40-1, 49, 53
  studies/theories 5-9

Everlasting Hatred, The (Lindsey) 39
evolution (theory of) 28–30
exclusive truth 3, 15, 90, 101, 113
exclusivism 15, 28, 94–5, 112
Existentialism 57–8

faith 1, 15, 18, 22, 26, 29, 33, 35–6, 38, 41–3, 54, 56–7, 90, 93, 97–9, 101, 102, 103, 109, 111–15, 122, 124, 127, 137–8, 148, 153–6, 158, 168, 174–6
faithful (to orthodox beliefs) 36, 40, 170
Falwell, Jerry 33, 38
family values 7, 32–3, 67, 70–1, 125, 132, 150, 198
Farrell, Justin 64–5
fascism 56
feminism xii
First Amendment 155
First Baptist Church 38
First Great Awakening 18, 21–2
First World War 29
Florida 38, 41
Focus on the Family 33
Folkways (Sumner) 50
Foreign Mission Board 113, 134
foreign policy 4, 34
Fox News 2
Frankfort (town) 111–12, 114, 237, 196
Freedom From Religion Foundation 35
Freedom of a Christian, The (Luther) 18
free speech 39, 102, 155, 191. *See also* hate speech
free will 26–7
Friedman, Harris 67–8
friendship ix, 39, 110 n.136, 186, 196
"From Accord to Discord: Arts Policy During and After the Culture Wars" (Wyszomirski) 63
Functions of Social Conflict, The (Coser) 50
fundamentalism 2, 10, 28–32, 34, 63, 67, 70, 128, 169, 172, 175
fundamentalist-modernist divide (nineteenth century) 28, 30–1, 67, 169
Fundamentals, The (booklets) 29
Furtick, Steven 41

Gabriel (angel) 20
Gabriel, Mark A. 39
Ganiel, Gladys 2, 9, 36, 112, 164, 179–80, 185–8
gay rights 33, 55, 59, 170
gender 37, 65–70, 83, 152, 170, 185, 188, 192–3
Germany 19, 50, 103
global warming 37
globalism 41
God
    Christian belief that Jesus is 3, 15, 87, 92, 97, 99, 103–5, 130, 133, 151, 197
    comparison with Allah 1, 39, 93, 104–5, 115, 125, 133–4
    and crucifixion/resurrection 9, 15, 92, 97, 104
    kingdom of 20, 25, 27, 29, 76, 110–12, 124, 133, 137, 151, 158, 183
    and moral authority argument 58, 62, 64, 67–8, 73, 76, 88, 105, 107, 119, 144, 159–60, 170
    right understanding of 115
    triune nature of x, xvi, 22, 76, 104–5
    will of 64
godlessness 29, 170
Good Friday 36
Gospel, the 17, 28, 33, 38–9, 42, 89–90, 99, 104, 124, 134, 150, 196
Grace Church 64
Graham, Billy 32
Graham, Franklin 1, 168
Great Awakenings 18, 21–4, 26
Great Commission 15, 30
Grillo, Michael 60
Guest, Mathew 2, 9, 32, 37, 119, 163, 179
Guide to Answering Islam (Janosik) 39
Guiness, Os 63
Gushee, David 37, 39, 171

Hadith 90
Half Devil, Half Child (film) 98
Hamlin, Cyrus 31
hate speech 2, 155, 177. *See also* free speech

healings   23
Hedonism   19
Heidegger, Martin   57
Helvic Confessions   26
hermeneutics   57, 168
Herrick, George   31
heterodoxy   58, 131
higher education   28–9
Hilliard, Clarence   33
Hitler, Adolf   130
Hobbes, Thomas   57
Holly, Israel   25
Holy Spirit   9, 21–3, 43, 75–6, 87, 97, 118–19, 122, 144, 159–60, 183, 184
Holy War   31
Homeschool   34. *See also* education
homosexuality   6, 36, 52–4, 63–4, 88, 160
honor-shame   99, 129, 130, 132, 137, 196
Hook, Sidney   58
Huguenots   19
Hull, William   34
humanism   35, 49, 56, 57–8, 64, 65, 66, 80, 86, 103, 105, 148, 168, 171
humanists   57, 66, 168
Hunter, James   6–13, 45–77, 80, 81, 84, 86, 91, 105–8, 119, 126, 140, 142–4, 155–6, 159, 161, 165–7, 182
Huss, Jan   17
hybrid identity   72, 86, 108, 118–19, 135, 143, 156, 161–2

identity theories
    social   11, 42, 48
    subcultural   6, 45, 48–9, 79, 107–9, 157, 158, 164
"Ideology, Moral Cosmology, and Community in the United States" (Ryle and Robinson)   67
ignorance/ignorant
    about Islam   90, 95, 123–5, 139, 150
    regarding understanding Evangelicalism   2
    stereotype of Evangelicals as   158, 169. *See also* anti-intellectual
images, worship of   24, 25
immigration/immigration reforms   34–5, 123, 173

Trump's ban   4, 39, 41, 173. *See also* terrorism
immorality   25
individualism   16, 18, 43, 58, 61, 67, 191
Indonesia   38
indulgences, selling of   18
ingroup/outgroup hypothesis   6–7, 11, 12, 49–52, 109, 158–9, 164–5, 181–2
Injil   91
insider movements (IMs)   42–3, 80, 94, 97, 98, 103, 105, 122, 128, 134, 135, 187
Institute for Religious Research   38
instrumentalism   46
intelligentsia   1, 176
interfaith dialogue   5, 7, 8, 12, 75, 77, 81, 83, 100–4, 107, 108, 109, 136–40, 142, 145, 147–8, 152–3, 174
interfaith movements   40, 137, 174
interfaith peace initiatives   40, 102–3, 138, 153
International Mission Board   113, 134
InterVarsity   34
Iran, in eschatology   34
Iraq war   38
Isaac (father of the Jews)   33, 39
Ishmael (father of the Muslims)   33, 39
Islam
    converts to Christianity (and Western culture)   3–4, 20, 27–8, 132–3
    and dhimmitude   102
    honor–shame culture in   132
    leaders as "sexual predators"   20
    literature by Evangelicals on   23–4, 39–40
    negative Evangelical views of   15, 19–20, 37–9, 132
    no compulsion in   104
    positive Evangelical views on   87, 111, 132, 139, 152, 159, 165, 167, 176
    religion/beliefs   ix, 5, 20, 26, 38, 87, 89–90, 92, 96, 99, 102, 114, 119, 124, 132, 135, 139, 154, 156, 158, 175, 192
    role in in biblical prophecies   23–4, 26

and terrorism   3–4, 35, 38–9, 41, 93, 110, 125, 128, 154, 163, 173, 187, 190
and violence   1, 16, 19–20, 26, 33, 38, 41, 89–90, 92–3, 96, 128, 139, 172
Islam and Terrorism (Gabriel)   39
"Islamic Awareness" classes   114, 115
Islamic Society of North America   170–1
Islamic State of Iraq and al-Sham (ISIS)   38, 92
Islamists   1, 49
Islamization   39, 42
Islamophobia   1, 37, 41, 90, 105, 164, 175–7
Ismaili   172
Israel
   Declaration of Independence, 1948   33
   missionary work in   33–4
Israel: Key to Prophecy (Hull)   33–4
Is There a Culture War? (Hunter)   46

Jacob (Isaac's son)   39
Jamestown   19
Janosik, Daniel   39
Jesus Christ. *See also* God
   Christological   40
   death of   15
   divinity of   15
   and Islam   3, 15, 17, 28, 31, 37–9, 42, 73–6, 87, 89, 92, 95–101, 104–5, 109–12, 115, 118–19, 122, 124, 126, 130, 132–5, 139, 144, 147, 149, 151, 159, 167, 183, 197
   Lordship of   42
   resurrection of   15
   revelation through   104
   salvation through   15, 135
   worship of   95
Jews   1, 20, 24, 33, 54, 104, 137, 139. *See also* Judaism
jihad   1, 20, 39
John (book of)   vi, xvi
Jones, Terry   38, 170
Judaism   19, 56
judgment of the Lord   18, 27, 34

Kant, Immanuel   57–8
Kidd, Thomas   21–2, 35, 173
Kingdom circle   112, 133, 183
kingdom of God   27, 29, 76, 111–12, 124, 133, 151, 158
Kriesberg, Louis   52, 165
Ku Klux Klan   155

Late Great Planet Earth, The (Lindsey)   33
laughter   23
lay people   17, 23, 112
leadership   23, 26, 51, 56, 59, 65, 83–5, 109–11, 113, 115–16, 118, 123, 131, 136, 138, 142–4, 146, 151, 154, 161, 164, 166, 171, 181, 183, 184, 190, 192-5
Lebanon   196
Leland, John   22
lesbian, gay, bisexual, and transgender   33, 55, 59, 64, 170
Lewis, Rebecca   42
liberal   29–31, 37, 49, 52, 55, 57, 59, 61, 64, 66, 70, 82, 87–8, 117, 122, 150, 167–8, 186
liberal theology   29, 37, 64
liberalism   57, 61
liberation theology   36. *See also* postcolonial theology
Lincoln, Abraham   15, 27
Lindsay, Michael   63, 116
Lindsey, Hal   33, 39
Locke, John   17 n.2
London   24, 196
Louisiana   169
Love, Rick   40
loyalists   26
Lucado, Max   36
Lucke, Glenn   59
Luther, Martin   18, 19
Lutherans   19

Machen, Gresham   61
Mainline denominations/Protestants/churches (decline of)   31, 66, 168, 170, 176
martyrdom   20, 98, 114, 187
McCallum, Richard   2, 172, 173, 176–7
McLaren, Brian   1, 35, 41, 171

Making Something of Ourselves (Merleman)   61
Manichaeism   63
Mark (Gospel of)   xv, 15
Marrant, John   23
marriage   36, 64, 88, 129, 160
Marsden, G. M.   29, 36, 164. *See also* resymbolization (of Progressives)
Martin, Steven   37
Marxism   56
mass shootings   41
Mather, Increase   23
McCallum, Richard   xiv, 2, 40, 172–4, 176
meaning   48, 59
meaninglessness   47, 79, 99
Meccan period   129
Medearis, Carl   39
media   ix, xi, 2, 4, 8, 32–4, 36, 47, 58–9, 82, 90–1, 107, 112, 114, 125, 168, 172–3, 176, 180, 185
Medinan period   129
mega-churches   8, 36–7, 39, 79, 90, 92, 113, 169
Mennonites   19
Mercy churches   107–8, 110–17, 119–21, 124, 131, 134, 136, 151, 169, 187–8, 190, 191–93, 195
Merleman, Richard   61
Methodists   22, 25, 26, 27, 111, 170, 181, 186
Middle East   1, 28, 38, 96, 99, 102, 153
Millennial generation   35
millennial kingdom   25
missiology   8, 11, 12, 42–3, 77, 91, 96, 100, 108, 112, 115, 124, 126, 128, 131–3, 137, 151, 157, 159
missional literature   39, 163
missionaries   28, 30–1, 42, 99, 114
missionary literature   28
mission trips   114, 125, 197
mock (other religions)   138
moderate views   100, 108, 136–7, 142, 151, 172
modernity   48–9, 64, 66, 113
Modernism   28, 29, 35–7, 46. *See also* postmodernism
Mohler, Albert   40

monotheism   3, 4, 15, 40, 95, 103
moral authority
   congregants'   118–22
   definition of argument   53–60
   more progressive than Evangelicals realize   96, 119, 144, 159–60, 163
   evidential analysis   8–9, 12–13, 73–7, 80–8, 94, 103, 104, 106, 109, 117–22, 125–8, 131–2, 138, 140, 142, 143–4, 154, 156, 159–63, 166, 182–4, 198
   leaders' *vs.* congregants'   160–2
   stated analysis   8–9, 46, 74–5, 80, 83–5, 117, 118, 120, 141, 142–3, 156, 159, 160, 162, 171, 183
   stated *vs.* evidential   143–9
   transcends politics   7, 167
moral cosmology   66–7
Moral Majority   33
moral nihilism   68, 69
Mormonism   54–5, 95, 130
Morris, Samuel   21
mosque   110, 115, 171, 196
Muhammad, prophet
   and blasphemy   ix, 93
   Art Exhibit and Contest   155
   belief in   76, 87, 93, 94, 107, 128–9, 147, 149, 152, 158, 168
   criticism of   3, 8, 20, 38, 39, 87, 94–6, 107, 115, 119, 128–30, 135, 136, 145, 150, 152, 154, 197
   early Evangelical perspective on   20
   refraining from negative judgments about   87, 119, 130, 154
   revelations of   3
   and violence   20, 38, 90, 92–4, 96
multiculturalism   53, 69, 153
Muslims. *See also* Islam
   belief that Christians should distance themselves from culture of   135
   community   2, 8, 42, 91, 110, 137, 164, 175, 192, 194
   culture   87, 97, 101–2, 111, 124, 132, 134–6, 146, 153, 172, 187
   diversity within   168, 172
   fear of   30, 37, 39, 41, 90, 123–5, 127, 146, 150, 176–7, 198

friends ix, 7, 39, 84, 110, 118–19, 122, 131–3, 136, 147–9, 175, 194, 196–8
follower of Jesus 42, 87, 95, 97–8, 100, 115, 117, 132–5, 196
identity 42–3, 99, 131, 134–5, 173
majority-countries ix, 4, 41, 97, 114, 132, 148, 173, 187, 194, 196
seek to learn from/approach as a learner 101, 104, 111–12, 133, 136–7, 145, 147–8, 153, 182, 197
refugees 4, 41, 97, 111, 114, 137, 149, 175, 196–7
honor of 99, 129–30, 137
and terrorism 3–4, 35, 38–9, 41, 93, 110, 125, 128, 154, 163, 173, 187, 190
women 92–4, 104, 107, 116, 129, 137, 145, 147–8, 152
Muslims, Christians, and Jesus (Medearis) 39

National Association of Evangelicals (NAE) 32
nationalism 4, 16, 38, 43, 173
naturalism 57, 68, 70, 165
Navigators 34
Nazi 155
Needham-Penrose, Judith 67–8
neo-monasticism 169
New England 20–1, 25
New Evangelicalism 26, 32–4, 168
New Evangelical Manifesto: A Kingdom Vision for the Common Good, A (Gushee) 37
New Evangelical Partnership for the Common Good (NEP) 37
New Evangelical Social Engagement, The (Steensland and Goff) 167–8, 171
New Monasticism and the Transformation of American Evangelicalism (Markofski) 169
Newsweek magazine 32
New World settlements 19
New York Times 39
nihilism 68–9
nondenominational 12, 109–10, 186
nones (religious) 35

9/11 attacks/aftermath 3, 35, 38–40, 43, 79, 110, 125, 163, 190
95 Theses (Luther) 18
nuclear weapons 33

Obama, Barack 32, 40–1
Occom, Samson 23
Okeley, William 20–1
Old Testament 58, 95, 127, 138
Olsen, Daniel 52, 63–4
One Faith No Longer (Yancey and Quosigk) 64
one-world government 34
open-air preaching 21
Orlando shooting 41
orthodoxy (Christian) 5, 28, 36, 42, 58, 61, 63–4, 94, 104, 131–5, 165
outgroup 6, 11–12, 15–16, 43, 45, 47–51, 60, 76, 109, 113, 158–9, 164–5, 181–2
"Outsourcing Moral Authority" (Thomas) 64–5

pacifism 26
Pakistan ix, 93, 87, 187
para-church 55
paradigm shift 112, 122, 133, 169, 183
Patriot 25–6, 38
peace/peacemaking 31, 39–40, 50, 96, 102–3, 110, 137–9, 148, 153, 167, 170
Pence, Mike 41
Pentecostalism 10, 34–5
persecution
  of Christians by Muslims ix, 41, 99, 132, 187
  in early colonial/US history 19, 22, 26
personal experience (as authoritative) 7, 53–4, 57–8, 61, 64, 66, 80, 82, 90, 122, 156, 159, 161, 166, 172, 180, 189, 197
"Perspectives on the World Christian Movement" course 134–5
Pew Research Center study 3, 4, 35, 38, 156, 173
phobia 177. *See also* Islamophobia; xenophobia
Pietists 19

Piper, John   40, 41, 95, 139
Plato   62
pluralism
  ideological   176
  modern   48
  religious   28
polarization   6, 13, 46, 56, 59, 62–3, 66–70, 80, 86, 140, 144, 152, 156, 157, 159, 161, 166
political activism   xi, 33
political conservatism   2, 27, 29, 33, 37–8, 55, 57, 59, 63–4, 67, 70–1, 87–8, 114, 122, 123, 139, 146, 150, 188
political freedom   38
polytheism   30, 107, 129
Pope   16, 20, 25, 103
pornography   54, 64, 65
postcolonial theology   35. *See also* liberation theology
postmodernism   35–7, 46, 68, 132–3, 135
power
  and conservatism   169
  Muslims lack   101–2, 111
  and orthodox appeal to authority   58
  and politics   24–5, 55, 60, 71, 88, 129
  and progressives   55, 58, 71–2, 76, 101, 171
  relations (Coser)   51
prayers   22, 27, 32, 33, 99, 113, 135, 137
predestination   18, 27
premarital sex   64
Presbyterians   22, 25, 27
presidency   xi, 4, 32–4, 39–41, 63, 150, 170, 173
Price, George McCready   30
progressive sources of authority   13, 54, 56, 58, 63–5, 72–4, 80, 84, 86, 91, 96, 119, 126, 141, 143, 156, 160, 162, 166, 168
progressive-traditional spectrum   11, 13, 46, 72–85, 91–2, 98, 104, 105, 108, 117–18, 125–8, 131, 135, 139–8, 150, 154, 155–6, 159–63, 166, 167, 174, 175, 183, 184, 186, 198
progressivism   5, 36, 45, 54, 55–8, 61, 66–8, 72, 76, 111, 118, 140, 144, 155, 156, 159, 161, 162, 166, 168, 171. *See also* dominant historical Evangelical perspective on Islam, deviated from
progressivist alliance   55–6, 57, 70
prophecy   26, 29, 34
pro-life policies   33
proselytization   xi, xii, 25, 28, 30–1, 40, 111, 117, 145, 147–8, 150, 197. *See also* Gospel, the
protection of rights of religious minorities   22
"Protestant Clergy and the Culture Wars: An Empirical Test of Hunter's Thesis" (Uecker and Lucke)   59
Protestantism   4, 10, 17–22, 26, 27, 56, 168
Proverbs (book of)   v, xiv, xv, *xvi*
Psalms (book of)   *xv*
Purgatory   25
Puritans   17 n.2, 19, 20, 22, 34
purpose   19, 45, 55, 57, 58, 61

Quakers   19, 22
qualitative methodology   5, 8, 46, 64, 75, 157, 162, 179, 181
quantitative methodology   5, 8–9, 21, 46, 75, 162–3, 171, 179
Quosigk, Ashlee   xi, xii, xiii, xv, 4, 11, 18–19, 36, 47, 64, 154, 161, 171–2, 175–6
Qur'an   1, 5, 8, 12, 58, 75–7, 79, 81, 87, 91–5, 97, 103–4, 107, 108, 109–10, 115, 119, 122, 124–8, 132, 135, 136, 142, 145, 147, 149, 151–2, 157, 158, 159, 168, 174, 175, 176, 182, 196
Qur'an and Christ (QAC) conference   110, 112, 132, 151, 169
Qureshi, Nabeel   39

race/racism
  ambiguity/fluidity   168, 189, 199
  Muslims as race rather than religious adherents   4, 41, 55, 168, 172–3
  and colorblind   189
  focus on   4, 55, 66, 168, 168, 172–3, 189, 199

formation project   189, 199
  and sample   55, 189, 199
relations (Coser)   51
Ramadan   21
Reagan, Ronald   33
reconciliation   40, 110, 167
Red Letter Christians   37, 138
Reformation   17–19, 21, 23
Reformed Church in America   30
refugee ministries   111, 114, 193
relativism   31, 35–6, 47, 62–3, 68, 176
religious freedom   19, 22, 25, 33, 38
religious identity xi, xii, xiii, 4, 42, 67, 71, 173
religious liberty (desire for)   22, 35
Religious Right   31–4, 37
Republican National Convention, Buchanan speech at   53, 63
Republican Party   35, 71, 88, 123, 150
researcher bias   xiii, 46, 186
Restructuring of American Religion, The (Wuthnow)   56
resurrection   15, 92, 97, 197
resymbolization (of Progressives) 56. *See also* Machen, Gresham
revelations   3, 6–7, 23–4, 104, 133, 148, 156, 159, 161, 166
revival   9, 21–6
Rimmer, Harry   30
"Road to Coronavirus Hell Was Paved by Evangelicals, The"   1
Roberts, Oral   32
Robertson, Pat   33
Robinson, Robert   66–7, 70
Roe v. Wade   71
Rome   20, 24
Russia   34
Ryle, Robyn   67

salvation   9, 15, 29, 89, 111
San Bernardino shooting   41
Satan   89, 129, 132, 196. *See also* devil
Saudi Arabia   3, 93, 97
schism   18, 27
school prayer   33
Science and the Good (Hunter and Nedelisky)   46, 69–70
scientific reductionism   70, 165
Scopes, John   30

Scopes Trial   30
Scots' Confession   26
Second Great Awakening   26
secularization   26, 29, 33–5, 49, 58–9, 65, 176
Seeking Allah, Finding Jesus (Qureshi)   39
self-fulfillment   36
self-sacrifice   35, 36
seminary   31, 66, 127
separatism   27, 34
sexuality   xii, 16, 20–1, 32–3, 36, 52–3, 55, 59, 64–5, 67, 70, 88, 116, 160, 168, 170, 188
sexual misconduct   188
Sharia Law   92–3, 97
Shi'is/Shia   28, 172
Sider, Ronald   33, 171
Simmel, George   50, 53, 165
Sinners in the Hands of an Angry God (Edwards)   20
Six-Day War   1967   33
skepticism   35, 134, 136, 152
slavery   20, 26–7, 43, 170
Smith, Christian   6, 7, 8, 12, 23, 36, 45–51, 76–7, 79, 81, 107–9, 113, 157, 158, 164–5
Smith, Joseph   85, 130
social constructionism
  criticism of   47
  and cultural relativism   47
  definition   46–8
  weak form of   47
social gospel   29–33, 111, 137. *See also* liberation theology, postcolonial theology
social identity theory   42, 48
social justice   33, 64, 95, 101, 111–12, 114, 136, 145, 167–8, 171. *See also* liberation theology, social gospel
sola Christus (salvation through Christ)   111
Southern Baptist Convention (SBC)   12, 22, 27, 33, 38, 71, 107, 110, 113, 134–5
Southern Intolerance (Ellison and Musick)   63
Soviet Union   114. *See also* Russia
Starks, Brian   67

state-supported churches 25
Stein, Arthur 51, 53, 165
Stewart, Katherine 1, 17
Stone, Lyman 41
Strangers in Their Own Land (Hochschild) 169–70
student ministry programs 34
subcultural identity theory 6, 45, 48–9, 79, 107–9, 157, 158, 164
subjectivism/subjectivity 5, 7, 54, 57–8, 156, 159, 161, 166
subjugation (of women) 92, 96
Sufi 172
Sumner, William Graham 50
supernatural happenings 23, 39, 65, 163
superstition 20
sura 92–3
syncretism 5, 16, 42, 75, 81, 99, 130–4. *See also* Chrislam, contextualization
Syria 38, 196
Syrian war 38, 196

Tawrat 91
taxation 21, 25
Tennessee (and the teaching of evolution) 30
terrorism 3, 4, 35, 38–41, 43, 63, 79, 93, 110, 125, 128, 154, 163, 173, 187, 190
terrorism literature 39, 163
Texas (place of Muhammad Art Exhibit and Contest) 155
theory (definition) 6
Third Jihad, The (Youssef) 39
"this-worldly" 56, 57, 168
Thomas, Jeremy 52, 63–3, 65–6, 74, 160
tolerance 2, 16, 36, 63–4, 66, 88, 96, 101, 115, 156, 164, 168–9, 187
torture 37, 101
Traditional Christians 9–13, 15, 19, 29-30, 32, 35, 36, 39–40, 61, 64, 74–6, 80–1, 86–9, 90–4, 98–100, 108–14, 117–19, 122, 124–5, 127, 131–40, 148–9, 153–5, 163, 167, 170–2, 175–6, 183, 198. *See also* conservative Christians/Evangelicals, dominant historical Evangelical perspective on Islam
traditional churches 35–6
traditional phraseology (progressivist usage of) 61. *See also* Machen, Gresham, resymbolization
traditional sources of moral authority 13, 56, 64–5, 72–4, 80, 84, 86, 91, 119, 126, 141, 143, 156, 160, 162, 166. *See also* dominant historical Evangelical perspective on Islam
trances 23
Trinity 43, 76, 104–5
Truman, Harry 32
Trump, Donald xi, 2, 4, 39, 41, 170, 173
Turkish Empire 21, 24, 31
"Two Approaches to Religion and Politics" (Starks and Robinson) 67
tyranny 24–5

Uecker, Jeremy 59, 81
uncertainty 35, 36, 94, 95. *See also* postmodernism
Unitarianism 31
United Church of Christ 31
universalism 31, 132, 133, 137–9
utilitarianism 67–8

Vines, Jerry 38
Virgin Mary 25, 104
visions 23, 39

Wallis, Jim 33, 171
war, NEP view 37
war on terror 3, 35, 38–9
Warren, Rick 40
Washington Post 41
Wellman, J. 38
Wesley, John 17 n.2, 21, 26
Western culture/societies/world 16, 26, 28, 31, 98, 101, 111, 132, 135, 154, 172
Westminster Confession 26
Whitefield, George 21
Who Is My Enemy (Camp) 39
Williams, Robin 51–2
Williams, Roger 20
Wolffe, J. 35, 164, 179

Woodberry, R. D. 36–7
World Relief 41, 133
World Values Survey 62
worship 22, 24, 25, 58, 94, 95, 99, 103–4, 112, 129, 133, 138, 182
Wuthnow, Robert 57, 70–1, 105
Wycliffe, John 17
Wyszomirski, Margaret 63

xenophobia 173. *See also* Islamophobia

"Young and the Restless? The Liberalization of Young Evangelicals, The" (Farrell) 64
Youssef, Michael 39

Zabur 91
zeitgeist 61
Zinzendorf-ers 22
Zwemer, Samuel 30–1
Zwingli, Ulrich 18